COINAGE AND HISTORY IN THE SEVENTH CENTURY NEAR EAST
4

Edited by
ANDREW ODDY, INGRID SCHULZE
and WOLFGANG SCHULZE

Proceedings of the 14th Seventh Century Syrian
Numismatic Round Table
held at The Hive, Worcester,
on 28th and 29th September 2013

Published in 2015 by the Seventh Century Syrian Numismatic Round Table, an informal group of numismatists and historians whose convenors are Andrew Oddy (waoddy@googlemail.com), Tony Goodwin (a.goodwin2@btopemworld.com) and Marcus Phillips and Susan Tyler-Smith (senmerv@hotmail.com)

© 2015: Copyright is held by the individual authors

Produced and distributed by:
Archetype Publications
c/o International Academic Projects
1 Birdcage Walk
London, SW1H 9JJ
www.archetype.co.uk

Printed by Short Run Press Ltd, Exeter, UK

ISBN: 978-1-909492-32-5

Cover design by Steve Lloyd of Morton & Eden Ltd
Front and rear cover illustrates an Arab-Byzantine Phase 2 fals of Skythopolis, see p. 153, fig. 2a.

This publication was made possible by very generous sponsorship from Morton & Eden Ltd., 45 Maddox Street, London W1S 2PE, to whom the Seventh Century Syrian Numismatic Round Table is very grateful.

The editors would also like to acknowledge the support of the following advertisers:
A H Baldwin & Sons Ltd, London,
Wilkes & Curtis Ltd, Tonbridge, Kent,
Stephen Album Rare Coins Inc., Santa Rosa, California,
Spink, London,
and of the UK Numismatic Trust who generously gave a grant to cover the hire of the lecture theatre in The Hive.

CONTENTS

Preface	iv
The Sasanian Empire at its Apogee in the 620s *James Howard-Johnston*	1
7th Century 'barbarous' Folles: a Secondary Mint in the Eastern Part of the Byzantine Empire under Persian Rule *Henri Pottier*	17
Some Aspects of 7thC Egyptian Byzantine Coinage *Tony Goodwin*	27
Byzantine and Early Islamic Coinage at Excavations in Jericho *Tasha Vorderstrasse*	37
Coinage and the Early Arab State *Marcus Phillips*	53
Symbolism and meaning on the early Islamic copper coinage of Greater Syria *Luke Treadwell*	73
Arab-Byzantine Coins from Excavations in Israel – an Update – *Gabriela Bijovsky*	95
Can we believe what is written on the coins? Enigmatic die links and other puzzles *Ingrid Schulze*	115
Notes on Two Imperial Image Obverse Types: The Falconer and the Seated Couple *David Woods*	137
The Phase 2 Coinage of Scythopolis under Mu'awiya and his successors *Andrew Oddy*	151
The Spear on Coins of the Byzantine-Arab Transition Period *Wolfgang Schulze and Andrew Oddy*	179
The Egyptian Arab-Byzantine Coinage *Tony Goodwin*	205
The Earliest Islamic Copper Coinage of North Africa *Trent Jonson*	217
Marks and isolated words on copper coins issued by the 'Treasury of Aleppo' in 146-148 H: a clue to the interpretation of marks on early Islamic coppers? *Lutz Ilisch*	241
The Coinage of the Seleucia Isauriae and Isaura Mints under Herakleios (ca.615-619) and related issues *Frank R. Trombley*	251
Previous publications of the Seventh Century Syrian Numismatic Round Table	273

PREFACE

This volume contains all but two of the papers presented at the 14th meeting of the *Seventh Century Syrian Numismatic Round Table* held in the recently opened shared public and university library building (known as The Hive) in Worcester in September 2013. Moving away from the Oxford/Cambridge/Birmingham axis was something of a gamble, but regular attendees found the new venue provided an extra interest and attendance was not affected by having to travel to the West Midlands. The meeting attracted 17 papers delivered by 14 speakers from 7 countries.

Those readers who have followed the fortunes of the *Seventh Century Syrian Numismatic Round Table* over the past 23 years will be aware that the meetings have developed from being a small group of curators, collectors and professional numismatists who shared their developing knowledge of the Arab-Byzantine coinage at a time when the subject had barely advanced since the publication of John Walker's British Museum catalogue in 1956. Now, those collectors who were feeling their way in this minefield have become recognised authorities and the meetings regularly attract historians of international repute. The result is a heady mix whose combined wisdom is shedding new light on the history of Greater Syria in the first century of the Hegira.

One thing that is notable in this volume is that papers presenting 'work in progress', which have been a feature that was encouraged in earlier round tables, are almost lacking. Virtually all the papers present complete studies of their topic, although that is not to say that some conclusions will not be revised by research in the future. It is significant that the number of pages resulting from the four round table meetings that have been published (see pp 273/4) has increased significantly with each succeeding round table. This is a measure of the interest now being taken in this series as the coins become ever more obtainable from web-based sources. Coins that were regarded as rare a few years ago can now be shown to be numerous, in spite of the 'hype' that is often applied to their descriptions on eBay and other virtual market places.

In recent years several large and important collections have been amassed in the USA, the UK and in Europe but the future of these is now uncertain because of the strictures placed on museums by the *UNESCO Convention on the Means of Prohibiting and Preventing the Illicit Import, Export and Transfer of Ownership of Cultural Property 1970*. One such collection is currently in the process of being sold by a well-known and respected American dealer and auction house. But other collectors who would like to see their collections preserved for the future and made available to scholarship are finding that museums are unable to accept them unless it can be shown that the coins have been exported from their country of origin before 1970. In the case of any collection of Arab-Byzantine coins, such an undertaking is impossible. This is a loss to scholarship although it does mean that the coins will be re-circulated in the future for the interest and enjoyment of collectors.

The problem with the UNESCO Convention is that it is designed to protect archaeological sites from illegal digging and architectural sites from desecration by the stealing of ornament and sculpture, and this is a laudable aim. Coins, however, are often found by agricultural and construction workers when going about their daily work and little purpose is to be served by banning their sale internationally. Even the use of metal detectors on agricultural land when 'controlled', as it is in the UK, serves to increase our knowledge of the past and often results in the discovery of new sites of potential historic interest. In the UK, hoards found by metal detectorists are reported to the authorities and museums are given an option to buy them at an agreed valuation. Those coins not required for public institutions are returned to the finders. Perhaps there is a lesson here for other countries.

Andrew Oddy   Ingrid Schulze   Wolfgang Schulze   January 2015

The Sasanian Empire at its Apogee in the 620s

James Howard-Johnston [1]

Europe and the Middle East had defences as strong as those of the Indian subcontinent and China in antiquity and the middle ages. Mountain ranges (Carpathians and Caucasus, the latter backed by the Taurus and Zagros), forests (covering the north European plain), a great river (the Danube) and two seas (Black and Caspian) between them constituted a formidable barrier facing the military heartland of Eurasia in the steppes. Iran lay outside these core sedentary lands in west Eurasia, serving as a massive outer bastion in the east, with its own natural defences on all sides. These took the form of the highlands of Media in the west, the two great ranges of the Elburz and Zagros on the north and the south which enfold the elevated interior basin, and the Kopet Dagh together with the arid plains and hills to the south which are cast across the eastern approaches. Within these naturally defined limits a distinctive Iranian culture developed in prehistoric times, which was securely fixed to its terrain and proved more than capable of extending its influence into peripheral zones, notably Khuzistan west of the Zagros, Adurbadagan north-west of Media, and Khurasan east of the Kopet Dagh.

The second Iran-based imperial power of classical antiquity was that created by Ardashir at the beginning of the third century AD. Inspired by the legendary Kayanian analogues of his distant predecessors, Cyrus and Darius, who founded the Achaemenid empire, Ardashir intensified and extended his authority from Persia proper in south-east Iran, and, after unifying the Iranian highlands, went on to conquer most of Mesopotamia, most of Transcaucasia and all of Khurasan.[2] The outer limits of this Sasanian empire were the watersheds at the head of the Tigris and Araxes in the west, the Persian Gulf and both its coasts in the south, the Caucasus and the Oxus in the north and east and, eventually, the Indus in the south-east. Natural defences were reinforced with manmade fortifications, long walls on each side of the Caspian in the north, a canal and associated forts guarding the desert approach to the lower Tigris in the south, and hard-point military bases commanding the principal potential avenues of invasion from the west (Nisibis and Dvin) and the east (Nishapur and Merv).[3]

The great powers which succeeded each other in the steppes to the north and east of the Sasanian empire, Kushans, Huns, Kidarites, Hephthalites and Turks, were effectually barred from entering inner Iran and its milch-cow in Mesopotamia, as were the Romans in the west and Arabs in the south. There were, however, exceptional times when extraneous forces succeeded in penetrating deep into Sasanian territory, as in 363 when Julian was able concentrate Roman forces against the Sasanians and came dangerously close to Ctesiphon, or in 484 when the Hephthalites were at their strongest and, after defeating and killing Peroz in open battle, were able to reduce Iran to tributary status, or in 573 when concerted attacks were launched on several fronts and much of Transcaucasia was overrun by the Romans.[4] It was probably the memory of these times of peril as well as a

---

[1] Emeritus Fellow of Corpus Christi College, Oxford: james.howard-johnston@history.ox.ac.uk
[2] J. Wiesehöfer, *Ancient Persia* (London, 1996).
[3] J. Howard-Johnston, 'The Late Sasanian Army', in T. Bernheimer & A. Silverstein, ed., *Late Antiquity: Eastern Perspectives* (Exeter, 2012), 87-127, at 87-108.
[4] J. Matthews, *The Roman Empire of Ammianus* (London, 1989), 130-87; T. Daryaee, *Sasanian Persia: The Rise and Fall of an Empire* (London, 2009), 22-5; M. Whitby, *The Emperor Maurice and His Historian: Theophylact*

determination to restore the strategic balance in the west, which impelled Khusro II both to embark on a long Roman war in 603, after he heard of the execution by the usurper Phocas of his benefactor, the Emperor Maurice, and to press on with the war, despite pleas for peace from Maurice's self-proclaimed avenger, Heraclius, in 610 and 615.

There is no single, comprehensive ancient narrative of the war. Despite its scale, it called forth no Herodotus or Thucydides of its own. However, the historical habit, which does not seem to have taken hold in Iran in antiquity, save for the dynastic history written down in the sixth century, was still in evidence in different parts of the Christian world in the seventh century, both within and beyond the limits of the premier Christian state, the east Roman empire. East Roman histories should have pride of place, since they include two – the anonymous *Chronicon Paschale* and the *Chronographia* of Theophanes – which drew extensively on contemporary documentary sources, but they are rivalled by two written in Transcaucasia - the *History of Khosrov*, traditionally but erroneously attributed to Sebeos, and a seventh-century work (dubbed the *History to the Year 682*) embedded in the tenth-century history of Movses Daskhurants'i – which are demonstrably based on high-grade contemporary or near-contemporary sources.[5] Useful supplementary material may be culled from saints' lives and miracle stories (especially the second book of the *Miracles of St. Demetrius* which is tantamount to a city history of Thessalonica), from histories written in Syriac, from snippets about eastern affairs in Latin sources and from long, but transmuted versions of historical reality in later Arab sources.[6] As for contemporary non-literary sources, there is some archaeological evidence, documentary papyri from Egypt in Greek, Coptic and Pahlavi, and large numbers of coins, Roman and Persian. The Roman coinage has been thoroughly catalogued and analysed in the recent past. Not so, alas, the Persian. The *Sylloge Nummorum Sasanidarum*, a collaborative project directed by Michael Alram and Rika Gyselen which is publishing catalogues of the collections in Paris, Berlin and Vienna, has only reached the death of Kavad I in 531. For the long and dramatic reign of Khusro II we have to fall back on the short handbook of *Sasanian Numismatics* published by R. Göbl in 1968, a miscellany of articles on aspects of Khusro's coinage, and an illustrated list (alas, without commentary) of the coins in the Tehran collection (one dinar and over 2,500 drachms, catalogued by mint).[7]

This last and greatest of Roman-Persian wars opened with a grand Persian offensive in spring 603 on two fronts, north and south of the Armenian Taurus. The northern field army, which was defeated with considerable ease when it moved out of the Dvin plain on to Roman territory, may have been no more than a decoy force, while the main blow was struck in the south against the outermost layer of the multi-layered defences developed by the Romans over past centuries. Dara, the main forward base, built menacingly close to the frontier a century earlier, was the principal objective. Khusro, who took personal charge of operations, was perhaps striving to emulate the

---

Simocatta on Persian and Balkan Warfare (Oxford, 1988), 250-8.
[5] *Chronicon Paschale*, ed. L. Dindorf, CSHB, 2 vols. (Bonn, 1832), trans. M. & M. Whitby, *Chronicon Paschale 284-628 AD*, TTH 7 (Liverpool, 1989); *Theophanis chronographia*, ed. C. de Boor, 2 vols. (Leipzig, 1883-5), trans. C. Mango & R. Scott, *The Chronicle of Theophanes Confessor: Byzantine and Near Eastern History AD 284-813* (Oxford, 1997); *Patmut'iwn Sebeosi*, ed. G.V. Abgarjan (Erevan, 1979), trans. R.W. Thomson in R.W. Thomson & J. Howard-Johnston, *The Armenian Chronicle Attributed to Sebeos*, TTH 31 (Liverpool, 1999); Movses Daskhurants'i, ed. V. Arak'eljan, *Movses Kałankatuats'i: Patmut'iwn Ałuanits' Ashkarhi* (Erevan, 1983), trans. C.J.F. Dowsett, *The History of the Caucasian Albanians by Movses Dasxuranc'i* (London, 1961).
[6] J. Howard-Johnston, *Witnesses to a World Crisis: Historians and Histories of the Middle East in the Seventh Century* (Oxford, 2010).
[7] R. Göbl, *Sasanian Numismatics* (Braunschweig, 1971); M. Alram, R. Gyselen *et al.*, *Sylloge Nummorum Sasanidarum: Paris-Berlin-Wien*, I *Ardashir I. - Shapur I.* and II *Ohrmazd I. - Ohrmazd II.*, Öst.Ak.Wiss., Phil.-hist. Kl., Denkschriften 317, 422 (Vienna, 2003, 2012); N. Schindel *et al.*, *Sylloge Nummorum Sasanidarum: Paris-Berlin-Wien*, III.1-2 *Shapur II. - Kawad I./2. Regierung*, Öst.Ak.Wiss., Phil.-hist. Kl., Denkschrift 325 (Vienna, 2004); V.S. Curtis, M.E. Askari & E.J. Pendleton, *Sasanian Coins. A Sylloge of the Sasanian coins in the National Museum of Iran (Muzeh Melli Iran), Tehran*, II *Khusrau II - Yazdgard III*, Royal Numismatic Society Special Publication 49 (London, 2012).

achievement of his grandfather who had captured it in a brilliant campaign in 573. His task was made easier by the revolt of Narses, the senior Roman general in the Levant, against the usurper Phocas. Narses established himself in Edessa, well to the rear of Dara, and admitted Khusro into the city, for a carefully choreographed ceremony in which he (Narses) handed over Theodosius, eldest son of Maurice, or someone alleged to be Theodosius, into the protection of Khusro.[8] Once Dara fell in 604, Persian forces could continue to chip away at Roman defences south of the Armenian Taurus, while to the north they renewed their efforts to recover the western part of Persarmenia which had been ceded to the Romans in 591. Two campaigns, in 604 and 605, brought them to the old frontier in Armenia, on the Araxes-Euphrates watershed. After a pause for reorganisation and additional recruiting, this laborious attritional advance resumed on both fronts. Roman forces fought stubbornly but were pushed back. Key Persian gains were Theodosiopolis in the north (608) and Edessa in the south (609).[9]

By spring 610, Persian forces were approaching the innermost line of Roman defence, along the old Flavian *limes*, which ran south from Trebizond past Satala to the point where the Euphrates turned south, and then followed the river as it cut across the grain of the landscape, leaving Melitene and its plain to the west, and then, after reaching the plains of northern Syria, described a great curve south-east.[10] That summer and autumn they made their second key breakthrough. As in the opening campaign, they succeeded in deceiving the Romans with a feint, in this case a thrust in early August across the Euphrates to seize a bridgehead round Zenobia, far downstream from their main intended crossing-point on the direct route to Antioch and the Mediterranean. Domestic troubles, taking the form of a rebellion against Phocas, which originated in north Africa in 608 and had been gathering momentum in 609 and 610, helped to distract the Roman authorities and commanders in the field. For it was towards the end of summer that the rebels, led by Heraclius, son of the Exarch of Africa, embarked on their final advance, by sea, on Constantinople. The main Persian attack was launched around the beginning of October. Antioch fell on the 8th, Apamea on the 15th and Emesa a few days later.[11] With their seizure of this substantial bridgehead in northern Syria, the Persians reached the sea and divided the Roman empire in two, gaining for themselves a decisive advantage of inner lines. Thenceforth they would be able to switch forces at will between the fronts facing Asia Minor in the north and the Levant in the south. Any Roman response would inevitably be delayed, reinforcements having to be dispatched by sea. At which point the Persians might simply redirect their efforts to the other front. The more alluring direction of attack was to the south. There lay the industrial and commercial heartland of the Roman empire, within the Persians' military reach, all too exposed since there was no natural defensive line athwart the settled lands for the Romans to use.

Initially the Persians paused in the south, attacking instead in the north. An expeditionary force, commanded by one of Khusro's two great generals, Shahen, crossed the Euphrates from western Armenia and advanced on Caesarea, capital of Cappadocia, which he occupied for a year, 610-11. This campaign has the hallmarks of another grand diversionary operation, intended to focus Roman attention on Caesarea, while the Persians consolidated their hold on northern Syria and prepared for a push south. It was only in 613, after the extrusion of the Persians from Caesarea (the attempt to trap them there failed), that Heraclius was able to launch an attack on the Persian bridgehead and to attempt to reopen the land routes between Asia Minor and the Levant. This Roman counteroffensive failed. The field army was defeated not far from Antioch and forced to withdraw west, through

---

[8] Principal source: Ps. Sebeos, 107.1-108.9, with **Hist.Com.**, nn.27-8.
[9] Principal source: Ps. Sebeos, 108.10-111.31, with **Hist.Com.**, nn.28-30.
[10] T.B. Mitford, 'Cappadocia and Armenia Minor: Historical Setting of the *Limes*', in H. Temporini, ed., **Aufstieg und Niedergang der römischen Welt**, II.7.2 (Berlin, 1980), 1119-1228.
[11] **Chronicon ad annum 724 pertinens**, ed. E.W. Brooks, CSCO, Scriptores Syri 3, Chronica Minora 2 (Louvain, 1960), 77-155, at 146.11-18, trans. A. Palmer, *The Seventh Century in the West-Syrian Chronicles*, TTH 15 (Liverpool, 1993), 17.

Cilicia and across the Taurus to the interior plateau of Asia Minor.[12] At which Persian forces resumed their advance, capturing Damascus on the inland side of the Lebanon and Anti-Lebanon ranges and Caesarea, capital of Palestine, on the coast. In 614, they took a further step, fraught with danger. In response to an urgent appeal from the Jews of Jerusalem as well as news of the killing of the small Persian mission in the city, Shahrbaraz, Khusro's leading general, intervened to halt a pogrom started by Christian young men at a time of heightened religious antagonism before Easter. The city fell after a three-week siege. Tales of atrocities and sacrilegious destruction were broadcast by the Romans, with potential repercussions in Mesopotamia, with its large Christian as well as Jewish populations. The city *was* sacked. Buildings *were* damaged. There was inevitably looting and bloodshed. But the Persian high command did what it could to minimise both, before organising the deportation of the city notables (including Patriarch Zacharias), useful trades and potential troublemakers. The army then returned to its base in Caesarea.[13]

The decisive year, the year in which Khusro resolved on the destruction of the Roman empire, was 615. The weakness of the Romans was made manifest by the sweeping advance of an army commanded by Shahen, who cut across Asia Minor and established his camp at Chalcedon, on the Asian side of the Bosporus, within sight of Constantinople. It was then admitted in an extraordinary document, a grovelling plea for peace sent by the Senate to Khusro. There were no territorial demands, no insistence on Persian evacuation of the occupied provinces. The Romans, through their supreme constitutional body, were offering to become Persian clients, leaving it for Khusro to nominate an emperor of his choice and clearly expecting to have to hand over large sums in tribute.[14] Everything that Khusro might have hoped to attain at the start of the war was on offer. But that same year the complacency which he and the leading elements in the Sasanian state might have felt was dissipated by the news of events in the east. A large Turkish army invaded Khurasan, possibly after arranging for a provocation by their local Kushan clients which would lure out the Persian regional commander, a distinguished but elderly Armenian general. There was no organised Persian resistance and the Turks were able to sweep along the northern edge of the Iranian plateau as far as Rayy capital of Media, and round the north-west angle, past the future site of Qom, to Ispahan in Persia proper. Here was a timely reminder of the geopolitical weakness of the Sasanian empire, caught between a long-established imperial power in the west and a new, nomadic confederation which could mobilise large, formidable fighting forces from the steppes.[15] In winter 615-16 Khusro took his fateful decision, rejected the Roman offer, incarcerated the Roman ambassadors and prepared to finish off his western adversary.[16]

After the withdrawal of Turkish forces, a punitive expedition was undertaken against the local Kushans and their Hephthalite king in 616. A victory in open battle opened the way for distant raids to Balkh, Herat and Tukharistan.[17] With the position stabilised in the east and Sasanian prestige restored, the final campaigns of conquest could be started in the west. Palestine had been occupied in 616. Preparations could be started for the penultimate task, the conquest of Egypt, achieved in 619-20 (after yet another diversionary attack in the north in 617), and the final one, the conquest of

---

[12] Principal source: Ps. Sebeos, 112.9-19, 113.12-22, 114.27-115.4, with ***Hist.Com.***, nn.30-1, 34.

[13] Principal sources: Ps. Sebeos, 115.5-116.7, with ***Hist.Com.***, n.34; Strategius, ed. & trans. G. Garitte, *La prise de Jérusalem par les Perses en 614*, CSCO, Scriptores Iberici 11-12 (Louvain, 1960); ***Chron.Pasch.***, 704.13-705.2; ***Khuzistan Chronicle***, ed. I. Guidi, CSCO, Scriptores Syri 1, Chronica Minora 1 (Louvain, 1960), 15-39, at 25.4-21, trans. T. Nöldeke, *Die von Guidi herausgegebene syrische Chronik*, Sitzungsberichte der kais. Ak. Wiss., Phil.-hist. Cl. 128 (1893), no.IX, at 24-7.

[14] ***Chron.Pasch.***, 706.11-709.23; Ps. Sebeos, 122.12-123.7, with ***Hist.Com.***, n.37; *Nicephori Patriarchae Constantinopolitani breviarium historicum*, ed. & trans. C. Mango, CFHB 13 (Washington, D.C., 1990), cc.6.7-7.10 (London ms., cc.6.6-7.5).

[15] Ps. Sebeos, 101.1-102.20, with ***Hist.Com.***, n.21.

[16] Ps. Sebeos, 123.8-9; Nic., c.7.10-22 (London ms., c.7.5-15).

[17] Ps. Sebeos, 102.25-103.13, with ***Hist.Com.***, n.21.

Asia Minor (initiated in 622).[18] The climactic campaign would be undertaken in alliance with the Avar khaganate, a great nomad power centred on the Carpathian basin and independent of the Turks. Two armies would converge on Constantinople from east and west. With the fall of its capital and the loss of all its provinces to Persians and Avars, the Roman empire would cease to exist.

Roman resistance was to be expected until that final moment, when the nerve centre of the empire was taken. The boldness with which Heraclius counterattacked in 624 was less expected. It was a daring, impudent campaign, in which he cut loose from Roman territory and ranged widely over Transcaucasia, causing extensive damage and seeking to gain the support of local Christian rulers. It forced Khusro to halt offensive operations in Asia Minor in 625, and direct all available forces against Heraclius. Eventually he was hunted down by three armies but not without inflicting defeats on them.[19] He showed real dash as a military commander, but the actions of his army, the last armed body which the Roman empire could put into the field, were plainly no more than the final spasms of a dying organism. In spring 626, both of Khusro's senior generals, Shahrbaraz and Shahen, returned to the attack, Shahrbaraz leading the way in the south, driving Heraclius and his troops westward across northern Syria and through Cilicia up into Cappadocia, while Shahen advanced in the north on eastern Asia Minor. The end was near. The final grand campaign to take Constantinople was under way. In the Balkans, an Avar host, some 80,000-strong, was assembling with a formidable array of siege engines.[20] The Sasanian empire was at its apogee.

The Roman Middle East and the traditional Roman sector of Transcaucasia were not brought under Sasanian control with a view to their use as bargaining counters in future negotiations with the Romans. Once the decision had been taken to root out Roman power and, presumably, in the long run to extinguish all live memories of a Roman state, every effort had to be made to impose Sasanian authority on once-Roman provinces. They were being annexed. Sasanian rule was intended to last. This required a military presence large enough to deter the provincials from taking up arms against the new ruling power and to back the civil authorities with force if necessary. Garrisons must be established at nodal points, from which they could move out swiftly to scotch troubles. At the same time, care must be taken, initially, not to disturb the traditional structures of Roman government. If the Persians were to economise on the resources, military and administrative, which they committed to the occupied provinces (troops must be husbanded for the final campaign of conquest), they had to work within the existing system. Above all, it was vital that they should win over the active co-operation of city notables, who traditionally ran local government, and should do everything possible not to antagonise the population at large.

General considerations such as these seem to have shaped Persian policy, to judge by the scanty available evidence. Old provincial capitals, such as Edessa in Osrhoene and Caesarea in Palestine, remained seats of government. There is no evidence of any change to provincial boundaries or functions. Troop deployments were not obtrusive, so that there is very little evidence about them.

---

[18] Restoration of order in Palestine (presumably after the imposition of direct rule): B. Flusin, *Saint Anastase le perse et l'histoire de la Palestine au début du VIIe siècle*, 2 vols. (Paris, 1992), II, 177-80. Conquest of Egypt: *Chron.724*, 146.26-7(trans.17-18); *Khuz.Chron.*, 25.22-26.12 (trans. 25-6) *inter alia*. Attacks on Asia Minor: Ps. Sebeos, 113.23-28, with *Hist.Com.*, n.32; George of Pisidia, *Expeditio Persica*, ed. & trans. A. Pertusi, *Giogio di Pisidia Poemi*, I. *Panegirici epici*, Studia Patristica et Byzantina 7 (Ettal, 1960), 84-162.
[19] Theoph., 306.19-312.8; Ps. Sebeos, 124.11-126.5, with *Hist.Com.*, nn.39-40. *Cf.* J. Howard-Johnston, 'Heraclius' Persian Campaigns and the Revival of the East Roman Empire, 622-630', *War in History*, 6 (1999), 1-44, repr. in J. Howard-Johnston, *East Rome, Sasanian Persia and the End of Antiquity* (Aldershot, 2006), no. VIII.
[20] *Chron.Pasch.*, 716.9-726.10; Ps. Sebeos, 126.6-10, with *Hist.Com.*, n.41; George of Pisidia, *Bellum Avaricum*, ed. & trans. Pertusi, 176-224; sermon of Theodore Syncellus, ed. L. Sternbach, *Analecta Avarica*, 298.1-320.9, Rozprawy Akademii Umiejętności, Wydział Filologiczny, 2 ser., 15 (Kraków, 1900). *Cf.* J. Howard-Johnston, 'The Siege of Constantinople in 626', in C. Mango & G. Dagron, ed., *Constantinople and its Hinterland* (Aldershot, 1995), repr. in Howard-Johnston, *East Rome*, no.VII.

All we can say is that the numbers were large, since their evacuation, at the end of the war, was an elaborate operation which took several months. As it was a precondition for the establishment of peace, the order to move out must have been issued soon after Heraclius' letter accepting Persian peace proposals (received at Ganzak in Adurbadagan on 3rd April 628) reached the court of Khusro's heir, Kavad Shiroe. The evacuation of Egypt was completed in June, that of Palestine and Syria was probably under way when Shahrbaraz, the commander-in-chief of the occupation forces, met Heraclius at Arabissus in the interior basin of the Anti-Taurus in July to decide the frontier and other matters.[21] We know that the occupying forces in Egypt were in control of many cities in the Nile valley and that they included *pāspānān* ('guards', 'lookouts' – probably garrison troops), *tansardārān* (chiefs of bodyguards), and a *kanārang* (commander) of cavalry.[22] The troops stationed at Caesarea of Palestine were housed in a special fortified compound outside the city, thereby minimising friction with the local population. The authority of the city governor, a local notable, was imposed effectively at Edessa, presumably because he could call on nearby Persian forces under the command of a *marzban* (regional governor).[23]

Once Persian control was assured, there was little difficulty in incorporating the annexed Roman provinces into the Sasanian empire. Like its Roman counterpart, it was managed effectively from the centre, through a tiered administrative system, in which the military, the judicial, fiscal and civil authorities exercised separately delegated powers, not necessarily at the same level, and were severally accountable to the centre. The highest tier was military. The empire was divided into four great commands – Khurasan (East), Nemroz (South), Khwararan (West) and Adurbadagan (north) – each with its own *spahbed*. Several clay sealings imprinted with the images (mounted), names and titles of *spahbeds* have survived from the later sixth and early seventh century (see figures 1 and 2).[24] The commands were defined in terms of subordinated civil provinces, which are listed in the Armenian geography of Anania of Shirak, written not long after the Arab conquest of Mesopotamia and Iran. The principle underlying the division was that of allocating roughly equal resources, in terms of population and production, to each of the commands. Because of the unequal geographical distribution of resources – very much weighted towards the west, Media, Adurbadagan and Transcaucasia north of the Zagros and Taurus, Khuzistan and Mesopotamia to the south – the southern and eastern commands were far larger than the northern and western.[25] It was almost as if the system of commands had been devised with a view to the incorporation of the adjoining Roman territories north and south of the Taurus. Only with the inclusion of western Armenia and the whole of Asia Minor, would the Adurbadagan command match Khurasan in size. The same was true for the western command, which would only balance the southern in terms of territory, with the inclusion of Syria, Palestine and Egypt. Thereafter, Asia Minor and Egypt would act as two great outer bastions for this greatly enlarged Sasanian empire. The distance to Bithynia and the Thebaid was no greater than to Balkh, Sistan and the Indus valley. Authority would be no less effectively

---

[21] **Chron.724**, 146.28-30, 147.18-24 (trans. 17-18).
[22] J. de Menasce, 'Recherches de papyrologie pehlevie', **Journal Asiatique**, 241 (1953), 185-96, at 188-92; A.G. Perikhanjan, 'Pekhlevijskie papirucy sobranija GMII imeni A.S. Pushkina', **Vestnik Drevnei Istorii**, 77 (1961), 78-93, at 91-3.
[23] **Vita S. Anastasii**, ed. & trans. Flusin, **Saint Anastase**, I, 56-63, with commentary in II, 231-43; J.B. Chabot, ed. & trans., **Chronique de Michel le Syrien, Patriarche Jacobite d'Antioche (1166-1199)**, 5 vols. (Paris, 1899-1924), V, 403-4, 408 (trans. II, 402-3, 411); J.B. Chabot, ed., Anonymi auctoris **Chronicon ad annum Christi 1234 pertinens**, CSCO, Scriptores Syri, 3.ser., 14 (Paris, 1920), 230.17-231.13, trans. Palmer, **Seventh Century in the West-Syrian Chronicles**, 133-5.
[24] R. Gyselen, **La géographie administrative de l'empire sassanide: Les témoignages sigillographiques**, Res Orientales 1 (Paris, 1989); eadem, **The Four Generals of the Sasanian Empire: Some Sigillographic Evidence** (Rome, 2001); eadem, **Nouveaux matériaux pour la géographie historique de l'empire sassanide: Sceaux administratifs de la collection Ahmad Saeedi**, Studia Iranica, cahier 24 (Paris, 2002).
[25] A. Soukry, ed., **Géographie de Moïse de Corène** (Venice, 1881), reproduced in facsimile as *Ashkharhatsoyts (AŠXARHAC'OYC'), the Seventh Century Geography Attributed to Ananias of Shirak*, ed. R.H. Hewsen (Delmar, NY, 1994), 40. Translation and commentary in R.H. Hewsen, *The Geography of Ananias of Širak (AŠXARHAC'OYC'): The Long and Short Recensions*, Beihefte zum Tübinger Atlas des vorderen Orients B.77 (Wiesbaden, 1992), 72, 226-34.

exercised from the imperial capital in Mesopotamia. The annexed provinces were being brought under firm Sasanian control, which would not be subject to intermittent slackenings and tightenings.

Figure 1:
(a): clay sealing of Veh-Shapur (General of the South) (private collection UK);
(b): drawing of an identical seal from Rika Gyselen, ***The Four generals of the Sasanian Empire: Some Sigillographic Evidence,*** *Rome, Istituto Italiano per l'Africa e l'Oriente, 2001*

Figure 2:
(a): clay sealing of Vistahm (General of the West) (private collection UK);
(b): drawing of an identical seal from Rika Gyselen, ***The Four generals of the Sasanian Empire: Some Sigillographic Evidence,*** *Rome, Istituto Italiano per l'Africa e l'Oriente, 2001*

The upper echelons of provincial government were, we may be sure, taken over by Persian officials. Outside Egypt, all that can be seen is the presence of governors, but it is plain that they exercised effective power in the localities. Thus, at Edessa, a city which had put up sterling resistance before capitulating in 609, the head of one of the principal local families, evidently identified as leader of an anti-Persian party, was deported together with his widowed mother and detained for a time in

Ctesiphon. Tough measures could be taken which might affect a whole city, for example the appropriation of a massive amount of silver revetment from the cathedral of Edessa (reported to have weighed 112,000 [or 120,000] pounds) as a reprisal for intrigues against the city governor.[26] It may be inferred that the main levers of local power, administrative and fiscal, were taken over, that revenues which had hitherto flowed into Roman coffers were diverted to help fund the Persian war effort.

Effective management of local affairs and appropriation of tax revenues are documented for Egypt. By a fortunate chance, a senior Persian official, a certain Shahralanozyan, figures in several papyri, Greek as well as Persian, and his reported activities provide invaluable glimpses of Persian administration in action. His area of responsibility covered the Fayyum, where he was based, and much of the Nile valley from Arcadia, if not further north, to the Upper Thebaid in the south. He appears to have had plenipotentiary powers. A subordinate, who dealt with the fiscal authorities of Oxyrhyncus and Cynopolis, was answerable to him. He also carried out tours of inspection, to judge by one letter announcing his imminent arrival in a country district, and authorised the issue of transport warrants. The *dadwar* or legal official responsible for drafting and sealing the warrants was another of his subordinates. The hypothesis advanced above that Persian authority reached deep into provincial society is borne out by this small collection of documentary material.[27]

Persian authority was, however, exercised in traditional ways within the established framework of provincial and local government. Every effort was made to ensure continuity of administrative practice. A striking example is provided by the policy adopted towards Jerusalem after the city was reoccupied for a second time in the course of 616. It might have been expected that the Persians would allow free Jewish movement into the holy city, given that Jews had proved more welcoming than Christians when they first entered Palestine and that it was an appeal from the Jews with established residence in city which had led to their initial intervention in 614. They did nothing of the kind, but rather issued a general order forbidding Jewish immigration into the city. Stability was evidently reckoned to depend on maintaining the existing balance between Christians and Jews in the city. A change of policy ran the danger of causing widespread and deep resentment among Christians in Palestine and further afield. The Sasanian government was well aware that it must respect Christian sensibilities, not least because of large and influential Christian constituencies in Mesopotamia. The equally important Babylonian Jewish community might be vociferous in its complaints, but it would not forget that many Jews in Palestine owed their lives to the Persians.[28]

This attention to Christian sensibility is also evident in other respects. The large number of Monophysites in Syria, who had been deprived of officially appointed bishops by the Roman authorities, formed a potential pro-Persian constituency which was well worth cultivating. This was duly done by the Sasanian authorities, but rather ham-handedly, since several of the new bishops who were parachuted in from Mesopotamia were resented by their rural congregations.[29] In addition there was no aversion to the appearance of the cross on coinage issued in occupied Egypt. Twelve-nummia pieces of the usual stubby Alexandrian sort were issued in large quantities (figure 3).

---

[26] Mich. Syr., V, 403-4 (trans. II, 402-3); *Chron.1234*, 223.16-30, 230.17-29 (trans.124, 133-4).
[27] Perikhanjan, 'Pekhlevskijskie papirucy', 88-9; *The Oxyrhyncus Papyri*, 77 vols. (London, 1898-2011), LV 3797 (with comments of J.R. Rea [77-8]); D. Weber, 'Ein bisher unbekannter Titel aus spätsassanidischer Zeit?', in R.E. Emmerick & D. Weber, ed., *Corolla Iranica: Papers in Honour of Prof. Dr. David Neal Mackenzi ...* (Frankfurt, 1991), 228-35, at 228-32; A. Gariboldi, 'Social Conditions in Egypt under the Sasanian Occupation (619-629 AD)', *La parola del passato: rivista di studi antichi*, 64 (2009), 321-350.
[28] Ps. Sebeos, 117.2-20, with *Hist.Com.*, n.35.
[29] Mich. Syr., V, 389-91 (trans. II, 379-81); *Chron.1234*, 224.28-225.9 (trans. 125-6).

*Figure 3: 12 nummi coins struck in Alexandria during the Persian occupation
left 20.04g, right 7.40g (scale x2)*

The attribution can be made confidently on the basis of the anomalous type (beardless frontal bust, armed, with small cross on top of crown or helmet, between star and crescent on the obverse, long cross on globe on reverse). The inclusion of two crosses should be viewed as a deliberate measure to reconcile the population to Persian rule.[30]

New coins were not minted by the Sasanian authorities in Syria and Palestine. There was a plentiful stock of Roman coins (gold and copper) conveying traditional political and religious messages, which continued to be topped up from Constantinople in the first four years of Heraclius' reign. Undoubtedly drachms would have arrived in large numbers, as salaries and pay for Persian officials and troops. It is unlikely that many entered the local circulating medium, which consisted exclusively of copper and gold coins, during the Sasanian occupation – although in due course, after the merger of the Roman and Sasanian monetary systems under the Caliphate, drachms did find their way west in large quantities, as is shown by their presence in Syrian hoards dating from the middle of the eighth to the early ninth century.[31] The only new coins minted in the Levant in relatively small quantities – they formed no more than 0.4% of the Syrian coin-stock in 630 – were struck with all sorts of spurious mintmarks at what was probably a clandestine mint, operating at or close to Emesa.

The quality of workmanship varied, presumably as the danger of detection rose and fell. Interspersed among imitations of old types of Justin II, Maurice and Phocas, which would not arouse suspicion, it minted local copies of current official Roman coins, bearing the images of Heraclius and his son, Heraclius the New Constantine (figure 4).[32] It was perhaps no more than a gesture of defiance by dissident elements, issued in the hope of fomenting sedition, at times of heightened anxiety in 614 (the year of the sack of Jerusalem), 618 (preparations for the invasion of Egypt) and 622-4 (the start of the conquest of Asia Minor).[33] Such hopes were vain. The Persian occupation seems to have been accepted as a brute fact by the great majority of the population.

The Persians thus were content, in the first place, simply to decapitate Roman provincial administrations and to provide the necessary military backing for the effective imposition of their authority. Reforms to administrative structures, to bring them into line with long-established Sasanian norms, were deferred for the moment, at the very least until the victorious conclusion of

---

[30] J.R. Phillips, 'The Byzantine Bronze Coins of Alexandria in the Seventh Century', *NC* 7 ser., 11 (1962), 225-41.
[31] M. Abu-l-Faraj al-Ush, ***The Silver Hoard of Damascus*** (Damascus, 1972); R. Gyselen & L. Kalus, ***Deux trésors monétaires des premiers temps de l'Islam*** (Paris, 1983); M. Abu-l-Faraj al-Ush, ***Trésor de monnaies d'argent trouvé à Umm-Hajarah*** (Damascus, 1972); R. Gyselen & A. Nègre, 'Un trésor de Gazīra (Haute Mésopotamie): Monnaies d'argent sasanides et islamiques enfouies au début du IIIe siècle de l'hégire/ IXe siècle de notre ère', ***Revue Numismatique***, 6 ser., 24 (1982), 170-205.
[32] H. Pottier, *Le monnayage de la Syrie sous l'occupation perse (610-630)*, Cahiers Ernest-Babelon 9 (Paris, 2004).
[33] Pottier, ***Monnayage***, 56 (table VIII).

the war. Assimilation of the population, in the first place of the governing elites, may have been a long-term aim, but it would take several generations.

Figure 4: Coins struck in Syria during the Persian occupation in years 2, 3, 6 and 12 Coin (a) imitates Phocas, (b) imitates Heraclius and Heraclius Constantine, (c) imitates Justin II, and (d) imitates Maurice (scale x1.5)

Questions, though, remain about taxation. Heavy demands were undoubtedly being generated by the enlarged, wartime armed forces, both those dispersed in garrisons across the former Roman provinces and those operating in the field, at a time when the war was approaching its climax – not to mention the many units guarding other frontiers, engaged in internal policing duties and stationed in the metropolitan area. Increases in expenditure required commensurate increases in tax revenue, which could only be topped up with a limited and probably constant amount of freshly mined bullion (mine production being hard to increase in a short time). Were the new subjects of the King of Kings taxed at the same rate as under the Romans? How was the gold and copper coinage which they paid, at whatever rate, changed into silver drachms for disbursement by the Sasanian state? How great an increase in revenue and expenditure was required to keep the war going after 615? How much of the increase fell on the core territories of the Sasanians, in Iran and Mesopotamia? Was too high a proportion of available resources there being drained off into the war effort?

The only available gauge of the level of expenditure – on salaries, pay, payments for goods and services *etc.* – is the volume of overall mint output. This can be documented from variations in numbers of drachms minted per regnal year of Khusro II in hoards concealed at times of crisis at the end of the Sasanian era (five all told) and under early Islam (six all told).[34] Emergency hoards are likely to contain samples of the local coin-stock at the time of burial. If there is a consistent pattern in hoards concealed in different localities at different times, that pattern can be taken as representative of the general coin-stock, itself reflecting ups and downs in overall mint output. Such

---

[34] Late Sasanian hoards: Susa I, *Mémoires de la mission archéologique de Perse*, 25 (1934), 68-76, 84-7; Seleucia, H. Göbl, 'Der Sasanidische Münzfund von Seleukia (Veh-Ardašer) 1967', *Mesopotamia,* 8-9 (1973-4), 229-60; Susa II, R. Gyselen, 'Note de métrologie sassanide: les drahms de Khusrō II', *Revue Belge de Numismatique*, 135 (1989), 5-23; R. Gyselen, 'Un trésor de monnaies sassanides tardives', *Revue Numismatique*, 6 ser., 32 (1990), 212-31; Quetta, H.M. Malek, 'A Seventh- Century Hoard of Sasanian Drachms', *Iran*, 31 (1993), 77-93. Early Islamic hoards: n.31 above for those concealed in Syria; Babylon, H. Simon, 'Die sāsānidischen Münzen des Fundes von Babylon: Ein Teil des bei Koldeweys Ausgrabungen im Jahre 1900 gefundenen Münzschatzes', *Acta Iranica*, 3 ser., 12, Textes et mémoires 5, Varia 1976 (Tehran-Liège, 1977), 149-337.

consistency *is* discernible not only across the four hoards recovered in the course of excavations, two at Susa, one at Seleucia and one at Babylon, but also across the others, chance finds with or without recorded provenances.

Overall mint output can be no more than a rough and ready indicator of trends in expenditure and taxation – rough and ready because the proportion of old drachms reminted may have varied greatly from year to year and from mint to mint. The ups and downs in mint output cannot therefore provide more than an indication of the general trend in the level of expenditure over a period of five years or so and a rough idea of the level of increase or decrease in expenditure. Nevertheless some significant trends are revealed by the hoards – first an increase in drachm output from regnal year 24 (613-14) to a peak around year 28 (617-18), in what was a key phase in the war, when Persian forces were engaged on three fronts, raiding deep into Asia Minor (615 and 617), pushing south in the Levant and preparing for the invasion of Egypt (619), and facing the Turks and their Kushan clients in the east (615-16). A second surge in coin production, signalling a second phase of high expenditure, occurred, not unexpectedly, as the war approached and entered its critical phase from regnal year 31 (620-1). This second surge in minting and expenditure was on a par with the first, a sign perhaps that output was at the maximum feasible level.[35]

Part of the increased revenue funding the first surge in expenditure may well have come from the provincials of Syria and Palestine after they were brought under Persian rule (613-616). Likewise an accretion of funding from Egypt after its conquest (619-21) may have contributed to the second surge. The conversion of the gold received from ex-Roman taxpayers into silver was presumably handled by money changers and bullion traders – but of them, of the processes involved and of the places, whether inside or outside the empire (in India, say), where the exchanges were made, we know nothing. As for the incidence of taxation, the evidence, both literary and documentary, suggests that the main burden fell on Sasanian taxpayers within the boundaries of the old empire. One of the main items on the charge-sheet against Khusro II (which is summarised in a wide range of sources in Greek, Armenian, Syriac and Arabic) concerned taxation – its high level and the severe measures taken against those in arrears. This was evidently a *leitmotiv* of the political opposition which developed in the late 620s.[36]

The regime must have been tempted to squeeze newly acquired subjects in annexed territories, to ease the pressure at home. There is evidence from Egypt that the temptation was resisted and that taxes were not raised to exorbitant levels after the Persian take-over. Papyri do not, alas, provide any evidence about the *embole*, the extraction of large quantities of grain for shipment overseas. It is likely, though, that it was scaled down, as demand was reduced. For Persian forces based in the Levant almost certainly required less of Egypt's surplus than had Constantinople. As for the tax paid in gold, some tantalising pieces of evidence are to be found in the archive of the Apion estate at Oxyrhyncus. Three documents date from the 623-4 tax year, with a fourth providing a point of comparison before the Persian conquest. It is a fascinating small dossier. A local official, Marinus, was responsible for forwarding to the Persian authorities revenue raised in cash from the two cities of Oxyrhyncus and Cynopolis, on opposite banks of the Nile. Marinus dealt directly with a Persian official, Razbana, who was answerable in turn to a senior postholder whom we have already encountered, Shahranalyozan. The tax was paid in three instalments, between October and May. Figures are given for two instalments in 623-4. An initial payment of 3,962 solidi, made in October 623, was 2,016 short of the required total of 5,978 solidi. A fierce dunning letter from Razbana

---

[35] The ups and downs of overall drachm production can best be gauged from the three late Sasanian hoards which were excavated (Susa I, Seleucia, Susa II) – see the graph at R. Gyselen, 'Un trésor de monnaies sassanides tardives', ***Rev.Num.***, 6 ser., 32 (1990), 212-31, at 220.

[36] MD, 145.3-17 (trans. 89-90); M.J. de Goeje *et al.*, ed., ***Annales quos scripsit Abu Djafar Mohammed ibn Djarir at-Tabari***, 1 ser., II (Leiden, 1881-2), 1047.5-8, trans. C.E. Bosworth, ***The History of al-Tabari***, V ***The Sasanids, the Byzantines, the Lakmids, and Yemen*** (Albany, NY, 1999).

demanding prompt payment duly extracted the balance owing three weeks later in early November.[37] Part-payment of the third instalment, amounting to 5,040 solidi, is acknowledged in a receipt dated April-May 624 and issued in the name of Shahranalyozan.[38]

The documentation is not unproblematic. Lacking an official receipt for the first payment, we cannot be sure whether it was made on behalf of one city or both of them. If it only came from one, the total sum paid in the first instalment would have amounted to around 10,000 solidi rather than a little under 6,000. Then there is the puzzling discrepancy between the amount owing on the first instalment in October, which is divided equally between the two cities, and the imbalance in their contributions to the down-payment on the third instalment in April-May – Oxyrhyncus put in four times as much as Cynopolis. Presumably that imbalance would have been redressed in a later payment, Cynopolis contributing much more than Oxyrhyncus. That would bring the total again to around 10,000 solidi. The only alternative – to postulate significant variations (1) in the proportion paid by each city and (2) in the total sum produced, from instalment to instalment – seems highly improbable, implying as it would excessive discretion on the part of the tax authorities, which would in turn increase the potential for corruption. It looks then as if the two cities paid around 30,000 solidi in cash in the 623-4 financial year, a figure which was somewhat higher than the annual gold payment required from them before the arrival of the Persians. They were assessed at 24,500 solidi in a document which, though not precisely dated, was probably issued by the Roman authorities earlier in the seventh century – there is no indication of Persian presence and the *embole* was in full swing (the cash value of the two cities' contribution amounting to 35,000 solidi, at the rate of 10 *artabae* to the solidus).[39] If like is being compared with like and the suggested dating of the assessment is correct, taxes in gold imposed on two cities of the middle Nile valley in one year of the Persian occupation had risen by some 25%, an increase which was almost certainly offset by a significant reduction in the *embole*.

There are, as has been stressed, several uncertainties in this argument, not to mention the obvious danger in generalising from a single attested case to Persian policy throughout the Roman Middle East through the whole period of the occupation. But the evidence which chances to survive in the Apion archive does appear, at first sight, to confirm the hypothesis that the Persians refrained from squeezing their new subjects too hard.

Sasanian coins, like those of most ancient, medieval and modern regimes, conveyed ideological messages in their imagery and legends, stressing, from the first, the divine election of kings and the importance of Zoroastrianism. They could also convey more ephemeral political messages, designed to enhance the status of particular kings at particular times. No king had more cause to make use of special issues than Khusro II, as he gradually battered the Roman empire into submission. He issued two distinct types of gold ceremonial coins, the second of which has a silver analogue and a silver variant. The first type, which is confined to dinars, appears to refer forward to future victory. Khusro appears on both sides of the coin: a frontal rather than the usual profile bust on the obverse; a full-length figure, likewise looking out, on the reverse, with his hands resting on the hilt of a long sword with its point on the ground (figures 5 and 6). The legends credit him with increasing *khwarrah* (royal glory) and, on the reverse, with freeing the world from fear. Coins of this type were struck for ceremonial distribution in regnal years 13 (602-3), 33 (622-3) and 34 (623-4), at the opening of the war and at the start of its final phase, when attacks were launched into Asia Minor.[40] They downplay Khusro's role as agent of the gods: the wings of Verethragna have been

---

[37] P. Oxy LI 3637, XVI 1843.
[38] P. Oxy LV 3797.
[39] P. Oxy XVI 1909.
[40] K. Mosig-Walburg, 'Sonderprägungen des Xusrō II. vom Typ Göbl V/6 und VI/7', *Iranica Antiqua*, 28 (1993), 169-91, at 169-77, 184-90. I leave to the side the twenty coins dated year 36 which appeared on the market between 1992 and 1997.

removed from his crown and he, a mere human being, replaces the fire altar with attendants which is customary on the reverse. The long sword points surely to the human feats of valour which are expected.

Figure 5: Ceremonial dinar of Khusro II of year 33
(Staatliche Museen zu Berlin, Münzkabinett, on-line catalogue)

Figure 6: Ceremonial dinar of Khusro II of year 34
(photograph courtesy of the Hermitage Museum)

The second type, by contrast, stresses Khusro's divine empowerment and devotion to the true faith. It is found on one and half dinars, dinars and drachms issued in year 21 (610-11), the year when his forces crossed the Euphrates and reached the sea, thereby dividing the Roman empire in two (figure 7). It thus probably marked the victorious conclusion of the first phase of the western war. On the obverse, there is a profile bust of Khusro (bearded), wearing his usual crown with the wings of victory. The reverse shows a frontal bust of a beardless man, whose head and hair are haloed in flames. The legend announces Khusro's success – 'Khusro, King of Kings, has increased *khwarrah*' (obv) and 'has increased Iran, well-omened' (rev).[41]

---

[41] R. Gyselen, 'New Evidence for Sasanian Numismatics: the Collection of Ahmad Saeedi', in R. Gyselen, ed., *Contributions à l'histoire et la géographie historique de l'empire sassanide*, **Res Orientales** 16 (Bures-sur-Yvette, 2004), 49-140, at 64-5; K. Mosig-Walburg, 'Sonderprägungen Khusros II. (590-628): Innenpolitische Propaganda vor

Figure 7: Ceremonial dinar of Khusro II of year 21 (CNG sale 81 lot 748)

The reappearance of the title King of Kings on a coin for the first time since the fifth century signals the extraordinary success which Khusro had achieved by the summer of 610, with the incorporation of all Roman territory east of the Euphrates. While the identity of the flame-haloed figure on the reverse is disputed, there can be little doubt that the flames which rise vertically are those of the sacred fire, normally represented in miniature on top of a fire-altar on the reverse of the drachm. The placing of a bust in the fire had a precedent, in the reverse type of drachms issued by Ohrmazd II and his successors down to Yazdgerd I, where a minuscule bust can be seen inside the flames on top of the altar (figure 8).[42]

Figure 8. Drachm of Ohrmazd II with a bust in the flames of the sacred fire (CNG Auction 304 lot 206)

Flames and bust, enlarged on Khusro II's special issue and detached from the altar, may have carried a second meaning, representing the radiating light or glory (*khwarrah*) of a divinely appointed and divinely guided King of Kings.[43] The message conveyed was triumphalist and was

---

dem Hintergrund des Krieges gegen Byzanz', in R. Gyselen, ed., *Sources pour l'histoire et la géographie du monde iranien (224-710)*, **Res Orientales** 18 (Bures-sur-Yvette, 2009), 185-208, at 189-94, 198.

[42] **SNS**, II, 362-7, III.1, 89, 215-19, 250-1, 268-9, 288-91, 321-5. The small bust moved to the front of the altar on the reverse of Bahram V Gor's drachms, before disappearing after his reign (**SNS**, III.1, 347-50).

[43] *Cf.* R. Gyselen, 'Un dieu nimbé de flammes d'époque sassanide', **Iranica Antiqua**, 35 (2000), 291-314. For *khwarrah* and its representation, see T. Daryaee, 'The Use of Religio-Political Propaganda on the Coinage of Xusrō II', **American Journal of Numismatics**, ser. 2, 9 (1997), 41-53, at 46-9.

clearly intended for a wider audience than courtiers, hence the striking of drachms as well as gold coins.

Two years later (612-13), another special drachm was issued, this time with Khusro's bust turned from the right to face the viewer on the obverse.[44] It was presumably the consolidation of the Persian hold on northern Syria which was being celebrated. On two subsequent occasions, the same type (with frontal bust of Khusro) was issued but with a change to the legend on the reverse, almost certainly to celebrate and commemorate two further successes, the first actual, namely the occupation of the whole of the Roman Levant (years 26-8, 615-18), the second in prospect but assured, the imminent fall of Constantinople (years 36-7, 625-7). The legend on the reverse now described Khusro as 'of the good religion' rather than 'well-omened'.[45] Despite this additional emphasis on his Zoroastrian faith, there was hubris in the special issues of years 36 and 37. Khusro was announcing victories before they had been won, assuming that Constantinople could not possibly hold out.

Figure 9: Ceremonial drachm of Khusro II of year 23 (courtesy CNG list of September 2012)

Figure 10: Ceremonial drachm of Khusro II of year 36 (courtesy Peus auction 380, November 2004, lot 642)

---

44 H.M. Malek, 'The Sasanian King Khusrau II (AD 590-628) and Anāhitā', *Nāme-ye Irān-e Bāstān*, 2 (2002), 23-40.
45 Gyselen, 'Un dieu nimbé de flammes', 309-10; Gyselen, 'New Evidence', 64-5; Mosig-Walburg, 'Sonderprägungen Khusros II.' (2009), 190-1, 193-4.

This was an eminently reasonable assumption to make in early summer 626. Two Persian armies were converging on Asia Minor, Shahen's advancing through Transcaucasia toward the interior plateau of Asia Minor, Shahrbaraz's pursuing Heraclius' expeditionary force westward and up on to the plateau through the Cilician Gates. Heraclius then veered off north-east, giving Shahrbaraz free passage towards the Bosporus where he was to link up with the Avars on the European side. There was nothing much to fear from Heraclius and his troops. Their numbers, limited at the outset, were doubtless depleted and their energy diminished after two years of unceasing action in the field. This time, Heraclius would be hunted down and cornered, having nowhere to flee.[46] It was true that he had managed to make contact with the Turks. A Turkish army even ventured across the Caucasus and raided eastern Transcaucasia that summer, but Khusro was not daunted by the menacing diplomatic note which he received, simply replying with an equally menacing note of his own. If the Turks persisted in seeking war, he would unleash his victorious forces against them. They should put little faith in the Roman fugitive who had managed so far to evade capture. The two great Persian generals who had destroyed the Roman empire would be turned east and woe then betide the Turks.[47]

Khusro was justifiably confident. The special drachms commemorating his victories were serving to broadcast the news of his achievements in the west, especially perhaps to the far-flung provinces fronting the steppes and the badlands of the south-east (hence the decision of a later ruler of Zabulistan to model issues of his own on these special drachms).[48] His western victories were thus used to bolster his reputation in the east and elsewhere in his empire. They also served to inflate his pride to danger level. Towards the end of his reign he is portrayed by the written sources as arrogant, unsympathetic to the strains of war on troops and taxpayers, and all too ready to resort to force in dealings with his great subjects. His was a classical case of hubris which would all too soon be followed by nemesis.[49]

He was evidently very conscious of the extraordinary scale of his success in war, only matched by the greatest of his predecessors, Shapur I in the third century. He was already planning to have monumental rock reliefs carved at the two ideological nodes of the empire, Bisutun in Media where Darius had recorded his achievements and Naqsh-i Rustam in Persia where his third-century predecessors had recorded their achievements below the tombs of ancient great kings. Work was well advanced at both sites a little over year later, when, in autumn 627, by a military stroke of foolhardy genius, Heraclius invaded Mesopotamia from the north and sent Khusro scuttling from his palace at Dastagerd to the safety of Ctesiphon behind the Nahrawan canal. The cliff surface at both sites had been excavated to create large screens for the depiction of Khusro's triumphs, the screen at Bisutun (not quite finished) being the largest ever carved.[50]

One aches to know how Khusro would have commemorated the annihilation of Rome for all time. Would there have been a panoramic battle scene (as in Piero della Francesca's depiction of the Battle of Nineveh), with the king himself striking down Heraclius at its centre? Or would Khusro have sat enthroned on one side, ready to receive the submission of representatives of all the conquered provinces headed by a delegation of senators, while Ohrmazd and Verethragna looked on benignly from the other side? Instead all we can do is to marvel at the grandeur of the screen carved out of the living rock at the base of the Bisutun cliffs with its large viewing platform, look on a void, not even 'two vast and trunkless legs of stone', and seek out the few capitals which have survived from the palace which Khusro was building nearby.

---

[46] Howard-Johnston, 'Siege of Constantinople', 131-3.
[47] MD, 133.16-134.18, 140.17-143.20 (trans. 81-3, 86-8).
[48] R. Gyselen, 'Un dieu nimbé de flammes', 298-301.
[49] MD, 145.3-17 (trans. 89-90); Tabari, 1042.1-1043.1, 1046.8-1047.17.
[50] J. Howard-Johnston, 'Pride and Fall: Khusro II and His Regime, 626-628', in G. Gnoli, ed., *La Persia e Bisanzio*, Atti dei Convegni Lincei 201 (Rome, 2004), 93-113, at 94-6, repr. in Howard-Johnston, *East Rome*, no.IX.

7th Century 'barbarous' Folles;
a Secondary Mint in the Eastern Part of the Byzantine Empire under Persian Rule

Henri Pottier [1]

The analysis of the coinage of folles in Syria during the Persian occupation was published in 2004 in 'Cahiers Ernest-Babelon'[2] and complemented by a paper in 2010 in *RN*.[3] These folles were struck in what was designated the 'Syrian mint'. In practice, these coins were probably struck in two different mint places, both depending on the same authority, as indicated by the fact that both were struck to the same weight standards, which differed from the imperial ones.

During the research on the Syrian folles, some imitations of Heraclius and Heraclius Constantine's folles were recorded which clearly were not part of the 'Syrian' mintage for various reasons: different style, different weight standards and use of immobilized dates. As a consequence we recorded them in a separate chapter AA3, entitled 'Barbarous imitations'.[4]

Now, due to the kind contribution of members of the Seventh Century Syrian Numismatic Round Table, the number of known specimens has reached 39, which seems enough to start a first analysis.

Generally the term 'barbarous' is used for masking the absence of an answer to the following questions: by whom, when, where and why were these folles struck? However, the barbarous adjective is judiciously used to characterize the style of the figures represented on the obverses of the folles that clearly show that the die engravers were unskilled.

The aim of this paper is to try to give a more civilized, or at least a less barbarous, picture of these coins.
The classification and the analysis of the 'Syrian' folles produced in Syria during the Persian occupation (610-30) have been made easier since it was demonstrated that their dates and officina numbers were really meaningful. Unfortunately, this is not the case for the barbarous folles where the dates and officina number are just copies of models locally circulating at that time.

As a consequence, the only criteria we used for classification and dating proposal are:

- Iconography
- Mark of value M or m
- Pseudo-mintmark
- Similarity of immobilised dates
- Die links
- Metrological data
- Origin of the recorded coins

---

[1] Henri Pottier is an independent scholar   henri.pottier@skynet.be
[2] H. Pottier, ***Le monnayage de la Syrie sous l'occupation perse (610-630)***. *Coinage in Syria under Persian rule*, Cahiers Ernest-Babelon 9, CNRS éditions, Paris, 2004, with a *Historical introduction: the Persian Near East (602-630 AD)* by Clive Foss
[3] H. Pottier, ***Le monnayage de la Syrie sous l'occupation perse (610-630) Complément***, *RN* 2010, pp. 447-476.
[4] H. Pottier, op. cit. fn. 2, pp. 87, 139 f., Pl. XVII

We consider four different series of similar crude style. The representation of the two figures is clumsy or caricatured, or even erroneous: sometimes their feet are turned right when they are facing or the globus cruciger is reduced to a simple cross in their right hands. The style of some obverses is comparable to the style of some Pseudo-Byzantine coins struck in Greater Syria after the Arab conquest.

The obverse iconography of the various series imitates the imperial folles of Heraclius and Heraclius-Constantine minted during the regnal years 3 to 6, i.e. between October 612 and 616. It indicates that the production of barbarous folles started after 612, unlike the Syrian coins, minted shortly after the Persian occupation that first imitate the obverses of Phocas folles.

Series 1. Rv. m

The mark of value m characterizes the first type of barbarous folles like it did for the first type of Syrian coins. The model imitated for the reverse certainly was the follis minted in Antioch under the reign of Phocas. This is confirmed by the pseudo-mintmark THEUP as well as by the immobilized dates Ϛ/I or II/Ϛ from the last regnal years of Phocas. This series is also characterized by particularly blundered obverse inscriptions where most of the letters are replaced by meaningless signs.

Three of the five obverse dies from series 1 are linked with specimens from two other series, reinforcing its status as the first series. The average weight is 10.41 ± 1.25g, similar to the imperial standards of Phocas as well as of Heraclius folles dated 3 to 6, i.e. 10.97g. The reference to Antioch indicates that the barbarous mint was located in the Eastern part of the Byzantine Empire.

Series 2. Rv. M – heavy module – pseudo-date 8

The mark of value M matches the reverse of the imperial folles of Heraclius. However, the immobilized dates refer to the latest regnal year 8 (ϚII or YIII) of Phocas. One of the obverse dies [6] could be a crude imitation of Phocas and Leontia.

The pseudo-mintmarks derive from NIKO, CON or KYZ, generally in a blundered form. The recorded officinae A, Γ and Δ are meaningless, probably copies of imperial models. Among these, the imperial Antioch folles, particularly under Mauritius Tiberius, were mainly produced by the officinae Γ and A. Three of the 13 obverse dies are linked to folles of the series 1, confirming that both series are produced by the same mint.

This barbarous series is the most numerous. The average weight is 11.64 ± 0.65g, again similar to 11.26g, the imperial standard of the second type of Heraclius folles minted during the regnal years 6 to 14.

Half-follis XX

The only recorded half-follis has XX as the mark of value, similar to the type of mark used during the reign of Phocas. The reference to Phocas is also expressed by the blundered obverse inscription starting with IIOCOΛ. However, we classify it, as well as a follis struck with the same obverse die, in the Heraclius series 2 due to the fact that its iconography is not in accordance with the imperial figure of Leontia: she should hold a sceptre resting on her right shoulder and should wear a basilissa crown with prependulia. Furthermore, the half-follis weight of 5.67g corresponding to a follis weight of 11.34g is similar to 11.64g, the average weight of the series 2.

Series 3. Rv. M – light module

This series is characterized by a very crude style, more blundered inscriptions and sometimes without a date. Nevertheless, seven of the eight specimens are die linked: two of the three obverse dies are linked to the series 1 and 2 as well as to the XX half-follis of series 2. Two of the reverse dies are linked to series 2, confirming that all these series are produced by the same mint.

When the date is mentioned, it is Ч/II, as in series 2. The officinae A and Γ here again are probably meaningless. The average weight is 8.13 ± 0.9g, similar to 8.25g, the imperial standard during the regnal years 15 to 19.

Series 4. Rv. M – pseudo-date 3

The mark of value as well as the date III now correspond to the reverse of the imperial model. However, the mintmarks here are illegible and the officinae A, Γ and Є are probably meaningless. There are no die links to show that series 4 belongs to the same mint as the other series, but this could be due to the limited number (6) of known specimens as some similarities in style suggest a relation with series 1 to 3. Furthermore, the absence of die links could justify the chronological order: the dies manufactured during the last phase could obviously not appear in the previous series.

Compared with the previous series, the weight 9.97 ± 0.63g is coming back close to the weights of series 1, but also close to the imperial standard of the regnal years 20 and 21. However, here again the conclusion should take into account the limited number of known specimens.

Tentative conclusions

The derivation of the barbarous coins from the iconography of Heraclius and from Antioch folles under Phocas leads us to compare these series with the 'Syrian' folles minted in Northern Syria (Emesa?) during the Persian occupation from 610 to 630. The common reason for the establishment of both irregular mints in the Eastern part of the Empire is, without doubt, the need for currency for trade in the occupied provinces after the closure of the Antioch mint and in the absence of coinage supply from the other imperial mints.

Apart from this common origin, the output of the two mints presents different characteristics:

1. The production of the Syrian mint is higher than the barbarous one; currently the number of barbarous folles recorded is 39 while the number of Syrian specimens is more than 300. Even with a larger production, the 'Syrian' coins seem to circulate in a quite limited area in Northern Syria, specimens having been found in excavations and hoards located in Apamea and Tell Bisa (i.e. close to Emesa). No specimen has been found either in the excavations in Antioch or in Gerasa.
2. The obverse figures of the first barbarous series imitating Heraclius and Heraclius-Constantine mean that the mint activity started after 612. If the reason for starting minting two years later than at the Syrian mint is that the Persian occupation occurred two years later, the location of the barbarous mint could be Palestine. Hitherto, unfortunately the provenances of the 39 known coins have not been recorded. The proportion of Syrian coins circulating in Syria around 630 is estimated at about 0.5% of the total amount of Byzantine coins locally in circulation. If the production of barbarous coins is 10 times lower, the absence of barbarous coins in the excavations made in Palestine is not necessarily significant.

3. The coins where the immobilized dates no longer refer to Phocas but rather to Heraclius has been classified as a fourth series, but in the absence of die links this classification is questionable. A strange characteristic of series 4 is that four of the six specimens are overstruck on earlier imperial Byzantine folles.
4. Even if the style of the emperor's design is barbarous and cruder than the 'Syrian' style, the barbarous production follows some standards similar to those applied in Constantinople, which is not the case for the Syrian mint.

Heraclius regnal years	3 to 6	6 to 14	15 to 19	20 to 21
Imperial Weight average (g)[5]	10.97	11.26	8.25	10.54
Barbarous Weight average (g) /series	10.41	11.64	8.13	9.97
95% confidence interval (g)	9.15-11.67	10.99-12.29	7.23-9.03	9.34-10.60

Comparison with imperial standards of Heraclius folles

The similarities of the barbarous weights standards with those applied in the various phases of the imperial production lead us to tentatively date the various barbarous series in accordance with the dates of the corresponding imperial phases. This weight correlation contributes to a less 'barbarous' aspect for this secondary mint.

Catalogue

The numbering of the coins and the dies is made according to the method applied in *Cahier Ernest Babelon* and *RN Complément*.

The linked obverse or reverse dies are registered with bold numbers.
N* indicates that the coin (N) was already published in *Cahier Ernest-Babelon*.
N** the coin (N) was already published in *RN Complément*.

The origin of the specimens is indicated as follows:

Private collections
AO   A. Oddy (UK)
HP   H. Pottier (B)
JPB J. - P. Blicq (B)
MD M. Donnevald (L)
NF   N. Fairhead (UK)
PP   P. Pavlou (UK)
RL   R. Lemaire (B)
SM   S. Mansfield (UK)
TG   T. Goodwin (UK)
TN   T. Natschke (G)
WL W. Leimenstoll (G)
WS W. and I. Schulze (G)

Publications
X26 *MIB 3*
Album S. Album and T. Goodwin, SICA 1

Public collection
WLM Westfälisches Landesmuseum Münster (inv. no. 16902)

Trade
AA   AA auction
eB   eBay auction
CNG Classical Numismatic Group auction

---
[5] C. Morrisson, *Catalogue des Monnaies Byzantines de la Bibliothèque Nationale*, Paris, 1970, p. 260.

AA3   'Barbarous' Ae Catalogue

coin n°	obv-rv dies	obv - *rem.*	rv - (date)	mintmark	off	mass (g)	origin	remarks
1. m								
1.1*	3.1-1	B [..] - TNOV	II/Ч	q /OЭHτ		10.41	HP	2 fig. inverted
2*	3.2-2		ANN-Λ/И/H	cON'		12.15	NF	
3.(1)*	3.3-3	CIO - ΛTƆV	AИИ - O/Ч/cI	?		7.12	HP	2 fig. inverted
3.2**	3.3-3	"	"			11.74	HP	
3a**	3.4-3a	[ ] - HNTC	ANNO - [ ]	τHЄЧP		9.66	HP	
3b	3.4a-3b	I - ΛΠ - NNI	ИИ - ЄYΛ	?		10.9	eB	
3c	3.4b-3c	*blundered inscr.*	ANNO-[ ]	*inv*KHO		10.92	TG	
2. M	**(ᘛII heavy)**							
4*	3.3-4		ИИИ - ᘛ/II	OИIX	Г	10.61	PP 20	2 fig. inverted
5.1*	3.4-5	[ ]CHv-HNT	AИИ - ᘛ/II	OHK(*inv*)	Г	10.23	RL	
5.2*	3.4-5	"	"			10.76	NF	
5.3	3.4-5	"	"			14.13	TG2	
6*	3.5-6	ЄOИI - ЄNL	AN - [ᘛ]/II ?	O ?	A	10.05	HP	
6a	3.6-4	IIOCOΛ –ITCNC	ИИИ - ᘛ/II	OИIX	Г	13.56	Trade	
7*	3.6-7	"	H/H/V	?	Г	12.70	NF	
8*	3.7-8		[ ]-III/Ч	OHIN	A	11.55	MD	
9*	3.8-9	[NCI- IIΛ.ΛIЄII]	ANN-Iᘛ(*inv*)	IЄ[..]	A	?	X26	star above **M**
10**	3.9-10	I - cIPЄRAI	ANN - [ᘛ]/II	oNK	Г	12.10	TN	
11	3.10-11	[…]	ANNO-U/II/I		Г	11.03	AO	overstr.
12	3.11-12	SCLIU-O.[CRP]	ANNO - [ ]	[CO.]	A	11.41	AO	twice overstr.
13	3.12-13	OΛCI - NN	[ ] - ᘛII	KYZ	Δ	11.26	WS	
14	3.13-14	NA - N I	AИИ - [ ]	[CON]	Δ	12.81	TG5	overstr. J II */M
15	3.14-15	[…- .AVI]	ANNO - ᘛ/II	CON	A	11.65	JPB	overstr.
16	3.15-16	ЄOИI - ЄNΛ	ΛOI - ИΔVI	YTV	A	10.69	TG7	2 fig. inverted
17	3.4a-20	I – Λ/Π - NNI	INV - CNЭ	И Пг	A	11.64	Trade	
XX								
17a	3.6-17	IIOCOΛ - [..]	XX			5.67	WS	

3. M	**(Ⴚll light)**							
18	3.16-18	vNN - CO[S..]	ANN-Ⴚll	[..H]	Г	6.64	AO	star above M
19.1	**3.6-4**	IIOCOΛ – [..]	ИИИ - Ⴚ/ll	OИIX	Г	9.37	CNG	
19.2	**3.6-4**	IIOCOΛ – [..]	ИИИ - Ⴚ/ll	OИIX	Г	8.62	Trade	
20	**3.6-19**	IIOCOΛ – [..]	*inv*Ⴚ/ll- AИИ	?	Г*inv*	8.03	Album	rv inverted
21.1	**3.4a-20**	I - Λ/Π - NNI	INV - CNƏ	И Пr	A	6.56	WS	
21.2	**3.4a-20**	"	"			9.39	WL	
22	**3.4a-21**	"	oN - ΛHИ	?	A	8.02	AA	
23	**3.4a-22**	"	[ ]o - IHΛ		A	8.79	eB	
4. M	**(III)**							
24	3.17-23	[ ] - ΛCЄN	NN - II/I ?	?	A	9.14	TG6	
25	3.18-24	ИИ - VTOO	ANNO - III	?	Є	9.93	TG3	overstr. Maur. T.
26	3.19-25	[vN..] - [N]H	ANN - II/I	?	Г	9.53	TG1	overstr. Phocas
27	3.20-26	NH-[.]A	ANN - [.]/I	[.O.] ?	A?	11.2	WLM	
28	3.21-27	IЄBP - [IISH]	[ ]-[II/I]	?	[ ]	9.50	AO	3 times overstr.
29	3.22-28	[ ] - CONP	ANNO - II/I	?	Є	10.53	AO	overstr. Maur.T.

25   26   27   28

29

WILKES & CURTIS
a modern tradition

10% BUYER'S PREMIUM

TIMED ONLINE AUCTIONS

wilkesandcurtis.com

PO Box 566
Tonbridge
TN9 9LR

+44 (0)7538-476757

mail@wilkesandcurtis.com

Some Aspects of 7thC Egyptian Byzantine Coinage

Tony Goodwin [1]

Introduction

The Egyptian 7thC copper coinage was effectively categorised by J. R. Phillips in 1962 and almost all of his conclusions still stand, but there remain a few problem areas and some of these are the subject of this paper. All coins are illustrated approximately 1.5x actual size and are from private collections unless otherwise stated.

The end of the 6th century coinage and the reign of Phocas

The distinctive Alexandrian copper coinage consisting of dodecanummia (12 nummi), and much less common fractions, was introduced either by Justin I or Justinian I in the mid 6th century. The basic design of the coins, with a profile bust and reverse denomination numeral **IB**, remained unchanged for the rest of the century and towards the end of Maurice's reign the mint was clearly functioning well. Fig. 1 shows three almost identical coins from what is probably the last issue of Maurice. These are well engraved and struck, and bear a consistent legend, unlike much official Alexandrian coinage.

Fig. 1: The last issue of Maurice Tiberius (582-602).
Obv: bust r. with consistently written legend around **DNAΠICPPA**.[2]
Rev: **I-B** *with cross between and* **AΛЄΞ** *in exergue. MIB 107b.*
Coin a 3.52g. 12h., Coin b 3.75g. 12h., Coin c 3.02g. 12h.

However, at some time around 600, either during disturbances at the end of Maurice's reign or at the beginning of the reign of Phocas, the Alexandrian mint appears to have ceased operations and no coins were issued in the name of Phocas (602-610). Wroth seems to have been the first to suggest that this gap could be filled by an extensive series of irregular coins which copy 6th century

---

[1] Tony Goodwin is an independent scholar: a.goodwin2@btopenworld.com
[2] This is an abbreviation of "Dominus Noster Mauricius Perpetuus Augustus", with an oddly written letter **R** which looks more like a **Π**. This should not be regarded as a blundering, but is more likely to be a local Egyptian letter form. These odd letter forms (based on Coptic or local Greek and Latin cursive scripts) turn up with increasing frequency on later 7thC Egyptian Byzantine and Arab-Byzantine coins.

types.³ This suggestion was adopted by Philip Grierson for the Dumbarton Oaks catalogue,⁴ and since then there has been a tendency in excavation reports for all irregular profile bust dodecanummia to be assigned to the reign of Phocas.

A selection of these irregular coins is shown in Fig. 2 and an undoubtedly regular dodecanummium of Justinian (coin a) is illustrated first for comparison. Coin b is representative of a large number of coins in the name of Justinian, with busts of coarser style and often slightly blundered legends. These are generally of full weight and, I think, should also be regarded as regular coins, which may date to later in the reign or may even be the product of a subsidiary mint. Coins c, d and e are definitely imitations, but coin c is typical of a large group of imitations which are of more or less full weight. Examples are often found which weigh over 5g., which would have been unusually heavy by the end of the 6thC.⁵ It therefore seems highly likely that at least some of these heavier imitations are roughly contemporary with their prototypes, i.e. 6thC rather than early 7thC. Coins d and e are lighter and cruder and could plausibly date from the reign of Phocas, but again a 6thC date for some of them cannot be ruled out. Coin f is a tiny cast imitation of a type often found in Israel and which may have been minted in Caesarea. A discussion of these interesting little coins is beyond the scope of this article, but their dating could well be different from the Egyptian imitations and needs to be considered as a separate problem.⁶

Another possibility that cannot be totally ruled out is that a few imitations date from after the Arab conquest, but I cannot find any evidence to support this idea and the fact that many lightweight coins are overstruck by Heraclian hexanummia (see next section) means that they were certainly being produced before 610.

Excavation evidence is also beginning to suggest a regional element to the Egyptian imitations and in the Antinoöpolis finds published by Castrizio a high proportion of the profile bust dodecanummia appear to be imitations, suggesting that some of them may be of Upper Egyptian manufacture. All the profile bust imitations that I have handled personally appear to be struck rather than cast, but Noeske recently published a wonderfully preserved pottery mould for casting profile bust imitations found at Suhag in Upper Egypt.⁷

In conclusion therefore, whilst some profile bust imitations were almost certainly struck during the reign of Phocas, many of them are probably earlier in date. Caution is therefore necessary in using these imitations to date hoards or excavation finds. Clearly considerably more research is needed in this area.

---

³ Wroth 1908 pp. 177-178.
⁴ Grierson 1968 p. 150 and pp. 192-195. All the imitations are listed under the catalogue number DOC 106.
⁵ I checked the weights of a group of 99 dodecanummia of Maurice's last issue (see Fig. 1 above), which were part of a hoard of several hundred dodecanummia apparently deposited early in the reign of Heraclius. The mean weight of these was 4.06g and only 6% weighed over 5g. 53 profile bust imitations from the same hoard, which generally seemed rather more worn than the Maurice coins, had an almost identical mean weight of 4.00g, but 17% of them weighed more than 5g. Not too much can be deduced from this somewhat superficial statistical analysis, but it does indicate that significant numbers of relatively heavy imitations were in circulation and it seems very likely that these were produced earlier in the 6th C.
⁶ For an up-to-date discussion of the Palestinian imitations see Bijovsky 2013 pp. 297-307.
⁷ Noeske 2009 p. 211 fig. 45.

Fig. 2: Imitations of 6th C dodecanummia
Coin a. Regular coin of Justinian I (527-565), Obv: bust of emperor r., **DNIVSTINIANVSPPAV**
Rev: **I-B** *with cross between and* **AΛЄΞ** *in exergue. 4.02g. 1h. MIB 165.*
Coin b. As a but of coarser style and with slightly blundered legends. 3.83g. 6h.
Coin c. Imitation of either Justinian or Justin II, as a, but with cruder bust and blundered obverse legends. 4.42g. 6h.
Coins d and e. Imitations of uncertain 6th C emperors, generally as a, but with crude bust, completely blunderd obverse legends and blundered mint name. 3.20g. 11h. and 1.85g. 5h.
Coin f. Crude cast lightweight imitation from Israel. 0.99g. 6h.

The first issues of Heraclius

Fig. 3: The first dodecanummia of Heraclius (613 or later).
Coin a. Obv: facing busts of Heraclius and Heraclius Constantine, blundered legend **ƌƌM hЄRACL…** *(or similar) around. Rev:* **I-B** *with cross-above-***N** *between and* **AΛЄΞ** *in exergue. 5.69g. 7h. MIB 201 (CNG sale 233 lot 551).*
Coin b. Obv: as coin a. Rev: **I-B** *with cross-on-steps between and* **AΛЄΞ** *in exergue. 4.50g. 6h. MIB 200 (CNG coin shop 859051).*

The first dodecanummia issued under Heraclius show the emperor with his son Heraclius Constantine and therefore cannot be earlier than 613, the year that Heraclius Constantine was crowned (Fig. 3). This leaves a surprising gap of at least 3 years at the start of the reign with apparently no Egyptian coinage.[8] In fact, given the importance of Alexandria as a staging post in the Heraclian revolt, we might also expect Alexandrian issues in the year or two before 610, but the only possible candidate is a series of non-Egyptian style folles which were either minted at Alexandria or Alexandretta in Syria (Fig. 4).[9] These coins do not look like any other products of

---

[8] A 'Heraclian revolt' dodecanummium offered in the Lanz sale of 4th June 1993 (lot 939) has rightly been dismissed by Hahn and Metlich (2009 p. 72) as an imitation similar to those discussed in the next section. They also correct the attribution in MIB of a dodecanummium in the Dumbarton Oaks collection which apparently has a facing bust (Hahn and Metlich 2009 p. 72 footnote 172). The DO catalogue identifies it as an issue of Phocas (Grierson 1968 Phocas Cat. 105) and MIB as the first Alexandrian type of Heraclius (MIB 199), but it is without much doubt no more than a regular two bust type (MIB 200) struck off-centre, so that only one bust is clearly visible.

[9] Opinion appears to swing between these two alternatives. Grierson (1968) favoured Alexandretta, whilst Hahn and Metlich (229 p. 71) argued strongly for Alexandria. In my view the arguments are not really decisive on either side.

the Alexandrian mint, so if they were produced in Alexandria, it must have been by a temporary mint associated with the army. Regardless of the location of the mint, there is no doubt that they were not intended for circulation in Egypt.

Fig. 4: Follis of the Heraclian revolt, Alexandria or Alexandretta mint.
Obv: Facing crowned busts of Heraclius and his father the Exarch Heraclius, ƌMN ERACLIO CONSULII *. Rev:* **M** *with cross above, officina* **A**, **ANNO-XIIII** *(indictional date14 =610/11) either side and* ΑΛΕΞΑΝΔ *in exergue. 7.41g. 6h.*
MIB 16b.

However, there is another possibility for closing the gap at the start of the reign of Heraclius. The first type of Heraclian hexanummium is shown in Fig. 5a and, as already mentioned, is often found overstruck on lightweight profile bust imitations (Fig. 5b). It is usually considerd as contemporary with the first dodecanummium and the legend is given in almost all catalogues as ƌƌm hERACL... or similar, indicating two domini and therefore a date of 613 or later.[10] However, the legend is almost always heavily blundered and in examining over 30 examples where the first part of the legend is visible I have been unable to find a single one which definitely begins ƌƌm. On examples where a reasonable amount of legend is visible it appears to be simply a blundered abbreviated version of **dominus heraclius**.[11] It is therefore quite possible that these coins were issued from the start of Heraclius' reign in 610, or even conceivably a year or so earlier as Heraclius is not named as Augustus and the title "dominus" was used on other coins of the revolt.

a   b

Fig. 5: The first hexanummium of Heraclius.
Coin a. Obv: cross-on-steps, blundered legend around. Rev: large **S** *with no legends.*
2.05g. MIB 210 (CNG sale 5.5.2010 lot 1620).
Coin b. As coin a, but overstruck on a profile bust imitation similar to Fig. 2e. 2.48g.

Some support for the introduction of the hexanummium early in the reign of Heraclius is provided by a group of Byzantine Alexandrian coins from the Graeco-Roman Museum in Alexandria published by Samira Abd al-Raouf Abbas in 2005, which she concluded was probably either a

---

[10] The Constantinople folles of years 1-3 (MIB 158) which show Heraclius alone have legends beginning ƌ N, an abbreviation for DOMINUS NOSTER, but when Heraclius is joined by Heraclius Constantine (MIB 159, 160) from year 4 (613/14) the start of the legend changes to ƌƌ NN to indicate two domini.
[11] In 1980 Simon Bendall published brief details of a hoard of 60 hexanummia and concluded that there appeared to be two types of legend, although the legends were usually incomplete and difficult to read. The first, for Heraclius alone, began ƌOMIN or ƌOMINU (confirmed by my own investigations), whilst the second named the two emperors. If both legends can be confirmed, this would strengthen the case for a start date before 613 for the hexanummia.

hoard or coins from a single site in Alexandria. Out of 1139 coins 1012 were of Heraclius and 933 of these were hexanummia. This preponderance of hexanummia is unusual and the group could well represent a sample of the coinage in circulation a few years into Heraclius' reign when hexanummia had been minted for several years but dodecanummia had only just started to be minted.[12]

In conclusion therefore it appears quite likely that around 610 the authorities in Egypt started to mint the new hexanummia as part of a programme to sort out the monetary chaos then prevailing. Very lightweight imitations were presumably de-monetised and imitations weighing around 2g restruck as hexanummia.

Irregular coins of Heraclius

Fig. 6: Imitations of Heraclius dodecanummia.
Obv: Crude busts of Heraclius and Heraclius Constantine, generally without surrounding legend.
*Rev: **I-B** with cross-on-steps between and blundered **ΑΛЄΞ** in exergue (all retrograde for coin d).*
Coin a 4.15g 6h; Coin b 4.15g 12h; Coin c 5.66g 5h; Coin d 4.11g 5h (imitating MIB 200).

The regular MIB 200/201 coins show considerable variation in style and usually have slightly blundered obverse legends (see for example the two very different obverses in Fig. 3), but they are competently engraved and have properly written mint names.[13] Quite distinct from these is a series of irregular coins of much cruder style which have received very little attention in numismatic literature. These often lack obverse legends altogether and almost always have blundered mint names. Four fairly typical examples are shown in Fig. 6 and appear to be the work of at least four different die engravers. Unlike the profile bust imitations there are no very lightweight examples and the average weight is only a little lower than that for the regular coins. They are not particularly common in museum collections and in two hoards of Heraclian dodecanummia that I have examined they account for less than 10% of the total number of coins of the MIB 200 type.[14] In contrast around half the MIB 200 type coins in the 'San Colluto Hoard' from Antinoöpolis appear to be irregular.[15] How can we account for this difference? The obvious explanation is that most of

---

[12] All the published excavations that I know of contain far more dodecanummia than hexanummia and the same is true of Heraclian hoards, most of which were probably deposited during the Persian invasion after 618.
[13] See Goodwin 2003 for a division into three main styles of obverse bust.
[14] Details of the first 'hoard' were published in Goodwin 2003 and the second (unpublished) was seen in trade in 2012.
[15] See Castrizio 2010 pp. 25-28. This hoard comprised 309 coins of which 306 were Egyptian Byzantine issues, almost all dodecanummia. There were 73 Heraclius dodecanummia of MIB 200 type and, from an examination of the plates, I was able to classify 31 of these as 'almost certainly regular' and 30 as 'definitely irregular'. The remaining 12 were

the irregular coins were minted in Upper Egypt and are therefore more common there. An alternative explanation is that most currently known examples of MIB 200 (including the two hoards which I examined) were deposited during the Sasanian invasion around 618 and that the irregular coins are a little later in date and so not present in these hoards. Castrizio dates the deposit of the San Colluto hoard to probably around 641, so the irregular coins in that hoard could have been produced during the Sasanian occupation. Considerably more evidence is required before drawing firm conclusions, but my present feeling is that both these explanations could be valid.

It is worth mentioning that irregular imitations of hexanummia also exist and two examples are shown in Fig. 7. Coin a is of normal weight and reasonable style, but it has a completely garbled obverse legends and a retrograde reverse. This coin should probably be regarded as irregular, but I have not had the opportunity of examinining large numbers of hexanummia, so I cannot completely rule out the possibility that it was struck by the official mint. Coin b is definitely an imitation and is of cast fabric, but it is of unknown provenance and so could possibly be a Palestinian imitation. Again more evidence is required before drawing any conclusions about irregular hexanummia.

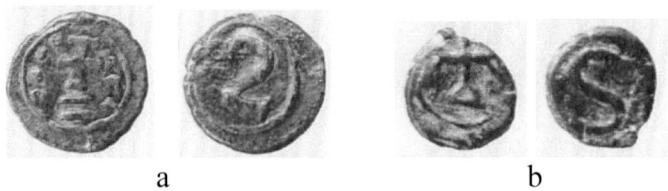

a   b

Fig. 7: Imitations of Heraclius hexanummia.
Coin a: as Fig. 5a, but legends completely blundered and reverse S retrograde. 2.58g.
Coin b: crude cast copy with no legends and obverse cross resting on a triangle. 1.84g.

Who struck the irregular coins?

In the foregoing discussion of irregular coins I have used the terms 'irregular coin' and 'imitation' more or less synonymously, which underlines our present uncertainty as to their exact status. The Heraclian imitations are clearly not the product of the Alexandria mint, but they could perhaps be the products of officially sanctioned 'mints' operating elsewhere in Egypt, perhaps during the Sasanian occupation, in which case they could be regarded as an Egyptian parallel to the extensive series of coins struck by the 'Syrian Mint' under Sasanian rule.[16] Alternatively they may be no more than totally illegal forgeries, mostly produced at a time when central control was weak.

For the earlier profile bust coins we have the additional possibility that some of them were struck at an official mint in Alexandria during the reign of Phocas as there are no definitely 'official' coins to compare them with.

With our present state of knowledge I think it would be dangerous to settle on just one of these interpretations. In 7thC Syrian numismatics we have recently seen a number of instances where coins which would previously have been classified as 'contemporary imitations' have been shown to be part of a coherent series minted with at least a degree of official approval. So it is tempting to regard at least some of the irregular Egyptian coins in the same light, but I think for the moment it would be unjustified. Further information on finds from specific sites is urgently required and metrological analysis of coins already in collections may cast some light on the problem, but it may well be that we will never be able to fully answer the question of who struck these coins.

---

difficult to classify from the images. Castrizio dates the deposition of the hoard to around 641, but, as the MIB 200 type coins appear to be the latest, a slightly earlier date seems possible.
[16] Fully described in Pottier 2004.

The last issues of Constans II

For Constans II we have the opposite problem from that at the start of the reign of Heraclius, namely rather a lot of coins compressed into rather a short time. The chronology of the period can be summarised as follows:

   640 September: Siege of Alexandria begins.
   641 January: Heraclius dies, Heraclius Constantine becomes senior emperor.
   641 April: Heraclius Constantine dies, Heraclonas becomes senior emperor.
   641 September: Constans II crowned.
   641 October: Heraclonas dies, Constans II becomes senior emperor.
   641 November: treaty of Alexandria.
   642 September: Alexandria occupied by the Arabs.
   645 Spring: Alexandria retaken by the Byzantines.
   646 Summer: Alexandria retaken by the Arabs.[17]

So far as Egypt was concerned, therefore, Constans II's reign lasted less than a year and into this period we need to fit two types of dodecanummium, the second of which is very abundant and exists in two main varieties (Fig. 8).

Fig. 8: The Alexandrian coinage of Constans II.
*Coin a. Obv: Facing imperial bust wearing chlamys and holding globus cruciger. Rev: **I-B** with cross-above-**M** between and **AΛЄΞ** in exergue. 7.84g. 6h. MIB 188 (CNG sale 288 lot 573).*
*Coin b. Obv: Standing emperor holding long cross and globus cruciger. Rev: **I-B** with cross-on-globe between and pellets to left and right, **AΛЄΞ** in exergue. 7.00g. 6h. MIB 189 (CNG sale 304 lot 425).*
*Coin c. Obv: Standing emperor holding long cross and globus cruciger. Rev: **I-B** with cross-on-globe between and **AΛЄΞ** in exergue. 8.65g. 6h. MIB 190.*

The first type (Fig. 8a) has a facing bust and could conceivably be an issue of Heraclonas. In the Dumbarton Oaks catalogue Grierson attributed all the early facing beardless bust coppers of Constans II to Heraclonas, but the correct attribution has since been conclusively demonstrated for the Constantinople and Sicily coins.[18] In the case of the Alexandrian coin the position is less clear; we know from an overstrike that it pre-dates the standing emperor type, and the bust is close to that on Constans' first solidi with a crown that has a prominent circlet or jewel surmounted by a cross

---
[17] The Egyptian chronology of this period is still largely based on the work of Butler (1902 revised edition 1908), but appears to be widely accepted among historians. A detailed chronology of the period 639-642 can be found in Trombley 2013 pp. 19-23.
[18] Grierson 1968 Heraclonas Cats. 5-9.

rather than the plain cross found on the Constantinople folles.[19] An attribution to Constans II therefore seems more likely, but Heraclonas cannot be totally ruled out. The second type uses an obverse image of a standing emperor similar to the first Constantinople folles of Constans II and may represent a conscious decision to align the Alexandrian coinage with that of the capital at a time when the former was under threat. There are two varieties; the first (Fig. 8b) has an obverse image of reasonably good style and has a pellet on either side of the **I-B** on the reverse; the second (Fig. 8c) lacks the reverse pellets and has a cruder obverse image executed in a rather linear style. Both these varieties are common and crucially both varieties are found at sites throughout the northern half of Egypt.[20]

It is difficult to believe that this variety and volume of coinage could have been distributed widely in Egypt during a single year in which the city of Alexandria was surrounded by Arab occupied territory, but I think that there is an obvious alternative explanation. It is that the Arabs simply kept the mint open in Alexandria after they occupied the city under the terms of the treaty agreed in November 641. They retained the mint personnel and continued to produce dodecanummia of Constans II – not really Pseudo-Byzantine imitations but coins which were indistinguishable from those already struck under Byzantine rule.[21] In Syria the Arabs were happy to import Byzantine coins, but in Egypt they had the opportunity to take over a city with a functioning mint. We should remember that the city was transferred by treaty, which presumably stipulated that infrastructure was left intact. It is quite possible that all of the second variety were produced under Arab control, but we have no way of telling for sure, and I would be very reluctant to label the first variety as Byzantine and the second as Arab-Byzantine. We can only speculate about how long Constans II dodecanummia continued to be minted in Alexandria, but a feasible end date would be the Byzantine re-occupation in 645/46. The Byzantines might well have destroyed the mint or removed the mint personnel when they finally left the city in the summer of 646.

Conclusions

Of the four main areas discussed, three have implications for dating coin finds:
1. There are a number of different series of profile bust imitations, some of which probably date to the 6thC. It is not therefore justifiable to date them all to the reign of Phocas.
2. The first issue of Egyptian coinage under Heraclius in about 610 may well have been the common hexanummium with a cross-on-steps reverse.
3. After the Arab occupation of Alexandria in 642 the mint probably continued to operate for a few years, striking dodecanummia of Constans II which are indistinguishable from those struck under Byzantine rule.[22]

---

[19] Throughout Heraclius' reign the obverse of the Alexandrian coppers was usually based on that of the current Constantinople solidi rather than the Constantinople folles.
[20] The excavation evidence is limited, but Castrizio (2010) records 12 from Antinoöpolis including both varieties and Milne in Quibell 1912 records 42 (identified as Type II of Heraclius) from Saqqara (pp. 37-42), although there are no illustrations, so some of these could be Arab-Byzantine imitations. Surprisingly Noeske (2000) only records 2 from Abu Mina compared with around 70 of Heraclius, but it is more than likely that pilgrimage to the site was interrupted during 641/642.
[21] These coins should not be confused with the smaller, lighter Type I Arab-Byzantine coins which copy the Constans II standing emperor type. These are described in my article on the Egyptian Arab-Byzantine coinage elsewhere in this volume.
[22] I am very grateful to members of the Round Table who contributed to the discussion following the presentation of this paper and particularly Steve Mansfield who read a draft and made numerous helpful suggestions.

Bibliography

Abd al-Raouf Abbas, S., 2005, 'Some Overstruck Coins from the Time of Heraclius' in Duyrat and Picard (eds.) *Études alexandrines* **10,** *L'exception égyptienne?*, pp. 339-357, IFAO Paris.

Bendall, S., 1980, 'A Hoard of Heraclian Six Nummi', *Numismatic Circular* **LXXXVIII**, p. 661.

Bijovsky, G., 2013, *Gold Coin and Small Change: Monetary Circulation in Fifth – Seventh Century Byzantine Palestine*, Trieste.

Butler, A., 1902, revised edition 1978 by P. M. Fraser, *The Arab Conquest of Egypt and the Last Thirty Years of the Roman Dominion*, Oxford.

Castrizio, D., 2010, *Le Monete della Necropoli Nord di Antinoupolis (1937-2007)*, Firenze.

Domaszewicz, L. and Bates, M., 2002, 'Copper Coinage of Egypt in the Seventh Century' in Bacharach, J. (ed.), *Fustat Finds*, pp. 88-111, Cairo.

Goodwin, T., 2003, 'A Hoard of Seventh Century Byzantine Dodecanummia', *Numismatic Chronicle*, pp. 355-357 and pl. 47.

Grierson, P., 1968, *Catalogue of the Byzantine Coins in the Dumbarton Oaks and Whittemore Collection* **Vol. 2**, Washington.

Hahn, W., 1975 and 1981, *Moneta Imperii Byzantini 2 and 3*, Vienna, referred to as 'MIB'.

Hahn, W. and Metlich, M., 2009, *Money of the Incipient Byzantine Empire Continued*, Vienna.

Metlich, M. and Schindel, N., 2004, 'Egyptian Copper Coinage in the 7th Century AD. Some Critical Remarks' in *ONS Newsletter* **179** pp. 11-15.

Noeske, H.-C., 2000, *Münzfunde aus Ägypten* **I**, Berlin.

Noeske, H.-C., 2009, 'Finds of coins and Related Objects from the Monastery of Apa Shenute at Suhag', *Dumbarton Oaks Papers* **63,** pp. 210-219.

Phillips, J., 1962, 'The Byzantine Bronze Coins of Alexandria in the Seventh Century', *Numismatic Chronicle*, pp. 225-241.

Pottier, H., 2004, *Le monnayage de la Syrie sous l'occupation Perse (610-630),* Paris.

Quibell, J. E., 1912, *Excavations at Saqqara – the Monastery of Apa Jeremias*, Cairo.

Trombley, F., 2013, 'Fiscal Documents from the Muslim Conquest of Egypt', *Revue des Etudes Byzantines* **31**, pp. 5-38.

Wroth, W., 1908, *Catalogue of the Imperial Coins in the British Museum* **Vol. 1**, London.

STEPHEN ALBUM RARE COINS

SPECIALISTS IN ISLAMIC, INDIAN, & ORIENTAL COINS
SINCE 1976

EXPERTISE

We are universally regarded as the world's premier experts in Islamic coinage.

DIVERSITY

We hold three major auctions per year, release multiple fixed-price lists per year, and attend numerous U.S. and international trade shows.

INTEGRITY

As members of the IAPN and other major organizations, we can be relied upon to be a trustworthy resource, whether you are buying or selling. Decades of experience have earned us this sterling reputation.

Pictured At Left:
A selection of Arab-Byzantine coins from our past auctions.

Stephen Album Rare Coins, Inc.
PO Box 7386
Santa Rosa, California, 95407, U.S.A.
TEL: 1-707-539-2120
FAX: 1-707-539-3348
info@stevealbum.com
Member: IAPN, ANA, ANS, ONS, RNS, CSNA, AVA, MCS
www.stevealbum.com

Byzantine and Early Islamic Coinage at Excavations in Jericho

Tasha Vorderstrasse [1]

Introduction

This article will examine the numismatic evidence from Byzantine and Early Islamic Jericho that comes from archaeological excavations.[2] Despite Jericho's importance as a settlement in Palestine, particularly in the Early Byzantine period, the coins from different archaeological excavation sites have never been examined in detail. The reasons for this become evident when one begins to look at the archaeological evidence. Most of the coins from excavations have only been published as descriptions, meaning it is difficult to make specific statements about coin circulation of specific types. Nevertheless, the coins have been published in enough detail that it is still possible to make statements about coin circulation in the Late Roman, Early Byzantine, and Early Islamic periods. Further, the evidence seems to indicate that both Late Roman and Early Byzantine coins continued to circulate in the Early Islamic period. This article will not only look at previously published evidence from archaeological sites for coins circulating in the Early Byzantine and Early Islamic periods but also from recent excavations by the University of Chicago at Khirbet el-Mafjer and Tell al-Hassan. The evidence from these excavations will provide further information about coinage and coin use in these periods. The article will first look at the settlement of Byzantine and Early Islamic Jericho, before turning to the previously published and the new coin evidence. It will conclude by examining the significance for the coin circulation and what this tells us about the site in the Byzantine and Early Islamic periods.

Byzantine and Early Islamic settlement in Jericho

Jericho is one of the oldest continually inhabited settlements in the world and as such, has attracted considerable attention from archaeologists. The site became particularly important in the Early Byzantine period, as Jericho and its environs attracted monastic and pilgrimage activity. Churches and monasteries belonging to different Christian denominations were built in Jericho and its surroundings. The urban centre of Jericho was focused on the area that is now known as Tell al-Hassan. After the Islamic conquest, Tell al-Hassan remained the main centre of occupation in the Early Islamic period, as it had been in the Early Byzantine period. Furthermore, a fortress was erected at Tell Abu al-'Alayiq, as well as a military encampment and water devices, and the palace complex was built at nearby Khirbet el-Mafjer. Scholars have argued for a major downturn in the settlement of Jericho after the Islamic conquest, with the number of monasteries dwindling and the town shrinking,[3] but these statements need to be examined further.

Despite the construction of the Umayyad palace complex at Khirbet el-Mafjer and the fortress at Tulul Abu el-'Alayiq, by the Crusader period Jericho is described by archaeologists as being a

---

[1] Research Associate, University of Chicago: tkvorder@uchicago.edu
[2] I would like to thank the Palestinian National Authority Department of Antiquities and Cultural Heritage for allowing me to examine the coins and their hospitality during the day I examined the coins in Ramallah with Dr. Hamdan Taha. I would also like to thank the excavators of the Tell al-Hassan site, Michael Jennings and Anthony Lauricella, for all their help with the material and Dr. Donald Whitcomb for all his advice and assistance.
[3] Augustinović (1951); Chitty (1966): 82-83; Hirschfeld (1992): 11-12, 16, 90; Schick (1995): 324; Sion (1996); Cirelli and Zagari (2000): 365-366; Dietz (2005): 145; D'Andrea and Sala (2011c): 55-60; Nigro (2011): 21, 23. For a list of monasteries in the region see Hirschfeld (1990).

small village around Tell al-Hassan. Al-Muqadasi, however, lists Jericho as one of the cities of Filastin including it with Jerusalem, Nablus, etc. and it is likely that some of the monasteries continued after the Islamic conquest. The Crusader period once again appears to be a time of expansion with the construction of a number of fortresses and monasteries in the area. Although new construction occurred, it has been suggested that it was not particularly densely settled.[4] Jericho is described in the Crusader period by Daniel the Abbot in 1106-1107 and also Theoderic in 1172 as a 'small village'.[5] The Crusaders re-occupied abandoned Greek Orthodox monasteries outside Jericho while other Greek Orthodox monasteries continued to function around the oasis.[6]

Coin circulation at Jericho: Tell al-Hassan and the surrounding area

Tell al-Hassan is thought to be the centre of occupation at Jericho in both the Early Byzantine and Early Islamic periods. It is currently located under modern Jericho and therefore has not been excavated in a large amount of detail. The main excavations are those conducted by Baramki at the church, the Russian excavations at the Russian Museum near Tell al-Hassan, and the rescue excavations conducted by the Palestinian National Authority Department of Antiquities and University of Chicago graduate students (see below).

If the theory of a dramatic reduction in the monasteries and town of Jericho is correct, one would expect to see a reduction in coin circulation in the Early Islamic period. An examination of the archaeological evidence, however, indicates that this is not the case. If one examines the centre of the town, Tell al-Hassan, first in the Early Byzantine and then in the Early Islamic periods, the archaeological evidence points to continuous coin circulation. In early excavations at Tell al-Hassan, Baramki found fifteen coins in a church, including six Early Byzantine coins (two of these coins were minted in Nicomedia and one in Constantinople) and six coins that he labels as Umayyad (these are probably Post-Reform). While the earlier coins are published in detail, the Early Islamic coins were only described vaguely.[7] Nevertheless, the coin evidence suggests that the church continued to be used into the Early Islamic period.

Period	Number of coins
Early Roman	1
Late Roman	2
Early Byzantine (1 coin Justin, 1 Justin II, 1 Heraclius?)	6
Umayyad (post Reform?)	6

Table 1: Coins from Baramki's Tell al-Hassan excavations (Baramki 1936: 89)

More recent excavations in 2012 were made by the Palestinian National Authority Department of Antiquities and the University of Chicago graduate students Michael Jennings and Anthony Lauricella as part of a rescue excavation. They opened two small squares: one square was 100 square meters and the other was 190 square meters, with depths of 1 and 2 meters respectively, comprising of one commercial area and another that was residential/industrial. Even though it was not a big exposure, over three hundred coins were found. The coins have, for the most part, been cleaned, but it is what could best be termed as light cleaning. This means that some identifications at this point are still fairly preliminary as many of the coins have not been cleaned thoroughly. Some of them are still very dirty and this has meant that some of the identifications were based more on size and thickness than inscriptions. The coins that were found include Late Roman, Early Byzantine, a very small number of Arab-Byzantine coins, and Post-Reform Umayyad/Abbasid and

---

[4] Nigro (2011): 24-26; Avni (2014): 197, no. 129, 204.
[5] Wilkinson (2002): 313; D'Andrea and Sala (2011c): 59-60.
[6] Jotischky (1995): 78, 80-81.
[7] Baramki (1936): 89.

a few later medieval and early modern issues. The Late Roman and Post-Reform Umayyad/Abbasid consist of the largest categories.

Period	Number of coins
Roman	1
Late Roman	34
Late Roman?	65
Early Byzantine	17
Standing caliph	1
Post Reform Umayyad/Abbasid	55
Late Islamic	2
Modern	2
Unidentified	130
Total	307

Table 2: Coins from Jennings and Lauricella excavations

It is likely that many of the Late Roman/Early Byzantine coins found at the site continued to circulate and were used into the Early Islamic period. A total of 17 Byzantine coins were found, of which several are still completely unidentified, dating from the reign of Anastasius/Justin to the reign of Phocas. The coins come from a wide variety of mints: Constantinople, Nicomedia, Cyzicus, Thessalonica, and Antioch. Constantinople is by far the largest mint, followed by Nicomedia. The Byzantine coins cluster in two groups. The first consists of early 5th century coins, primarily of Anastasius and Justin I, although there is also one joint coin of Justin I/Justinian, which were mainly minted in Constantinople, although Nicomedia is also represented with two examples. Then there is a gap from 527 until the 550s, when the coins begin again with Justinian (both minted in Constantinople), and then another gap until the 570s with Justin II (minted in Constantinople and Nicomedia) and then coins of Maurice and Phocas. It is interesting that the later coins are all minted at Nicomedia, Antioch, and Kyzicus (which suddenly starts playing a role in the coins from the site) with none from Constantinole. Despite the relatively small number of Byzantine coins overall from the total coin numbers, we have a fairly good selection of both rulers and mints. The only Arab-Byzantine coin is a standing caliph coin that appears to be minted in Amman. The number of coins increases again in the early Islamic period, and they seem to be primarily from local mints.

Ruler	Dates	Mint
Anastasius/Justin I	499-527	Unclear, A officina
Anastasius/Justin I	499-527	Constantinople
Anastasius/Justin I	499-527	Constantinople
Justin I	518-527	Nicomedia
Justin I	518-527	Constantinople
Justin I and Justinian	527	Nicomedia
Justinian	552/3	Constantinople
Justinian	559/560	Constantinople
Justin II	573/4	Nicomedia
Justin II	574/5	Constantinople
Justin II	575/6	Nicomedia
Justin II?	570/571	Unclear
Maurice	589/590	Antioch
Maurice	601/602	Kyzicus
Phocas	603/604-610?	Kyzicus
Unclear	6th/7th century	Thessalonica

Table 3: Byzantine coins from Tell al-Hassan excavations

In addition, further work by Beliaev near Tell al-Hassan at the Russian Museum site which started in 2010 has also revealed large numbers of coins at a site that is described by the excavators as a monastery. The Russians have been active on excavations in Jericho since the 19th century. The excavations at the Russian Museum, however, have largely been ignored by others working on Jericho. The reason for this is that the earlier excavations have largely not been published or published in Russian, meaning that they have not entered into the archaeological discourse. The Russian contribution to the archaeology of Palestine has remained largely unknown.[8] The Russian activity in Jericho began with the work of the Archimandrite Antonin Kapustin (1817-1894), who worked in Palestine in 1864-1894 and helped acquire land for the Russian state. He was interested in Christian archaeology and history, including numismatics, and conducted excavations in Jerusalem and also in Jericho. Subsequent excavations were also never published.[9]

In 2010, the Russians began work there again and found some 200 coins. This included both single finds dating from the Hasmonean period onwards, as well as a Byzantine hoard. In total they found 26 Late Roman coins (they term the $4^{th}/5^{th}$ century coins as Byzantine but presumably mean Byzantine period rather than Byzantine coinage), 60 Early Byzantine coins and an Early Byzantine hoard that was deposited some time after the 590s. In addition, there were thirteen 7th century coins dating after the Islamic conquest (presumably all Arab-Byzantine since no Byzantine coins are mentioned) and coins of the 8th century.[10] The coins have not been published in detail. Therefore, it is clear that a large number of coins have been documented at or near Tell al-Hassan, except when Baramki excavated the church, where one would not necessarily expect to find many coins. Although both the Russian and the other excavations at Tell al-Hassan showed a relatively large number of coins for the area of the excavation, the coin finds are not parallel. The Russian excavations shows a large number of Early Byzantine coins, with a smaller number of later coins, while the Tell al-Hassan coins are more comparable with the rest of the Jericho excavations that are not necessarily in the same area.

Period	Number of coins
Hasmonean	8
Roman/Late Roman (2nd-4th centuries)	22
Late Roman ($4^{th}/5^{th}$ centuries)	4
Byzantine ($6^{th}/7^{th}$ centuries)	60
7th century coins	13
Post-Reform Umayyad/Abbasid (8th cent)	9

Table 4: Coins from Russian Museum excavations (Beliaev 2011)

Ruler	Number of coins
Anastasius	18
Justin I	16
Justinian	9
Justin II	10
Maurice	3

Table 5: Bronze coin hoard from Russian Museum excavations. 56 examples, last coin dates to 593/4 (Beliaev 2011)

---

[8] The Russian activities in Jericho are missing from D'Andrea and Sala's (2011a, 2011b, and 2011c) extensive overview of excavations, catalogue of list of sites, and bibliography of the sites. This is despite the fact the current Russian excavations are mentioned in the same volume. See Taha (2011): 286-287.
[9] Guruleva (1998); Beliaev et al (2009); Frary (2013): 141-150.
[10] Beliaev (2011): 77-78.

The evidence for coinage at the centre of Jericho confirms the archaeologists' statements that it was occupied in both the Early Byzantine and Early Islamic periods. It is unclear if the centre of the town shifted slightly away from the site of the Russian Museum in the Early Islamic period as the number of coins was fewer there than at the site excavated by Jenning and Lauricella. Nevertheless, assessing the significance of the Russian material is problematic due to the fact that the coins have not been fully published. It is not clear exactly what date the 7th century coins are, although they may be Arab-Byzantine. Therefore, one must wait for further details in future publications.

Coin circulation at Jericho: Tulul Abu el-'Alayiq

The most extensively published coins from Jericho come from the site of Tulul Abu el-'Alayiq. The site can be divided into two areas: south and north. The entire site of Tulul Abu el-'Alayiq was occupied by the three Herodian palaces excavated by Netzer. The southern part of the site, however, was also the site of a fortress in the Early Islamic period. After abandonment in the Byzantine period, the site was reoccupied in the 8th and 9th centuries AD.[11] The coins from the Late Roman/Early Byzantine period are very meagre which matches what was found in the field but in the Early Islamic period one can see a revival following the construction of the fortress there.[12]

There have been several different excavations at the site of Tulul Abu el-'Alayiq but only one other has revealed a large number of coins. In Kelso and Baramki's excavations, they found only 7 coins including two 6th century coins and two Post-Reform Umayyad coins, as well as two later coins.[13] In Pritchard's excavations, however, 254 coins were found including only a small number of Late Roman coins, followed by no Early Byzantine coins, a small number of Arab-Byzantine, including a Pseudo-Byzantine coin of which no photograph was published, an Arab-Byzantine coin that Miles did not attribute to a mint but a similar coin has been identified by Album and Goodwin as being from Amman on the basis of its fabric and style of the obverse. In addition, there are a large number of Post-Reform Umayyad coins and a few Abbasid coins. The Post-Reform Umayyad mints were located throughout Palestine and Syria, as well as Egypt.[14]

Again, the excavations by Netzer at the Herodian palaces also identified Late Roman, Byzantine, and Early Islamic coins. Both the Late Roman and Early Byzantine coins were much worn and where the mint could be identified, they were from Constantinople. The 13 Post-Reform Umayyad coins were minted in both Palestine as well as Syria.[15] The worn coins of the Late Roman and Early Byzantine period may have therefore circulated in the Umayyad period.

Period	Number of coins
Late Roman	1
Early Byzantine (6th century)	2
Post-Reform Umayyad	2
Later Islamic	2

Table 6: Excavations at Tulul Abu el-'Alayiq (Kelso and Baramki 1955b: 20-41)

---

[11] Kelso and Baramki (1955a): 4; Schick (1995): 324; D'Andrea and Sala (2011b): 99-105.
[12] Meshorer (2004): 289.
[13] The Umayyad coins are not specifically stated to be Post-Reform Umayyad, but given the fact that they are in fact identified as being Umayyad and 8th century means that they are necessarily Post-Reform Umayyad coins. Kelso and Baramki (1955b): 41.
[14] Johnson (1958): 29; Miles (1958); Cirelli and Zagari (2000): 365; Album and Goodwin 2002: 97. Five of these coins, which are Post-reform Umayyad, Miles (1958): Pl. 61, nos. 8, 11, 14 and Pl. 2, nos. 4 and 6 are now in Tübingen. These have now been published in Ilisch (1993) without reference to their context. I would like to thank Lutz Ilisch for this information.
[15] Meshorer (2004): 305-307.

Period	Number of coins
Late Roman (4th century)	3
Arab-Byzantine	2
Post-Reform Umayyad	159
Abbasid	12
Defaced (probably Post-Reform)	78

Table 7: Excavations at Tulul Abu el-'Alayiq (Johnson 1958; Miles 1958)

Period	Number of coins
Seleucid	6
Hasmonean	594
Herodian	172
Roman	69
Revolt	2
Nabatean	1
Late Roman	12
Early Byzantine	5
Post-Reform Umayyad	11

Table 8: Excavations at Tulul Abu el-'Alayiq (Meshorer 2004)

Coin Circulation in Jericho: Khirbet el-Nitla and Tell al-Sultan

Khirbet el-Nitla, which may be the Biblical Galgala (although this is disputed), was located slightly to the east of Jericho.[16] In the Early Byzantine period there was a village and monastery and these continued into the Early Islamic period.[17] The coins from Khirbet el-Nitla were almost entirely illegible and out of 84 coins, only 19 could be read at the time of publication. The coins were primarily Late Roman and Early Byzantine, with a few coins of the 8th century. The publication does not specify whether or not these coins were post-reform Umayyad or Abbasid period, but it is likely they are Post-Reform Umayyad.[18]

Period	Number of coins
Late Roman (4th Century)	5
Late Roman (5th century)	5
Early Byzantine (6th century)	7
Early Islamic (8th century)	2

Table 9: Coins from Khirbet el-Nitla excavations (Baramki 1955)

At Tell al-Sultan, assessing the evidence is again problematic. The current Italian excavations have not reported finding any Islamic coins, but rather coins of the 4th/5th century that continued to circulate 'much later'. These coins were found together in a burial and probably were the contents of someone's coin purse.[19] It is possible that these coins circulated into the Islamic period. Equally, Sellin and Watzinger also report finding 4th and 5th century money (which they inaccurately refer to as 'byzantinisch' in a grave that were probably buried in a sack. The poor preservation of the coins did not permit further identification.[20] In addition, Sellin and Watzinger found copper coins from the Umayyad period, without ruler, mint, or date. Although they are not described, they are clearly

---

[16] Pringle (1993): 221-222.
[17] Baramki (1955): 50-52; Pringle (1993): 221-222; D'Andrea and Sala (2011b): 134-135.
[18] Baramki (1955): 52.
[19] Zagari (2000): 362, 365.
[20] Sellin and Watzinger (1913): 166.

Post-Reform Umayyad. Unfortunately, the numbers are not given.[21] It may be related to the houses that are associated with the Byzantine and Early Islamic period, but this is unclear.[22] Since these coins have never been fully published, it is difficult to assess their significance, but there are some limited signs the site was possibly occupied in the Late Roman or Early Islamic periods.

Period	Location of coins
4th/5th century	Burial (Italian excavations)
4th/5th century	Burial (Sellin and Watzinger)
Post-Reform Umayyad	Unclear (Sellin and Watzinger)

Table 10: Coins from Tell al-Sultan excavations (Sellin and Watzinger 1913; Zagari 2000)

Khirbet el-Mafjer and surroundings: Palace, Monastery, and Synagogue

The site of Khirbet el-Mafjer is arguably one of the most famous monuments in the Umayyad Middle East, with its extensive palace and bathhouse buildings. Despite its importance as an architectural and artistic monument, the site was never fully published and the main publication, written by Hamilton, did not mention any coins.[23] One might expect that objects as significant as coins would be mentioned in publications, but Hamilton fails to mention other significant objects that they discovered in the course of excavations. The question therefore remains whether or not any coins were actually found because there is no mention of any coins in the publications, including Baramki's unpublished dissertation.[24] It is interesting to note that in Baramki's other publications of materials from Jericho, he does mention the coins he found in great detail, even if he does not do more than describe them in general (see above). Therefore, one has to ask whether he found any coins at all.

The number of coins found at the modern excavations at Khirbet el-Mafjer is not particularly large. The fact that coins were found there in modern excavations could argue that the original excavations also found coins and that these were never published. They are not in the Rockefeller Museum, however, where most of the excavation materials are now stored. The small number of coins found in the modern excavations suggests that if any coins were found in the original excavations, they may have been few in number, which could explain why they were never mentioned. Recent excavations in 2006 revealed only two coins, one of which was a silver coin of the post-reform period minted in Damascus in 705, and the other described as a lead coin.[25]

One might have expected that such an important site would have produced a correspondingly large number of coins, but this is not the case. If one turns to the modern excavations, there is only one coin that can be dated before the Post-Reform Umayyad period. As I already noted in the introduction, since the complex is supposed to have been built at the beginning of the 8th century, this is not surprising. Only one coin has been found that dates to the Byzantine period. It is of Heraclius, dates between 612 and 616 and was minted in Nicomedia. The coin is badly worn suggesting that it continued to circulate some time after it was struck, which would not be surprising since the site postdates the coin. It is possible that this coin came from the monasteries and cells that date to the Byzantine period that were located near the palace site,[26] but this is not clear. It may point instead to the continued circulation of Byzantine coins in later contexts which has been well documented.

---

[21] Sellin and Watzinger (1913): 169.
[22] D'Andrea and Sala (2011b): 152-153.
[23] Hamilton (1959).
[24] Baramki (1955).
[25] Taha (2011): 296.
[26] Bar-Adon (1972): 115-116; Sion (1996): 249, 262, site C; Hirschfeld (1990): 22-23; D'Andrea and Sala (2011b): 126-128.

Period	Number of coins
Early Byzantine	1
Post-Reform Umayyad/Abbasid	10
Unidentified	2

Table 11: Khirbet el-Mafjer coins from Taha and Whitcomb excavations

Baramki's other excavations near the Khirbet el-Mafjer area at a synagogue revealed 10 coins, the vast majority of which were Post-Reform Umayyad. The one Late Roman coin that was found is categorized as being 'badly worn'[27] suggesting that it had continued to circulate into the Early Islamic period. It is interesting to see that the coin numbers from the synagogue are almost the same as at the site of the palace. The coins would suggest that the synagogue dates to the 8th century or later, making it contemporary with the palace.

Period	Number of coins
Late Roman	1
Post-Reform Umayyad	9

Table 12: Coins from the synagogue (Baramki 1938)

Coin circulation at Jericho

There are several things we can note when we compare the coins found at Jericho across the different sites. First, we can see that that almost all of the sites had similar types of coins, even if the numbers are different. Second, we can see that most sites had Late Roman coins, usually but not necessarily Early Byzantine, Post-Reform Umayyad and/or Abbasid, but generally not Arab-Byzantine. There are two exceptions to this: Tulul Abu el-'Alayiq, where there are very few Late Roman coins, in one case no Early Byzantine, and a large number of Early Islamic; and the Russian excavations, where there were some Late Roman and a large number of Early Byzantine, and began to decline in the 8th century. One assumes that this is a result of changing settlement patterns from the seventh to the eighth centuries, although this would need further investigation.

The difficulty in comparing the various sites with each other however is the lack of specificity in many of the publications. They do not tell us anything about the different mints represented, with the exception of Miles' work on the Islamic coins, and even that, the most complete of anything currently published on coins of Jericho, neglects to publish photographs with the result that we do not know what type of Arab-Byzantine coins were found at the site. The descriptions suggest one Pseudo-Byzantine coin (presumably with blundered legends) and another that is described as a standing caliph on the obverse and an M on the reverse. In the case of the Early Byzantine mints represented at Jericho, we can only speak of a small number of coins, since the mints remain largely unreported because the coins are only described in the most general of terms. This has led me to guess about certain identifications – assuming that 'Umayyad' coins means Post-Reform Umayyad, for instance, even though I am not certain of that. We cannot know if this was because the authors of these reports were not numismatists and did not know the mints involved, if they were not interested in coins, or if the coins were so badly preserved that they could not read them. In the case of the Russian excavations, where the number of Byzantine coins was much larger than the Late Roman or the Post-Reform Umayyad, there were a number of coins dated to the 7th and 8th centuries that seem to date after the Islamic conquest, but it is not clear if the thirteen 7th century examples are Arab-Byzantine coins or not. If this is the case, then there is clearly a downturn into the 8th century, with only 9 examples and then nothing until the 12th century. Given the lack of specificity about the coins from the 2010 excavations, there is no evidence for anything else.

---

[27] Baramki (1938): 75; D'Andrea and Sala (2011b): 127.

The question is why there is a gap in the coins found in the seventh century at most of the sites with only two Arab-Byzantine coins found at Tell al-Hassan and two at Tulul Abu el-'Alayiq respectively. Of course, due to the lack of specificity about the coins labelled as 'Byzantine' by the different archaeologists, it cannot be discounted that some additional Arab-Byzantine coins were found but simply not identified by the excavators. Nevertheless, even taking this into account, the numbers would not appear to be overly large. There is simply a gap in the evidence. The question is why this may be the case.

The archaeological evidence from Tell al-Hassan and elsewhere would seem to confirm the idea that one of the reasons that there were not a large number of Arab-Byzantine coins circulating in Jericho was that the population was actually using Late Roman/Early Byzantine coins instead and therefore did not use the later coins in large numbers. The Early Byzantine coins found at Jericho are all dated to prior to the Islamic conquest (assuming that general dating such as 'Byzantine, 6th century' is accurate) and there are no coins of Constans II at all. The Russian excavations suggest that actually in some parts of the site Arab-Byzantine coins might have circulated, however. The excavators of that site do not suggest that the Byzantine coins are circulating later, although this would be probable in my opinion.

In addition to hoards and coins that copy early Byzantine coins, there is also archaeological evidence for the continued circulation of Late Roman and/or Early Byzantine coins. One can see this at other sites such as at Nevé Ur near Beth She'an, where the excavators report finding an Early Islamic village that was built on virgin soil where there was no previous Byzantine site. The coins found included Late Roman and Early Byzantine coins as well as Arab-Byzantine and Post-Reform Umayyad coins.[28] This clearly points to the continued circulation of Late Roman and Early Byzantine coins in the Early Islamic period at this site.

The importance of this for archaeologists is clear. One can certainly not use single coins or a small number of coins to date archaeological sites. The site of Nevé Ur stands as an excellent example of how to integrate the coins and archaeological evidence together. At the site, it was clear that the pottery and the coins did not entirely agree, since it was an Early Islamic site. Similarly, we should not assume that there was no settlement at Tell al-Hassan in the 7th century after the last Byzantine coin either.

The number of coins found at the two small areas that were opened at the excavation of Tell al-Hassan is surprisingly large, although finds of large numbers of coins from small sites are not unprecedented. At the monastery of Lot in Jordan, for example, excavators discovered 2183 coins, of which 561 were from two different hoards. The coins suggest that Late Roman coins continued to circulate into the Early Islamic period.[29] This is in contrast to the evidence from the monastery of Khirbet al-Deir, located to the east of Hebron and southwest of Jericho, where excavations only revealed two coins of Anastasius I and Justinian I, minted in Constantinople. Consequently Barkay

---

[28] Bijovsky and Berman (2002); Shalem (2002): 149, 153, 172, 174.
[29] Bowsher (2012): 317, 327, 329-330. Unfortunately most of the coins were not identifiable. The latest coins came from the time of Justinian and no coins of Justin I or Early Islamic coins were found. This is despite the fact that the church continued until the 8th century AD and the ceramics continued until at least the early 10th and possibly 11th century AD. The large number of coins at this site may be associated with pilgrimage, but this is unclear. But one should not assume that coins were not in use in the later period, since Late Roman coins are found in stratigraphic contexts that date from the 4th-10th centuries AD. Bowsher argues as a result that such small value coins continued to be used as currency after coins ceased to be supplied to site as a result of the Early Islamic conquest. Bowsher does not discuss this in detail but this statement obviously has important implications for the function of the monastery in the Early Islamic period. One sees similar patterns in Nubia, for example, where Late Roman coins continue to circulate long after they were initially minted. See Vorderstrasse (2012).

suggests that money was not used frequently there. Indeed, numismatic finds in monasteries are usually scarce.[30]

Coin evidence from Jericho and the historical record

The coin evidence reveals much important information about Jericho in the Early Islamic period that has been previously overlooked. Despite the fact that there seems to have been a large drop in the number of sites after the Islamic conquest, the number of coins actually increases after a gap in the Arab-Byzantine period. After the end of the 7th century, however, coins increase to significant numbers at some sites in the city although Jericho is generally thought to be a small village in this period (see above). One of the major sources used for reconstructing Jericho as a small village is the account of the late 7th century pilgrim Arculf, as related by Adomnán. While Adomnán partially based the description of Jericho on that of Jerome, he did include information that seems to have come directly from Arculf. This part of the account stated that all of Jericho was ruined except for the House of Rahab. Although Adomnán relates this as God's will, some scholars have suggested that Jericho was destroyed in the earthquake of 659/660, as described in the Syriac Maronite Chronicle.[31] Schick speculates that while some parts of Palestine may have been more quickly rebuilt, based upon literary descriptions, he does try to connect the earthquake with Arculf's description. Indeed, Schick suggests that many of the buildings in Jericho went out of use before the end of the Umayyad period.[32]

The statement that the House of Rahab remained standing is clearly a miraculous event, attributed to the fact that Rahab, the prostitute, hid Joshua's spies in the Biblical account (see Joshua 2:1-6). According to the Piacenza Pilgrim, who visited Jericho in 570, the House of Rahab was a guesthouse (*xenodochium*),[33] but this is likely to be connected to a tradition that Rahab kept an inn,[34] thereby explaining why one could reasonably stay in the house as a pilgrim. The fact that it would have survived all the ruins is perhaps surprising. It is also interesting that Arculf states that Jericho was in ruins and that between the ruined city and the Jordan River was an area densely populated by 'wretched' people of 'Canaanite' origin (*Cananeae stirpis homanitonum*). While the religion of theses individual is not mentioned, it is likely that they were not Christians or Jews.[35]

Even if we can accept Adomnán's characterization of Jericho as ruined (according to Arculf), there may be other reasons for his gloomy assessment. According to the recent archaeological work, the settlement concentrated in the north-western part of the oasis in the Early Islamic period.[36]

---

[30] Barkay (1999): 152-153.
[31] Adomnán. *De locis sanctis*. 2.13 (Meehan 1985: 84-85; Guagnano 2008: 144-145; D'Andrea and Sala (2011c): 59. This work is allegedly based on Arculf's journey but also other 4th-5th literary sources, in particular Jerome's translation of Eusebius' *Onomasticon* with additions that he used extensively. This includes his description Jericho. There is no current agreement on precisely how much of the journey is accurate and how much of the information contained therein can be relied upon. See O'Loughlin (1994); Limor (2000): 31; O'Loughlin (2000); Woods (2002); O'Loughlin (2007): 23-25, 174-175; Aist (2010): 162-163, esp. no. 12, 170; Avni (2014): 2-3. For the description of Jericho in Arculf see Geyer (1895): 17; Abel (1950): 330; Meehan (1958): 15 (which compares the texts concerning Jericho in Jerome and Adomnán side by side); O'Loughlin (1994): 35; Wilkinson (2002): 189-190, no. 63; Woods (2002): 26; O'Loughlin (2007): 173; Aist (2010): 170.
[32] Schick (1995): 126, 322-323.
[33] Piacenza Pilgrim. *Ps.-Antonini-Placentini Itinerarium*: 13 (Geyer 1965): 136. See Abel (1950): 330. For more on *xenodochia* in Byzantine Palestine see Voltaggio (2011), esp. p. 202.
[34] This is repeated in several texts including Josephus, *The Antiquities of the Jews,* Book V. 2, 7-8 and the Targum. See Abel (1950): 328-330. This seems to have come about because of the fact that the word *pundekita* in Aramaic, means both prostitute and innkeeper. See Feldman (1998): 444; Bodi (2013): 11. Alternatively, van der Kooij suggests that this arises from the notion that female innkeepers were the same as prostitutes. See Van der Kooij (2012): 255.
[35] O'Loughlin (2007): 173.
[36] Nigro (2011): 23.

Therefore, depending on which part of the town Arculf saw, he might well believe it was somewhat ruinous if various monasteries and churches had been abandoned after the Islamic conquest.

Conclusion

When one looks at the numismatic evidence from Jericho that has been published, the reason that the site has not been examined in detail becomes evident. While many locations in and around Jericho have been excavated, many coins have not been adequately published. Most coins have only been published in the most general way, making it difficult to compare the different parts of the site with each other. Nonetheless, tentative comparisons can be made, and strongly suggest certain patterns of circulation, including the continued use of Late Roman and Early Byzantine coins in the Early Islamic period. This continued use of coinage could explain the gap in Arab-Byzantine coins in the 7th century or it may be related to shifting settlement patterns. What does not seem to be the case is that Jericho went into a decline in the Early Islamic period, but rather than it remained an important town in the region and continued to be economically prosperous. Further excavations and studies of the coinage of this area will hopefully lead to a better understanding of the site in the 7th century.

Bibliography

Abel, F.-M., 'L'anathème de Jéricho et la maison de Rahab', *Revue biblique* 57 (1950), 321-330.

Adomnán, *De Locis Sanctis*, (ed. D. Meehan), *Adamnan's De Locis Sanctis*, Scriptores Latini Hiberniae Volume III, Dublin, 1958; (ed. M. Guagnano), *Adomnano di Iona, I luogui santi*, Bari, 2008.

Aist, R., 'Adomnán, Arculf and the Source Material of *De locis sanctis*', *Adomnán of Iona: Theologian, Lawmaker, Peacemaker,* (eds. J. M. Wooding, R. Aist, T. O. Clancy, and T. O'Loughlin), Dublin, 2010, 162-180.

Album, S. and Goodwin, T., *Sylloge of Islamic Coins in the Ashmolean. Volume 1. The Pre-Reform Coinage of the Early Islamic Period*, Oxford, 2002.

Ariel, D. T., 'Coins from the Surveys and Excavations of the Caves in the Northern Judean Desert', *Survey and Excavations of Caves in the Northern Judean Desert (CNJD) - 1993*, (ed. L. Wexler), Jerusalem, 2002, 282-304.

Augustinović, A., *Gerico e dintorni*. 1951.

Avni, G., *The Byzantine-Islamic Transition in Palestine: An Archaeological Approach*, Oxford, 2014.

Bar-Adon, P., 'The Judaean Desert and Plain of Jericho', *Judaea, Samaria and the Golan: Archaeological Survey 1967-1968*, (ed. M. Kochavi), Jerusalem, 1972, 92-149 (Hebrew).

Baramki, D. C., 'An Early Byzantine Basilica at Tell el-Hassan-Jericho', *Quarterly of the Department of Antiquities of Palestine* 5 (1936), 82-89.
'An Early Byzantine Synagogue near Tell es-Sultan, Jericho', *Quarterly of the Department of Antiquities of Palestine* 6 (1937), 73-77 with notes by M. Avi-Yonah, 'An Early Byzantine Synagogue near Tell es-Sultan, Jericho', *Quarterly of the Department of Antiquities of Palestine* 6

(1938), 73-77. The date is 1938 not 1937, that is the date on the actual journal cover even though logically it should be 1937.

'The Excavations at Khirbet en-Nitla', *Excavations at New Testament Jericho and Khirbet en-Nitla*, (eds. J. L. Kelso and D. C. Baramki), The Annual Schools of Oriental Research Vols. XXIX-XXX, New Haven, 1955, 50-52.

Barkay, R., 'The Coins', *The Early Byzantine Monastery at Khirbet ed-Deir in the Judean Desert: The Excavations in 1981-1987*, (ed. Y. Hirschfeld), Qedem 38, 1999, 122-123.

Beliaev, L. A., 'Proyekt "Vizantiyskiy Iyerikhon": raboty 2010 g. i perspektivy issledovaniy', *Rossiyskaya arkheologiya* (2011), 71-85.

Beliaev, L. A., Butova, R. B., Lisovoy, N. N., 'Arkheologicheskiye pamyatniki Russkoy Palestiny po arkhivnym materialam 1870–1910-kh godov', *Rossiyskaya arkheologiya* (2009), 46–57.

Bijovsky, G. and Berman, A., 'The Coins from Nevé Ur', *'Atiqot* XLIII (2002), 177-184.

Bodi, D., 'The Encounter with the Courtesan in the Gilgameš Epic and with Rahab in Joshua 2', *Interested Readers: Essays on the Hebrew Bible in Honor of David J. A. Clines*, (eds. J. K. Aitken, J. M. S. Clines, and C. M. Maier), Atlanta, 2013, 3-18.

Bowsher, J. M. C., 'The Coins', *Sanctuary of Lot at Deir 'Ain 'Abata in Jordan: Excavations 1988-2003*, (K. D. Politis), Amman, 2012, 317-336.

Chitty, D. J., *The Desert a City: An Introduction to the Study of Egyptian and Palestinian Monasticism under the Christian Empire*, London and Oxford, 1966.

Cirelli, E. and Zagari, F., 'L'oasi di Gerico in età bizantina e islamica. Problemi e proposte di ricerca', *Archeologia medievale* 27 (2000), 365-376.

D'Andrea, M. and Sala, M., 'Bibliography of the Sites in the Jericho Oasis and its Surroundings', *Archaeological Heritage in the Jericho Oasis. A Systematic Catalogue of Archaeological Sites for the Sake of their Protection and Cultural Valorisation*, (eds. L. Nigro, M. Sala, and H. Taha), <<La Sapienza>> Studies on the Archaeology of Palestine & Transjordan 7, Rome, 2011a, 171-268.

D'Andrea, M. and Sala, M., 'Catalogue of the Sites in the Jericho Oasis and its Surroundings', *Archaeological Heritage in the Jericho Oasis. A Systematic Catalogue of Archaeological Sites for the Sake of their Protection and Cultural Valorisation*, (eds. L. Nigro, M. Sala, and H. Taha), <<La Sapienza>> Studies on the Archaeology of Palestine & Transjordan 7, Rome, 2011b, 95-170.

D'Andrea, M. and Sala, M., 'History of Travels, Tours and Explorations in the Jericho Oasis from the Earliest Pilgrims to the Current Archaeological Activities', *Archaeological Heritage in the Jericho Oasis. A Systematic Catalogue of Archaeological Sites for the Sake of their Protection and Cultural Valorisation*, (eds. L. Nigro, M. Sala, and H. Taha), <<La Sapienza>> Studies on the Archaeology of Palestine & Transjordan 7, Rome, 2011c, 55-94.

Dietz, M., *Wandering Monks, Virgins, and Pilgrims: Ascetic Travel in the Mediterranean World, A.D. 300–800*, University Park, Pennsylvania, 2005.

Feldman, L., *Josephus's Interpretation of the Bible*, Berkeley and Los Angeles, 1998.

Frary, L. J., 'Russian Missions to the Orthodox East: Antonin Kapustin (1817-1894) and his World', **Russian History** 40 (2013), 133-151.

Geyer, P., **Adamnanus, Abt von Jona. Sein Leben. Seine Quellen. Sein Verhältnis zu Pseudoeucherius de locis sanctis. Seine Sprache**, Augsburg, 1895.

Guruleva, N. N., 'Arkimandrit Antonin kak numizmat', **Numizmaticheskii sbornik 1998. K 80-letiiu V. M. Potina**, St. Petersburg, 1998, 235-243.

Hamilton, R. W., **Khirbat al Mafjar: an Arabian mansion in the Jordan Valley**, Oxford 1959.

Hirschfeld, Y., 'List of Byzantine Monasteries in the Judean Desert', **Christian Archaeology in the Holy Land New Discoveries: Essays in Honour of Virgilio C. Corbo OFM**, (eds. G. C. Bottini, L. Di Segni, and E. Alliata), Franscican Printing Press: Studium Biblicum Franciscanum Collectio Maior 36, Jerusalem. 1990, 1-90.
The Judean Desert Monasteries in the Byzantine Period. Yale University Press: New Haven and London. 1992.

Ilisch, L., **Sylloge Numorum Arabicorum Tübingen – Palästina – IVa Bilād aš-Šām I**. Tübingen 1993

Johnson, S. E., 'A Catalogue of Roman Coins', **The Excavation at Herodian, Jericho, 1951**, (J. B. Pritchard), The Annual of the Schools of Oriental Research Vols. XXXII-XXXIII, New Haven, 1958, 24-28.

Jotischky, A., **The Perfection of Solitude: Hermits and Monks in the Crusader States**, Pennsylvania State University, 1995.

Kelso, J. L. and Baramki, D. C., 'The Excavation of New Testament Jericho (Tulul Abu el-'Alayiq', **Excavations at New Testament Jericho and Khirbet en-Nitla**, (J. L. Kelso and D. C. Baramki), The Annual Schools of Oriental Research Vols. XXIX-XXX, New Haven, 1955a, 1-19.

Kelso, J. L. and Baramki, D. C, 'The Pottery of New Testament Jericho (Tulul Abu el-'Alayiq and Khirbet en-Nitla', **Excavations at New Testament Jericho and Khirbet en-Nitla**, (J. L. Kelso and D. C. Baramki), The Annual Schools of Oriental Research Vols. XXIX-XXX, New Haven, 1955b, 20-41.

Kenyon, K., **Excavations at Jericho Volume Three: The Architecture and Stratigraphy of the Tell**, Jerusalem, 1981.

Van der Kooij, A., 'Josephus, Onkelos, and Jonathon: On Agreements between Josephus' Works and Targumic Sources', **Studies on the Text and Versions of the Hebrew Bible in Honour of Robert Gordon**, (eds. G. Khan and D. Lipton), Supplements to Vetus Testamentum 149, Leiden, 2012, 253-267.

Limor, O., 'Arculf', **Trade, Travel, and Exploration in the Middle Ages: An Encylcopedia**, (eds. J. Block Friedman and K. Mossier Figg), New York, 2000, 31.

Marchetti, N. and Nigro, L., **Excavations at Jericho, 1998. Preliminary Report on the Second Season of Excavations and Surveys at Tell es-Sultan, Palestine**, Quaderni di Gerico 2, Rome, 2000.

Meshorer, Y., 'The Coins', **Hasmonean and Herodian Palaces at Jericho. Final Reports of the 1973-1987 Excavations** *Volume II* (eds. E. Netzer, R. Laureys-Chachy, and Y. Meshorer) Jerusalem, 2004, 289-312.

Miles, G. C., 'A Catalogue of Islamic Coins', ***The Excavation at Herodian Jericho, 1951***, (J. B. Pritchard), The Annual of the Schools of Oriental Research Vols. XXXII-XXXIII, New Haven, 1958, 29-41.

Nigro, L., 'Introduction', ***Archaeological Heritage in the Jericho Oasis. A Systematic Catalogue of Archaeological Sites for the Sake of their Protection and Cultural Valorisation***, (eds. L. Nigro, M. Sala, and H. Taha), <<La Sapienza>> Studies on the Archaeology of Palestine & Transjordan 7, Rome, 2011, 1-54.

O'Loughlin, T., 'The Library of Iona in the late Seventh century: The evidence from Adomnán's *De locis sanctis*', *Eriu* 45 (1994), 33-52.

'Palestine in the Aftermath of the Arab Conquest: The Earliest Latin Account', ***Holy Land, Holy Lands, and Christian History: Papers Read at the 1998 Summer Meeting and the 1999 Winter Meeting of the Ecclesiastical History Society***, (ed. R. N. Swanson), Studies in Church History 36, Oxford, 2000, 78-90.

Adomnán and the Holy Places: The Perceptions of an Insular Monk on the Locations of the Biblical Drama, New York, 2007.

Piacenza Pilgrim. *Ps.-Antonini-Placentini Itinerarium* (ed. P. Geyer), *Itineraria et Alia Geographica*. Corpus Christanorum Series Latina 175. Turnhout. 1965. 129-153.

Pringle, D., ***The Churches of the Crusader Kingdom of Jerusalem. A Corpus. Volume 1. A-K (Excluding Acre and Jerusalem)***, Cambridge, 1993.

Schick, R., ***The Christian Communities of Palestine from Byzantium to Islamic Rule: A Historical and Archaeological Study***, Princeton, 1995.

Sellin, E. and Watzinger, C., ***Jericho: Die Ergebnisse der Ausgrabungen***, Leipzig, 1913.

Shalem, D., 'Nevé Ur – An Early Islamic Period Village in the Bet She'an Valley', *'Atiqot* XLIII (2002), 149-176.

Sion, O., 'The Monasteries of the Desert of the Jordan', *Liber Annuus* 46 (1996), 245-264.

Taha, H., 'Appendix A. Archaeological Excavations in Jericho, 1995-2010', ***Archaeological Heritage in the Jericho Oasis. A Systematic Catalogue of Archaeological Sites for the Sake of their Protection and Cultural Valorisation***, (eds. L. Nigro, M. Sala, and H. Taha), Studies on the Archaeology of Palestine & Transjordan 7, Rome, 2011, 269-304.

Voltaggio, M., '*Xenodochia* and *Hospitia* in Sixth-Century Jerusalem. Indicators of Byzantine Pilgrimage to the Holy Places', ***Zeitschrift des Palästina-Vereins*** 127 (2011), 197-210.

Vorderstrasse, T., 'Coinage and Monetary Economy in 7th Century Nubia', ***Arab-Byzantine Coins and History*** (T. Goodwin), London 2012, 169-181.

Wilkinson, J., ***Jerusalem Pilgrims before the Crusades***, Warminster, 2002.

Woods, D., 'Arculf's Luggage: The Sources for Adomnán's "De locis Sanctis" ', *Ériu* 52 (2002), 25-52.

Zagari, F., 'Appendix H: Remarks on the Byzantine Occupation of Tell es-Sultan', ***Excavations at Jericho, 1998. Preliminary Report on the Second Season of Archaeological Excavations and surveys at Tell es-Sultan, Palestine***, Quaderni di Gerico 2, Rome, 2000, 355-381.

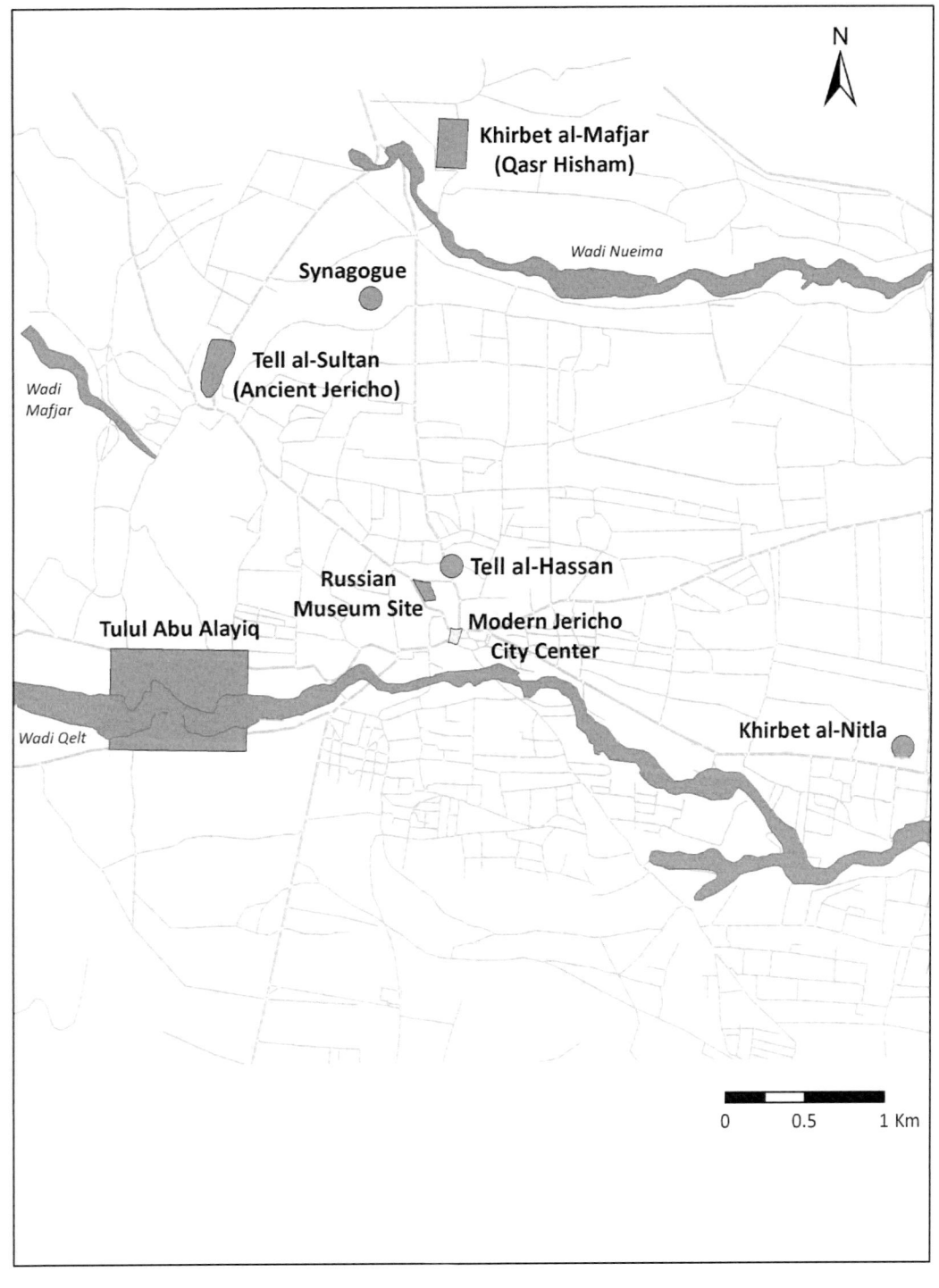

Map of sites in Jericho mentioned in the text.[37]

---

[37] Thanks are due to Michael Jennings for this map.

BALDWIN'S
The Name for Numismatics

Proudly buying and selling the best in numismatics, Baldwin's maintains a stock at the very highest level. You can browse our coins, medals and books 24 hours a day, any day, online.

www.baldwin.co.uk

399 Strand, London, WC2R 0LX
++ 44 (0)20 7930 6879   ++ 44 (0)20 7930 9450
coins@baldwin.co.uk

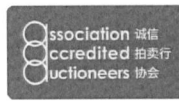     

Part of The Stanley Gibbons Group PLC

Coinage and the Early Arab State

Marcus Phillips [1]

This paper is more or less the same as the version I gave at the Round Table meeting. Personal circumstances have prevented me from making any revisions or improvements. The only exception is some addition to the discussion on land ownership for which I am grateful to Hugh Kennedy.

Introduction

The Arabic tribes who conquered the territories of the Byzantine and Sasanian empires found, in both cases, a centralised coin using fiscal system which they immediately exploited. The coinage they inherited had not only been an imperial monopoly but also an important expression of the ruler's personal sovereignty. Why then were the Arabs in the west content to use the coins of a state with which they were at war? Why, even after they had begun to issue their own copper, were they so diffident about striking gold? These questions were always in the background when I was updating the list of coin finds which appeared in the previous volume of the proceedings.[2] Similar questions apply to the east. Why did the Arabs continue to use the image of a dead and vanquished Sasanian ruler? Why is it that the first Arabs to put their names on the coins are the provincial governors? In the longer term why did the currency system that emerged under the Umayyads differ so much from that of the successors of the Roman Empire in the west?

The reforms of ʿAbd al-Malik marked a decisive change in the nature of Arabic (now Islamic) political consciousness. Coining, in precious metal at least, became once more a state monopoly. In many ways the new coins made a decisive break with the traditions of Rome and Persia. The ruler's name, temporarily, and his image, permanently, disappeared. Unlike in the west where the successor states used the language and script of the empire they had replaced, the Arabs used their own. Nonetheless they could not entirely escape the influence of the empires they had supplanted. In trying to understand the nature of the influences which determined the development of early Arab coinage they should not be considered in isolation. Not only should the changes be related to what preceded them but it helps our understanding if we compare how the coinages of the other contemporary successor states developed.

The Medieval State

In the conclusions I sketched out at the end of my update on the finds of Byzantine coins in Syria,[3] I used the words 'state' and 'statehood'. These are modern concepts with modern legal definitions.[4] As Stefan Heidemann reminds us, medieval Islam had no word for 'state' or 'empire'.[5] Nonetheless the third volume of the *Studies in Late Antiquity and Early Islam* is subtitled 'States, Resources and Armies' and in their discussion of the nature of early Islamic polities at least two recent authors,

---

[1] Marcus Phillips is co-editor of the **Numismatic Chronicle**   senmerv@hotmail.com
[2] Phillips, 'The import of Byzantine coins to Syria revisited'.
[3] Phillips, 'The import of Byzantine coins to Syria revisited', at pp. 58–9.
[4] Cf. Foss, 'Muʿāwiya's state', p. 91 for the modern legal definition.
[5] Heidemann, 'Evolving representation', p. 149, n. 1. They used the terms *dār al-Islām* and *dār al-ḥarb* for the territory inside and outside Islamic jurisdiction respectively. 'None the less the government of the caliph with Islam as the state religion can nevertheless be defined as 'imperial'.

Robert Hoyland and Clive Foss, have used the word 'state' in their titles.[6] Hoyland deals mainly with the Islamic nature of the Arab state before the reforms of ʿAbd al-Malik. Foss is more concerned with the extent to which Muʿāwiya's state was centralised and whether it functioned efficiently.

What is meant by the word 'state' with regard to early-modern Europe, particularly the Carolingian and Ottonian empires and the Anglo-Saxon kingdoms, has been the subject of a substantial body of literature in the west. Here the discussion may have become somewhat over-sophisticated: one author, Gerd Althoff, subtitles his book on the Ottonian and Salian empire as *Königsherrschaft ohne Staat.* [royal power without a state].[7] British writers with their customary reluctance to use abstractions differentiate the classical state with its urban base and bureaucratic structures with the essentially rural and customary base of the medieval one. Seeking to define the essence of royal power in the early medieval state, Rory Naismith has the following formulation:[8]

> *The history of the 'state' in the early Middle Ages is by and large synonymous with the complex interaction of kings and other powerful agencies and institutions. Power and political organisation were founded principally on control of agricultural resources especially land and on the social relationships of those with land. Kings wielded superiority as major landowners and as the focal point in this hierarchy of social relationships.*

This is more or less what Althoff meant by 'royal power but no state' but the question is how far Naismith's carefully worded definitions represent something different from the situation of the medieval Arab ruler. There is one obvious point of difference. In Late Antiquity the church was directly integrated into the machinery of the state but in the medieval west it became an autonomous institution. Its ecclesiastical organisation was distinct from the secular monarchy and nobility and it could defend its corporate interests from a territorial redoubt by force if necessary. Its command over the beliefs and values of the masses was immense. In making Islam the ideological basis of Arab rule ʿAbd al-Malik co-opted the new religion so successfully that the distinction between church and state would have been meaningless to a medieval Muslim authority. For the Romans, the official church created its own problems because it meant that obscure Christological disputes rapidly morphed into an attack on the authority of the state itself. Tension between lay and religious authority may have existed in Islam but it was not institutionalised as in the west.

The transition from Public to Private

This formula comes from the title of an article by Michael Hendy.[9] This transition, he thought, did not just apply to the coinage but to the whole structure of the late Roman state. The implication of the change as far as the function of money was concerned was far reaching though the idea has not been without its critics. Again quoting Naismith:[10]

> *Minting changed being a primarily fiscal tool serving the tax needs of a centralized state, to being a mechanism for the collection of rents by private landowners and the circulation of private supplies of cash. This shift from tax to rent has been traced across the early Middle Ages from several perspectives and for a number of regions. However, the speed and nature of the process were shaped by local circumstances. Survival of terminology did not always herald the survival of institutions, and what was true of one*

---

[6] Hoyland, 'New documentary texts and the early Islamic state'; Foss, 'Muʿāwiya's state'.
[7] Althoff, 'Die Ottonen: Königsherrschaft ohne Staat'.
[8] Naismith, 'Money and Power', p. 16.
[9] Hendy, 'From public to private'.
[10] Naismith, 'Gold coinage', pp. 288–9.

> *kingdom – or even one city – need not have been true for all. One might also question the sharp division between 'public' and 'private' and consider the proposition that 'private' minting may still, on some levels, have served 'public' purpose.*

One aspect of the ethos of minting throws the distinction into a very sharp contrast indeed. In 369 the Roman emperor Valentinian I (364–75) expressly forbad private individuals from having their own gold coined in the mints. He ordered that all such gold and coins should be confiscated.[11]

The ruling may have been subsequently modified but one and a half centuries later the Ostrogothic ruler of Italy Theoderich (493–526) took a similar view.[12]

Two hundred years later the founder of Carolingian rule Pepin the Short (752–68), who was trying to re-establish royal control over the coinage, laid down the rate which private individuals could receive for bullion (silver by now) brought to the mint and what fee the mint should charge.[13] He thus institutionalised the very process the Romans had tried to stop and, in so doing, set the pattern for minting in Europe for centuries.

One might expect that Khusrau II's attitude to private citizens having the bullion coined at his mints would have been the same as Valentinian's but there is no evidence either way.

According to al-Balādhuri's source:

> *Al-Hajjah inquired about the procedure of the Persians in the matter of coining dirhams, and then erected a mint and then assembled men to do the stamping. He used to coin money for the Sultan and out of the good metal obtained from spurious coin alloyed silver and counterfeit coin out of the gold bullion which was collected for him. He allowed merchants and others to have silver pieces coined for them, and kept as profit what remained after paying the wages of the workmen and the coiners. He marked the hands of the coiners.*[14]

It is not clear, at least in this version, whether al-Hajjaj, although he enquired about the Sasanian system, followed it. The decision to allow merchants to have their silver coined may have been a departure from Sasanian practice which is why it is mentioned. Likewise coining gold hardly fitted in with the Sasanian system. There may be a hint that private individuals could have silver coined but not gold. Marking the coiners either by branding or tattooing may suggest that they were state functionaries or may just reflect they were regarded with suspicion.[15] Finally there is always the possibility that al-Balādhuri is mirroring the situation as it existed in his own time. All that does seem clear is that under the 'Abbasids, and earlier, the Arabs, as in the medieval west, were happy to let private citizens have their own silver made into coin. We can only guess whether or not the Shahanshah would have approved.

Some other aspects of coinage

As already pointed out with respect to Foss' article, discussions about the nature of the state have concentrated on fiscal and administrative matters. In this context coinage is discussed as a function of the tax system. So, as a change, I would like to look at some other aspects of coinage which

---

[11] Mommsen and Meyer (eds), 'Codex Theodosianus', p. 473, ii, 21 7; discussion in Hendy, 'Public to private', p. 35.
[12] Naismith, 'Gold coinage', p. 288.
[13] Capitulary of Vernon 754/5. Jesse, 'Quellenbuch', p. 9, no. 28.
[14] Hitti and Murgotten, p. 266.
[15] Thus a few lines further on, 'Yusuf ibn Umar… kept the coiners and money changers under close surveillance, cutting the hand and branding the flesh.'

attract less attention but which have bearing on the nature and policies of the authority which issued them.

They are:
> The significance of names and imagery on coins,
> Coins and public opinion,
> The changing status of the three coinage metals.

These will be discussed in the context of Late Antiquity and the seventh century.

Names on Coins

In a well known passage Procopius of Caesarea made his disapproval of the behaviour of the Frankish kings of Gaul very clear:

> *As gentlemen of leisure they attend the chariot races at Arles and they continue to use gold from the mines in Gaul to mint nomismata with their effigy instead of that of the Roman autocrator. Yet the Basileus of Persia himself who enjoys complete freedom with regard to his own silver coinage would not stamp his image on gold coins. Even though he has plenty of gold in his kingdom it is not right that he, or any other Basileus in the barbarian world, should put his likeness on a gold stater. The barbarians, with whom his subjects trade, would not accept such money. The Franks continue to do this.*

This is a very familiar passage to most people though the translation differs slightly from the version in the *Loeb Library*. It was provoked by the issue of signed gold solidi by the Frankish king Theodebert (533–48)[16]:

Figure 1: Theodebert of Metz, solidus, Deutsche Bundesbank[17]

It is generally taken as an express association of the emperor's name and image with the acceptability of the solidus, even among barbarian peoples. Of course the rulers of the successor states in the west had been issuing gold for some time (fig. 2) but always in the emperor's name. So names are significant. If you had asked any contemporary Byzantine authority 'why does the ruler of the Arabs not put his name on his gold coins?' the answer would presumably have been 'because he does not dare to' even when his armies were besieging Constantinople itself. On the other hand the ruler of the Arabs was not trying to get his coins accepted among the gold using barbarians of the west.

---

[16] Procopius, 'History of the Wars', Dewing (ed.), vol. 4, pp. 438–9, vii. 33.5–6. For the background to the Theodebert issue see Grierson and Blackburn, MEC I, p. 116.
[17] All pictures in this article are slightly enlarged.

Figure 2: Gaul, Pseudo-Imperial solidus in the name of Justinian, SMB 18202211

As already pointed out the first Arabs to put their names on coins were provincial governors. Both Muʿāwiya and ʿAbd al-Malik issued silver coins with their names but they were outnumbered by those of the governors, many of them quite obscure figures. In addition some of the people who issued signed coins, such as Qaṭarī, were the most dangerous and implacable of the caliph's enemies (fig. 3).

Figure 3:
(a) Muʿāwiya, drachm DA Darabjird, frozen year 43H, Album auction 14 (September 2012) lot 70;
(b) ʿAbd al-Malik, drachm DA Darabjird 64YE–75-76H, Album auction 18 (January 2014) lot 139;
(c) Ziyād ibn Abī Sufyān, drachm DA Darabjird 43H, CNG auction 288 (October 2012) lot 623;
(d) Qaṭarī b. al-Fujāʾa, drachm DA Darabjird 76H, CNG Triton X (January 2007) lot 902

Compare the Armenian soldier Mzhezh who briefly occupied Sicily after the assassination of Constans II in 668. He issued not only solidi but also fractions with his own name (Latinised as Mezezius) and portrait and with the title AUGUSTVS[18] (fig. 4). Theodebert used the titles REX and VICTOR. Thanks to James Howard-Johnston we know that Mzhezh was effectively the creature of Muʿāwiya who had engineered Constans' assassination. He strikes the gold coins in his own name which Muʿāwiya did not. Clearly there are manifest cultural differences at work but what are they?

---

[18] Grierson, 'Semissis of Mezezius'. Howard-Johnston, 'World Crisis', pp. 126, 225, 492. Mezezius had been proclaimed as emperor by his troops but Augustus implied a coronation at Constantinople.

a b

Figure 4: Mezezius, usurper in Sicily
(a) Solidus, Gemini auction II (Jan. 2006) lot 531; (b) Semissis, Grierson, NC 146 (1986), Pl. 25D

Moving even further west we reach the extreme case. Speaking of Merovingian Gaul, Robert Latouche commented 'Never in our history has the conception of the state known so complete an eclipse.'[19] Whose names do we find on their coins? Answer: the moneyers. In so far as there was any authorisation behind the coin that the user could accept it was the name of the private citizen issuing it.[20]

On the other hand the absence of a name on a gold coin could have dire consequences! The laconic *Chronicle* of the Coptic bishop John of Nikiu finds time to mention the following:

> *And some said: 'The death of Heraclius is due to his stamping the gold coinage with the figures of the three emperors—that is, his own and of his two sons on the right hand and on the left—and so no room was found for inscribing the name of the Roman empire.' And after the death of Heraclius they obliterated those three figures.*[21]

There is another point which links this reference with the much discussed allusion in the *Maronite Chronicle* to people rejecting coins because they did not have crosses.[22] In both cases the authors claim that there was an adverse public reaction to innovations in the design of coins. This leads us on the question of coins and public opinion.

Coins and Public Opinion

There is no doubt that people in the ancient world examined their coins more closely than we do. What did they look for and did the state seriously try and exploit this? The Greeks, and it seems the Roman Republican world, at least to judge by the names they used, knew coins primarily from their image: 'owls', 'archers', 'quadrigati', etc. This applies to the statement that, at the time of the reform, al-Hajjaj ordered that taxes should be paid in 'Khusro dirhams' as a means of withdrawing them from circulation. John Walker, I would argue, was wrong to equate these only with Arab-Sasanian coins – in this context the term surely applied to any Sasanian style coin regardless of the inscription.[23]

---

[19] Latouche, 'Birth of Western Economy', p. 129.
[20] Discussion in MEC I, pp. 100–1; Naismith, 'Gold coinage', p. 290–1; Hendy, 'Public to private', pp. 65–8. During the period c.575–c.675 some 800 mint-places and 2,000 moneyers are named on the coins. With the exception of the silver coins of Provence, which cite local Patricians, the only names are those of the moneyer and the mint. There may have been some sort of implied guarantee by the local lord. In theory, on the other hand, moneyers' activities were defined in law and the mints were seen as public institutions. The whole subject has recently been discussed in several important papers in Jarnut and Strothmann (eds), 'Die Merowingischen Monetarmünzen'.
[21] John of Nikiu, 'Chronicle', CXVI 3. I am grateful to Tony Goodwin for reminding me about this and pointing out that 'empire' is a mistake for 'emperor'.
[22] Palmer, 'Seventh Century in West-Syrian Chronicles', p. 32.
[23] Walker, 'Arab-Sassanian', p. cxlix.

In the Roman Empire, coins were used to convey any number of messages about the emperor and his successes. There has been a certain amount of argument about the level at which this was authorised and what its impact might have been. What seems to be the latest discussion of the question, as far as the earlier Roman Empire is concerned, is that of Michael Crawford who was, of course, able to draw on a wide range of numismatic and written evidence.[24] His rather stark conclusions are that, while the emperors no doubt issued general directives, what appeared on the coins was down to individual artists and officials at the mint trying to do their best for their patron. The general public took very little notice. As far as the emperor was personally concerned, statutes and buildings had a much higher profile as did his patronage of the arts and attendance at certain ritual sporting events. This explains why Procopius is so disapproving of the Frankish lords attending the chariot races.

What did the coin using public care about? Was the coin issued by a respectable authority? What is the element in the design that proves that it was? In the case of the Roman Imperial series, a tradition carried on into the Byzantine era, it is the head of the emperor. Significantly the only time that the design of a coin is mentioned in the masses of references to coins in the Theodosian code it relates to the portrait. People had to be reminded that although the head on some coins was smaller than usual it did not mean that they were worth any less.[25]

What we find in the seventh century in both contemporary sources, and in the more extensive later ones, is the considerable attention paid to modifications in the designs on coins. In the most high profile case both Greek and Arabic authorities agree that such changes helped provoke a full scale war (fig. 5).

Figure 5: Shahada solidus, Numismatica Genevensis auction 6 (November 2010) lot 285

What I have argued is that references of this sort in the texts are the exception not the rule. Is this just chance or has something changed? There are two points here. First the aggressive and high profile nature of the Heraclius propaganda machine; second the ritualistic aspect of coin use which has very little echo in the west.

The cult of Heraclius as the 'New Constantine' was novel in that, as far as I know, no Roman emperor tried to reinvent himself in this way and it was put in to practice very thoroughly. One example is the publicity surrounding the saga of the True Cross.[26] I have heard it suggested that the story of Heraclius rescuing the True Cross after Khusrau II had taken it is a complete myth. I am waiting to see this in print.

After his victory over Khusrau II, the 'New Constantine' increased the weight of the follis and introduced a new obverse design depicting himself in military dress holding a long cross in his right hand and with his other hand on his hip (fig. 6a). The obvious implication is that this symbolised his military prowess. Another, much rarer type exists with the emperor holding a sword instead (fig. 6b

---

[24] Crawford, 'Roman imperial coin types and the formation of public opinion'.
[25] Mommsen and Meyer (eds), 'Codex Theodosianus', ix 22, AD 343 'the solidi on which our images appear and for which there is universal veneration must as of the same value'.
[26] Vividly described by Soyanov, 'Apocalypticizing warfare', at pp. 386–94.

and c). This type was first published in 2001, though at least one example had previously appeared at auction, and probably only around ten examples are now known.[27]

a   b   c

Figure 6:
(a) Heraclius with hand on hip, follis year 20, CNG auction 87 (May 2011) lot 1220;
(b) Heraclius with sword, follis year 20, Morton & Eden auction 68 (June 2014) lot 148;
(c) Heraclius with sword, half follis year 20, private collection

It appears to have preceded the common type showing the emperor with his hand on his hip since an example is known from the mint of Thessalonica dated year XX (629/30) which was closed around this time and does not issue the common type. We can only surmise, since there is no reference to the coin in the extant literary sources, that it was not popular and was quickly withdrawn. The earlier emperors had armour and spears but there was no precedent for a sword. This sudden adoption of military types is all the more remarkable in that it was going against a trend whereby armour was replaced by civilian dress. After Leo III (717–41) emperors ceased to wear military dress on coins for over three hundred years. It came back into fashion in the eleventh century when Constantine IX (1042–55) had himself depicted in scale armour with a sheathed sword on his silver (fig. 7a) without arousing comment; but when Isaac Comnenus (1057–9) was shown with a drawn sword on his gold (fig. 7b) he was attacked for his impiety in hinting that it was through his sword and not divine grace that he had achieved power.

a   b

Figure 7:
(a) Constantine IX, Miliaresion, CNG auction 300 (April 2013) lot 354;
(b) Isaac Comnenus, Histamenon Nomisma, CNG auction 61 (September 2002) lot 2286

---

[27] Lampinen, 'A new variety of Heraclius follis'. A particularly fine example recently fetched a high price (Hammer: £1200) at auction (fig. 6b). It would be interesting to know how many dies and officinae exist.

By contrast ʿAbd al-Malik gave great prominence to the sword held by the so-called Standing Caliph (fig. 8). According to a garbled account in Maqrizi, this seems to have caused offence in some quarters.[28]

Figure 8: ʿAbd al-Malik, drachm 75H, Morton & Eden auction 54 (April 2012) lot 23

The ruler we know as Constans II was officially known as Constantine III and he not only adopts the *en touto nika / ananeos* legend on his folles but temporarily abandons the portrait in favour of a standing figure. It was still the image of the Emperor but he has dissociated himself from his name and title. When Tony Goodwin and I published our original survey of the finds of Byzantine copper coins in Syria one of the most intriguing aspects, and one which received very little attention, was the presence of the *Inper Const* folles in Syria and Cyprus and nowhere else (fig. 9). What was missing was an explanation. I found it difficult to think of any reason why this particular type should be chosen to be sent to Syria. When I looked at all the new find evidence it was obvious that the picture was basically right but it needed modifying in that the type is originally destined for Cyprus whose strategic importance I had overlooked. Michael Metcalf,[29] has suggested that it was deliberately chosen to be sent to the garrison in the immediate expectation of Arab attack. So the name and portrait of the emperor was seen as a special morale booster.[30]

Figure 9: Constans II, Inper Const follis, private collection

Considering the squalid appearance of these small copper coins it seems incredible that they could be considered as a suitable propaganda medium. Why not used the gold? To some extent Heraclius did so by putting the young Heraclius Constantine, and later Heraclonas, on the solidi, not to mention the increasingly grotesque beard on his own bust. The problem, as hinted at by Procopius, is that there is a risk of changing the design of an internationally accepted coin. People are suspicious of change, particularly with a valuable item. The radical departure in design that occurs with the *Servus Christi* solidus of Justinian II (fig. 10) must have been approved by the emperor himself.

Figure 10: Justinian II, Servus Christi solidus of Constantinople, CNG coin shop 733391

---

[28] Goodwin, 'Arab-Byzantine Coinage', p. 160
[29] Metcalf, 'Coins from Saranda Colones', pp. 206–7.
[30] Phillips, 'The import of Byzantine coins to Syria revisited', p. 50.

I would therefore argue that during the seventh century there was an intensification of the level of imperial propaganda on coins as part of a coordinated programme which is why we see this increase in references in the literature.

There was another more obscure force operating. The parable of the Tribute Penny[31] is always taken as a demonstration of the importance of the Imperial image and title. This is of course a Christian parable but the background is Jewish and the place where one does find references to the symbolic importance of the portrait on a coin is the Talmud. There is a strange passage, mentioned by Crawford, certainly not found in all versions, which states that, on account of the persecution of the Jews by Hadrian in and around 132AD, coins with his portrait should not be handled at least as long as the portrait remained recognisable. When that ceased to be the case due to wear, the coin could be used.[32] At the time of 'Abd al-Malik's reforms it is claimed that certain 'Companions of the Prophet' objected to putting the name of God on coins which might be touched by impure hands.[33] Whoever wrote this had no idea what pre-reform coins looked like so where is the tradition coming from? The answer is that it derives from Jewish traditions concerning the handling of coins and hostility to images. I am fully aware of the liturgical function of coins in the Western tradition but I cannot think of anything as extreme as this. Could this be one factor to help explain why Mzhezh in Sicily finds it culturally acceptable to strike his own gold while the ruler of the Arabs does not?

Even more remarkable is that this sudden development in numismatic propaganda, reflected in a willingness to risk changing established designs, was not confined to Byzantium. Whether the spectacular facing bust Khusrau II drachms with the Anahita (or is it Mithra?) reverse (fig. 11a) reflect triumphalism or desperation (both seem to have been suggested) they certainly mean something.[34] These drachms were issued in very small numbers but they inaugurated a sudden willingness to adapt royal portraiture which had remained stereotyped since the family coins of Vahran II. There had been changes but significantly only on the coins of usurpers. Whether the decision to present boys such as Ardashir III (fig. 11b) as beardless was borrowed from the depiction of the young Heraclius Constantine I do not know but it is a possibility.

a　　　　　　　　　　　　　　　　　　b

Figure 11:
(a) Khusrau II, drachm facing bust year 23, CNG auction 90 (May 2012) lot 916;
(b) Ardashir III, drachm young bust WYHC year 1, CNG auction 313 (October 2013) lot 143

The Status of the Three Metals

Modern authors now agree that early in the fourth century a fundamental change took place in the metallic composition of Roman coinage. In the words the anonymous author of *De rebus bellicis*:

---

[31] Matthew 22, 15–22.
[32] Crawford, 'Roman imperial coin types', p. 56.
[33] The best known version of this tradition is in al-Maqrizi (trans De Sacy, p. 25). Discussion in Bacharach, 'Signs of sovereignty', p. 22 and p. 30, nn 76–7, who emphasises the hostility related to words rather than images.
[34] Mosig-Walburg, 'Sonderprägungen Khusros II'.

> *In the age of Constantine [the Great (307–37)] extravagant public spending prescribed gold for petty transactions instead of bronze, which previously was highly valued.*[35]

It is not simply that the use of gold increased dramatically but the role of copper was diminished. A parallel development which consolidated the domination of gold was an increasing emphasis on it in payments to and from the state. This was reinforced by the practices of *adaeratio* and *coemptio*: commutation of taxes in kind into cash, and forced purchase of goods by the state, respectively.

This coincided with a marked demarcation in attitude to the three metals as reflected in the laws regarding coin forgery (the penalties for which grew ever more severe) in the Theodosian Code.[36] In the article I am following, Philip Grierson summed it up thus:

> The forgery of gold was regarded as a personal act of sacrilege against the sovereign.
> Forgery of silver was regarded as a form of fraud.
> Forgery of bronze was regarded as wrong in that it lead to a loss of profit on the mints.

The Justinianic code, which essentially preserved what was thought to be of permanent value in that of Theodosius, kept the distinction between gold and copper. I do not know if anyone has ever argued that it was more than just coincidence that the adoption and universal use of gold should have coincided with the conversion of the empire to Christianity but it may be why coined gold acquired this supernatural quality. It helps explain why the Arabs in Syria are ready to strike bronze but hesitate for a long time over gold.

Curiously the references to the punishment of coin forgers in al-Balādhuri do not specify the metal, though from the context I assume he is talking about silver. In one case he specifies that the forger 'counterfeited the government inscription' though the rest of his references relate to clipping rather than forgery.[37] At all events there is nothing in al-Balādhuri or, as far as I am aware, in other medieval Islamic jurisprudence to match the savagery of the punishments for forgery that existed in western Europe. Grierson argued that when European coinage changed from gold to silver in the seventh and eighth centuries the aura of sacrilege, which in the Roman empire, had surrounded the gold coinage was transferred to less noble metals 'and the strange and barbarous history of the medieval law of counterfeiting began'. By this he meant boiling people alive, pouring molten lead down their throats and other horrors. In Islam forgery was essentially theft and usually punishable by the loss of a hand.[38]

What I have tried to do so far is to sketch some cultural, and perhaps transcendental, attitudes to coin which the Arabs would have encountered in the lands they occupied. I would also emphasise the highly unusual, if not unique, ideological nature of the designs on the coins prevailing at this time. It emphasises the sheer weight of cultural and political inhibition that had to be overcome before the caliph could strike official gold, quite apart from the practical problem of getting his coins accepted. In the east, in contrast to the west, the Roman emperor was still there 'armed and dangerous' and, as the caliph was fully aware, the recipient of the real allegiance of many of his own subjects.

When ʿAbd al-Malik finally did issue his own gold coin, the anonymous three figure type (fig. 5), he still did not put his name and/or title on it. He chose for his prototype a coin with no obverse

---

[35] *De rebus bellicis* quoted Naismith, 'Gold coinage', pp. 2–3.
[36] This paragraph is based on Grierson, 'Roman law of counterfeiting'.
[37] Hitti and Murgotten, pp. 267–9.
[38] There seems to be no general study of the punishment of coin forgers. For a detailed analysis of the influence of Roman law over customary law and practice in the Low Countries and further east, complete with gruesome details, see De Graaf, 'Den valscher den ketel (?)'.

legend because he did not have to worry about substituting one, though he and his advisers must have known it would suggest an allusion to the Trinity.

Muʿāwiya's State

Here I am dependent on the aforementioned article by Clive Foss. If I am, at times, critical of Foss's conclusions I have to acknowledge my obligation to his lucid and comprehensive marshalling of the sources.

The debate is over whether Muʿāwiya merely presided over a loose tribal confederation or whether he operated something more organised. All the writers seem to agree that ʿAbd al-Malik created the Islamic State so the debate seems to have resolved itself to the degree to which Muʿāwiya started the process.

Foss divides Muʿāwiya's 'state' into three geographical areas: Egypt, Syria and Persia. In each case he is concerned to stress the continuity of Arab rule with that of their predecessors. In Egypt he argues that the papyri prove the continuity of a tax raising system and the personnel who operated it. This area, for reasons of space, I leave to be dealt with by others.

Persia

I have stressed that the so-called Arab-Sasanian coinage is essentially that of provincial governors, not to mention other groups implacably opposed to the Umayyads. In spite of this there does seem to be a high level of metrological consistency. It cannot be considered 'private' in the Merovingian sense. But it certainly deviates from the coinage of the Sasanians.

The Arabs showed no indication of wanting to tamper with the design of the coinage until the last Sasanian *Shahanshah* was dead (651/31). As far as coin supply was concerned there was plenty of Sasanian material available. They begin by using theologically neutral terms such as 'valid' (fig. 12a), 'in the name of God' (fig. 12b) and interestingly they put them in the same place as Khusrau II had inserted the enigmatic *apd* (fig. 12c).

a   b   c

Figure 12: Drachms with (a) jayyid, The NY sale 20 (January 2009) lot 475; (b) bismillah, CNG auction 182 (February 2008, lot 279; (c) apd, CNG auction 319 (January 2014) lot 176

This was Khusrau II's most important innovation; the difficulty is that we do not fully understand the purpose behind it. That the Arabs were dependent on Sasanian mint personnel is obvious enough but, in so far as the people using the coin could regard it as coming from an authoritative source, the guarantee from the very first is in Arabic. As far as the image is concerned the Arabs were not hostile, just indifferent. Ten years after Yazdgard III's death, and shortly after the accession of Muʿāwiya, the first governor to put his name on the coins, ʿAbd Allāh b. ʿĀmir, broke the key connection between legend and portrait (fig. 13a).

a   b

Figure 13:
(a) ʿAbd Allāh b. ʿĀmir, drachm DA Darabjird 43H, St James auction 19 (October 2011) lot 1588;
(b) Ziyād ibn Abī Sufyān, drachm DA Darabjird 43H, CNG auction 288 (October 2012) lot 623

It is only in 665/45 when Ziyād ibn Abī Sufyān (fig. 13b), a former enemy, was appointed governor of Baṣra that Foss, relying heavily on Ṭabarī, sees Muʿāwiya comprehensively reasserting state authority.[39] The fortuitous discovery of old Sasanian records made it possible to reinstitute the tax system. Dissidents were brutally dealt with, civil engineering projects undertaken, and the postal system reconstituted. Stability, however, was still partly dependent on the safety valve of more conquest of land. Ziyād remained loyal but, even taking Ṭabarī at face value, one can categorise this as authority delegated to an excessive degree, backed by Syrian enforcers, rather than any organised hierarchy, and heavily dependent on Persian administrators. The same model repeated itself with al-Hajjaj b. Yusuf and ʿAbd al-Malik. In between, the ease with which rebels groups, Zubayrids (fig. 14a) and Kharajites (fig. 14b), were able to take over public jurisdictions, including mints, underlines the distinctly personal nature of Ziyād's rule.

a   b

Figure 14:
(a) ʿAbd al Malik b. ʿAbdallāh, drachm BYSh Bishapur 66H, Baldwin ICA 23 (Dec. 2012) lot 28;
(b) Qaṭarī b. al-Fujāʾa, drachm DA Darabjird 76H, CNG Triton X (January 2007) lot 902

How do the coins contribute to our understanding of this situation? Al-Balādhuri mentions a coin forger issuing a coin not bearing the 'government inscription'.[40] A curious phrase when the only coins he would have been familiar with would have been the post reform dirhams. I would suggest that one can interpret the so-called 'Arab-Sasanian' coins as a mixture of public and private. The

---
[39] Foss, 'Muʿāwiya's state', pp. 77–9.
[40] Hitti and Murgotten, p. 268.

name of the governor or caliph, in Pahlavi, being not so much private as personal, the guarantee, the 'government inscription', being in Arabic. The yardstick of statehood, I would argue, is the extent to which the caliph's representative was able to assert and extend central state power against the spontaneous grain of tribal society. This meant establishing a 'public' authority outside the complex web of private jurisdictions. This tension is symbolised on the coins. The marginal Arabic inscription on these coins is always very neat and clear and, to repeat, it centres on the place where Khusrau had made his important innovation. The portrait is of less significance, so much so that when the propaganda war hotted up, unlike the 'War of Images' in the west, it was a 'War of Words' in which the Kharijites wrote 'To God alone the judgement', and the Zubayrids 'Muhammed is the Messenger of God', the latter subsequently adopted by ʿAbd al-Malik. What we do not know is how many people could actually read them. As far as the, mostly Persian, individuals who handled the coins were concerned they remained 'Khusrau drachms'.

Syria

In Syria, as we all know, there is a dearth of written sources. Foss underlines the continuity of personnel on the evidence of the Nessana papyri which is similar to that of Egypt. The poll tax was an innovation but one borrowed from the Sasanians. So we fall back on the coins and in particular the gold. Here there have been some developments on the ground as it were. In an earlier article Foss argued that the 'mutilated cross' solidi, that is imitations of Byzantine solidi but with the crosses removed from both obverse and reverse, were official issues of Muʿāwiya[41] A number of 'mutilated cross' solidi have recently appeared (fig. 15a-d) and I would argue that the overall effect has been to undermine Foss' argument that these represent an official coinage.

a   b   c   d

Figure 15: 'Mutilated cross' solidi
(a) Focas imitation, Morton & Eden auction 63 (April 2013) lot 6;
(b) Heraclius imitation, Morton & Eden auction 63 (April 2013) lot 7;
(c) Heraclius imitation, Dix Noonan and Webb, 29 September 2008, lot 6332;
(d) Heraclius imitation, Baldwin ICA 24 (May 2013) lot 3999

The types and styles are too random and varied to support the idea of any kind of centralised issue. One new coin, in particular, combines the obverse of Heraclius and Heraclius Constantine (with the young bust) and the reverse with the pole on steps and, what has been read, on the three figure types, as the supposed indictional date of year 12 (fig. 15b). For the present I am inclined to agree

---

[41] Foss, 'A Syrian coinage of Muʿāwiya'.

with the comments of Stephen Lloyd, the cataloguer, that the coin reinforces Michael Bates' view the engravers neither understood nor cared about the significance of what they were copying.[42]

Unfortunately it is difficult to glean any information about the provenance of these 'new' coins. Some of them seem to be from 'old collections' tempted out by the high prices being paid, but two of them are said to have been consigned by people allegedly unaware of what they were. One is said to have come from Egypt another from Syria. None so far have been found in Israel. Until we have some reputable hoard evidence the chronology of these is very uncertain.

So how do we explain the assertion in the Maronite Chronicle that Muʿāwiya issued coins without crosses which the public rejected?[43] Goodwin and I have come to the same conclusion. The chronicler saw the coins and, given the nature of the imperial gold coinage, it never crossed his mind that they could be anything but official. In reality they were gold Pseudo-Byzantine coins.

Foss, however, overlooks what I would argue is an important element. Whatever state ʿAbd al-Malik may or not have created after his victory in the second Civil War, unless one assumes some important innovations by the two short-lived intermediate rulers (Yazīd I, 680–3, and Muʿāwiya II, 683–4), which seems unwarranted, the state that he inherited in 684/64 was that of Muʿāwiya. This included the obligation to pay tribute to the Byzantines.

Ever since 677 and the disastrous defeat of Muʿāwiya's attempt to conquer Constantinople, the Arabs had been forced to pay tribute, on and off, to the Byzantines.[44] This had begun as a mere token sum of 3,000 solidi a year. Taking advantage of the eruption of the second *fitna*, Justinian II forced a revision of the treaty in 686.[45] The revenues of Cyprus, Armenia and Iberia were to be shared, and a vast 365,000 solidi was to be paid each year to the Romans. The scale of this sum, if at all accurate, is extraordinary. ʿAbd al-Malik also had to find the resources to pay his army now embroiled in the second Civil War. The hoard evidence indicates a sharp falling off in the import of Byzantine gold coins after 680. ʿAbd al-Malik's potential sources of tax income have recently been analysed by Michael Humphreys on the basis of available estimates from the Byzantine period.[46] He points out that in 686 only Syria and Egypt were under Marwanid control, and that there is considerable doubt over how much of the revenue of Egypt the caliphs were ever able to extract for the treasury in Damascus.

Humphreys stresses the ideological weakness in relying on media inherently bound to the Christian-Roman symbolic world combined with the fact that the Marwanids' enemies had already used the coinage of the Sasanian world to proclaim a more strident Islamic identity. It was this pressure that led to the various innovations in coinage design that then took place.

Although there is evidence that ʿAbd al-Malik frantically overhauled the tax system (reflected in contemporary apocalyptic literature), to begin with at least he had to make do with what he had inherited. He must have been able, in the short to medium term, to draw on an emergency reserve either in the form of tax or his own personal fortune. My guess would be that it was a combination of the two. Muʿāwiya came from a family which had owned land before the time of Islam. The early caliphs were great property developers. A Syriac writer from the eighth century tells us Hisham, the last really effective Umayyad ruler, drew more from his private estates than from the

---

[42] Other recent examples: Heraclius two bust imitation: Baldwin ICA 11, 13 July 2006, lot 13; three standing figure imitation: Timeline auction, 19 June 2013, lot 273.
[43] Palmer, 'Seventh century in West-Syrian chronicles', p. 32. There is also the puzzling reference to silver coins minted by Muʿāwiya. Conceivably the chronicler happened to see some Sasanian or related coins and assumed they were some sort of official issue though this seems rather far fetched.
[44] Bates, 'First century', pp. 251–2; Howard-Johnston, 'World Crisis', pp. 494–7.
[45] Theophanes, 363; Mango and Scott, 'Chronicle', p. 506.
[46] Humphreys, 'The 'War of Images' revisited', at pp. 239–41.

taxation of the whole empire.[47] Perhaps they were not so different from early western rulers after all. At all events, Muʿāwiya had clearly created a substantial resource base on which ʿAbd al-Malik was able to draw.

Foss shows convincingly that Muʿāwiya was a capable politician who managed to reconstitute and maintain an effective machinery of government. What he does not show is that he was much of an innovator, certainly not one who would have undertaken an extensive issues of gold coins as long as he had access to Byzantine ones. Conversely, if like Foss, you take the Maronite Chronicle at face value, he tried to introduce new coin types but gave up when he encountered opposition. This does not sound like a state builder.

Looking forward to the Umayyads and ʿAbbasids, in two key aspects at least, the coinage continued the traditions of the Roman Empire. It had a spread of denominations, was universally negotiable, and was guaranteed by a central authority. Hugh Kennedy memorably contrasted the caliphate of al-Muʿtaṣim (833–42) 'where taxes were collected from all over the empire and brought to the capital where they were used to pay an elite professional military force' with the situation in France a century later where effective royal power (and control of the coinage) had almost ceased to exist.[48] There were considerable limits to the centralisation and uniformity of ʿAbbasid government. It was exercised over a diverse variety of social formations and cultures and Kennedy later preferred to use the term 'Muslim Commonwealth'. His description of the key role of the provincial governors and the interaction both with the centre and the local elites certainly recalls the old Colonial Office.[49]

The crucial element of land ownership, so important in the west, also applied to the east even though towns were far more important. I have already emphasised the importance of the early caliphs' personal estates. They also created what became large cities such as Kufa, Basra and Baghdad. An important innovation, again recently highlighted by Kennedy, was the *qatīy'a* developed to regularise private ownership of landed estates and property. It arose from the urgent need to repair and conserve the irrigation system in Mesopotamia which had been destroyed by the wars of the seventh century. The creation of cities such as Baghdad, which was dependent on grain from the area, would have impossible without this infrastructure. Rather than finance it through taxation, the Umayyad caliphs leased it to individual entrepreneurs under certain conditions. It later became the personal property of the developer and was both transferable and hereditable. Unlike the system that developed in the west, cultivated land was never granted in return for military service. The development of previously uncultivated land, on the other hand, was also carried out under the *qatīy'a* system.[50] This takes us somewhat beyond the scope of the present paper. I mention it merely to underline the point that power based on the ownership of land, emphasised by Naismith, was also significant under the Umayyads and ʿAbbasids.

Conclusion

One of Michael Hendy's last constructive articles is entitled 'East and West: Divergent models of coinage and its use'.[51] In spite of the title I do particularly recommend it. Not always the most lucid of writers, his dogmatism, not to mention his bad manners, were getting the better of him. He does, however, make the following challenging conclusion:

---

[47] Kennedy, 'The Prophet and the Age of the Caliphates', p. 111.
[48] Kennedy, 'Financing of the military', p. 361.
[49] Kennedy, 'Decline and fall', p. 28.
[50] Kennedy, 'Feeding of the five hundred thousand'.
[51] Hendy, 'East and West', p. 675.

It has not escaped the author's notice that while Byzantium and the west have both been included within the scope of this paper the contemporary Arab world has not: the situation there remains to be fitted somehow–but necessarily–into this schema. But that function rests with somebody in possession of the requisite tripartite expertise: a rare quality indeed.

I would not for one minute suggest that these brief and rather disconnected remarks fill the gap which Hendy highlighted, anymore than I would necessarily agree with his views on the nature of coinage. Rather they are a plea for early medieval numismatists, not to mention the self-styled 'monetary historians', to try and gain perspective by examining the contrast between developments in the east and the west. Drawing conclusions about the nature of the transition from ancient to medieval on the basis of what happened to the coinage is all very well, but these conclusions will always be limited if societies are studied in isolation. Finally the historical importance of coinage is not simply a matter of its fiscal function in a given context. Cultural and social forces have sometimes played a surprisingly important role. Greater awareness of this can only enhance the contribution of numismatics to historical understanding.

Bibliography

G. Althoff, **Die Ottonen: Königsherrschaft ohne Staat**. Kohlhammer Urban-Taschenbücher vol. 473 (Stuttgart, 2000).

J.L. Bacharach, 'Signs of Sovereignty: the Shahāda, Qur'anic verses, and the coinage of ʿAbd al-Malik (65-86/685-705),' **Muqarnas** 27 (2010), pp. 1-30.

M.L. Bates, 'History, Geography and Numismatics in the First Century of Islamic Coinage', **SNR** 65 (1986), pp. 231-263.

C.N.L. Brooke, B.H.I.H. Stewart, G. Pollard, T.R. Volk, **Studies in Numismatic Method Presented to Philip Grierson** (Cambridge, 1983).

M.H. Crawford, 'Roman imperial coin types and the formation of public opinion', in Brooke et al., **Studies in Numismatic Method…**, pp. 47-64.

C. de Graaf, 'Den valscher den ketel (?); Bestraffingen van muntmisdrijven in Holland, Zeeland en Utrecht ca 1300 – ca 1600', **JMP** 82 (1995), pp. 77-179.

C. Foss, 'A Syrian Coinage of Muʿāwiya?', **RN** 158 (2002), pp. 353-66.

C. Foss, 'Muʿāwiya's state' in Haldon (ed.) **Money, Power and Politics**, pp. 75-96.

T. Goodwin, **Arab-Byzantine coinage**. Studies in the Khalili Collection 4. (London, 2004).

P. Grierson 'A semissis of Mezezius', **NC** 146 (1986), pp. 231-2.

P. Grierson, 'The Roman law of counterfeiting', in R.A. Carson and C. H. V. Sutherland (eds), **Essays in Roman Coinage Presented to Harold Mattingly** (Oxford, 1956), pp. 240-61. Reprinted in **Scritti**, pp. 107-128.

P. Grierson, **Scritti, Storici e Numismatici** (ed. E.A. Arslan and L. Traviani) Spoleto, 2001.

P. Grierson and M. Blackburn, **Medieval European Coinage** vol. I (Cambridge, 1986).

J. Haldon (ed.), *Money, Power and Politics in Early Islamic Syria. A Review of Current Debates* (Farnham, 2010).

S. Heidemann, 'The evolving representation of the early Islamic Empire and its religion on coin imagery', in A. Neuwirth et al. (eds.), *The Qur'ān in context: Historical and Literary Investigations into the Qur'ānic milieu* (Leiden, 2010), pp. 149-95.

M. Hendy, 'From public to private: the western barbarian coin images as a mirror of the disintegration of late Roman state structure', *Viator* 19 (1988), pp. 29-78. Reprinted Hendy, *Economy*, no. 7.

M. Hendy, *The Economy, Fiscal Adminstration and Coinage of Byzantium*. Variorum Reprints: Collected Studies Series 305 (Northampton, 1989).

M. Hendy. 'East and West. Divergent models of coinage and its use', in: *Il secolo di ferro: mito e realtà del secolo X*. Settimane di Studi del Centro Italiano di Studi sull'Alto Medioevo 38, (Spoleto 1991), pp. 637-75.

P.K. Hitti, and F. Murgotten (ed. and trans.). *The origins of the Islamic state: being a translation from the Arabic, accompanied with annotations, geographic and historic notes of the Kitâb futûḥ al-buldân of al-Imâm abu-l Àbbâs Aḥmad ibn-Jâbir al-Balâdhuri*. Studies in History, Economics and Public Law 68 (New York, London, 1916-24).

J. Howard-Johnston, *Witnesses to a World Crisis* (Oxford, 2010).

R. Hoyland, 'New documentary texts and the early Islamic state', *Bulletin of the School of Oriental and African Studies* 69 (2006), pp. 395-416.

M. Humphreys, 'The 'War of Images' revisited. Justinian II's coinage reform and the Caliphate', *NC* 173 (2013), pp. 229-44.

J. Jarnut and J. Strothmann (eds), *Die Merowingischen Monetarmünzen als Quelle zum Verständnis des 7. Jahrhunderts in Gallien* (Paderborn, 2013).

W. Jesse, *Quellenbuch zur Münz-und Geldgeschichte des Mittelalters* (Halle, 1924).

John of Nikiu, *The Chronicle of John, Bishop of Nikiu*, trans. by R.H. Charles (The Text and Translation Society, Oxford University Press, 1916).

H. Kennedy, *The Prophet and the Age of the Caliphates* (London, 1986).

H. Kennedy, 'The financing of the military in the early Islamic state', in A. Cameron (ed.), *The Byzantine and Early Islamic Near East III: States, Resources and Armies* (Princeton, 1995), pp. 361-78.

H. Kennedy, 'The decline and fall of the first Muslim empire', *Der Islam* 81 (2004), pp. 3-29.

H. Kennedy, 'The feeding of the five hundred thousand: cities and agriculture in early Islamic Mesopotamia', *Iraq* 73 (2011), pp. 177-99.

P. Lampinen, 'A new variety of Heraclius follis', *NCirc* 109, 1, (February, 2001), p. 5.

R. Latouche, *The Birth of Western Economy* (London, 1961).

C. Mango and R. Scott, *The Chronicle of Theophanes Confessor* (Oxford, 1997).

D.M. Metcalf, 'Byzantine, Islamic and Crusader coins from Saranda Colones', *NC* 163 (2003), pp. 205-26.

T. Mommsen and P. Meyer (eds), *Codex Theodosianus* (Berlin, 1904-5).

K. Mosig-Walburg, 'Sonderprägungen Khusros II (590–628): Innenpolitische Propaganda vor dem Hintergrund des Krieges gegen Byzanz', *Res Orientales* 18 (2009), pp. 185-208.

R. Naismith, *Money and Power in Anglo-Saxon England* (Cambridge, 2012).

R. Naismith, 'Gold coinage and its use in the post-Roman West', *Speculum* 89, 2 (April 2014), pp. 273-306.

A. Palmer (ed. and trans.), S. Brock and R. Hoyland, *The Seventh Century in West-Syrian chronicles*. Translated Texts for Historians 15 (Liverpool, 1993).

M. Phillips, 'The import of Byzantine coins to Syria revisited', in Goodwin (ed.), *Arab-Byzantine Coins and History*, Papers presented at the Seventh Century Syrian Numismatic Round Table (London, 2012), pp. 39-72.

Procopius, *History of the Wars*, H.B. Dewing (ed. and trans.), 5 vols. (London and Cambridge, MA: Harvard University Press (1961-8), vol. 4, pp. 438-39.

Y. Soyanov, 'Apocalypticizing Warfare: from political theology to imperial eschatology in Seventh- to Early Eighth-Century Byzantium', in K.B. Bardakjian and S. La Porta (eds), *The Armenian Apocalyptic Tradition. A Comparative Perspective. Essays Presented in Honor of Professor Robert W. Thomson on the Occasion of His Eightieth Birthday* (Leiden, Boston Mass., 2014), pp. 379-433.

J. Walker, *A Catalogue of the Arab-Sassanian Coins* (London, 1941).

SPINK

LONDON
1666

LEADING COLLECTABLES AUCTION HOUSE ACHIEVING RECORD BREAKING AUCTION RESULTS AND RENOWNED NUMISMATIC PUBLISHER

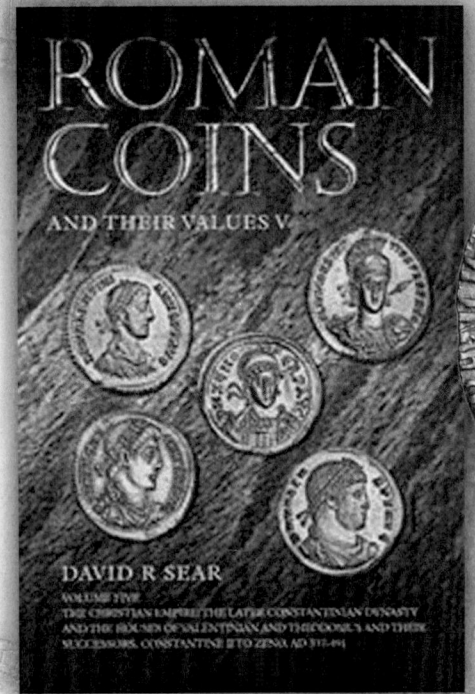

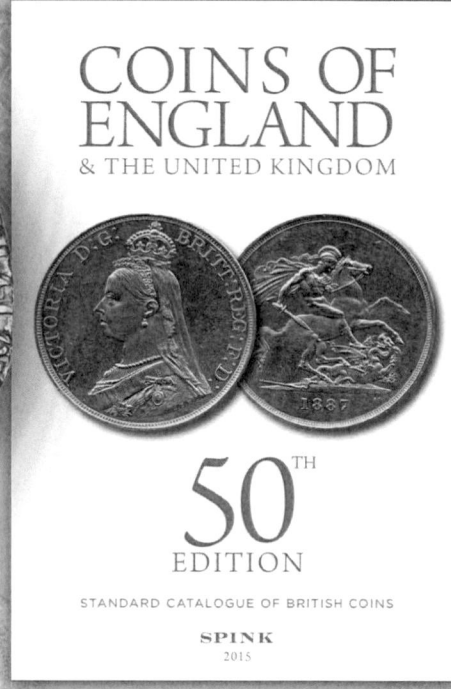

HENRY VII (1485 - 1509)
SOVEREIGN
RECENTLY SOLD AT
SPINK FOR £372,000
A WORLD RECORD FOR A TUDOR COIN

SPINK HAS BEEN A LEADING PUBLISHER OF NUMISMATIC REFERENCE WORKS FOR OVER 100 YEARS. WE PUBLISH LITERATURE ON ALL SUBJECTS PERTAINING TO THE COLLECTION OF BRITISH, ROMAN AND WORLD COINS, MEDALS AND TOKENS.

For more information, please contact Jennifer Mulholland:
Tel: (0)20 7563 4046 | Email: books@spink.com
If you are interested in consigning your items, please contact Richard Bishop:
Tel: (0)20 7563 4053 | Email: rbishop@spink.com

SPINK London | 69 Southampton Row | Bloomsbury | London | WC1B 4ET

WWW.SPINKBOOKS.COM

Symbolism and meaning on the early Islamic copper coinage of Greater Syria

Luke Treadwell [1]

Introduction

The study of early Islamic coinage has made much progress in the past twenty years, with new catalogues and thoughtful commentaries on monetary production, circulation and function. Particularly spectacular advances have been made in respect of the early Islamic coppers, which must rank as one of the most intensively studied series of Islamic coinage of any period. Now that the task of bringing order to this challenging body of numismatic material is fully under way, scholars are increasingly turning their minds to the question of what the designs and inscriptions on the copper coinage might have meant to the issuers and users of these coins at the time that they were struck.

The available material presents considerable difficulties: by contrast with the carefully regulated and transparently comprehensible imagery of Late Antique coinage, early Islamic figured coinage appears to be immensely complicated. Stock images, mostly of imperial figures recognisable in their basic outlines from Byzantine coinage, recur in many different mints. Yet few of these images are imitations in the sense of being copies of particular prototypes, for all of them show evidence of some degree of adaptation of the originals. Inscriptions are invariably garbled and often composed of isolated letters distributed at random on the die. Devices such as asterisms, squiggly lines, pellets and other shapes are common on many dies. The coinage is 'mute' in the sense that inscriptions rarely refer to, let alone identify, the figured images: neither do they give unequivocal information about the date of issue or, prior to the onset of the Imperial Image Phase,[2] the mint location. The existence of 'unofficial' issues which adopted the imagery of the coins of official mints further complicates the picture.

Much effort has been devoted to wrestling some coherence and sense out of this intractable series of coins. The approach adopted has been to assume that buried within this material are examples of coins that are attributable to identifiable issuers and to named mints and that once enough coins have been understood through painstaking research, this evidence will permit a better understanding of the bulk of the coinage.[3] The underlying premise of this approach is that some of the imagery on

---

[1] Luke Treadwell, University Lecturer in Islamic Numismatics and Senior Assistant Curator of Islamic Coins, Ashmolean Museum Oxford: luke.treadwell@orinst.ox.ac.uk

[2] In this paper, I adopt the terminology ('Pseudo-Byzantine' and 'Imperial Image') used by Goodwin in his introduction ('Arab-Byzantine coinage') to Album, S. and Goodwin, T., ***The Pre-reform coinage of the early Islamic period*** (Sylloge of Islamic coins in the Ashmolean vol. 1), Oxford, 2002. Schulze and Oddy have recently proposed a concise and simplified terminology (in which Phases 1 and 2 correlate to 'Pseudo-Byzantine' and 'Imperial Image') (see their article 'Terminology for the transitional coinage struck in 7th century Syria after the Arab conquest', ***Arab-Byzantine coins and history****: papers presented at the 13th Seventh Century Syrian Numismatic Round Table,* ed. T. Goodwin, Archetype Publications, 2012, pp. 187-200). But since I wish to highlight the function of coinage imagery, I find the *SICA* terminology more appropriate to my topic: I also wish to distinguish in what follows between the Imperial Image coinage of the official mints of Greater Syria and the products of the curious pseudo-Damascus mint and its analogues. Numbered phases seem ideal in terms of objectivity and clarity, but when describing developments that occurred within single phases, it is convenient to revert to the old terminology.

[3] For Syrian coppers with isolated names (Saʻid and Muhammad) that may be those of local governors see Goodwin, T., 'The chronology of the Umayyad Imperial Image coinage: progress over the last 10 years', ***Arab-Byzantine coins and***

these coins conveys coherent messages which can yield important information: thus the widespread presence of crosses is sometimes taken to indicate Christian agency behind the production of coinage. Similarly, it has been suggested that some types of figure, particularly those that diverged most sharply from the Byzantine numismatic canon, such as the 'Falconer' type, must have been intended to reflect an aspect of the identity of the issuer.[4]

In this paper, I will begin from the opposite premise. I will assume that the difficulties of identifying coherent messages in the imagery and inscriptions of early Islamic copper coins reflect the fact that they were, for the most part, not intended to be coherent. I seek to demonstrate this fact by re-examining recent arguments in favour of coherence and suggesting that they are probably unsustainable. My argument will concentrate mainly on imagery rather than inscriptions, however, since inscriptions, in the form of complete words, were largely absent from the copper coinage, before the 'Imperial Image' phase – with the exception of the *al-wafa lillah* series, extensive citations did not appear on the copper coins until the introduction of Standing Caliph coppers in 74 AH. Finally I will turn to the problem of accounting for a coinage that was so different from the Late Antique coinage which preceded it and from which it derived most of its imagery.

I should underline an important point here – my observations will be largely confined to the copper coinage for the sake of clarity and concision. The imagery and inscriptions of early Islamic precious metal coinage is a different matter altogether. From its inception under the caliph Mu'awiya, who struck the so-called 'Mutilated Cross' solidi, up to the introduction of epigraphic coinage at the end of the 70s AH, the gold and silver coinage bore images and/or inscriptions which projected ideas relating to caliphal authority and the status of the religion of Islam.[5]

In what follows, I look first at the copper coinage of Greater Syria, which until 74 AH showed no sign of caliphal control and may be described as an urban coinage. In the second section, I offer a few brief comments on the Standing Caliph type (or as I would prefer to call it, the Caliphal Image type). Here I deal with two recent proposals concerning the identity and chronology of the standing figure type on copper coins: first, the theory that the Standing Caliph figure represents the Prophet rather than the caliph and second, the dating of the Twin Standing Caliph issue of Jerash to the beginning of 'Abd al-Malik's reign. In conclusion, I suggest that the imagery of the copper coins contained, for the most part, a remarkably low semiotic charge.[6]

As a working hypothesis, I will argue that the imagery and inscriptions on copper coins were largely denotative and only rarely connotative. By this I mean that images were selected for inclusion on the coins in order to *denote* the fact that the metal flans on which they were placed via

---

history: papers presented at the 13th Seventh Century Syrian Numismatic Round Table, ed. T. Goodwin, Archetype Press, 2012, pp. 89-107. For the name 'Abd al-Rahman on a Standing Caliph issue of Sarmin, see Goodwin, T., 'A Standing Caliph fals issued by 'Abd al-Rahman at Sarmin', **Coinage and History in the Seventh Century Near East**: *proceedings of the 12th Seventh Century Numismatic Round Table,* ed. A. Oddy, Archetype Press, 2010, pp. 41-43. Mints were only identified by name from the Imperial Image phase, although the claim has been made by H. Pottier, and I. and W. Schulze that Hims was the principal mint for the pseudo-Byzantine coppers (see their article, "Pseudo-Byzantine coinage in Syria under Arab rule (638-c. 670)", **Revue Belge de numismatique**, 154, 2008, pp. 98-155).
[4] Oddy, A., 'Arab imagery on early Umayyad coins in Syria and Palestine: evidence for falconry', **Numismatic Chronicle**, 151, 1991, pp. 59-66; Oddy, A., 'Symbolism and design on early Umayyad coinage', **Arab-Byzantine coins and history**: *papers presented at the 13th Seventh Century Syrian Numismatic Round Table,* ed. T. Goodwin, Archetype Publications, 2012, pp. 109-123.
[5] See Treadwell, W. L., ''Abd al-Malik's coinage reforms: the role of the Damascus mint', **Revue numismatique**, 165, 2009, p. 357-381: and Treadwell, W. L., 'From caliphal imagery to aniconism: image and text on early Islamic coins and other objects' (forthcoming).
[6] For a critical assessment of the widely accepted idea that the Umayyads developed a 'caliphal iconography' in which the numismatic image of the Standing Caliph played an important role, see Treadwell, W. L., 'The formation of religious and caliphal identity in the Umayyad period: the evidence of the coinage', in **The Blackwells Companion to Islamic art and architecture**, eds. Flood, B. and Necipoğlu, G. (forthcoming).

the impression of the die were in fact coins: thus the repertoire was largely restricted to images that circulated on Byzantine and pseudo-Byzantine coinage in the Byzantine Near East. Only rarely do we find coin types that were *connotative* of ideas that went beyond the coins themselves: the primary example being the so-called Standing Caliph type (74–77 AH).[7]

Let me clarify my use of terminology at the outset. I use the term 'symbol' below to mean an image, figured or abstract, elaborate or simple in form, that refers to a readily perceptible referent which has a meaning that exists outside the coin on which the symbol is placed. Thus the Standing Caliph figure is clearly distinct from the Byzantine-style ruling figures that exist on earlier coins: he has no crown and wears distinctive clothing. The figure is drawn in such a way as to project dynamism and alertness; he is well armed so that he can confront his enemies. The figure *symbolises* the authority and efficacy of the caliphal institution.[8] For all other forms, including the generic figures found on their obverses – of which the standing emperor and the imperial bust are the most common examples – as well as the small letters and decorative elements that appear on many copper coins, I prefer to use the term 'emblem' or 'device': because they are not used to project ideas in the same way as the symbolic forms to which I have just referred.

My terminology differs fundamentally from that adopted by others who have written on early Islamic coinage, among them a pioneer in the field of early Islamic copper coinage, Andrew Oddy. Oddy refers to those objects which I would prefer to call 'emblems' as symbols, using the term in the same sense as we might when we refer to the 'symbols of the periodic table'.[9] Oddy proposes that these symbols must have encoded a system of meaning: in other words that the different combinations of such emblems on the coinage of Hims, for example, reveal information on some aspects of mint organisation, serving perhaps as die identification systems for officinae, die engravers or mint supervisors. Oddy would argue that the publication of more material may eventually reveal useful insights into the production system. However he also subscribes to the idea that the presence of several dies with similar images and combinations of 'symbols' within a coin series proves that such images must have made some sense to the coin producers: otherwise no-one would have bothered to duplicate dies of the same kind. He also believes that some dies were so different from their distant prototypes, and included so many new features, both of human physiognomy and other details, that these features must have been added by an engraver who had a particular idea in mind which he wished to represent: for example a figure that encapsulates some characteristics which were central to the issuer's claimed identity.[10] Similar arguments in favour of coherent messages conveyed by copper coins have been made by Ingrid and Wolfgang Schulze in respect of the *al-wafa lillah* and 'Orans' types respectively.[11]

I take a different view of these coin types, seeing them largely as the product of engravers working in the unmonitored environment of an exceptional mint (or as I would prefer to say, cluster of mints – see below). I will argue that these engravers produced many dies of varied types which reflected the extent of their creative imagination, but were for the most part unrelated to the desire to produce

---

[7] In this article, as the title makes clear, I limit my discussion to the coinage of Greater Syria: transitional coins struck in other regions than Syria, such as Iraq, for instance the 'Orans' drachms, and Umayyad Iranian coppers, are excluded from extensive consideration.
[8] As a second example of a connotative image, we might take the image on the reverse of the 'Mihrab and 'Anaza' (or Caliph Image 2 type in my preferred terminology) drachm, which shows a weapon placed upright within an arch supported by two columns. It projects a concept that might be described as the 'triumph of Islam', as confirmed in the inscription to either side of the spear (*nasr / allah*).
[9] See Oddy, A.,'Symbolism and design on the early Umayyad coinage', ***Arab-Byzantine coins and history:*** *papers presented at the 13th Seventh Century Syrian Round Table,* ed. T. Goodwin, Archetype Press, 2012, pp. 109-123.
[10] Oddy, 'Arab imagery'.
[11] See I. Schulze, 'The *al-wafa lillah* coinage: a study of style (work in progress)', in ***Coinage and history in the Seventh Century Near East 2****: proceedings of the 12th Seventh Century Syrian Numismatic Round Table,* ed. A. Oddy, 2010, pp. 111-121: W. Schulze, 'The Syrian "orans figure" copper coins', *Arab-**Byzantine coins and history:** papers presented at the 13th Seventh Century Syrian Round Table,* ed. T. Goodwin, Archetype Press, 2012, pp. 131-144.

imagery (or inscriptions) that had a connotative impulse. Before I engage the question of 'meaning' in these numismatic images in more detail, however, I will briefly address one exceptional image type, which has hitherto been largely ignored in the secondary literature. This type, the Enthroned Emperor issue of Damascus, does seem to represent an unexplained anomaly. It, alone of all copper images produced before 74 AH, appears to have been deliberately formed in order to project a message of some kind. If this image was 'meaningful' in the way that I suggest, it would form the sole exception to the general rule that the imagery of the Imperial Image phase, like the preceding pseudo-Byzantine phase was denotative, rather than connotative.[12]

The Enthroned Emperor type of Damascus

The Enthroned Emperor type of Damascus was struck during the Imperial Image coinage phase, now commonly dated to the late Sufyanid era (early 60s AH) (see figure 1).

Figure 1: Enthroned Emperor type of Damascus with 'Bird-on-T' to the left (CNG sale 88, lot 1779)[13]

Goodwin argues that the Enthroned Emperor image may well have been the first of the copper types struck by the capital mint of the Umayyads in the Imperial Image phase.[14] He concludes this on the basis of the fact that these coppers are relatively rare; that they are never found as overtypes on other issues; and that at least one such coin is known to have formed the undertype of another Imperial Image type, struck in the mint of Hims.[15] Goodwin's tentative suggestion that the Enthroned Emperor might have been loosely based on the prototype of the Antioch follis of Justinian I is difficult to accept, since the two types are quite dissimilar in terms of the imperial regalia borne by the seated figure and the form of the throne. Another way of approaching the problem of the genesis of this image, in the absence of either close numismatic or sigillographic prototypes,[16] would be to see it as a confected image that draws elements from two different coinage types that were in circulation at the time of its production. The torso of the seated figure certainly resembles the general outline of the Standing Emperor type that is commonly found in the pseudo-Byzantine coppers, with the globus cruciger in the left hand; while the sceptre held in the right hand and the form of the throne with its two slender vertical uprights recalls the seated figures

---

[12] To introduce the Enthroned Emperor type as a possible (connotative) 'exception' before establishing the (denotative) 'rule' may appear counterintuitive and needlessly confusing. However I have chosen to discuss the Enthroned Emperor first because the most interesting element in this image, the 'Bird-on-T', was incorporated into some variants of the later issues which I will discuss below, namely the 'Orans' coppers and the 'Falconer' coppers.
[13] Coins illustrated in this article are not shown to scale.
[14] Goodwin, 'Arab-Byzantine coinage', in Album and Goodwin, ***The pre-reform coinage***, p. 82.
[15] Goodwin, 'Arab-Byzantine coinage', p. 86.
[16] No similar prototype is to be found among Byzantine coins or seals. The only bird commonly used on Byzantine coins appears on the *scipio*, the eagle-topped consular sceptre: but this is clearly an eagle and always has its wings extended (see I. Koltsida-Makri, 'The representation of the eagle on lead seals and its provenance', in ΔΕΛΤΙΟΝ ΤΗΣ ΧΡΙΣΤΙΑΝΙΚΗΣ ΑΡΧΑΙΟΛΟΓΙΚΗΣ ΕΤΑΙΡΕΙΑΣ, Athens, 2003, pp. 411-416.)

of the heavy-flan Scythopolis and Jerash issues (see figure 2), which themselves were modelled upon a Justin and Sophia follis of Nicomedia.

Figure 2: (Left) Pseudo-Byzantine Standing Emperor copper (obverse) (Ashmolean Museum)
(Right) Scythopolis heavy flan copper (obverse) (Foss, Arab-Byzantine coins, p. 53)

If the engraver did indeed draw on elements of these two types for his new die, we still have to explain the appearance of the 'Bird-on-T' (or a bird on a perch), which appears to the left of the throne on all dies of the Enthroned Emperor type from the Damascus mint. It seems that this bird was introduced onto this type *before* being copied from this type onto some later Standing Emperor types of Damascus and some issues of the pseudo-Damascus mint. This may be argued not only on the basis of Goodwin's proposal for the chronological precedence of the Enthroned Emperor type, but also on the grounds that in this type the bird is always in correct proportion to the scale of the seated figure, whereas in later types, it is often elongated to the extent that it measures about half the height of the standing figure, in order to fill the left-hand side of the coin.

What should we make of the 'Bird-on-T'? As the only element in the Imperial Image coinage that appears to be an invention of the engraver, rather than an adaptation of a prototype(s), we have to ask what his purpose was in placing the creature next to the seated figure. It seems reasonable to interpret the bird in its original form as a bird of prey, or a hawk, seated upon a perch, even if its later manifestations do not support such an identification. One might surmise that the hunting bird was either associated with the city of Damascus or was somehow considered appropriate as an adjunct to the enthroned figure.

Could the bird have been associated with the Umayyads, given that this was their capital mint? The presence of Christian regalia on the seated figure might at first sight suggest that the seated figure could not have been perceived as representative of Umayyad authority. But Christian regalia are found on most Imperial Image types, including an early issue of Hims which also contains the phrase *bismillah* (In the name of God) in the field to the left of the standing figure who supports a staff with a cross at its tip.[17] Indeed the persistence of Christian regalia on Imperial Image coppers, all of which also bear the name of the city in which they were minted, suggests that the Muslim governors of those cities were indifferent to the proliferation of Christian symbols on their copper coins. In these circumstances, it is possible that an inventive engraver, whose die designs were only loosely monitored by mint officials, could have introduced the bird, either as a city emblem or a sign of Umayyad ruling prowess, and juxtaposed it to the seated figure as a way of indicating the identity of the seated figure. What appears to be a glaring contradiction to modern eyes, in other words a 'Christian ruling figure' set next to an emblem associated with Islamic governance (at the

---

[17] See Oddy, A., 'The "Constans II" bust type of Arab-Byzantine coins of Hims', **Revue numismatique**, ser. 6, 29, 1987, pp. 192-197.

level of the city or the ruler), may not have been perceived as such in the late Sufyanid period. The numismatic form of the 'Christian ruler' may have been perceived instead as a generic ruling figure.

But the precise signification of the bird on the perch is elusive. The few sources we have on falconry in the Umayyad period suggest that the sport became popular among the Muslim elite after the conquest and it was the Umayyad caliphs who first promoted it and practised it in addition to other types of hunting that had been popular in the Jahiliyya. Yazid b. Muʿawiya (d. 64 AH) was said to have been addicted to the sport.[18] Could hunting with birds of prey have been perceived as a characteristically 'Arab' pursuit and thus acquired a special meaning for the Umayyads? The case is difficult to make on currently available evidence: but this exceptional numismatic image does require an explanation. The original 'Bird-on-T' appeared on the first named issue of the caliphal capital. The consistency of this image on the Damascus copper and its deliberate placement next to the seated figure hint at a definite, if still enigmatic, message which the engraver, or his superiors, wished to convey. The same cannot be said of the copper types to be discussed in the following section, which included a plethora of different types, most of which were adaptations of existing types and figures (including that of the 'Bird-on-T', as we shall see).

The *al-wafa lillah* Series, the 'Orans' Coppers and the 'Falconer' coppers

These types belong to a body of coins which I propose to call the pseudo-Damascus 'mint cluster'. These comprise the pseudo-Damascus coinage itself (currently being researched by Tony Goodwin),[19] which includes the 'Falconer' type, as well as associated coinages, such as the 'Orans' type. I treat this group as a single entity, even though not all of it can be proven to have been struck at the same mint (e.g. there are no links between the 'Orans' type and the pseudo-Damascus issues), because it shares some significant features: it appears to originate from the Jund al-Urdunn and it shares many decorative features, including the emblems that appear on the reverse dies. The third coin type which I include in this group, the *al-wafa lillah* series, is exceptional in that it does not share the variety of the preceding mints: it has a consistent typology of Standing Emperor obverse (with or without the inscription), with a cursive m reverse below which the inscription always appears in the exergue. In spite of the features that distinguish the *al-wafa lillah* series,[20] however, I include it in the following discussion because of its chronological and geographical proximity to the pseudo-Damascus coinages, and because, like the pseudo-Damascus types, it has recently been identified as a coinage with connotative value, that is a coinage whose forms and inscriptions were designed to project a message connected to the identity of its issuer.

The pseudo-Damascus coinages are very different from contemporary copper issues. They lack viable mint names and their imagery is more often adaptive rather than imitative of the prototypes they follow. In the case of the pseudo-Damascus mint itself, new elements were added to standard forms, such as that of the standing emperor, and the fields of both sides of the coin, but especially the reverse, are commonly filled with stars, crescents, crosses, squiggles, box-forms etc., arranged in haphazard form in every conceivable part of the die. At the same time, some of the designs appear to be finely executed and full of detail, including large faces with luxuriant moustaches, crowns filled with ornaments, elegant birds on perches.

Why were the pseudo-Damascus mint and related coinages so different from the norm? Why were these issues so loosely organised and why was such latitude allowed to the die engravers? The mint itself looks like it was set up and managed by agents who had little idea of or interest in the

---

[18] *E I* (second edition), 'Bayzara'. See also R. Smith, 'Hunting poetry (tardiyyat)' in *Abbasid belles lettres*, ed. J. Ashtiany et al., Cambridge, 1990, pp. 167-184.
[19] See Goodwin, T. and Gyselen, R., *The Irbid Hoard of Arab-Byzantine Coins* (forthcoming).
[20] I am grateful to Tony Goodwin (email comm.) for reminding me of the distinctive features of the *al-wafa lillah* series.

traditional model of copper coinage production. The resulting coinage looks more like a token coinage than a 'city' coinage: perhaps a coinage that was organised for a market place or a network of markets, where the appearance of the coins was of minor importance, since the coins themselves were only used within a restricted context. This appears to be borne out by the relatively restricted area of finds in which these coins have been retrieved. One can imagine an engraver sitting by the entrance to the market, producing dies that were quickly employed to strike up quantities of such 'tokens' which merchants, both vendors and purchasers, might buy in order to be able to trade in the market. Such an informal mode of coin production probably lacked a high level of quality control, leading to a quick turnover in die usage, which in turn demanded a higher than average production of dies.

The use and adaptation of motifs borrowed from contemporary issues from the capital mint of Damascus, as well as the use of the capital's mint-name itself, does suggest an important point about the status of the mint and its products. These coins consciously adopted the name of the capital mint even though they were conspicuously not the products of that mint themselves. Such wanton disregard for regulatory proprieties does seem exceptional. But it does not rule out the model of a coinage produced and used by a group of merchants who had an interest in keeping their markets alive and vigorous. Could the omission of the real mint-name even have been a deliberate attempt on the part of the issuer to avoid local taxes which were raised by the regional authorities on the use of 'city' coinages?

Goodwin has taken a leading role in trying to understand the monetary environment in which these irregular coins functioned. Since contemporary coppers all bore the name of the city in which they were struck, he has suggested that the absence of mint-names on the majority of these coins might be a clue to their extra-urban origins.[21] Yet the issue of such a prolific coinage in a rural or a desert environment is difficult to accept: copper coins are usually designed for exchange in return for low-value goods and services, such as are commonly available in towns and cities, rather than in the villages of the *badiya*. In response to this point, Goodwin suggests that while the coins were intended for circulation in settled environments, their particular features might be explained by the tribal origins of the persons who commissioned them and their random and loosely organised character, by the unstable political circumstances of the period in which they were issued. The two claims appear to be supported by the evidence of the coins themselves: hints of 'tribal' identity have been detected in some of the figures depicted on the coins, while the turmoil of the Zubayrid Civil War has provided an explanation for the disturbed political environment which allowed irregular coins of different types to flourish. Following this line of argument, it has been proposed that the inscriptions of the *al-wafa lillah* series served as propaganda for their issuers. The legend has been interpreted as a pious slogan employed by the pro-Zubayrid forces in Syria to bolster the Zubayrid faction which briefly contested control of the province for a year or so before the Marwanid victory at Marj Rahit.[22] A second type has recently been proposed as forming part of the so-called Zubayrid Syrian copper coinage: the 'Orans' coppers have been interpreted as the depiction of a praying figure, who represents the Zubayrid cause in Syria, displaying in graphic form the claim to exemplary piety which was also expressed in pious phrases on the Zubayrid silver coinage of Fars province and on the *al-wafa lillah* coppers.[23]

It must be emphasised here that all the interpretations summarised above have been offered with clearly stated caveats, which make plain the authors' acknowledgement that these are not proven cases, but working models, that offer speculative contextualisations of the coins. However there are questions that need to be asked about the underlying premises that support such reconstructions,

---

[21] Goodwin, T., 'The pseudo-Damascus mint: progress report on a die study', **Supplement to ONS Journal no. 193**, 2007, pp. 12-16.
[22] I. Schulze, 'The *al-wafa lillah* coinage'.
[23] W. Schulze, 'The Syrian "orans figure" copper coins'.

beginning with the general context, as well as more specific considerations relating to individual coin types.

The *al-wafa lillah* coppers

Ingrid Schulze has produced a systematic catalogue of these coins which she divides into two types (with and without obverse legend) and which she attributes to Natil b. Qays, leader of the pro-Zubayrid faction in the Syrian Civil War. These coins have been identified as rebel issues on the basis of their legend, which Schulze translates as 'Honesty belongs to Allah' or 'Loyalty to Allah', an expression which she deems appropriate to the Zubayrid cause.[24]

Foss has already questioned the attribution of the *al-wafa lillah* coinage to the Zubayrids on the grounds that the *jund al-urdunn* was consistently loyal to the Umayyads and thus not where one would expect to find a high concentration of Zubayrid copper coins.[25] Another important point which calls into question the Zubayrid attribution relates to the meaning of the inscription. There is widespread evidence for the use of the same phrase on small commonplace objects that were current in the markets of Jund al-Urdunn. There are several references in the published and unpublished literature to glass commodity measures and metal coin weights that bear the same inscription; as well as evidence for the use of the root *waw/fa/alif* and the word *wafa* alone on both weights and coins.[26] In all cases, the reference is to a well-known Quranic verse (Q.xxvi.181) (*awfu al-kayla wa la takunu min al-mukhsirin – Give full measure and be not cheaters*) in which the the verb (*awfu*) conveys the sense of giving full measure or settling a legal debt, whether in kind or coin. An appropriate translation of the phrase '*al-wafa lillah*' on these objects might be 'To give full measure is godly/right in God's eyes'. Given that this phrase occurs on contemporary weights, measures and coins and that we are dealing with a coinage that is intimately associated with the marketplace, it seems sensible to come down in favour of the market weights and measures as the source from which the die engraver derived the inscription. This in turn suggests that the phrase carried the same meaning on the copper coins as on the other market paraphenalia – in other words, an exhortation to the coin user to deal fairly when transacting exchanges involving these coins. Correct comportment in monetary matters was one of the messages conveyed implicitly in the inscriptions of the 'Abd al-Malik's later epigraphic coinage.[27] There seems to be no compelling reason to posit an extension of the original meaning of the phrase to include the wider issue of loyalty to God, let alone the attribution of such coins to a brief pro-Zubayrid interlude in Syrian history.

The *'Orans'* coppers

Another type which that has been attributed to the Zubayrids in Syria, is the so-called 'Orans' copper issue (see figure 3). Wolfgang Schulze argues in favour of an early suggestion of Shraga Qedar that the coins in question depict the figure of an 'Orant', holding his hands up in prayer, and proposes that the figure was a propaganda tool employed by the pro-Zubayrid forces that operated

---

[24] Schulze, I., 'The *al-wafa lillah* coinage', p. 111.
[25] Foss, C., 'Abdallah ibn Al-Zubayr and his Coinage, *Journal of the Oriental Numismatic Society*, 216, 2013, p. 16.
[26] See the use of the word *waf(in)* on the *jaza hadha dimashq wafiyya* copper types (Goodwin, *SICA* vol. 1, p. 86). See also *waf(in)* on the reverses of the Standing caliph issues of Jund Qinnasrin (See Goodwin in Album and Godwin, *The pre-reform coinage,* pp. 96-97). For the evidence from coin weights see Khamis E., *Weights and Scales from the Byzantine and Umayyad periods from Beth Shean, the Decorations and Inscriptions as Reflectors on the Changes in Administration and Culture,* unpublished MA thesis submitted to The Hebrew University of Jerusalem, (Hebrew), 1998, p.4 5, pl. 11, no.32: Amitai-Preiss N., *The Administration of Jund al- Urdunn and Jund Filastīn during the Umayyad and Early `Abbasid Periods according to Seals and Other Small Finds*, unpublished dissertation, 2007, Ben-Gurion University of the Negev, (Hebrew), Chapter 3: Weights, p. 218, No. b.
[27] Treadwell, W. L., 'Qur'anic inscriptions on the coinage of the Ahl al-Bayt from the second to the fourth century AH', *Journal of Quranic Studies*, 14/2, 2012, pp. 267-291.

briefly in Greater Syria in the year or so prior to the Marwanid victory at Marj Rahit (685).[28] But it is unlikely that the 'Orant' figure is anything of the kind.

Figure 3: 'Orans' copper type I (private collection)

Schindel and Hahn made clear their view that the origin of the figure was a pseudo–Byzantine type (Goodwin's Type E classification in *SICA* 1)[29] in order to refute the identification of the figure as the preacher John the Baptist in the controversial thesis of Volker Popp.[30] Schulze responded to this assertion by pointing out that the prototype must have been an Imperial Image type, rather than a pseudo-Byzantine type, since some of the dies include the 'Bird-on-T', which was first introduced to the mint of Damascus in the Imperial Image phase.[31] Schulze's objection may be valid on chronological grounds: but the Standing Emperor type of Damascus with 'Bird-on-T' could have served as the engraver's model just as well as the pseudo-Byzantine type suggested by Schindel and Hahn.

The wider point made by Schindel and Hahn is that the figure with upheld arms and splayed fingers looks like an adaptation of the standard Standing Emperor figure which is the most common of the Byzantine prototypes for Arab-Byzantine coinage. The proof of their argument lies in the staff topped with a cross and the freestanding cross, which have been carried over from the prototype onto the 'Orans' dies. However Schulze suggests that the construction of the 'Orant' figure was the primary intention of the engraver and that the engraver himself added elements of Christian regalia in order to *disguise* the identity of the 'Zubayrid Orant' and thus avoid the censure of the Marwanid authorities who had recently regained control of Syria. In other words Schulze accounts for the presence of Christian symbols on many of these dies by suggesting that such symbols were inserted onto the dies in order to 'Christianise' the appearance of the 'Orant'. But subterfuge on this scale, applied to a humble object of poor manufacture and low value is hard to credit. Had the Zubayrid faction in Syria intended to project their claims to piety on this coin type, they would surely have produced some dies at the beginning of the series on which the main features of the Zubayrid *imam al-salat* were clearly visible and perceptible as a reference to Zubayrid, rather than Marwanid, piety. In other words, the connotative function of the image could have been effective only if the symbolic referent (the Zubayrid imam) was discernible in the image. None of the coins in the copper 'Orant' series falls into this category.

---

[28] Schulze, 'The Syrian "orans figure" copper coins'.
[29] Goodwin, 'Arab-Byzantine coinage', p. 79.
[30] Schindel, N. and Hahn, W., 'Notes on two Arab-Byzantine coin types from seventh century Syria', **Numismatic Chronicle,** vol. 170, 2010, pp. 321-330.
[31] Schulze, 'The Syrian "orans figure" copper coins', p. 139.

If we compare these coppers with the Kufan and Basran 'Orans' drachms of Bishr b. Marwan, the difference is immediately apparent (see figure 4).[32] The Marwanid silver coins present the praying figure with both arms raised, surrounded by his congregants: all three figures are wearing clothing that differs from that of the fire altar attendants on the prototype – the transformation from Zoroastrian fire worship to Muslim prayer is unambiguous, and the identification of the Marwanid *imam* is further strengthened by the placing of the *shahada* in the obverse margin of the same type. In what was probably the earliest of the dies belonging to this series, the name of Bishr b. Marwan appeared in Arabic directly below the praying figure, where it acted as an identifying caption.

*Figure 4: 'Orans' drachm of Kufa (Akula) dated 73 AH
(Treadwell, 'The "Orans" drachms, Fig. A3, p. 263)*

Furthermore Schulze's suggestion that 'Abd al-Malik may have adopted the Zubayrid praying figure as portrayed in this copper type as the model for the Marwanid silver drachm is unfounded. The Kufan drachm was not an innovation by 'Abd al-Malik: it was a type struck far away from Syria, in south Iraq, by his maverick brother, Bishr b. Marwan, governor of the Mashriq from 73–75 AH. As I have suggested elsewhere, Bishr produced his 'Orans' image in order to address the specific circumstances of the reintroduction of Umayyad rule in a region that was still largely hostile to control from Damascus and deeply resentful of the past history of Umayyad rule in Iraq.[33]

As in the case of the 'Falconer' type and the Jerash Twin Standing Caliph (see below), the genesis of this intriguing copper form should be sought at the level of the die engraver, not the political actors of time. The type which Schulze catalogues as the Type II Orant, a standing figure with his right arm still grasping the staff with cross, while his left arm is raised above shoulder height with fingers splayed, could have been an intermediate stage between Standing Emperor prototype and the fully developed 'Orant' pose. Alternatively it could be an independent type, unrelated to the 'Orant', perhaps best characterised as the 'Saluting emperor'. It is difficult to prove either of these ideas when the identity of the engraver(s) responsible for these dies is unknown and die links between the two types are lacking, but the hypothesis is more plausible than the tenuous argument for the one-armed 'Orant' that Schulze constructs in order to bring Type II within the 'Orant' family.[34]

It is worth noting at this stage that the Schulzes' arguments in favour of a coherent series of Zubayrid inscriptions and images on both the *al-wafa lillah* and 'Orans' types is echoed in Goodwin's assertion that the pseudo-Damascus series as a whole may have been struck by the leader of the pro-Umayyad Banu Kalb 'as a reaction against' the issue of *al-wafa lillah* series by his

---

[32] For the 'Orans' drachms of Kufa and Basra, see Treadwell, W. L. 'The "Orans" drachms of Bishr b. Marwan and the figural coinage of the early Marwanids', in J. Johns (ed.), **Bayt al-Maqdis: Jerusalem and early Islam**, Oxford, 1999, pp. 223-270.
[33] Treadwell, 'The "Orans" drachms'.
[34] Schulze, 'The Syrian "orans figure" copper coins', p. 141.

pro-Zubayrid rivals, citing the recurrence of certain features of the *al-wafa lillah* coins on the pseudo-Damascus issues.[35] However it is doubtful whether one can extrapolate from the observation of common features belonging to both series an argument that posits adversarial intentions of a political nature between two rival factions. The pseudo–Damascus series certainly constitutes an exception in the Imperial Image phase: but the extraordinary diversity of imagery in the pseudo-Damascus mint and its unofficial imitations argues strongly against the ascription of connotative intent behind any of the many and varied images it contains. A well-known type from this curious mint is discussed next.

The 'Falconer' figure

The 'Falconer' figure is one of the most intriguing of all the pseudo-Damascus series, by reason of its apparently non-imperial, non-numismatic origins. Here, it seems, we finally dive below the surface layer of regnal numismatic imagery into the social life of the period. Oddy has proposed that the figure illustrates the Umayyads' love of the sport of hunting with birds of prey; that it was specifically tied to the Umayyad caliph Yazid I (b. Mu'awiya) who was said to be addicted to the sport; and that it was a product of a mint attached to one of the *qusur* on the desert fringes.[36] Can these claims be substantiated and if so, what do they tell us about the imagery of the pseudo-Damascus series?

Oddy believes that the large number of dies bearing variations of the 'falconer' figure suggests that the figure had 'real meaning'.[37] By this I assume he means that the figure was not just a whimsical invention of the die engraver's imagination, but a figure with connotative value: a figure that said something about the identity of the issuer or the mint which produced it. As noted above, Oddy's early article on the 'falconer' type proposed an attribution to an Umayyad caliph and suggested that it was struck in an Umayyad *qasr*. The recent linking of the 'falconer' type to other dies (standing emperor, enthroned emperor, two enthroned emperors etc.) belonging to the pseudo-Damascus mint argues against Oddy's attribution to an Umayyad palace mint,[38] but Oddy insists on the connotative value of the figure depicted, on the grounds that without such 'meaning' no mint would have taken the trouble to issue large numbers of dies bearing this figure.

In 2010 Schindel and Hahn noted the lack of consensus about the correct classification of the type and made their own suggestion that it should be classified as a Two Standing Figure coin, based on their claim that the standing figure, with its distinctive cinched waist, was derived from a Two Standing figure with Figure in Military Dress (TSFMD) issue of Heraclius or Constans. In the same article they suggested that the bird which sits on the figure's arm was copied from a rare ceremonial silver coin of Heraclius and Heraclius Constantine, in which the emperor receives a crown from a Victoriola that sits upon his left arm. They suggest that the Victoriola was either deliberately changed to a bird in the pseudo-Damascus die or misunderstood as a bird by the engraver.

Oddy questions Schindel and Hahn's explanations for the transformation of the figure of the Victory to a bird, for which neither explanation seems particularly plausible: one might add that if Schindel and Hahn were correct in their identification of the silver prototype, it would be the only silver donative coin to have provided a prototype for an Islamic copper coin. On the other hand, their identification of the TSFMD prototype appears sound – there is no other way, it seems, to account for the staff held by the left-hand figure or for the progressive reduction in size of the right-hand standing figure on some of the Islamic copper dies (from half-size torso in Schindel and Hahn Fig. 9 to head in *ibid.*, Fig. 10 – see below, figure 5). The problem is how to account for the bird.

---

[35] Goodwin, T., 'The chronology of the Umayyad Imperial Image coinage', pp. 93–94.
[36] Oddy, A., 'Arab imagery'.
[37] Oddy, 'Symbolism and design'.
[38] See Goodwin, 'The pseudo-Damascus mint', Fig. 6, for die-links.

Here, I would suggest, we do not have a mistaken imitation of a Byzantine prototype, but rather the intrusion of an established feature of the Imperial Image Damascus copper coinage. The bird is taken from the 'Bird-on-T' figure which is found to the left of the enthroned emperor and standing figure on the Damascus coppers (see above 'The Enthroned Emperor type of Damascus'). Its first appearance on the pseudo-Damascus dies probably occurred on the die illustrated in Schindel and Hahn Fig. 9. There the bird, with the horizontal platform underneath it still visible, but lacking the vertical support of the 'T', has been transposed from its position to the left of the seated figure on the Damascus coppers and placed in the only available space on the already crowded TSFMD prototype of Heraclius/Constans – in the upper right-hand corner, where space has been created for it by reducing the right-hand figure of the prototype to half its original size. The bird's profile has been reversed, so that it now faces the principal standing figure, as it also does on the Damascus prototype.

The clumsy intrusion of the bird, placed above the head of the shrunken right-hand figure and apparently poking its beak into the ear of the military figure strikes the observer as an exceptionally clumsy and ill-prepared image to place on a die: it is as if the engraver began working on the die before he had formulated a considered reaction to the problem of integrating the elements from his two prototypes. But as can be seen from the pseudo-Damascus dies already published by Oddy and Goodwin, this was not exceptional for the pseudo-Damascus mint, which has some examples of misplaced emblems on its obverses and several on its reverse dies.

Figure 5: Early 'Falconer' type dies
(Schindel and Hahn, 'Notes on two Arab-Byzantine coin types', Figures 9 and 10)

Once the initial die had entered use, it appears that an engraver, either the original engraver or another, decided to resolve the anomalies of the early die by lowering the bird and placing it on the extended arm of the military figure, while further contracting the already reduced right-hand torso into a bust, which was placed under the extended arm within a frame, suggesting a container that was carried by the military figure. The eyes and nose and mouth, clearly visible on the container on Schindel and Hahn's Fig. 10, disappeared in subsequent dies, to form a round featureless frame that hangs under the arm.[39] The resulting 'Falconer' figure formed from the adaptation of the Heraclean/Constans TSFMD prototype was later followed by sub-types which mimicked the original 'Falconer' figure, but employed different prototypes for the standing figure. One such sub-type was clearly based upon the Imperial Image standing figure of Damascus, which appears with its characteristic rightwards-pointing 'tail' and a residual orb placed underneath the bird (see figure

---

[39] Oddy ('Symbolism and design', p. 110) accepts Schindel and Hahn's theory of the progressive adaptation of the Byzantine two-figure prototype in his most recent treatment of the falconer type. But he insists on the appearance of the bag under the huntsman's arm as an independent addition of the die engraver, who he claims was intent on creating the figure of a falconer. He does not accept the argument which suggests that the 'bag' was nothing more than the final remnant, the head, of the shrinking bust. Oddy concludes that the only borrowing from a prototype was the hunter with the cinched waist: all other elements, including the bird and the hunter's bag, were added by the engraver with the intention of creating a falconer figure, which he designed in order to depict a heroic figure on the coin.

6 below). The 'Falconer' type developed new features as it evolved, including a square box-like crown that appeared on the standing figure's head as well as random letters and small emblems that appeared in various places on the dies; the bird also changed its features, at times wearing what appears to be a cox-comb (as in figure 6 below).[40]

*Figure 6: Later sub-type of the 'Falconer' series
(Oddy, 'Symbolism and design', Figure 1, no. 5)*

Where does this leave us when we return to the question of the meaning of the image? As the preceding paragraphs suggest, I would favour the theory that the 'Falconer' figure was a generic figure that seems to have been conceived fortuitously by an engraver who was dissatisfied with the way that the Damascus bird had been inserted on an early die and wanted to create an image that was easier to recognise. This he and his fellow engravers achieved by placing the bird on the hunter's arm and transforming the second standing figure into a container that was suspended from the same arm. Whether the association with the 'falconer' figure was constant in the minds of later engravers who altered the shape of the bird to make it look like a domestic fowl rather than a sleek bird of prey, is open to doubt. Oddy's ascription of meaning to the figure is correct to the extent that the figure is, at least in some dies, immediately comprehensible as a hunter using a bird of prey for the purpose of pursuing a quarry. But the idea that the 'Falconer' figure was a self-standing symbol of heroic virtue which was intended to represent the character of the issuer is borne out neither by the reconstruction of the die's evolution offered above, nor by the overall character of the pseudo-Damascus mint.

The same arguments deployed above should be used in respect of the identification of the 'Leontius' copper.[41] Here Oddy makes a tentative attribution of one of the pseudo-Damascus 'falconer' specimens (see figure 7 below), which he links to the activities of a Byzantine general, Leontius, in the Caucasus in the late 680s CE. Given that the 'falconer' types were issued in a mint that was probably located in Jund al-Urdunn, it is unlikely that a coin would have been issued in his name as far south as this: neither does the abbreviation LEON + K carry conviction as a naming/title inscription for a Byzantine general. The current fashion for identifying certain groups of coins as issues of anti-Marwanid rebels in the period of the Civil War is probably unwarranted (see above): the likelihood that a single die or die pair, linked to the pseudo-Damascus mint, should have been cut for an opponent of the regime is also implausible.

---

[40] See Oddy, 'Symbolism and design', Figure 1.
[41] Oddy, 'Symbolism and design', pp. 120-122.

*Figure 7: 'Falconer' type attributed to Leontius
(Oddy, 'Symbolism and design', Figure 1, no. 15)*

The Standing Caliph type on copper coins of Greater Syria

In this section I will comment briefly on two recent controversies that concern the identity and dating of the Standing Caliph figure. The main point to bear in mind in the following pages is one which has been emphasised repeatedly in the secondary literature but which nevertheless bears repeating here. The Standing Caliph and associated imagery stands out from the other numismatic images discussed above, because it was intimately associated with the Umayyad caliph himself, appearing as it does on precious metal, as well as base metal, coins.

Standing Caliph or Standing Prophet?

Over the past two decades, the argument has been made by more than one scholar that the familiar standing figure, which is referred to in the literature as the Standing Caliph, is in fact a portrait of the Prophet Muhammad. This idea has already been firmly rejected by Heidemann (2010), Ingrid and Wolfgang Schulze (2010) and Morrisson and Prigent (2013), but there is more that should be said on the matter. One reason for this is that the claim for the Prophetic identity of the image has been forcefully endorsed in the non-numismatic as well the numismatic literature – such a radical re-interpretation of a key image in early Islamic visual culture demands rigorous scrutiny.[42] We begin with a review of the debate so far.

Foss was the first scholar in recent times to raise the question.[43] Foss's first article suggested that the presence of the phrase *muhammad rasul allah*, which surrounds the standing figure on some coppers of Palestine and Mesopotamia (see figure 8a), justifies the identification of the figure as

---

[42] The issue was first raised by Foss ('Anomalous Arab-Byzantine coins: some problems and suggestions', ***Oriental Numismatic Society Newsletter***, 166, 2001, p. 9) and in more recent years has gained support from Hoyland, Humphreys and Natif. See Hoyland, R. G. 'Writing the biography of the Prophet Muhammad: problems and solutions', ***History Compass***, 5/2, 2007, pp. 581-602; Humphreys, M., 'The "War of Images" revisited. Justinian II's coinage reform and the caliphate', ***The Numismatic Chronicle***, 173, 2013, pp. 229-244 (see esp. pp. 242-243 where Hoyland's theory is adopted uncritically); Natif, M., 'The painter's breath and concepts of idol anxiety in Islamic art', in ***Idol Anxiety***, eds. J. Ellenbogen and A. Tugendhaft, Stanford University Press, 2011, p. 42, which baldly states 'There are even early Umayyad coins with the image of the Prophet Muhammad shown in a manner similar to the way in which the Byzantine emperor was represented on coins.' Refutations of the Prophetic identity of the standing figure have been offered by Heidemann ('The evolving representation of the early Islamic empire and its religion on coin imagery', in A. Neuwirth, N. Sinai and M. Marx, M. (eds.), ***The Qur'an in context: historical and literary investigations into the Quranic milieu***. Leiden: Brill, 2010, pp. 149-195, note 71); Schulze, I. and W., 'The Standing Caliph coins of al-Jazīra: some problems and suggestions', ***Numismatic Chronicle***, 170, 2010, pp. 331-353; and Morrisson, C. and Prigent, V., 'L'empereur et le calife (690–695): reflections à propos des monnayages de Justinien II et d'Abd al-Malik', ***Topoi*** (Suppl. 12), 2013, pp. 571-592.

[43] See Foss, C., 'Anomalous Arab-Byzantine coins', p. 9; *idem.*, 'The coinage of the first century of Islam', ***Journal of Roman Archaeology***, 16, 2003, pp. 757–58; *idem.*, ***Arab-Byzantine Coins: an introduction, with a catalogue of the Dumbarton Oaks collection*** (Dumbarton Oaks Byzantine collection publications), 12, 2008, p. 69.

Muhammad. He argued that in the Late Antique tradition, the name on a coin always identified the figure with which it was associated. However, in the case of these particular coppers, the phrase that is inscribed next to the standing figure is clearly not a caption to the image, but a pious phrase that forms an essential element of the Islamic testimony of faith, namely the assertion that Muhammad was the Prophet of God. This pious phrase was used in the early period on several coin types that had no images relating to Muslim personages (see for example the silver drachms of Bishapur and other Zubayrid/Khariji issues).[44]

The sole case in which the name 'Muhammad' appears without the epithet *'rasul allah'* occurs on a rare copper issue of Harran where the name is inscribed vertically to the left of the standing figure (see figure 8b), as well as vertically to the right of the reverse die.[45] The Harran type is the only possible candidate for the argument that the name identifies the figure. Even here, however, there are reasons to believe that the word was not intended to serve as a caption.

Figure 8: Standing caliph coppers of (a) Iliya (b) Harran (c) Ruha
*(Album and Goodwin, **The pre-reform coinage**, nos. 731, 687 and 688)*

Stylistic comparison with the contemporary issue of the nearby mint of al-Ruha (see figure 8c) suggests that the Harran type may have been an adaptation of the latter, which simplified the overcrowded fields of the al-Ruha coin by removing most of the inscriptions on both sides of the coin to produce a neater coin face that retained the name *muhammad* on the obverse and ensured there was adequate space to allow the mint-name to be easily read, while duplicating the same name on the reverse field. It has been suggested that the two occurrences of the name 'Muhammad' on the Harran copper might refer to the Prophet and the regional governor, Muhammad b. Marwan, respectively.[46] If the die engraver of the Harran coin did indeed believe the standing figure to be the Prophet, rather than the caliph, he appears to have been alone among all the engravers of contemporary copper dies in thinking so. Even if this were the case, it would be inadmissible to use such a slender piece of numismatic evidence, drawn from the outer margins of the Umayyad state, to imply that other standing figures on this type of coinage were representations of the Prophet,

---

[44] For the drachms of Bishapur, see Album, ***The pre-reform coinage***, pp. 21 and 25.
[45] See I. and W. Schulze, 'The Standing Caliph coins of al-Jazīra'.
[46] See I. and W. Schulze, 'The Standing Caliph coins', p. 343.

when as we will see below, other evidence is strongly in favour of identifying the figure as the caliph.

Once the Prophetic hare had been set loose by Foss, it soon caught the sharp eye of a historian anxious to find evidence for the biography of the founder of the Islamic *umma*. In an article written in 2007, Hoyland acknowledged the enormous difficulty of recreating the biography of the Prophet from textual sources that were based on stories which had circulated by word of mouth and only achieved written form many decades after the Prophet's death. At the end of his piece, Hoyland marshalled the evidence in favour of reading the standing figure on the coin as the Prophet and appended his remarks innocently, and without preamble, in a 'Postscript'.[47] The article proposes the Prophetic identity of the numismatic figure as a tantalising ray of hope to the reader, following the acknowledgement that the surviving texts offer little prospect of recreating the Prophet's life. What is more, we are told, if the image *was* that of the Prophet, the date of the coin on which it is placed means that it would have been made at a time when some of his contemporaries, although elderly, were still alive.[48] The implication is clearly that the image could well have been informed by eyewitness testimony to his appearance.

Hoyland accepts Foss's suggestion that the figure is identified by the inscription on the copper coins just discussed, but attacks the problem from a different perspective, namely the historical context of the relationship between 'Abd al-Malik and Justinian II and the Civil War which 'Abd al-Malik had just won against the Zubayrids. Hoyland thus moves the debate about the identity of the standing figure from the provincial coppers of Palestine and Mesopotamia to the heart of the caliphal enterprise, suggesting that the image on the Standing Caliph gold solidi, issues that were directly associated with the caliph himself, was that of the Prophet. His claim is that 'Abd al-Malik himself endorsed the use of the image of the Prophet on the first uniform type devised for Islamic coinage, which was designed to be used on coins of all three metals. This is a far more ambitious claim than Foss's earlier suggestion that a few provincial copper mints struck coins with images of the caliph. How does Hoyland make his case?

He assumes that the 'Standing Caliph' gold type was struck in response to Justinian's Christ Pantocrator issue, arguing that the Prophet's image would have been the appropriate response to the bust of Christ, for only the Prophet's image could 'challenge that of the image of Christ'.[49] While he is correct to point to the radical nature of the Byzantine reform that produced the Pantocrator type and justified in urging consideration of both coin types together, Hoyland ignored the fact that the precise dates of the Pantocrator issue were unknown at the time of writing and made the unwarranted assumption that 'Abd al-Malik produced the Standing Caliph as a riposte to his Byzantine rival, rather than as a response to the monetary needs of his emerging post-*fitna* state.[50] Second, Hoyland asserts that the name of Muhammad the Prophet had become '*de rigeur* on every official text…and pretty much standard in epitaphs and graffiti' after 'Abd al-Malik's victory in the Civil War. This is of course true and nowhere more so than on the Marwanid precious metal coinage, where it appears in the form of the *shahada* which is located in the marginal legend. He then extends the argument from inscription to image, claiming that it was more likely that the Prophet's image would appear on the caliph's coin, rather than that of the caliph himself, since the latter would have exposed the caliph to the charge that he was acting like an infidel king. But such a radical innovation as placing the Prophet's image on the coinage would have required a clear signalling of the Prophet's identity, just as the Christ Pantocrator was captioned on the Byzantine coin. No such labelling is present on either the copper or the gold issues of this type.

---

[47] Hoyland, 'Writing the biography of the Prophet Muhammad'.
[48] Hoyland, 'Writing the biography of the Prophet Muhammad', p. 596.
[49] *Ibid.*, p. 594.
[50] On this issue, see now Treadwell, W. L., 'Byzantium and Islam in the late 7th century AD: a "numismatic war of images"', ***Arab-Byzantine coins and history***, ed. T. Goodwin, Archetype Press, 2012, 145-156.

We should therefore revert to the received wisdom that the figure is an attempt to create an image of the caliph on the imperial Byzantine model, an impression strengthened by the marginal legend on many of the coppers which begins *li-'abd allah 'abd al-malik*... It should also be noted here that the earliest surviving written testimony in the Islamic record, that of Maqrizi's (15th century CE) *Shudhur al-uqud,* identifies the figure as a 'sword-bearing caliph'.[51] Hoyland's third point is less significant: the resemblance posited between the Christ figure and the Muslim figure in terms of coiffure and headgear are coincidentally accurate for the majority of cases, but this is a secondary attribute that would only carry weight if the preceding two points were proven. In fact, the early Muslim aversion to symbols of kingship provides a good explanation for the caliph's lack of a crown.[52]

Strong evidence in favour of the caliphal identity of the standing figure can also be found in the copper and silver coinage of the same period. The Standing Caliph copper types of Manbij (see figure 9) and Ma'arrat Misrin bear the inscriptions *khalifat allah* (Deputy of God) and *amir al-mu'minin* (Commander of the Believers) to either side of the standing figure, where the inscriptions clearly act as labels for the figure, identifying him as the caliph.[53] Two silver types, which I have designated Caliphal Image drachms 1 and 2, were struck at the same time as the solidi, and both support the theory of the caliphal identity of the figure (see figure 10 a and b).

Figure 9: Manbij Standing caliph copper
(Schulze, I. and W. 'The Standing Caliph coins of al-Jazira', Fig. 1)

Figure 10: (a) Caliphal image Drachm 1
(Gyselen, R., Arab-Sasanian copper coinage, pl. 15/VII
(b) Caliphal Image drachm 2
(Treadwell, 'Mihrab and 'Anaza', Cat. no. 4)

---

[51] See the phrase *wa daraba mu'awiya aydan dananir 'alay-ha timthalu-hu mutaqallidan sayfan,* in Maqrizi, *Shudhur al-'uqud,* facsimile text, L.A. Mayer, Alexandria, 1933, p. 4: and Maqrizi, *al-Nuqud al-islamiyya al-musamma bi-shudhur al-'uqud fi dhikr al-nuqud,* ed. Muhammad al-Sayyid 'Ali, Najaf, 1967, p. 9. The reference to Mu'awiya is anachronistic, but the identification of the sword-girt figure as the caliph is to be noted.
[52] Treadwell, W. L., 'The formation of religious and caliphal identity in the Umayyad period' (forthcoming).
[53] Goodwin, 'Arab-Byzantine coinage', p. 94.

Caliphal Image drachm 1 (otherwise known as the Standing Caliph drachm) shows an image of the standing figure on the reverse which, like the above-mentioned coppers, is flanked by two phrases to left and right, *amir al-mu'minin* and *khalifat allah*.[54] The standing figure on this silver coin is smaller than that on the gold coin, constrained as it is by the three dotted circles that surround the field. He is crudely rendered, with a disproportionately large head and an enormous scabbard that reaches up to his neck. Lack of space apparently forced the engraver to truncate, and in at least one die, to omit, one element of the figure's regalia – the knotted cord hanging from his middle.[55] It seems that the engraver inscribed the caliph's titles to either side of the field in order to confirm the fact that this rather clumsy standing figure was indeed the analogue of the standing figure on the gold coin. It is inconceivable that the caliphal titles would have been inscribed in such close proximity to a portrait of the Prophet, whose title, as is well known, was not *khalifa*, but *rasul allah*.

On the obverse of Caliphal Image Drachm 2 (otherwise known as the 'Mihrab and 'Anaza' drachm), the rightward-facing bust figure is clearly modelled on the bust of the Sasanian emperor on the Arab-Sasanian drachms which had been produced in the Damascus mint (and many other mints in Iran) prior to the issue of this Caliphal Image drachm.[56] On this coin, the emperor's winged crown was removed and replaced with a simple tasselled cap, while a shorter version of the sword held by the standing figure was placed in his hands. The figure is obviously an adaptation in bust form of the standing figure that was identified as the caliph (see preceding paragraph). Were we to accept the identification of the standing figure as that of the Prophet, its transposition into the long-familiar numismatic form adopted by the Sasanian emperor would make no sense at all. To place caliphal regalia in the arms of a bust that had clear Sasanian precedents was a risky undertaking for the Umayyad die designer, since it exposed the caliph to charges of endorsing a representation of himself as an imperial figure. To have transposed the Prophet's image into a form still recognisable as that of the Sasanian emperor would have entailed a much greater risk – that of anathematising the Prophet's status as the founder of the *umma* who struggled against kings and emperors.

To summarise, there are no strong arguments in favour of seeing a standing Prophet on either the copper or precious metal coinage and many reasons to doubt that the caliph would ever have taken such a radical step.[57] The Marwanid commemoration of the Prophet is a topic that has attracted strong scholarly interest in the past decades, triggered by numismatic evidence derived from Miles' interpretation of the 'Mihrab and 'Anaza' type.[58] But the case remains highly speculative, and it is

---

[54] Treadwell, 'The role of the Damascus mint', pp. 370-372.

[55] The cord is omitted altogether in the Bibliothèque nationale specimen illustrated in Gyselen's catalogue of Arab-Sasanian coins (see plate 15/VII in Gyselen, R., **Arab-Sasanian copper coinage**, Vienna, 2000).

[56] See several examples in Treadwell, W. L., '"Mihrab and 'Anaza" or "Sacrum and Spear"? A reconsideration of the iconography of an early Marwanid silver drachm", **Muqarnas**, vol. 22, 2005, pp. 1-28.

[57] Heidemann ('Evolving representation', fn. 71) claims that 'in the 7th century the inscription and the text are separated', a statement that is difficult to comprehend as it stands, but is apparently intended to refute Foss's claim that the inscription (*Muhammad*) functions as a label that identifies the adjacent image (of the Standing figure) on the copper coins of Harran (for further comments that clarify Heidemann's analysis of the relationship of numismatic text and imagery in the 7th century, see Heidemann, S., 'The Standing Caliph type – the object on the reverse', **Coinage and history in the Seventh Century Near East 2:** *proceedings of the 12th Seventh Century Syrian Numismatic Round Table*, ed. A. Oddy, 2010, pp. 23-34). Heidemann rejects Hoyland's theory of the Prophetic identity of the standing figure on the grounds that inscriptions were not used to identify images, but ignores Hoyland's principal arguments that relate to the so-called 'war of images' between caliph and emperor. Although Heidemann is undoubtedly right to insist on the caliphal identity of the figure, the Caliphal Image silver coins and the coppers of Manbij and Ma'arrat Misrin demonstrate that textual captions were occasionally used to identify figures on early Islamic copper and silver coins. See also the contribution of Morrisson and Prigent: 'L'empereur et le calife (690-695): reflections à propos des monnayages de Justinien II et d'Abd al-Malik', **Topoi** Suppl. 12 (2013), pp. 571-592. See esp. pp. 585-586 where the authors firmly reject the Prophetic identity of the standing figure, but partly on the erroneous grounds that the standing figure had appeared at the beginning of 'Abd al-Malik's reign on the commemorative Twin Standing Caliph issue of Jerash as per Foss – for the correct date of this issue, see below ('The Twin Standing Caliph issue of Jerash').

[58] See Whelan, E., 'The origins of the Mihrab Mujawwaf: a reinterpretation', **IJMES**, 18/2, 1986, pp. 205-223: Flood, F. B., 'Light in stone: the commemoration of the Prophet in Umayyad architecture', **Bayt al-Maqdis: Jerusalem and**

important that every new piece of evidence brought forward in favour of the notion of Prophetic commemoration is carefully examined. When carefully scrutinised against the evidence of all the Standing caliph coins, the case for Prophetic identity collapses.

The Twin Standing Caliph issue of Jerash: an accession issue of 'Abd al-Malik?

Commemorative coinage is a great rarity in Islamic numismatics: one rare example is the dirham of Amid struck in 286 AH whose legend reads ('…struck in the year of the reconquest of Amid…').[59] Foss has proposed to add another coin type to the short list of commemorative issues. In the Dumbarton Oaks catalogue of Arab-Byzantine coins, he suggests that the twin Standing Caliph issue (no mint, but attributable to Jerash rather than Scythopolis/Baysan) was struck at the beginning of 'Abd al-Malik's reign to commemorate the appointment of 'Abd al-Malik as caliph and his brother, 'Abd al-'Aziz, as heir apparent. Foss points out that the coin was 'struck by command of the caliph himself' and reminds us that 'Abd al-'Aziz was appointed heir apparent by Marwan b. al-Hakam at the same time that the latter appointed 'Abd al-Malik caliph.[60] The coin does indeed show two standing figures, both recognisable as analogues of the standing figure on the Standing Caliph solidus, with a vertical shaft on a stand between them (see figure 11). Foss states that it was probably struck at the very beginning of 'Abd al-Malik's reign in 65 AH to mark his accession to the caliphate.

Figure 11: The Twin Standing Caliph issue of Jerash
(Foss, Arab-Byzantine Coins, p. 60)

This intriguing theory, which gives a date as well as a location for this otherwise anonymous coin, nevertheless raises some problems. First, while there may be a tiny difference of scale between the two figures, this is barely perceptible on the coin: in effect, we have two identical and similarly sized standing figures *en face*. Is it likely that a Marwanid caliph would have commissioned a coin type which showed his appointed successor in identical pose to himself? Monarchs do not usually grant others, even significant others, the privilege of looking exactly like they do. The only other early Islamic coin to show a ruler and his son (and heir) known to me, is the donative medallion of Rayy dated 351 AH:[61] here father and son are clearly distinguished one from the other by the form of their crowns as well as the accompanying inscriptions. Second, the assertion that the legend

---

early Islam (Oxford Studies in Islamic Art, 9/2), Oxford, 1999, pp. 311-360. For a contrary view, which interprets the arch on columns as the sacrum rather than the mihrab, see Treadwell, '"Mihrab and 'Anaza" or "Sacrum and spear?"'.
[59] Album, S., *A Checklist of Islamic coins*, 3rd ed., Santa Rosa, 2011, no. 242m. For rare donative coinage that commemorated a caliph victory, see the caliph Mutawakkil's portrait medallion with the image of a camel on the reverse (Ilisch, L., 'Münzgeschenke und Geschenkmünzen in der mittelalterlichen islamischen Welt', *Münstersche Numismatische Zeitung*, 14/3, 1984, p. 17.).
[60] Foss, C., *Arab-Byzantine coins*, pp. 60-61: Foss first raised the possibility that this was an accession issue struck at the beginning of 'Abd al-Malik's reign in his article 'The Two-Caliph Bronze of Abd al-Malik', *Oriental Numismatic Society Newsletter*, no. 177, pp. 4-5. Foss's dating of this issue to c. 65/685 is accepted by Oddy (A. Oddy, 'The Twin Standing Caliph Fals', *Oriental Numismatic Society Newsletter*, no. 179, Spring 2004, pp. 10-11). For a reference to 'Abd al-'Aziz's heir apparency, see Marsham, A., *Rituals of Islamic monarchy: accession and succession in the first Muslim empire*, 2009, Edinburgh: Edinburgh University Press, p. 118.
[61] See Ilisch, 'Münzgeschenke', no. 19, p. 32.

li-'abd allah 'abd al-malik meant that the coin was 'commissioned' by the caliph is an overstatement. This was a formulaic phrase that appeared on many copper issues of the Standing Caliph type. It was certainly meant to be read as a statement of caliphal association with the image on the coin, but it does not imply that the caliph personally ordered the issue, which is what one might expect of a commemorative issue. It also remains to be explained why the Marwanid caliph would have commissioned a unique copper coin bearing such an image, in a minor mint in *jund al-urdunn*, which was far from his capital city.

A production-oriented approach to this coin leads us to a different interpretation of the image. As is well known, the Jerash and Scythopolis coppers (see above, figure 2) traditionally bore a representation of two seated figures, which were modelled on a Byzantine prototype struck in the mint of Nicomedia. When the Standing Caliph coinage was first issued in 74 AH, some specimens no doubt reached the mint of Jerash: either that, or a direct order was received in the mint to incorporate the Standing Caliph figure on the coinage of the mint.[62] The engraver or the mint master or some other official faced a dilemma: how to incorporate the new figures on both sides of the coin, while at the same time retaining the format of the existing local coinage with its two figures in order to maintain a formal link with circulating currency? He appears to have adopted a compromise solution which preserved the two-figure format, but transferred the Adapted Cross from its customary location on the reverse of the standard Standing Caliph type, to the obverse. In the place of the seated figures he engraved duplicates of the Standing Caliph to either side of the die: between them he placed an enigmatic form which clearly derives from the Adapted Cross but appears to add some new elements to it. The lower part of the Adapted Cross is modelled on the prototype, but the upper part seems to deviate from it to some extent, since it contains a pointed tip above a small circle/ellipsis.[63]

This experimental type does not appear to have been continued for long, as far as the surviving record suggests, even though the obverse type is found in combination with different reverses that contain Arabic and Greek inscriptions respectively.[64] The reason is not far to seek: the compromise effected in Jerash did not conform to the model followed at seventeen other mints in Greater Syria and made a nonsense of the Standing figure as a representation of the caliphal office.

This interpretation will not appeal to scholars who regard the coinage of the period as centrally controlled and carefully regulated. Indeed the duplication of imagery proposed here might appear to stretch the historical imagination to breaking point: how could an engraver have either misunderstood the prototype or been so ignorant of its significance as to make a double from a figure that represented the office of the sole ruler of the caliphate? The Jerash case appears to be an extreme example of indifference or miscomprehension on the part of the engraver which has been proposed in other cases (see above). However I would suggest that the emerging picture of the copper coinage, particularly that produced in the southern provinces of Greater Syria, shows that a great deal of latitude was given to the individual mints and in some cases to individual engravers, in

---

[62] The Standing figures on the Jerash issue appear to contain more detail in their clothing and regalia than most other copper Standing Caliph figures. This raises two possibilities: either that they were copied from the gold Standing Caliph rather than the coppers or that they were copied from drawings of the Standing figures.

[63] The vertical shaft on the stepped platform is puzzling. Its lower part does appear to replicate the Adapted Cross on Steps, with a globe on top of a vertical shaft. Yet above the globe there is quite clearly another element which appears to be oval in shape. It could be that the 'globe' on the shaft of the Jerash copper is a compacted version of the ellipsis which appears on the Standing Caliph coppers of the northern mints, reduced in width in order to fit between the two standing figures, while the 'oval' is the analogue of the globe on the Adapted Cross. Alternatively the whole figure may be intended as a conflation of cross and spear. The correct identification of these elements still remains to be ascertained. The engraver also added a new element to the Standing figures, in the form of the six-pointed stars which he placed upon their heads (See Foss, ***Arab-Byzantine coins***, p. 60).

[64] See Foss, C., ***Arab-Byzantine coins***, p. 61, Type B. I am grateful to Andrew Oddy for the following information: he reports that he has identified only one obverse die among the eleven specimens known to him and a single Arabic die (in addition to the Greek dies) (pers. comm. May 2014).

the design of their coinage, while little attempt was made to monitor their output. In these circumstances, it seems reasonable to accept the Twin Standing Caliph issue of Jerash as exactly that: a somewhat naïve attempt to accommodate the new type within the format of the existing coinage in the year of its inception (74 AH).[65] It seems that the reluctance that characterised the response of the Jerash mint to the Standing Caliph type was mirrored in another important local mint, Tabariyya, which never produced a Standing Caliph type.

Conclusions

As the preceding pages have made clear, I suspect that early Islamic copper coinage struck before 74 AH bore images that were denotative rather than connotative. The Standing Caliph coppers represented a significant change in that they employed an image of the caliph that promoted a clearly understood concept of the function and efficacy of the office of the caliphate (with the exception of the Jerash issue – see above). Why was the copper coinage so different from precious metal coinage in this respect?

First, the example of the copper coinage struck in the pre-conquest Persian interlude must have been an important precursor which influenced the nature of early Islamic coinage. The coins struck by the Persians had established the principle that locally-minted Byzantine-style coins could circulate in Greater Syria long before the Islamic conquests. This precedent was continued under Islamic rule, at first probably for no better reason than that the conquerors simply wished to preserve economic life in the cities which they had recently brought under their control. The continuing importation of genuine Byzantine coppers and solidi into Greater Syria in the early decades of Islamic occupation shows that this pragmatic attitude extended to approval by the Muslims, or at least a lack of resistance on their part towards, the use of their enemy's currency on a wide scale: it is also possible to make the argument that the Muslim authorities were powerless to change existing patterns of monetary circulation in these early years, given their preoccupation with the more pressing agenda of maintaining their authority over the newly conquered lands.

Early Islamic coppers were probably struck in mints that were administered by Christian personnel, some of whom no doubt had produced Syrian coinage before the arrival of the Muslims. The influence of Christian mintworkers may have contributed towards the conservative nature of the coinage imagery, but the fact that the Muslims did not move towards a change in the style of later copper coinage, in particular the coinage issued in the Imperial Image series, is remarkable. By the late Sufyanid period, they would surely have been capable, had they so wished, of co-ordinating a new style of copper, which would at least have eliminated the Christian symbols that appeared on the earlier coins. Yet all we see is a (possible) preliminary move towards the introduction of a new emblem ('Bird-on-T') in the capital mint: no attempt was made to remove Christian symbols from the coins in this period. This suggests a profound indifference on the part of the Muslim authorities to the content of the images on the coppers which did not match the close attention paid to the image of the Cross-on-Steps on the gold coinage of Muʿawiya and his successors. As is well known, copper coinage continued to diverge from precious metal in the post-reform period of Umayyad coinage: here, as Ilisch's studies of the mints of Filastin have shown, copper coins did not conform strictly to the aniconic format set by gold and silver coinage.[66]

In default of textual sources which might inform us directly about this question, we can at least point to some sources that hint at early Islamic attitudes towards imagery that might go some way towards explaining these anomalies. One such source is a story told in the annalistic history of the Christian Arab historian Eutychius (or Ibn Bitriq, d. 328–9/940) who describes an encounter

---

[65] See Humphreys, 'The "war of images" revisited', note 73, for a skeptical response to Foss's claim that the Jerash coin was struck at the beginning of 'Abd al-Malik's reign.

[66] Ilisch, L., ***Sylloge Numorum Arabicorum Tübingen*** **(vol. 1 – Palästina IVa Bilād aš-Šām I)**, Tübingen, 1993.

between the Patriarch of Qinnasrin and the Muslim conqueror of northern Syrian in the aftermath of the victory at Yarmouk during the reign of the caliph 'Umar I. Eutychius tells us that the general Abu 'Ubayda b. al-Jarrah concluded a peace treaty with the patriarch which stipulated that a column be set up to mark the boundary between the Muslim army camp and the territory of the Christian inhabitants of Qinnasrin. On top of this column was placed a statue of the Byzantine emperor enthroned in majesty. One day an Arab horseman who was practising his fighting skills inadvertently gouged out the eye of the statue with his lance. The Byzantines were deeply offended and demanded recompense from the Muslims. The Muslims were asked to make a statue of the caliph 'Umar which the Christians were then to be permitted to deface in the same manner. Abu 'Ubayda accepted the proposal without demur: a statue of 'Umar was made and its eye gouged with a lance, after which the Byzantines declared themselves satisfied. Abu 'Ubayda and his men expressed not the slightest objection to the defacement of Umar's image, which the Christian historian clearly found surprising.[67]

The story provides an interesting perspective upon Christian perceptions of early Muslim attitudes towards figured imagery and particularly towards imperial imagery. Indifference is a keyword in understanding Abu 'Ubayda's reaction to the patriarch's demand for restitution. Perhaps this account can help us to understand the persistence of Christian symbolism and the recycling of imperial imagery in early Islamic coinage. In a word, the Muslims did not share the same feelings towards the representation of regnal figures which informed the Byzantine development of imperial iconography in the 7th century. In 7th-century Byzantium the imperial icon rivalled the status of the saintly icon.[68] Such deeply embedded reverence for the image was not a feature of the early Islamic world. Indeed, there is good evidence that the early caliphs, especially Mu'awiya, were consciously averse to projecting themselves as kings in the mould of Late Antique rulership, because they knew that such pretensions would arouse the hostility of their subjects, not least among the tribal *shuyukh* on whose military capacities they relied to maintain their empire. Apart from a brief burst of creative activity in the mid-70s AH, the caliphs showed little interest in developing an iconography of power on the Byzantine model in the 1st/7th century: early Islamic copper coinage seems to reflect this trend.[69]

---

[67] Ibn Batriq, **Kitab al-ta'rikh**, 1909, Beirut, ed. Cheiko *et al.* p. 19.
[68] Belting, H., **Likeness and presence: a history of the image before the era of art**, Chicago, 1994, p 102.
[69] Although I was unable to attend the Syrian Numismatic Round Table in September 2013, I have received some informal responses to the first draft of this paper which was circulated to participants at that meeting. I am grateful to those colleagues who offered comments.

Arab-Byzantine Coins from Excavations in Israel

– an Update –

Gabriela Bijovsky [1]

As a result of discussions at the last round table in Oxford 2011, the Arab-Byzantine database of copper coinage at the Coin Department of the Israel Antiquities Authority (IAA) has been revised and updated. This article outlines the major changes in terminology, dating and attributions to the database. Even though the process did not drastically change the general picture, new insights will be presented here.

	Round Table Oxford 2011	Round Table Worcester 2013
Constans II	573 coins	307 coins
Constans II or Arab-Byzantine 1	?	212 coins
Arab-Byzantine 1	638 coins	863 coins
Arab-Byzantine 2	309 coins	282 coins
Arab-Byzantine 3		105 coins

Figure 1

The results of work during the last two years are summarized in Fig. 1, which shows the total of coins in each category following the terminologies adopted at the 2011 and 2013 round tables. As proposed in Oxford, the general terminology Arab-Byzantine (Phases) 1, 2 and 3 has been adopted to replace the common nomenclature: Pseudo-Byzantine, Bilingual/Imperial Image, and Standing Caliph series respectively. Coin identifications on the database have been rechecked and re-classified into three main groups: official imperial coins (mostly attributed to Constans II), Arab-Byzantine coins (following the new terminology) and a third group consisting of coins which, due to their bad state of preservation, have not been identified with any certainty. The main changes noticed in Fig. 1 are the reallocation of many Arab-Byzantine coppers previously attributed to Constans II, and the division between Arab-Byzantine 2 and 3 groups, which were not previously separated in the IAA database.

On this basis, new and more accurate distribution maps have been prepared.[2] The new map in Fig. 2 includes all sites and coin finds in Israel (sites from Gaza and the West Bank are not recorded in the IAA database).

---

[1] Curator at the Coin Department of the Israel Antiquities Authority (IAA), Jerusalem, Israel: gabriela@israntique.org.il
Maps were prepared by Danit Levi, IAA.
[2] The map presented in Oxford showed sites excavated by the IAA yielding more than 10 specimens following the original classifications. See G. Bijovsky, 2012, p. 75

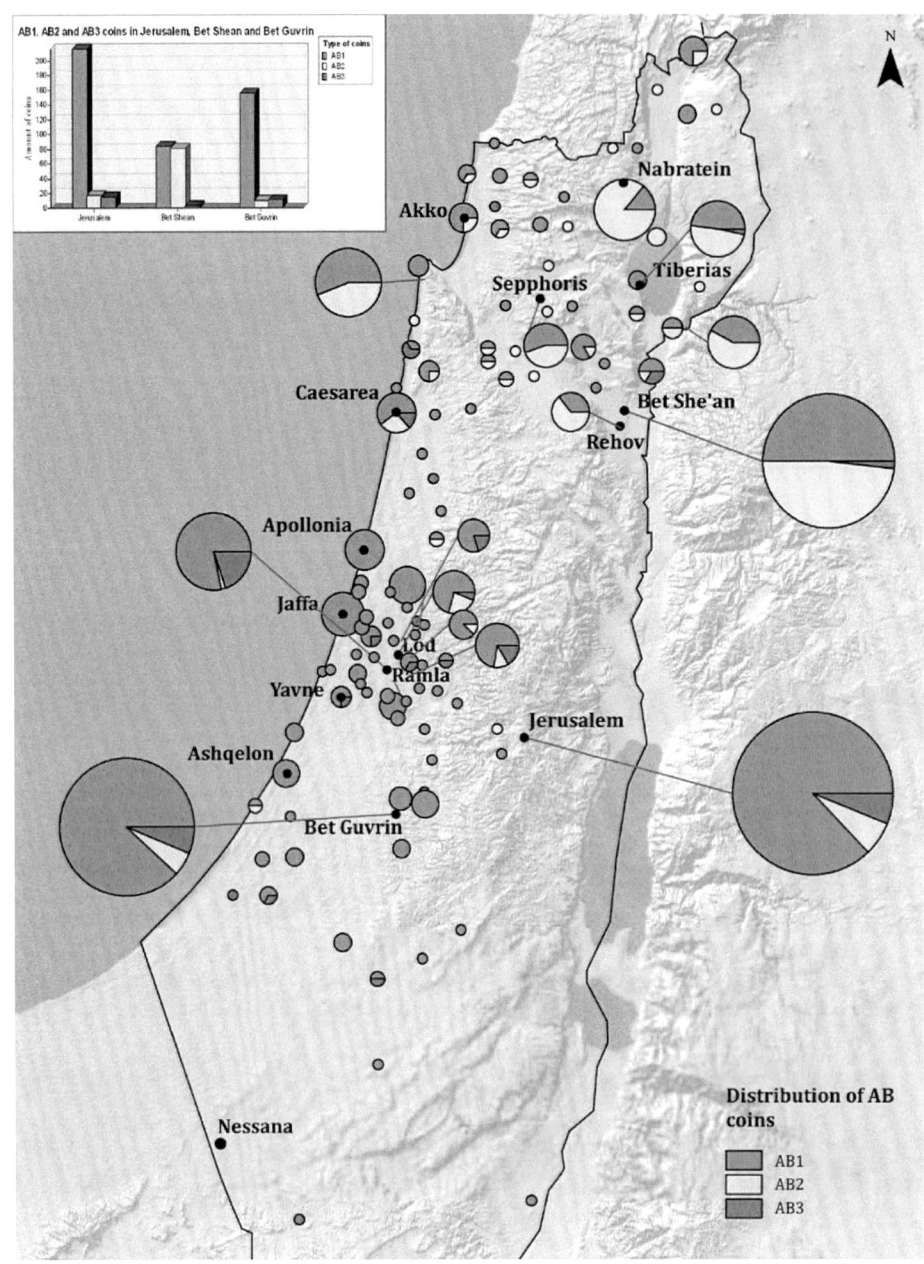

Figure 2

Since all scholars now agree that Byzantine coinage continued to be imported into Syria and Palestine well after the Arab conquest, the incidence of contemporary Byzantine official coinage is included here for comparison.

	Gold (most from hoards)	Copper
Focas	123 coins	234 coins
Heraclius	752 coins	623 coins
Constans II	248 coins	307 coins
Constantine IV	58 coins	7 coins
Justinian II	1 coin	1 coin

Figure 3

Figure 3 shows amounts for gold and copper coins of all seventh-century emperors. The largest quantities are found during the reign of Heraclius. Numbers clearly indicate that something happened to quantities of both gold and copper coinage after the reign of Constans II. Hitherto, the best explanation was the reduced import of Byzantine coins to the region. A closer examination of coin types of this emperor will enable us to discern exactly when this reduction took place. All provenanced gold coins of Constantine IV were recovered from the Bet Sh'ean hoard.[3] Copper coinage of this emperor is extremely rare: of the seven coins found in excavations, four are folles from Syracuse and three are decanummia from Constantinople. Only two coins of Justinian II are recorded in the database: a solidus from the Rehov hoard and a follis of unknown provenance.[4] In any case, coins of these last two emperors are relatively rare all over the Byzantine Empire, suggesting a reduction in mint production, as indicated at the 2011 round table.[5]

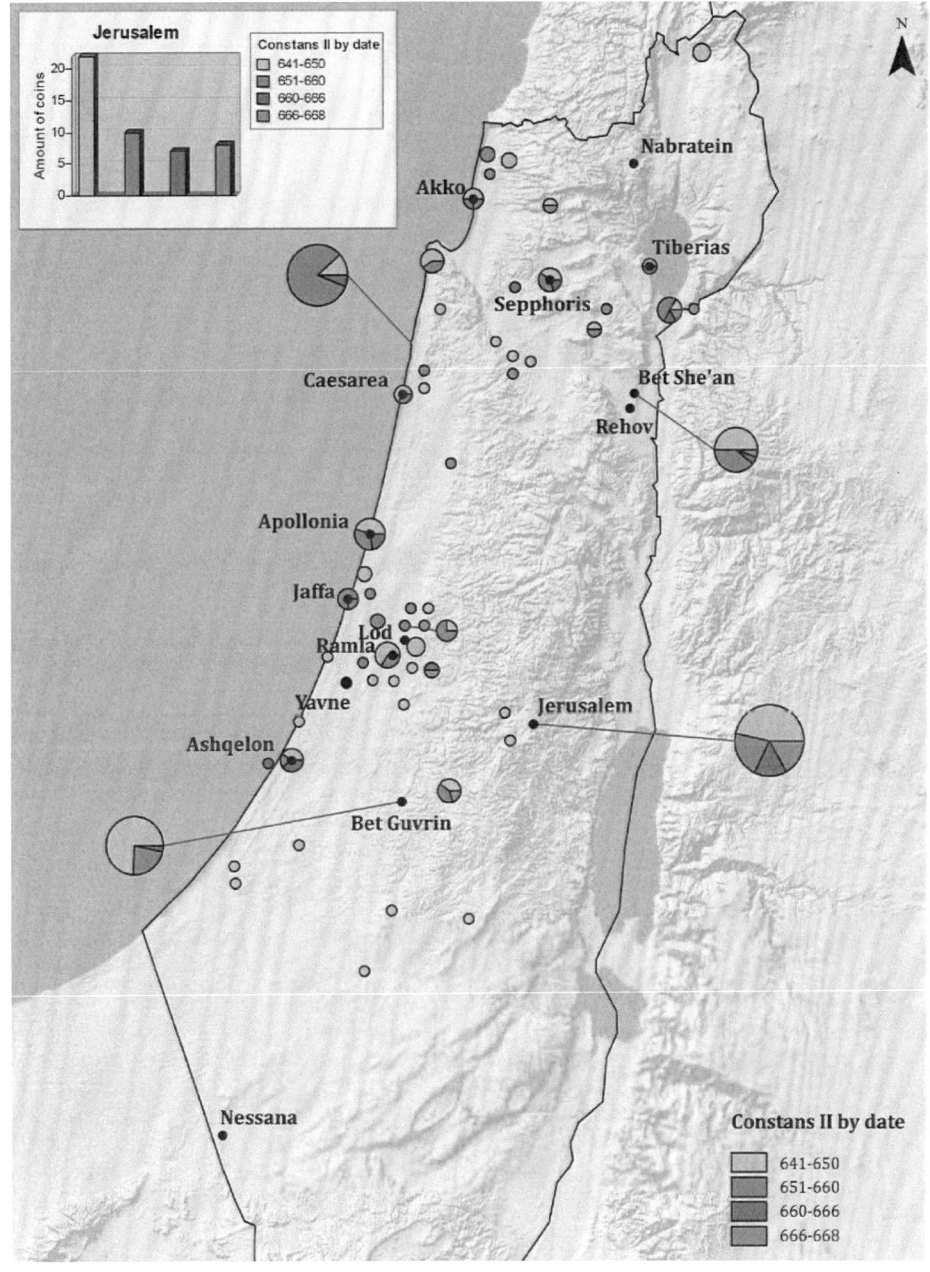

Figure 4

---

[3] G. Bijovsky, 2002, pp. 161–222.
[4] For the solidus in the Rehov hoard see, G. Bijovsky, 2012, pp. 147–158. The follis of uncertain provenance is IAA 58272.
[5] M. Phillips, 2012, p. 46.

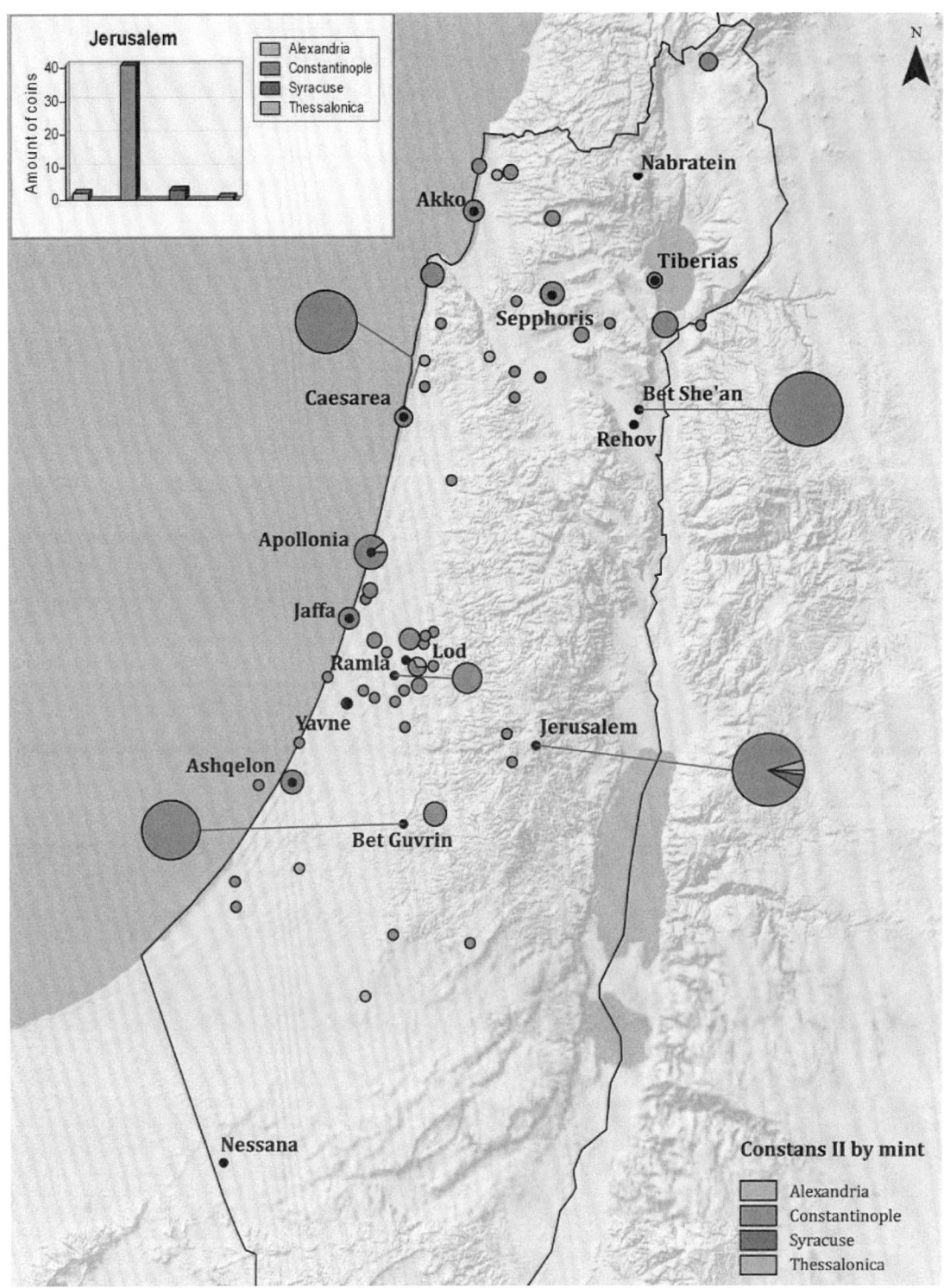

Figure 5

If we return to Constans II, Figs. 4 and 5 show the incidence of his **copper** coinage by date and mint. Constantinople is almost the only supplier of coins at every site (a total of 293 coins). In Jerusalem, however, we find coinage from other mints: Alexandria (10 coins), Thessalonica (two coins) and Syracuse (three coins), indicating the special cosmopolitan status of this city. In terms of denomination, about 95% of the coins are folles while only two half folles, 10 dodecanummia and seven decanummia are registered. For the sake of simplicity, copper coins of Constans II have been roughly divided chronologically into four periods following the *DOC* classification. As seen in the map in Fig. 2 the earlier groups by far predominate.

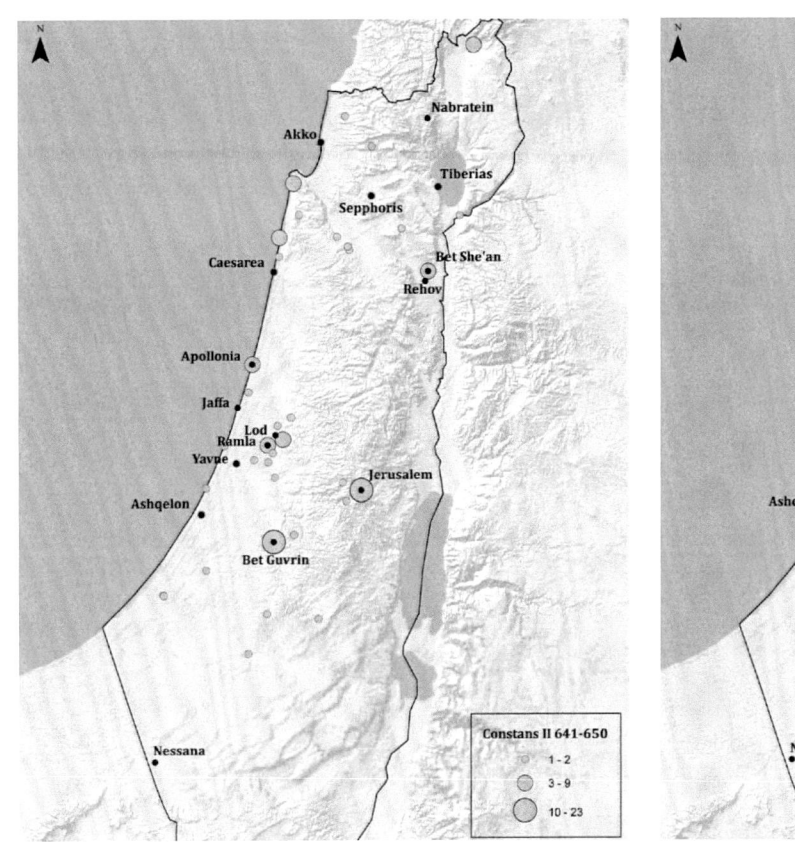 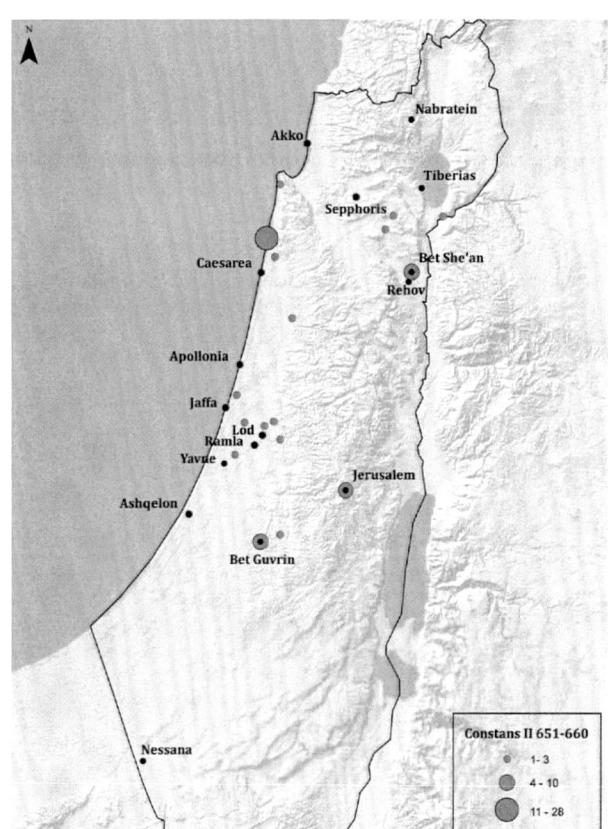

Figure 6   *Figure 7*

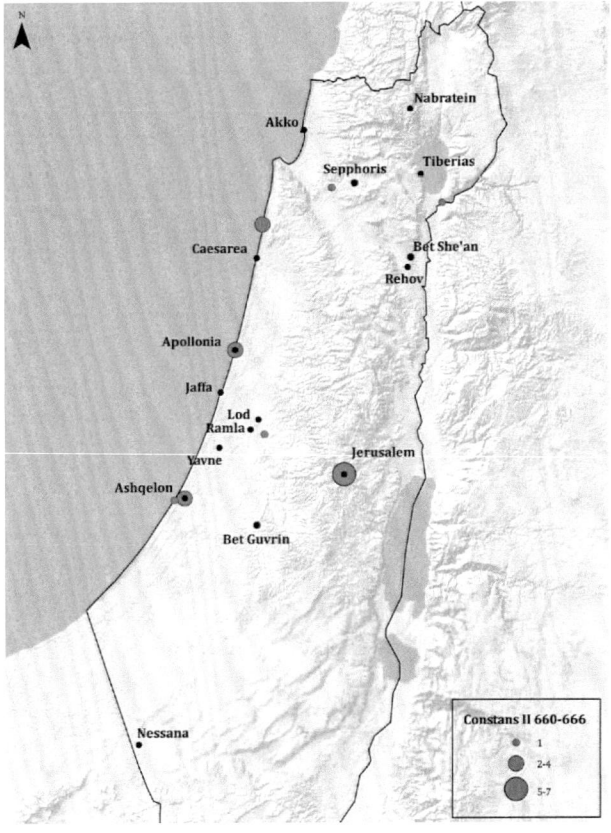 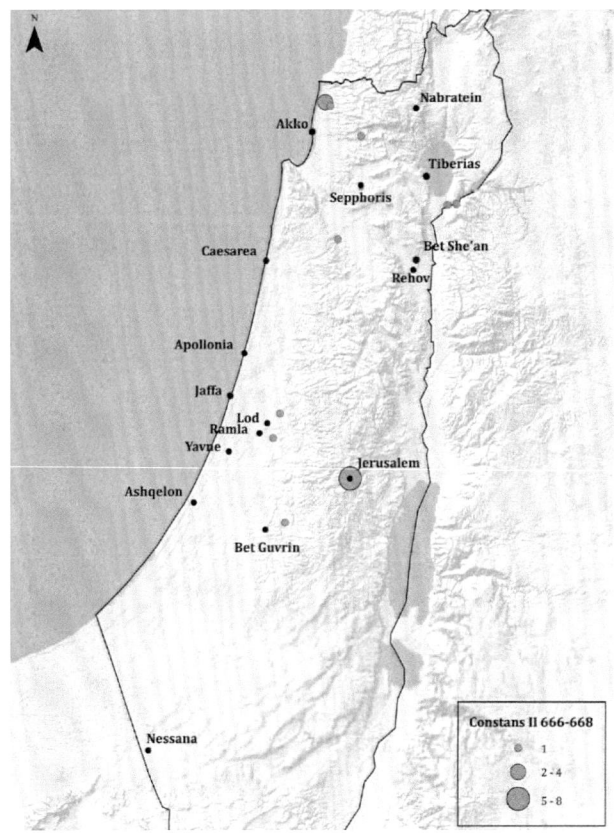

Figure 8   *Figure 9*

Coins from Constans II's classes 1-8 dating roughly up to 660 constitute the majority of finds (Figs. 6 and 7).[6] These are spread over the entire coastal strip as well as Galilee and Judea – areas which roughly correspond to the Byzantine provinces of Palaestina Prima and Secunda. The largest concentrations of coins were found in Jerusalem, Bet Guvrin and the Lod-Ramla-Yavne cluster. Analysis of these quantities reflects the administrative situation of this period when, during the years following the Arab conquest, coins of Constans II continued to flow into Palestine, but once in circulation they were not systematically withdrawn, simply because the Byzantine fiscal system was not in charge any more. Moreover, as stated by Marcus Phillips, it seems that the Arabs had no objection to using imperial coins.[7]

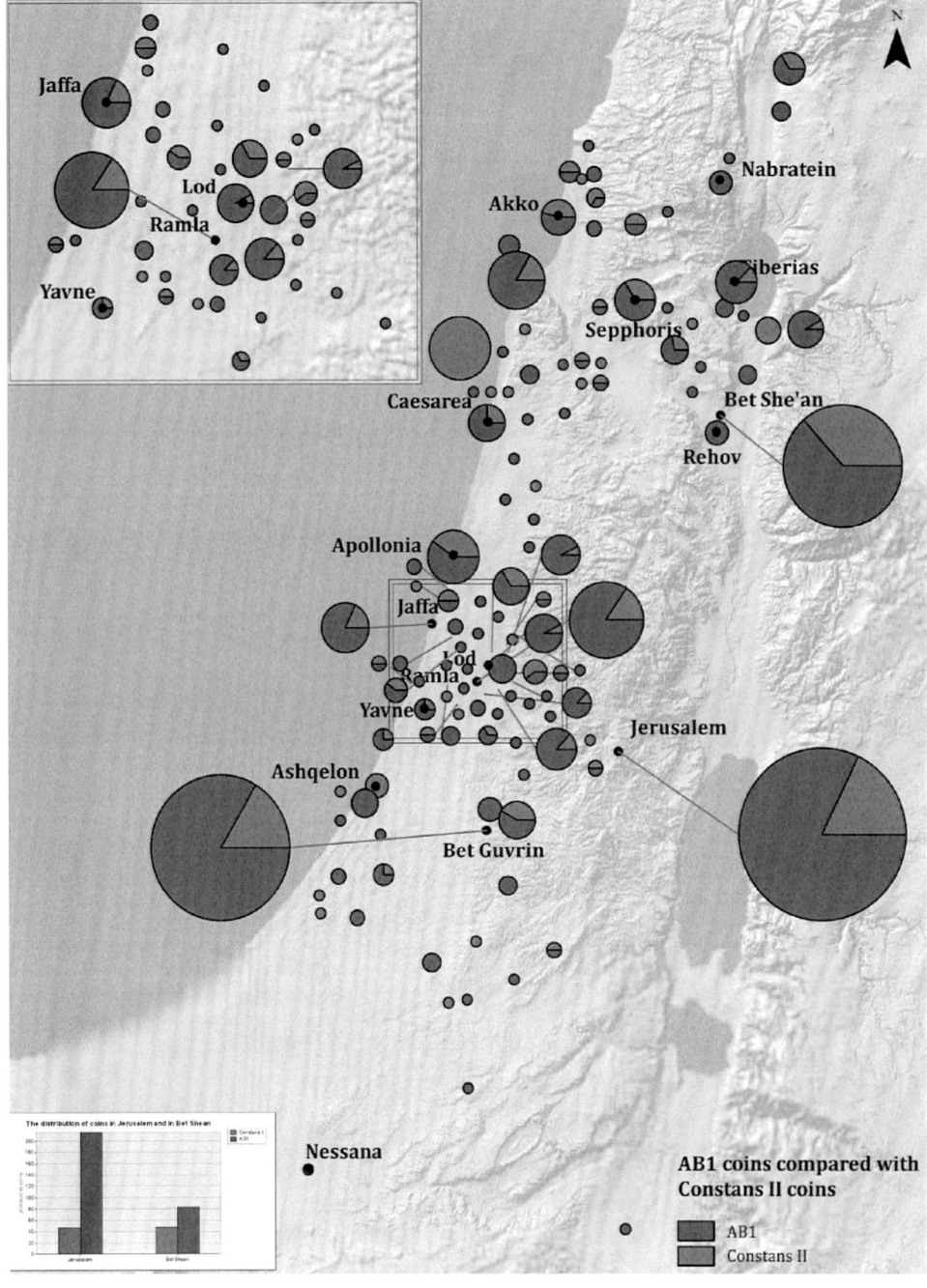

Figure 10

---

[6] 115 coins for the period 641–650 and 86 coins for the period 651–660.
[7] See fn. 5, p. 40, 56 and 59.

However, as shown in Figs. 8 and 9, after 660 there is a significant drop in the number of coin finds, indicating a drastic decrease in the importation of 'new' coinage to Palestine.[8] Jerusalem is still the site with largest quantities of coin finds while the incidence of coins at other locations is apparently random. Still, larger quantities of coins are recovered from sites along the coast, but this could be coincidental. Most coins are folles but seven coins are decanummia. Two major historical reasons are suggested for this decrease: first, the shift in attention to the imperial affairs in the West by Constans II in 660 and second, and more convincingly, is the fact that Mu'awiya was formally proclaimed caliph in 660/661 and started 'to reject the use of official Byzantine coins'.[9]

The increasing shortage of imported Byzantine currency does not imply that there was not still a huge demand for copper coins in Palestine. As already mentioned, the Arabs had no objection to using contemporary Byzantine coinage, but this reason is clearly not sufficient. When the distribution of Constans II coins is compared with that of the contemporary Arab-Byzantine 1 issues, dated roughly to 647–670 (Fig. 10), the picture that emerges is one of plentiful local minting spread over the entire region (even in the northern Negev) with large concentrations of coins found in Jerusalem, Bet She'an and the Lod-Ramla-Yavne cluster. In fact, the totals of Arab-Byzantine 1 are almost triple than that of Constans II coins.[10]

Almost every site yields coins from both types of coinage: imperial and local, usually showing higher percentages of Arab-Byzantine 1 coins. Few are the sites with coins exclusively of Constans II. The most illustrative example is the Dor shipwreck discovered during underwater excavations in the harbour of Tel Dor, which yielded 35 coins of Constans II.[11] Since this was most likely a consignment of coins being imported into Palestine it is therefore not surprising that no Arab-Byzantine coins are included.

A general analysis of the distribution of Arab-Byzantine 1 coins (Fig. 11) actually shows that the incidence of coin finds eventually correlates with centres of the Umayyad administration and/or mints in Bil'ad el Sham: Bet She'an/Scythopolis and Tiberias, which correspond to jund el-Urdunn while the cluster of Ramla-Lod-Yavne and Jerusalem, correspond to jund Filastin.

In terms of typology, Arab-Byzantine 1 coins imitating classes 1–8 of Constans II prevail. Folles of this emperor were apparently so popular that they constituted a ready prototype for imitations. Most Arab-Byzantine 1 coins in the IAA database are struck from crudely engraved dies on recycled Byzantine coins which underwent clipping (according to a weight standard which declined over the years). It seems that no Arab-Byzantine 1 coins were struck on regular new flans. This simple minting practice had many advantages: it enabled the rapid introduction into circulation of large quantities of coins, filling the vacuum created by the decrease in the import of imperial coinage. This entire series was not the result of clandestine counterfeiting. Some sort of local administration had to be responsible for this process, and based on the large concentration of finds and dies known, Arab-Byzantine 1 folles were most likely produced at a number of workshops somewhere in jund Filastin.

According to the map in Fig. 11 the incidence of Arab-Byzantine coins from Egypt was insignificant in quantity, only two coins found in Jerusalem and one in Mishmar David are known. In terms of a typological classification of coin groups within the massive Arab-Byzantine 1 coinage, I was not able to identify more than few coins of the Lazy B and LITOIE groups or workshops.

---

[8] 20 coins for the period 660–666 and 22 coins for the period 666–668.
[9] See fn. 5, p. 40–41.
[10] 278 coins of Constans II against 820 Arab-Byzantine issues.
[11] The site is marked at the map (Fig. 10) as a large circle on the sea to the north of Caesarea. For a description of the hoard see D. Syon and E. Galili, 2009, pp. 81–94.

A single follis of the Lazy B type was found at Lod and three LITOIE coins are recorded showing their wide geographical distribution.[12]

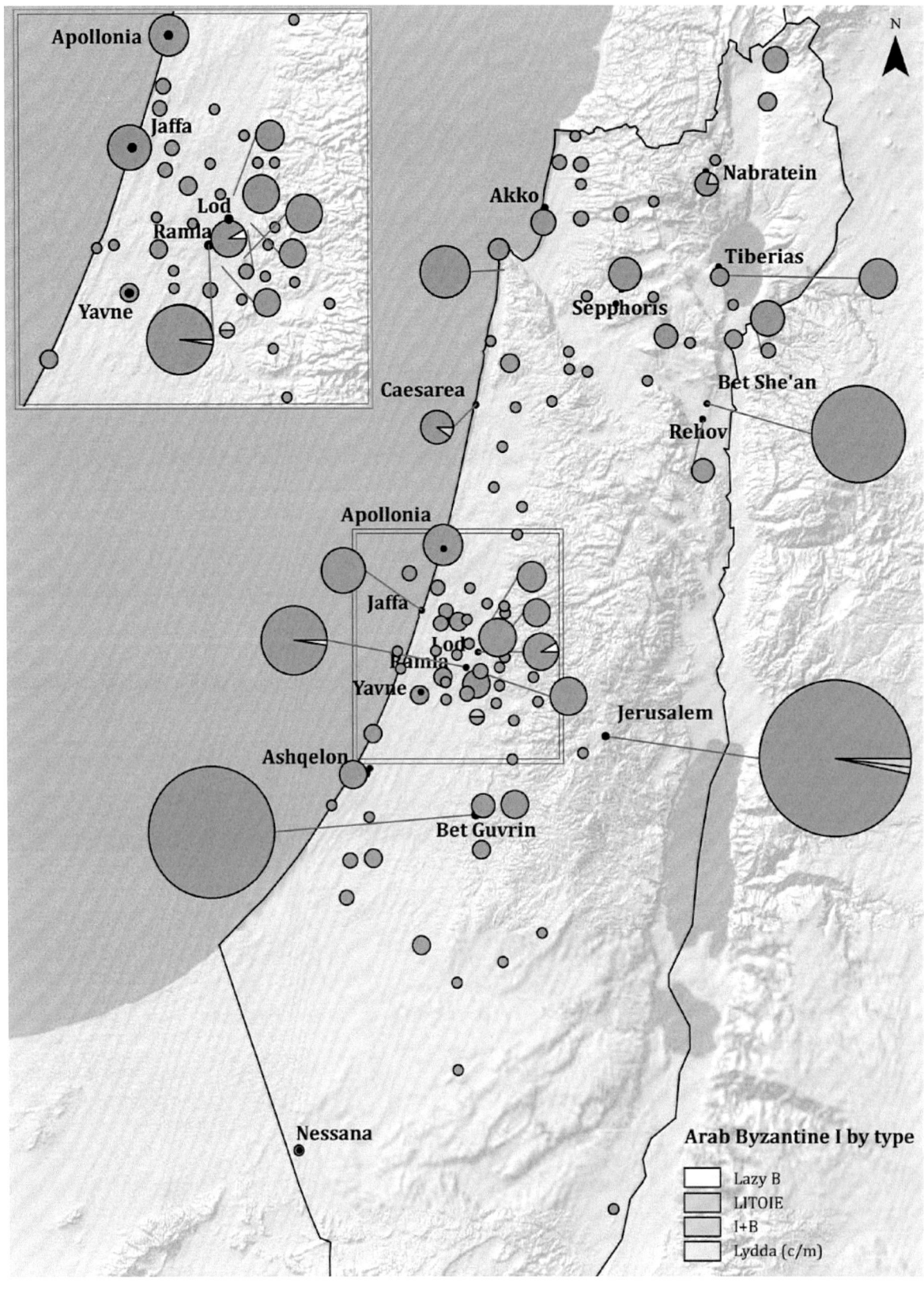

Figure 11

---

[12] The Lazy B coin is IAA 137522. The three LITOIE coins are IAA 80461 in northern Galilee at Nabratein, IAA 27168 on coastal Caesarea and IAA 31505 in inland Jerusalem.

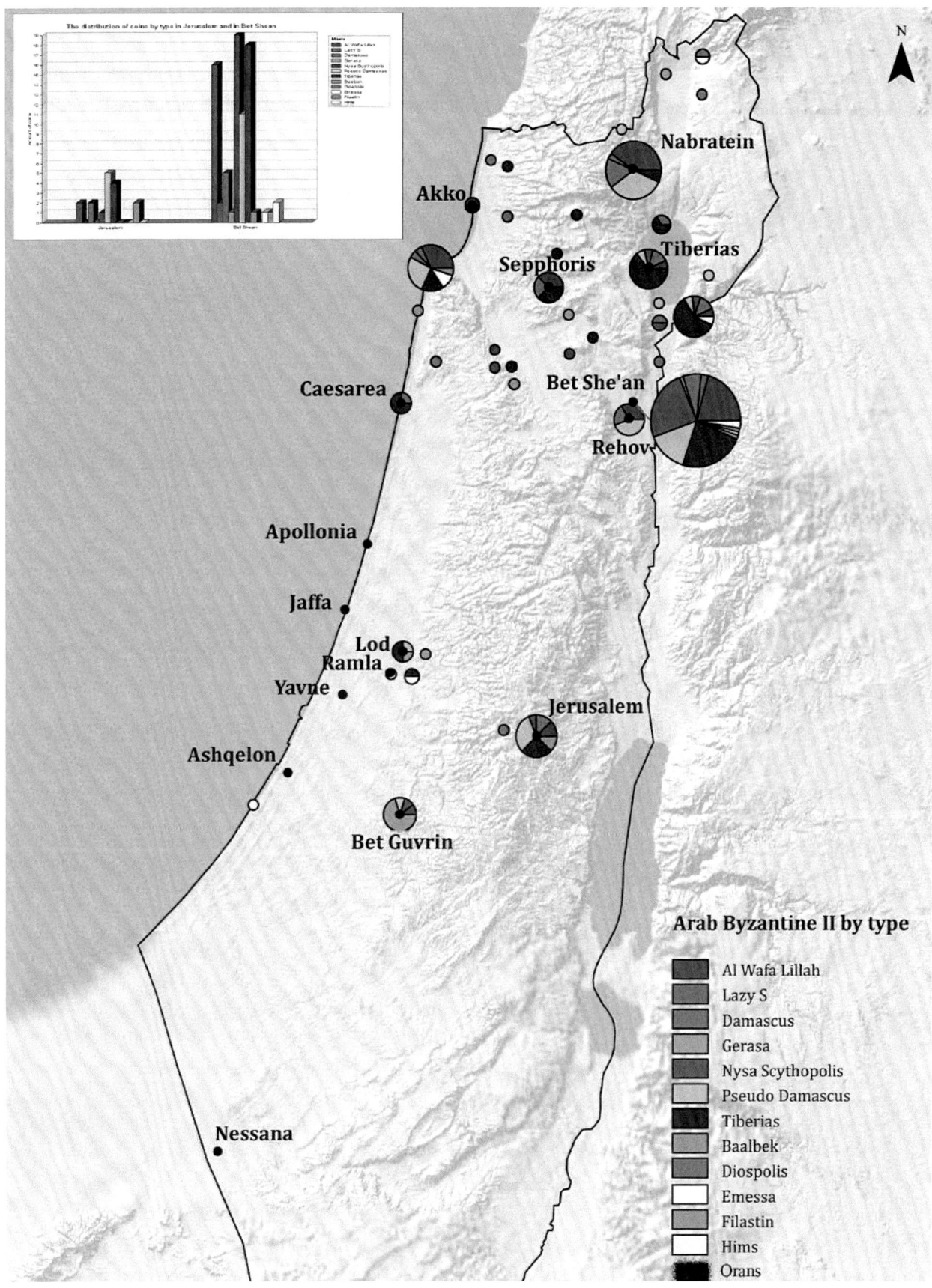

Figure 12

Fig. 12 shows the incidence of coins of the Arab-Byzantine 2 group. On one hand the total number of finds diminishes dramatically (250 coins), but on the other a vast diversity of types develops which can appear together at the same site. This is noticed in leisure places such as the baths of Hammat Gader, small villages such as Nabratein or Rehov, towns such as Qastra and Bet Guvrin, and cities such as Tiberias, Bet She'an and Jerusalem.

Many coin types bear mint names so that their places of issue are certain: Scythopolis, Tiberias, Jerash, Damascus, Ba'albeq, Hims and Diospolis. Goodwin rightly proposed to call them 'local city coins', the term used for the Roman Provincial coinage.[13] But if we accept this term, then it implies in my view that there was a central authority behind minting and distribution, perhaps during the reign of Mu'awiya as suggested by Foss or other shorter caliphates, as proposed by Goodwin.[14]

Of all Syrian mints, only Damascus (30 coins) and, to a certain degree, Hims (11 coins) appear in significant numbers, especially in the north. Other typological groups bear no mint names but may shed light on the locations of their mints based on their geographical distribution. This is the case for the *al-wafā lillāh* group, Lazy S, Pseudo-Damascus, Orans and square coins. Four coins of the Lazy S group are recorded: two at Bet She'an, one at Nabratein and one in Qastra, therefore we assume they were minted somewhere in jund el-Urdunn.[15] Only one coin of the Orans type 1 has been registered at Nabratein (IAA 80405). According to Wolfgang Schulze, this type is very rare and our coin does not add much information about the location of the original workshop. He remarks however, that the Orans type has some stylistic similarities to the Pseudo-Damascus and *al-wafā lillāh* groups, and he locates the mint somewhere in northern Jordan.[16]

Contrary to the majority of Arab-Byzantine 2 issues, which are generally struck on round regular flans, coins included under the title 'Filastin' constitute at least two distinctive groups struck on square shaped flans depicting the imperial figure and a cursive m. The first group, called "ugly square flan coins", was defined by Ingrid Schulze as a local emergency issue, produced most likely in Caesarea.[17] The second group, more nicely engraved, bears Greek letters and/or in some cases Arabic names, such as 'Amir' and 'Muhammad', which Tony Goodwin attributes to local governors.[18] This is a very homogeneous group with coin finds from Bet Guvrin and Jerusalem, suggesting that their mint and area of circulation was located somewhere in jund Filastin. Only one coin from the mint of Diospolis was discovered at Tel Horshan, to the north of Caesarea (IAA no. 60119). These coins are extremely rare.

By locating coin finds on comparative maps, it is possible to analyse circulation patterns in greater detail. The main Arab-Byzantine 2 local mints in jund el-Urdunn were located at Tiberias and Scythopolis (Fig. 13). It seems that while coins of Scythopolis remain concentrated at Bet She'an itself (25 coins), coins from Tiberias are much more numerous, not only in Tiberias but over several sites in Galilee: Caesarea, Jerusalem, Lod and Ramla (62 coins). The limited distribution of coins from Scythopolis is most likely related to the fact that coins were minted in larger and heavier flans, uncommon in other places. The fact that Goodwin refers to four coins minted in Scythopolis overstruck on the very largest Tiberias coins, might also indicate that coins from Tiberias were not only more numerous but also less valuable than those from Scythopolis.[19] Interestingly, almost the same number of coins from both mints was discovered in Bet She'an itself: 19 coins from Scythopolis and 18 coins from Tiberias.

---

[13] T. Goodwin, 2012, pp. 90–91.
[14] C. Foss, 2002; C. Foss, 2008, Chapter 5 and T. Goodwin 2012.
[15] Bet She'an: IAA 114142 and 114125; Qastra: IAA 75540 and Nabratein: IAA 80442.
[16] W. Schulze 2012.
[17] I. Schulze 2012.
[18] T. Goodwin 2012, 95–96.
[19] T. Goodwin 2012, 102.

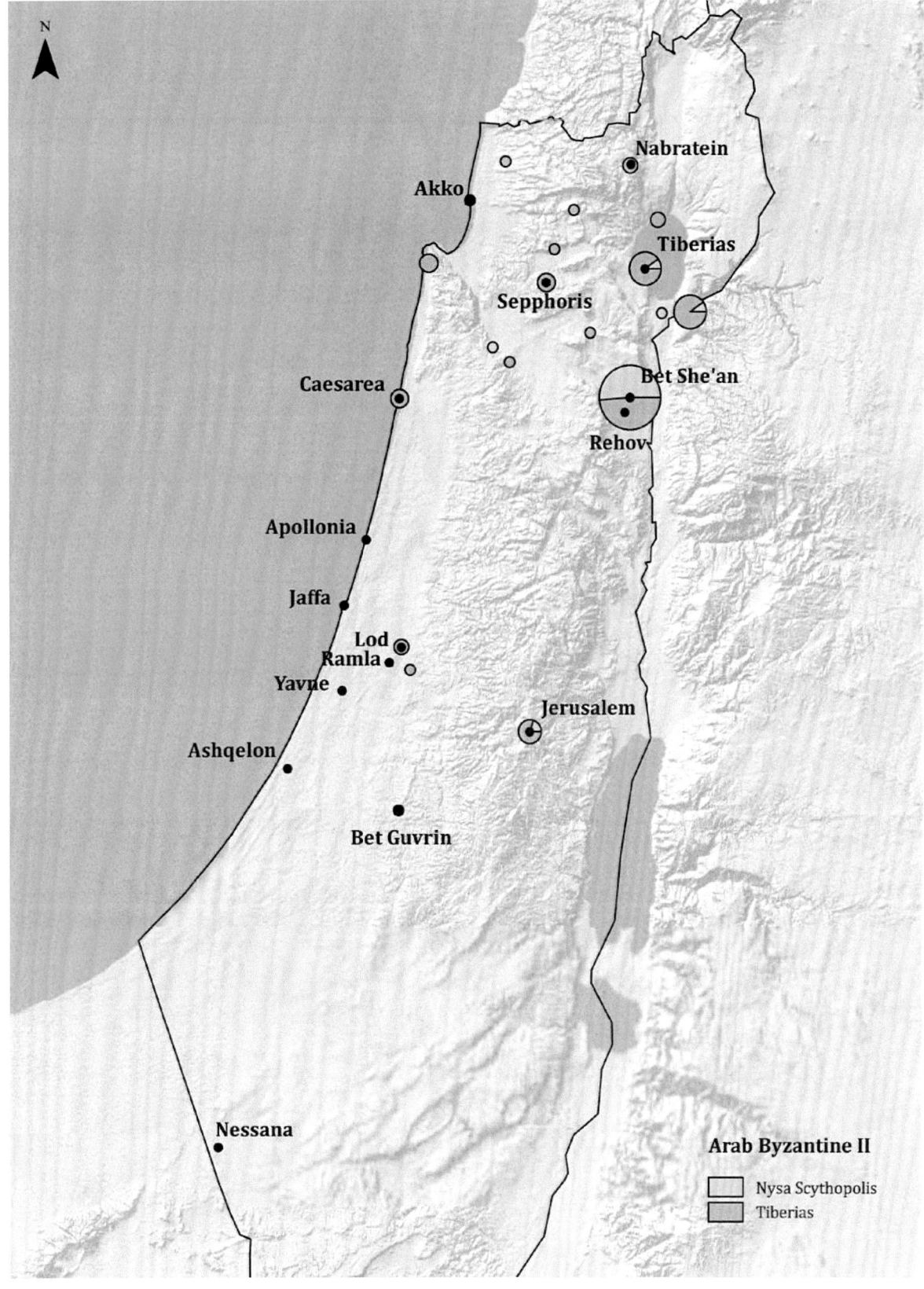

Figure 13

I believe that this is a provisional picture since this map does not include the huge quantities of coins discovered by the Hebrew University expedition at Bet She'an during the 1980-90 excavations. The sole Arab-Byzantine 2 coin from the mint of Jerash registered in the database was found in excavations in Bet She'an (IAA 42568).

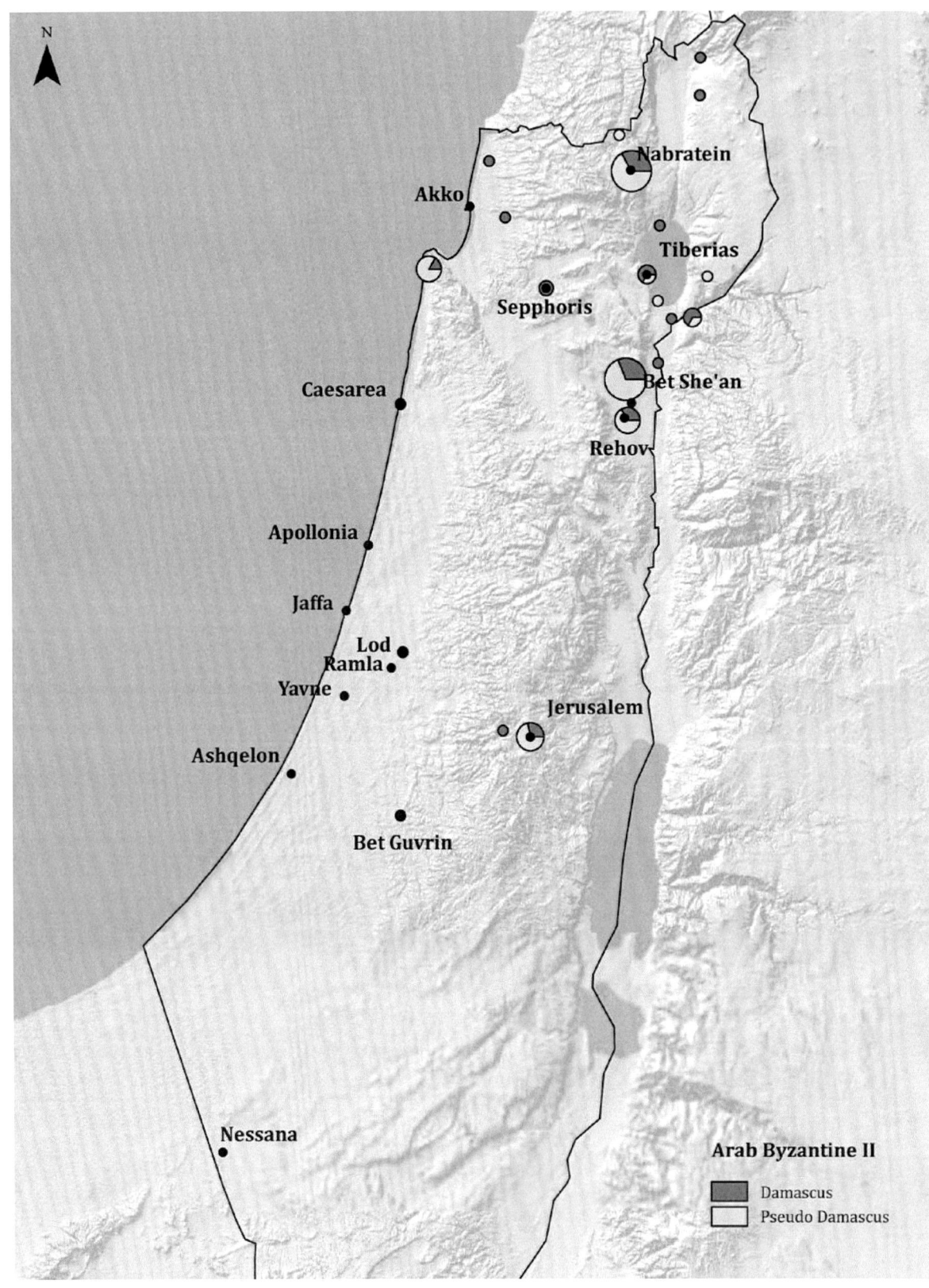

Figure 14

The map Fig. 14 compares the distribution of coins from Damascus (30 coins) with the pseudo-Damascus group (42 coins). Both groups predominate in northern Israel and Jerusalem. There are single isolated coin finds from both groups in Bet Guvrin and Kh. El-Beida (to the west of Jerusalem). But the general picture is one of distribution in the territory of jund el-Urdunn. Damascus is actually the only Syrian mint which appears in relatively large numbers in Palestine.

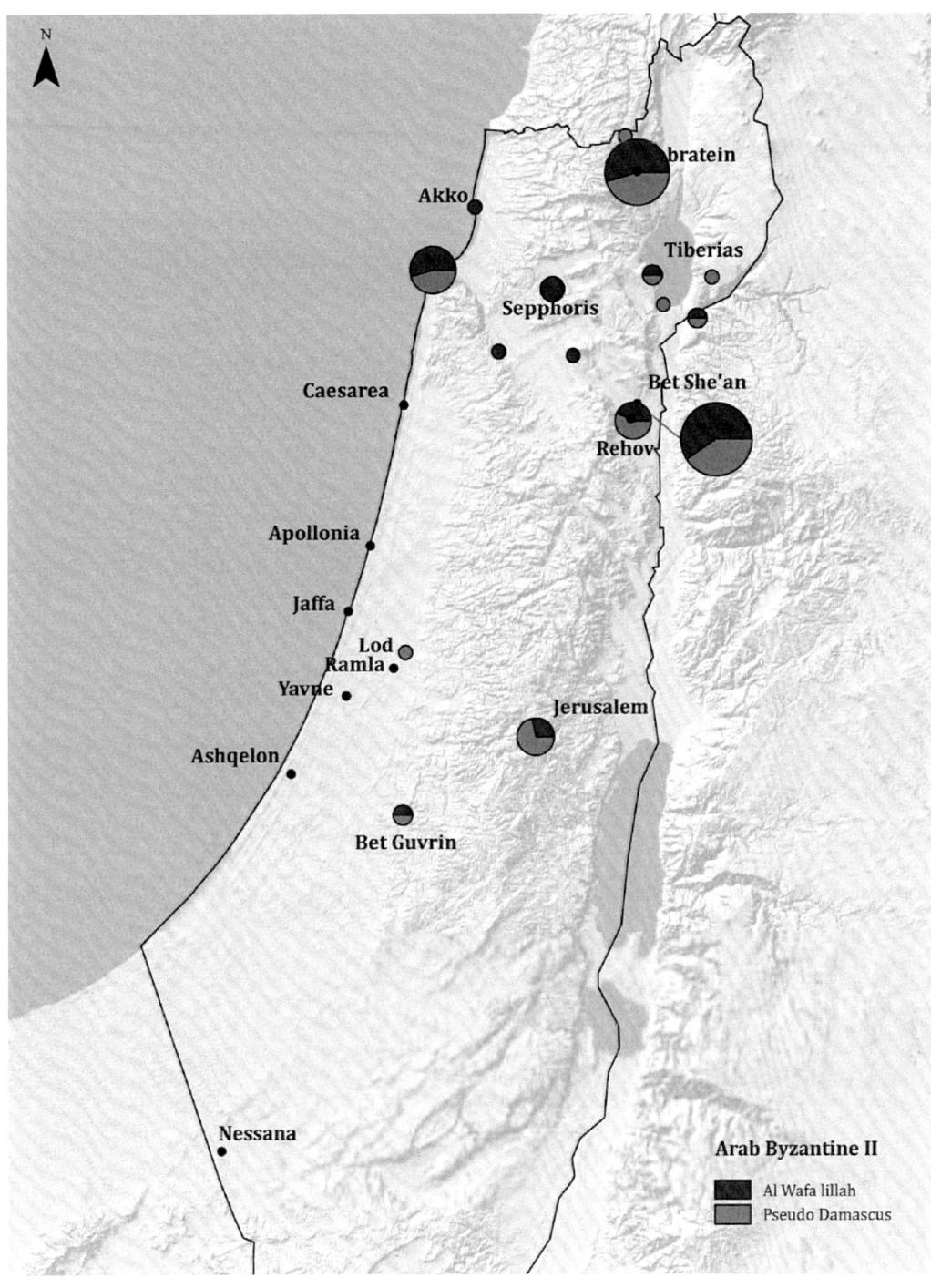

Figure 15

The third comparative map focusses on the distribution of coins of the *al-wafā lillāh* (48 coins) and the pseudo-Damascus groups (41 coins) (Fig. 15). Neither bear mint names but both have been attributed to particular entities: the Judem tribe which supported the Zubayrids for the former and the Kalb tribe who supported the Umayyads for the latter.[20] Both tribes were active in northern Israel and Jordan circa 684/685; therefore it is not surprising that their coinage series have many stylistic similarities in common. As is clear from the map, there is no reason to presume that the coins did not circulate contemporaneously. In terms of coin finds, both groups predominate in northern Israel and Jerusalem. Single isolated coin finds from both groups are found in Bet Guvrin and Lod, but the general picture is one of main circulation in the territory of jund el-Urdunn.

---

[20] See I. Schulze 2010 and Goodwin 2012, pp. 92–94.

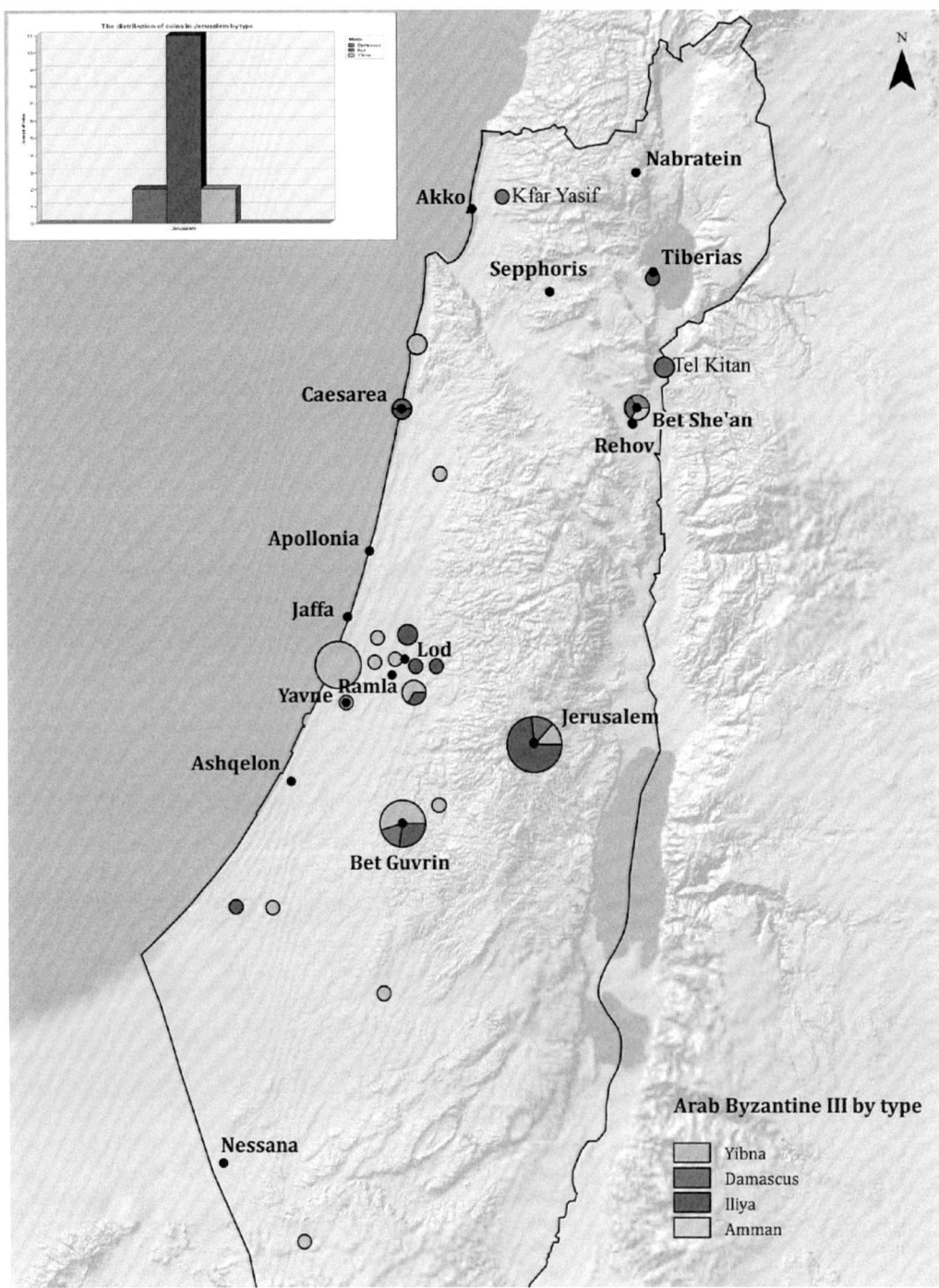

Figure 16

The next map shows the incidence of coins of the Arab-Byzantine 3 or Standing Caliph group (Fig. 16). Not coincidentally most finds are concentrated in jund Filastin. As far as we know, no Arab-Byzantine 3 coins have been minted in the territory of jund el-Urdunn. The few Arab-Byzantine 3 finds in this jund come from the mint of Damascus (at the sites of Kfar Yasif, Tel Kitan, Bet She'an), Iliya (Tiberias and Bet She'an), and one coin minted in 'Amman (Bet She'an). On the other hand, Arab-Byzantine 3 coins are popular within the territories of jund Filastin. Coins of this province are peculiar: they depict a standing caliph on the obverse and a cursive m on the reverse instead of the common symbol on steps, legends are in Arabic and they include mint names. For this reason some scholars believe the Arab-Byzantine 3 group from Palestine is the earliest in the series, a sort of transitional group between the Arab-Byzantine 2 types and the conventional Standing Caliph types Arab-Byzantine 3. The leading mints are at Yavne (33 coins) and Iliya (17 coins). To the latter we add a variant of five specimens which reads on both sides of the m the name

Filastin, and are also attributed to Iliya.[21] Coins from the mint of Diospolis are rare and no examples are recorded in our database.

These maps show the incidence of Arab-Byzantine 3 coins in more detail. For the Iliya mint, most coin finds are, as expected, in Jerusalem and the Lod-Ramla-Yavne cluster (Fig. 17).

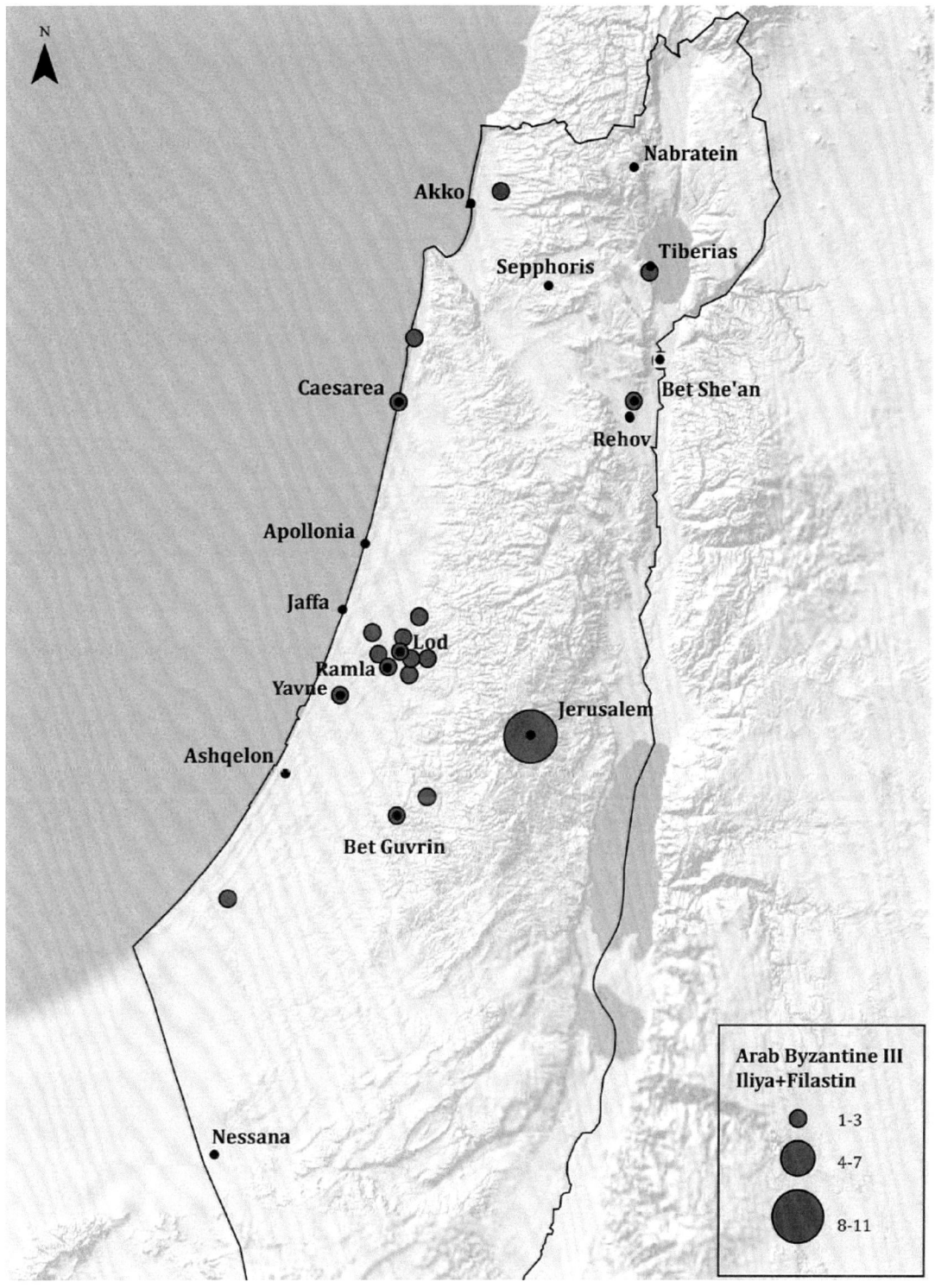

Figure 17

---

[21] T. Goodwin, 2005, p. 102, Type 1 No. 45.

The picture for the mint at Yibna is even more concentrated around the Lod-Ramla-Yavne cluster, with significant quantities in Bet Guvrin and scattered coin finds in the Negev and Galilee. Only two Yibna coins are recorded from Jerusalem (Fig. 18).

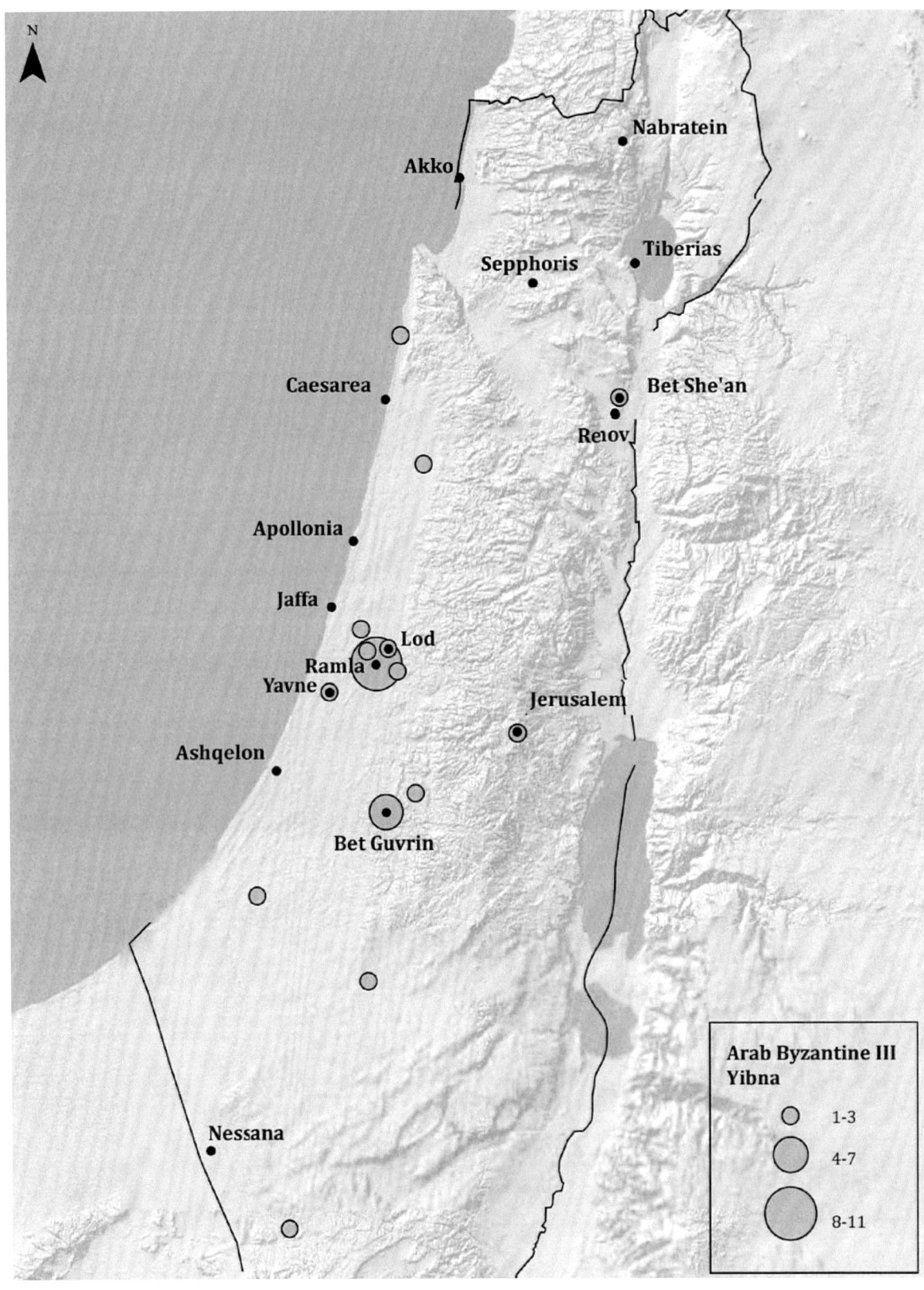

Figure 18

The last map of the Arab-Byzantine 3 series shows coin finds from the mint of Damascus, the only Syrian mint present in Palestine during this period (Fig. 19). Finds are sparse (9 coins) indicating they were not intended for circulation in this region. In short, the picture presented by the Arab-Byzantine 3 coinage is one of very local character.

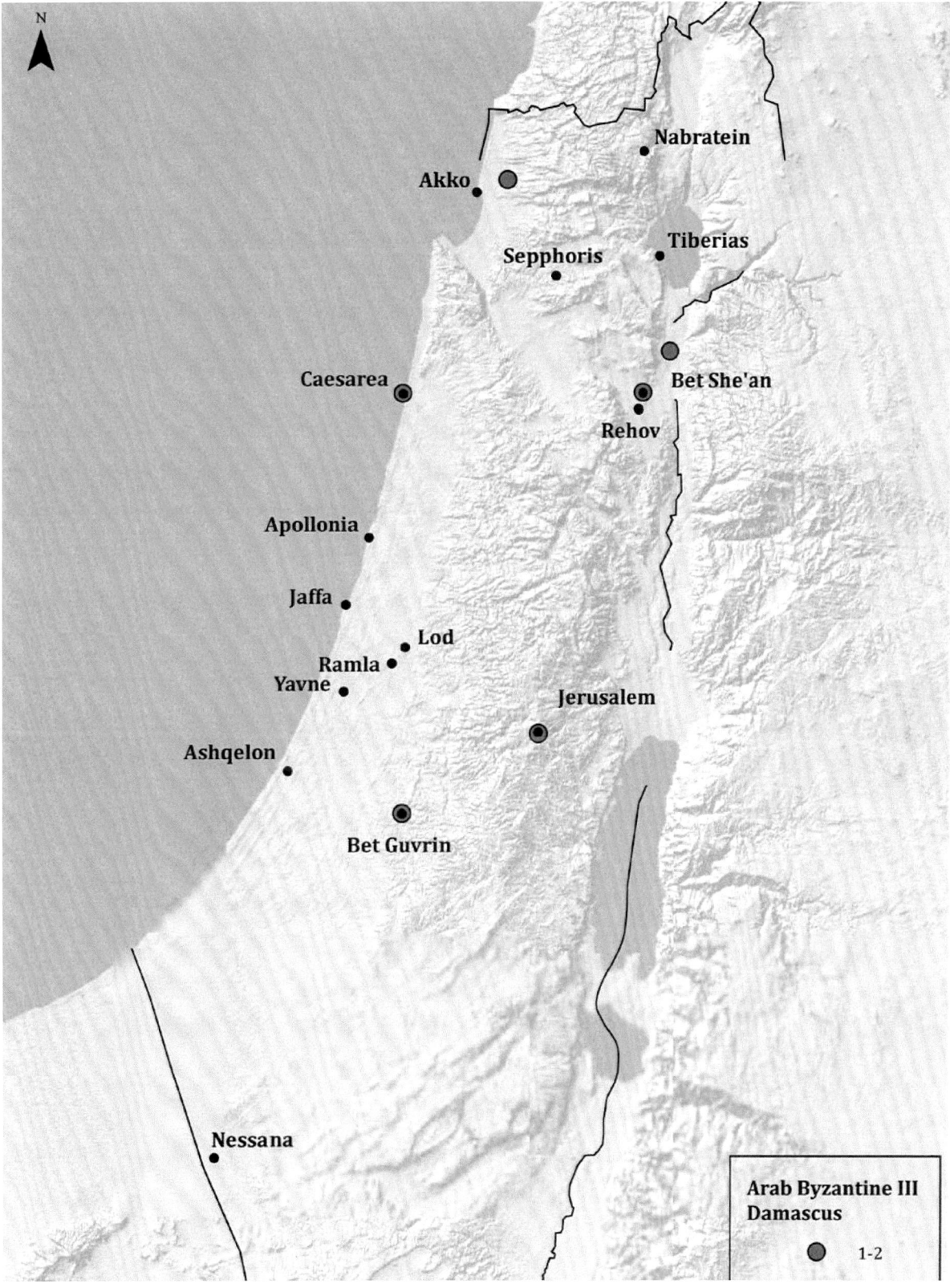

Figure 19

To sum up, we refer to the general map in Fig. 2 in order to see the relationships between the different series of coinage.[22] Arab-Byzantine 1 coins are by far the most numerous all over Israel, with especially large concentrations in Jerusalem, the Lod-Ramla-Yavne cluster, Bet Guvrin, Bet She'an, and Qastra, and with scattered isolated finds in the Galilee and northern Negev. It is

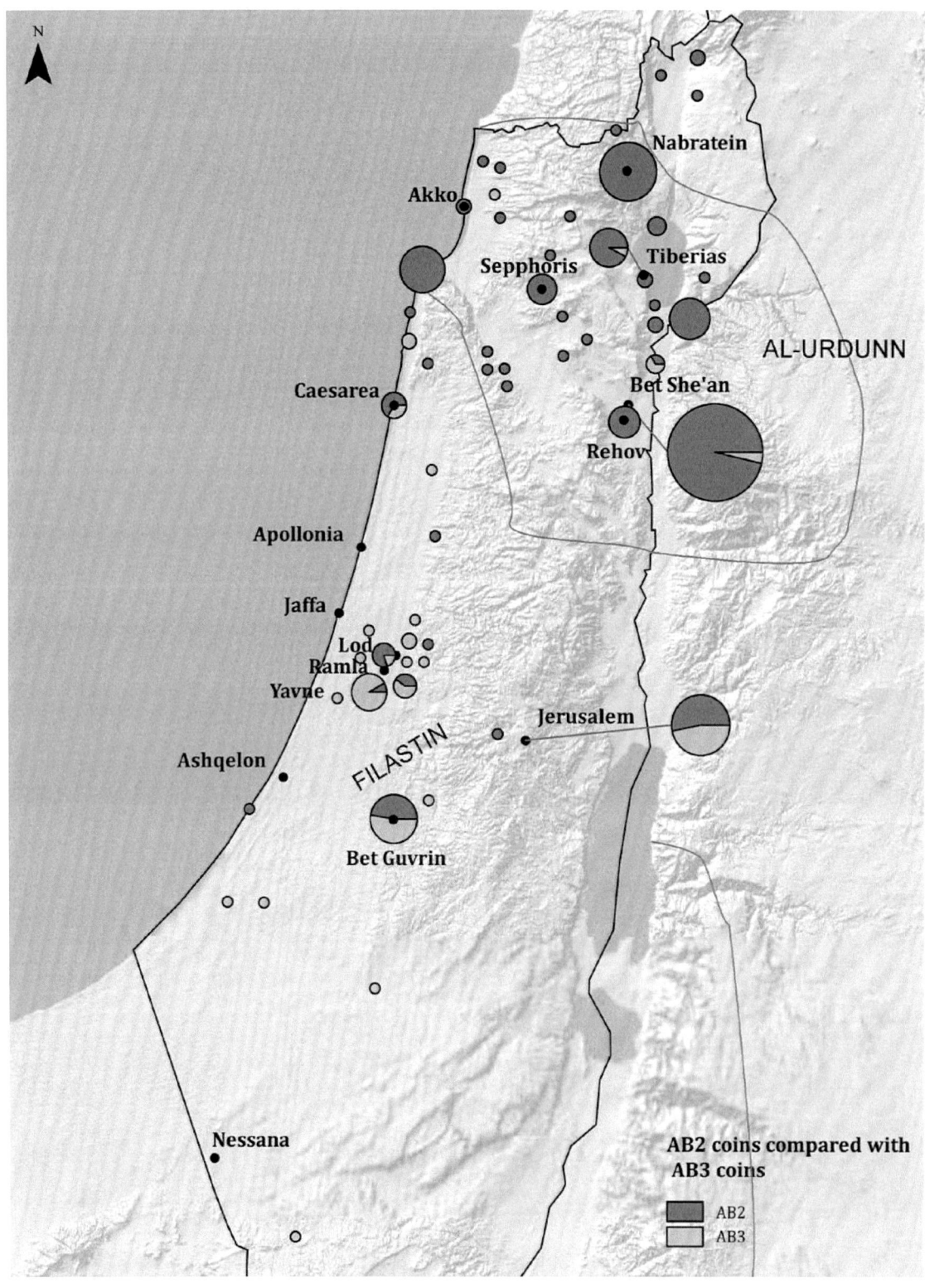

Figure 20

---

[22] The total numbers for each series are: Arab-Byzantine 1 – 820 coins; Arab-Byzantine 2 – 250 coins and Arab-Byzantine 3 – 65 coins.

difficult to conclude from this map however, how long Arab-Byzantine 1 coins were in circulation. In view of the smaller numbers of Arab-Byzantine 2 and Arab-Byzantine 3 coin finds (totals are together less than half of the Arab-Byzantine 1 coins!), I assume that Arab-Byzantine 1 coins remained in circulation side by side with the newly issued Arab-Byzantine 2 coins, which are the dominant group in northern Israel, and Arab-Byzantine 3 coins that prevail in the territories of jund Filastin.

The last map emphasizes the relationships between Arab-Byzantine 2 and Arab-Byzantine 3 series (Fig. 20). When the borders of both junds Filastin and el-Urdunn are added, the regionality of each series is striking. While the majority of Arab-Byzantine 2 coins circulated in jund el-Urdunn, Arab-Byzantine 3 coins were predominant in jund Filastin.

What are the implications of this distribution pattern? Is this only a geographical division or a chronological one as well? Is it possible that both series were issued simultaneously in Palestine and are not consecutive as accepted so far? Or should some extent of overlapping between the series be considered? What were the administrative considerations behind this division? These important questions require further research beyond the scope of this paper.

Bibliography

G. Bijovsky, 'A Preliminary Overview of Arab-Byzantine Coins from Excavations in Israel'. T. Goodwin (ed.), *Arab-Byzantine Coins and History, Papers presented at the Seventh Century Syrian Numismatic Round Table held at Corpus Christi College, Oxford on 10th and 11th September 2011.* London, 2012, pp. 73-80.

G. Bijovsky, 'A Hoard of Byzantine *Solidi* from Bet She'an in the Umayyad Period', *Revue Numismatique* 158 (2002), pp. 161-222.

G. Bijovsky, 'A Byzantine Gold Hoard from Rehob (H. Parwa)', *Israel Numismatic Research* 7 (2012), pp. 147-158.

D. Syon and E. Galili, 'Byzantine-period Bronze Coins from the Sea at Dor', *'Atiqot* 61 (2009), pp. 81-94.

C. Foss, 'A Syrian Coinage of Mu'awiya?', *Revue Numismatique* 158 (2002), pp. 353-365.

C. Foss, *Arab-Byzantine Coins. An Introduction, with a Catalogue of the Dumbarton Oaks Collection* (Dumbarton Oaks Byzantine Collection Publications 12), Washington D.C., 2008.

T. Goodwin, *Arab-Byzantine Coinage* (Studies in the Khalili Collection 4), London and New York, 2005.

T. Goodwin, 'The Chronology of the Umayyad Imperial Image Coinage. Progress over the Last 10 Years', T. Goodwin (ed.), *Arab-Byzantine Coins and History. Papers presented at the Seventh Century Syrian Numismatic Round Table held at Corpus Christi College, Oxford on 10th and 11th September 2011.* London, 2012, pp. 99-107.

M. Phillips, 'The Import of Byzantine Coins to Syria Revisited', T. Goodwin (ed.), *Arab-Byzantine Coins and History. Papers presented at the Seventh Century Syrian Numismatic Round Table held at Corpus Christi College, Oxford on 10th and 11th September 2011,* London, 2012, pp. 39-72.

I. Schulze, 'The al-wafā lillāh Coinage – A study of style', A. Oddy (ed.), *Coinage and History in the Seventh Century Near East 2.* London, 2010, pp.111-121.

I. Schulze, 'Ugly square flan coins – Another consistent group within the Byzantine-Arab Transitional coinage', T. Goodwin (ed.), **Arab-Byzantine Coins and History**. *Papers presented at the Seventh Century Syrian Numismatic Round Table held at Corpus Christi College, Oxford on 10th and 11th September 2011.* London, 2012, pp. 81-87.

W. Schulze, 'The Syrian "Orans Figure" copper coins', T. Goodwin (ed.), **Arab-Byzantine Coins and History**. *Papers presented at the Seventh Century Syrian Numismatic Round Table held at Corpus Christi College, Oxford on 10th and 11th September 2011,* London, 2012, pp. 131-144.

**A pdf FILE OF ALL THE MAPS IN THIS PAPER IN COLOUR IS AVAILABLE.
PLEASE EMAIL** waoddy@googlemail.com OR schulze@wg-s.de

Can we believe what is written on the coins?

Enigmatic die links and other puzzles

Ingrid Schulze [1]

The coins struck in Bilad al-Sham during Phase 2[2] of the Byzantine-Arab transition period are defined by meaningful Greek and/or Arabic inscriptions and a mint name.[3] Some smaller mints perhaps made this change in the 670s AD, possibly under a local authority, while the main period of minting started in the 680s AD, and the fact that the later coinage shows a certain degree of coordination allows us to assume caliphal authority.[4]

Thus, if we read Damascus (*dimashq*), Emesa (*ḥimṣ*), Baalbek (*baʿlbakk*) or Tiberias (*ṭabariya*) on a coin of Phase 2 we are inclined to believe that the coin was struck there. Possibly we make the restriction 'blundered legend' or 'irregular appearance', but the mint name itself is seldom questioned.

a b c d e

Figure 1 [5]

Figure 1 shows five reverses of Phase 2 coins, each one normal or regular looking and not at all suspicious. We see a coin from Hims (1a), one of Tiberias (1b), two of Damascus (1c and 1d) and one of Baalbek (1e). In the course of the first part of this article it will be demonstrated that most probably none of them was struck in the mint place written on them.

Die links between different mints?

Damascus – Baalbek
The very special relation between the Damascus and Baalbek mints has already been investigated by Tony Goodwin in his *Studies in the Khalili Collection Volume IV*.[6] An example for the difficulty of attribution is illustrated here (the mint name written on the coins is used for the caption – this does NOT mean an attribution):

---

[1] Ingrid Schulze is an independent scholar: ingridschulze@wg-s.de
[2] For the terminology used here see Schulze and Oddy (2012).
[3] Exclusions are e.g. the Pseudo-Damascus and the *al-wafā lillāh* coins. For more examples see Schulze and Oddy (2012) p. 196.
[4] For a detailed analysis see Goodwin (2005a) pp. 18-20.
[5] All coins are illustrated approximately 1.5x actual size; on figure 11 slightly less.
[6] Goodwin (2005a) p. 60 f.

Figure 2 [7]

Figure 2 shows a die link between Damascus and Baalbek. Interestingly it also links a two figure coin and a one figure coin. Each of the coins seen separately would be assigned to the mint that appears on the coin. But there are some details that do not completely fit with the main series of the two mints. On the two figure obverse the sceptres are pointing to the right instead of to the left as is usual, and the reverse inscription is blundered with ᚛ instead of the correct Є. The one figure obverse shows a double line beneath the globe and possibly a second globe, an obscure Greek inscription on the right, starting with an upside down **A** at 1 o'clock and a strange symbol or animal inside the spandrel of the double line. Due to the die link this obverse has to be attributed to the Baalbek-Damascus related series.

Curiously enough the die cutter made a second attempt:

Figure 3 [8]

---

[7] The die numbers of obverses and reverses are those of the Baalbek die study (Goodwin 2005a, p. 49 ff.).

[8] Many thanks to Andrew Oddy for providing me with the pictures of coins 3a and 3b after the 2013 meeting.

Again we see the double line with an uncertain symbol within the edge, a letter Ԑ to the right of the globe and unclear letters in the upper right field. Three different *dimashq* reverses are known, all badly preserved, and it is hard to find die links either to Damascus or to the Damascus-Baalbek related series. For stylistic reasons these three coins too should be attributed to the Damascus-Baalbek related series. Of course they need further research.

Some more coins of the Damascus-Baalbek related series show another phenomenon:

a	b	c	d
O8/R46b	O43/RD3b	O22/R69d	O22/R35d

Figure 4 [9]

On reverses 4a and 4b we see dots within O and *mim* respectively, giving the impression of birds-eyes; reverses 4c and 4d show dots and wavy lines either side of the cross. These decorative elements are never found on coins of Damascus and Baalbek, but they occur on coins of Hims:

Figure 5: Coins of Hims with birds-eyes and wavy lines

Finally a last example of the Damascus-Baalbek related series:

a	b
O29/R10b	O13/R3a

Figure 6

---

[9] Coin 4a is from the same pair of dies as Foss (2008) no. 62, attributed as regular coin from Baalbek.

Here we see O29 (figure 6a) and O13 (figure 6b) of the Khalili die study, with a small **o** and **ΛЄO** respectively on the right. In addition a small detail attracts attention: the curve of the line coming from the robe of the left hand figure. Normally this line is vertical between the two figures but here the line curves back on itself like a letter 'S'. This seems not to be very spectacular, but it will reappear later in another connection.

Let us sum up the small details found so far on coins of uncertain origin: sceptres pointing to the wrong side, double lines, wrong letters, letters upside down, dots, wavy lines – each of them so unobtrusive that most of the coins seen so far would have been attributed to the mint we read on them. It is a tribute to Tony Goodwin that he identified this group in his Baalbek die study. In the discussion about the origin of these coins he cautiously suggests the possibility that the mint of Baalbek was closed and transferred to Damascus.[10] But there are serious doubts. Why should the mint of Damascus use these additional features described above? Why the pictures changed and decorations were added which are only known at Hims? Can we believe in Damascus as the minting place for 'Baalbek' and 'Damascus' coins with completely unusual designs?

Damascus – Hims – Baalbek – Damascus
Another example shows the particular problem of attribution even more clearly. In 1995 Oddy and Pavlou[11] published the following die link:

Figure 7

The authors classified these coins as 'irregular issues or barbarous copies' and stated 'that at least one irregular workshop was producing imitations of more than one mint'. What is wrong with these coins? A Hims bust type obverse and a Damascus style standing figure are linked by a confusing reverse: it has no mint name, but the capital **M** and probably a retrograde *ḍarb* on the left point to Damascus. In the exergue however we see the Arabic *ṭayyib*, exclusively used in Hims and on the rare Tartus coins and as a countermark on coins of Scythopolis and Gerasa. The obverses differ from their prototypes insofar as on the bust coin the usual **ΚΑΛΟΝ** is replaced by **ΚΛИ** with a horizontal **K** which we will see later again; the Damascus style standing figure obverse shows a prominent dot in the left field, and usually the palm branch is on the left of the staff and not under the arm.

---

[10] Goodwin (2005a) p. 61.
[11] Oddy and Pavlou (1995).

This die link can now be extended:

Figure 8

Another bust coin (figure 8a) from the same obverse die has come to light; the reverse shows a retrograde Ɛ.

But this is not all:

Figure 9

The standing figure obverse of figure 7 also occurs with two different reverses of Baalbek (coins 9b and 9c) and one of Damascus (coin 9d).

Even this is not all:

Figure 10

The most exciting discovery and finally the reason for this article was a coin (10c) with the same confusing reverse but a two standing figure obverse. On this obverse we see again the curved line going to the wrong side, which I already emphasized in the description of figure 6, here ending in a significant stroke between the two figures. Of course this two figure coin must be seen as the product of the same workshop as the bust and the one figure coins. This two figure obverse seems to be quite abundant as it occurs with a reverse in a blundered Damascus-Baalbek style (10b) as well as with at least five different Damascus reverses. An overall view of this extraordinary link makes the complexity obvious (see figure 11).

This link is a striking example of the dilemma with the classification of Phase 2 coins. Some of these are regarded as 'barbarous copies' as mentioned above, others found their way into the literature as regular coins of Baalbek (coin 11g)[12] and of Damascus (coins 11n and 11o)[13]. Can we believe in Baalbek and Damascus respectively as the mints with the evidence of this link? The answer must be: no.

We know of irregular coins for practically every mint, but it seems dangerous to designate every coin which shows more or less blundered legends or clumsy depictions as unofficial or barbarous, but it also seems dangerous to accept blundered legends as 'usual' and therefore as 'regular', as is the rule for Damascus coins.

Where is the origin of this Damascus–Hims–Baalbek link? Certainly not in one of the three official mints named on the coins. Even if some of the reverse dies could be regarded as regular (as they have been), all the obverses show elements that do not fit into the main series of each type: the wrong curved line, the horizontal **K**, and a dot and palm branch in an unusual position. The not (yet) linked bust coins in the lower right of figure 11 (coins 11p to 11r) feature the horizontal **K** and may be part of the group. We do not believe in any of the mint names as the place where this group was struck, but we should consider another possibility. Due to similar features it might be possible that a

---

[12] Foss (2008) no. 63.
[13] Walker (1956) no 42 Pl. IV and Goodwin (2005a) p. 37 no. 24.

greater part of the Damascus-Baalbek related coins do have the same origin as the linked group shown in figure 11.

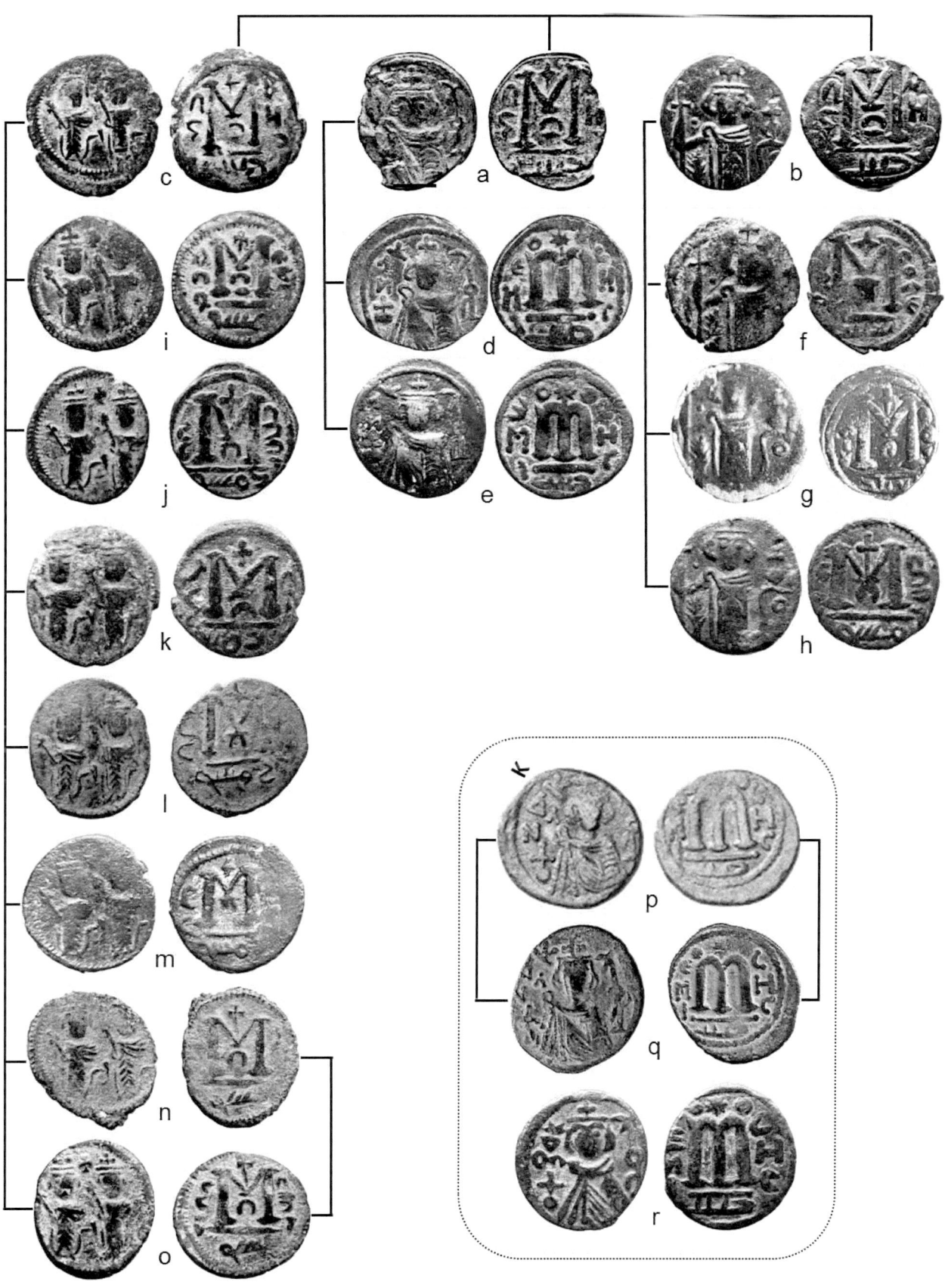

Figure 11

Tiberias – Damascus – Tiberias – Damascus

Another die link should be mentioned in this connection, originally found by Tony Goodwin and published by Marcus Phillips[14] and Wolfgang Schulze.[15]

Figure 12

This linkage between 'Damascus-' and 'Tiberias-looking' coins can now be extended by a three figure coin (12a).[16] These coins are extraordinary in style, weight and size and are not die-linked with the official coins of Tiberias and Damascus. Thus it is easy to follow the conclusion of Marcus Phillips that this is a special issue, struck neither in Tiberias nor in Damascus.[17]

So far we have seen three linked series:

1) Damascus–Baalbek
2) Damascus–Hims–Baalbek–Damascus
3) Tiberias–Damascus–Tiberias–Damascus

As already mentioned the assessments of these links in the literature are different: the first one is cautiously attributed to Damascus, the second one differs considerably between 'regular' and 'barbarous', the third one is regarded as a 'special issue'. I would like to plead that all coins shown in these linkages are 'special issues' which were not struck in the mint named on them, nor are they irregular/barbarous imitations. They all follow their own rules: pictures and legends of well-known coins from different mints were adapted and slightly modified with dots, wavy lines, double lines, turned letters etc. These additions would not have been used by an unofficial mint that hoped to pass its production off as 'official'. It seems that we are dealing with products of semi-official mints,[18] possibly controlled by local authorities. Consequently we are not dealing with die links between two or three mints, but only within the output of semi-official mints, which 'borrowed' elements of other mints. As there is a stylistic relation between links 1) and 2) concerning the two figure obverses with the wrong curved line it might even be that both link series are produced in the same semi-official mint. Further research and an extensive die study are needed to investigate this.

---

[14] Phillips (2010) p. 72.
[15] Schulze W. (2012) p. 138.
[16] Many thanks to Tony Goodwin who found this new connection and provided me with the information.
[17] Phillips (2010) p. 76.
[18] The possibility of semi-official mints was proposed by Lutz Ilisch, cf. SICA p. 85 fn. 30 and p. 86 fn. 34.

'Stylistic links'

Hims – Damascus

Beside die links there are also stylistic links, especially with elements of the coinage of Hims. In 1995, Tony Goodwin published an interesting coin with a Pseudo-Byzantine obverse and a blundered standing figure Hims reverse.[19] This coin connects Phases 1 and 2 of the Byzantine-Arab transitional coinage and was most likely struck in a mint which still struck Pseudo-Byzantine coins at a time when the official mint of Hims had started to produce standing figure coins.

Another example of stylistic relation is shown in figures 13 and 14 (coins a-d):

Figure 13

We see four obverses with a standing figure and **KAΛ-ON** either side with an integrated star. The main difference is that **O** and **N** changed their places on coin 13d. We expect these coins to be minted at Hims.

Figure 14

Surprisingly only on coins 14a to 14c can we read **ЄMH-CIC** for Emesa (Arabic *ḥimṣ*) while coin 14d shows **ΔAM** for Damascus in the exergue. The standing figure type of Hims with **KAΛON** on the obverse[20] is quite abundant; the Damascus coin with **KAΛON** on the obverse is extremely rare and to my knowledge only struck from this pair of dies. However, two details on the reverse of this coin are highly suspicious. The 'officina' **Δ** and crescent and star either side of the monogram are typical for Hims and some coins from Tartus[21]. As these features never occur on the Damascus main series we can be sure that this coin was not struck there.[22]

Back to the three Hims coins: coin 13/14c is also a little bit suspicious. The depiction of the figure and the clumsy letters with a retrograde **Є** do not quite fit in the main series of Hims. We have to wait for an extensive die study to clarify the status of this coin.[23]

---

[19] Goodwin (1995) no. 14; SICA p. 86 fn. 31.
[20] Oddy (2007) Class 1.
[21] Cf. Schulze W. (2013).
[22] Suggested to be irregular: SICA no. 563 and p. 86 fn. 33.
[23] Oddy (2007) p. 10.

Pseudo-Damascus – Hims

Also the Pseudo-Damascus mint(s) 'borrowed' elements from the coinage of Hims; here are some examples:

Figure 15

Coin 15a has a perfect Pseudo-Damascus obverse known with several reverse dies with m or M. This particular reverse die claims Hims as the mint. But we can exclude Hims as minting place for several reasons:

- The appearance of the figure has nothing to do with the one we are used to see on Hims coins.
- The combination of 'standing figure – cursive m' does not exist in the official mint of Hims.
- Dots between the uprights of the m never occur on official Hims coins.

In short: coin 15a is a Pseudo-Damascus coin imitating an irregular Hims reverse.

Coins 15b and 15c share the same obverse with a bird to the left and three tassels in the right field; the tassels indicate that we are NOT dealing with an official Damascus coin, although the reverse of 15b could pass off as an official Damascus reverse, 'blundered as usual'. The reverse of coin 15c, however, shows left of the M instead of *jā'iz* the Greek letters CHC which can be interpreted as part of ЄMЄ-CHC.[24] As these coins are not part of the official Damascus series, they must be either part of the Pseudo-Damascus series or the product of a semi-official mint, copying elements of Damascus, Pseudo-Damascus and Hims. Only a die study can possibly help to establish the origin of these coins.

Coins 15d and 15e are not die-linked, but here the reverses are very close in style and the dies were probably cut by the same hand. While coin 15d shows a nice standing figure in Pseudo-Damascus style, coin 15e looks irregular with traces of ЄMH-CIC either side of the figure.[25] It is hard to decide whether coins 15d and 15e were struck in the same mint or not.

Up to this point I have described some examples of adaptions of Hims elements on Pseudo-Damascus coins or semi-official coins, and the use of mint names which may mislead us.

---

[24] For the different spellings of ЄMЄCHC see Oddy (2007).
[25] A coin from the same obverse die but with a cursive m reverse was published by Goodwin (2005b, Cat. 23). In face of the crude reverse he believes that it is rather a late Phase 1 coin than a Phase 2 coin (p. 42). For another picture see CNG electronic auction 339 lot 456.

al-wafā lillāh and related coins

Figure 16 shows a combination of a die link and stylistic relationships. In my article about the *al-wafā lillāh* coins[26] I emphasised the stylistic relationships to other series. Here I can publish the first link from an *al-wafā lillāh* obverse (coin 16a) to one of the stylistically related series.[27] The new coin 16b is not yet die-linked to other series, but it shows a strong stylistic relationship to the 'lazy S' series (coin 16c), and from here we are stylistically not far from another enigmatic series (16d).[28] The *al-wafā lillāh* coin is in the collection of the Barber Institute, University of Birmingham, and is up to now unique. It is too early to draw any conclusions of the new link until the *al-wafā lillāh* part from the Irbid hoard has been published.[29]

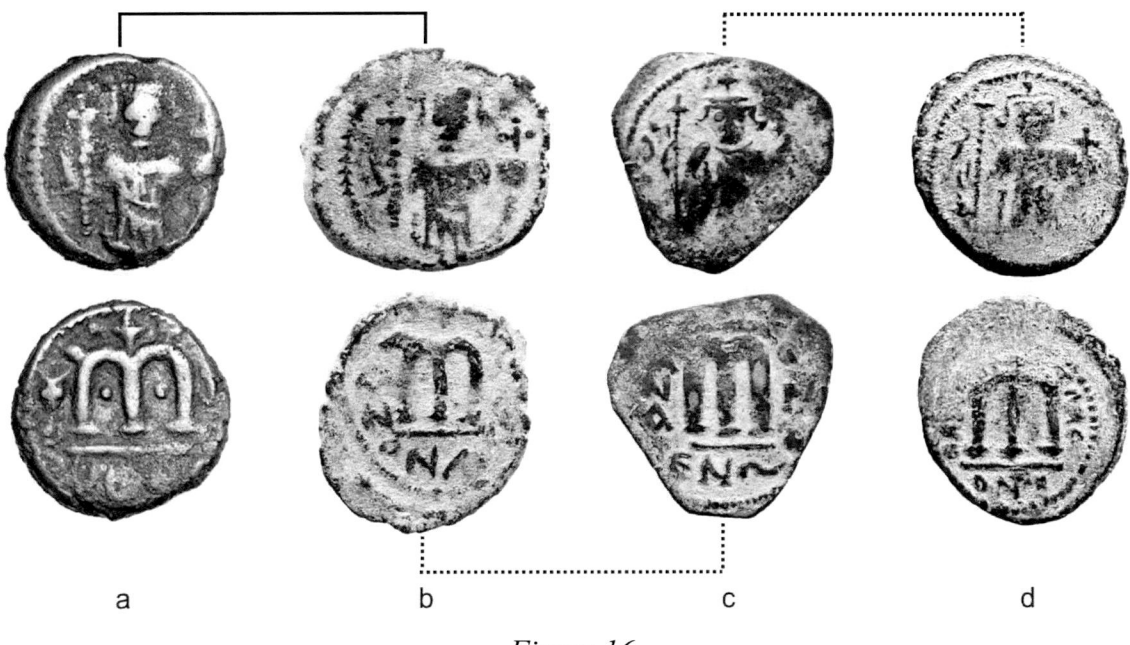

a　　　　　b　　　　　c　　　　　d

Figure 16

Mules?

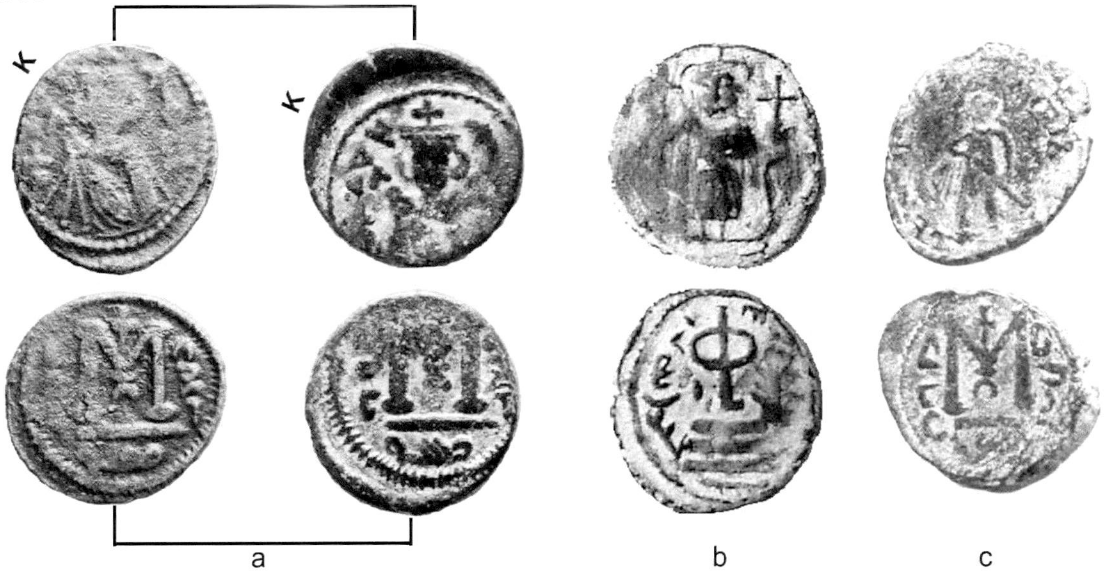

a　　　　　　　　　　　　b　　　　　　c
Hims/Damascus　　　　　Phase 1(2?)/Phase 3　Phase 3/Phase 2

Figure 17

---

[26] Schulze I. (2010a).
[27] Schulze I. (2010a) p. 118 fig. 12.
[28] Usually attributed to Tiberias. Cf. e. g. Meshorer (1966) or Qedar (1991).
[29] Goodwin and Gyselen, *The Irbid Hoard* (forthcoming).

Figure 17 shows mules which are coins made by using two dies which were not originally intended for each other. In this case they claim to be struck in different mints and phases of production.
But are these mules REAL mules?

The first two coins from the same pair of dies mixing a 'Hims bust' obverse with a Damascus reverse may be the product of a semi-official mint[30] where other coins with a Hims/Damascus relationship were struck because we see again the conspicuous 'horizontal **K**' (cf. above).
The other two coins are mixing obverse and reverse dies from different Phases. Coin 17b shows an obverse of Phase 1 or 2 and a Standing Caliph reverse (Phase 3). On coin 17c we see a Standing Caliph obverse and a Phase 2 reverse. At a first glance these coins seem to be the result of a turbulent transition phase in a single mint place. But until now no die links to the main series have been found, and the clearly irregular appearance of these coins makes it highly improbable that they are the result of an inadvertent mixing of dies in the official mint of Damascus and are thus to be regarded as semi-official or unofficial.[31]

Die links between different mints of Phase 3?

Qinnasrin – Aleppo – mintless (lillāh)
Now we enter Phase 3 of the Byzantine-Arab transitional coinage, the period of the Standing Caliph coins.

a
Qinnasrin

b
Aleppo

c
'lillah'

d
'lillah'

Figure 18

The problem illustrated here is close to that of figure 2 with the Baalbek-Damascus related coins: We would attribute the first coin (18a) without doubt to Qinnasrin and the second one (18b) to Aleppo, if we were not aware that both share the same obverse die. It is the third coin (18c) which makes this group even more dubious: instead of a mint name we see *lillāh*. This legend, the fact that all three coins have extreme low weights of less than 2g, and the very unusual depiction of the caliph's figure and his robe, makes them candidates for a semi-official or unofficial mint, although the inscriptions are complete and correct.[32] The last coin (18d) is not die-linked to the group, but here too we see only *lillāh* instead of a mint name; the style is very crude.[33]

---

[30] SICA p. 85 fn. 30 and p. 86 fn. 34.
[31] This is in contrast to Ramadan (2010a).
[32] This is in contrast to Goodwin (2013).
[33] For more die links of Phase 3 coins in the Jund Qinnasrin cf. Goodwin (2010) and Schulze W. (forthcoming).

Mintless – Manbij

Figure 19

In contrast to the previous example, in this linked group (figure 19) everything is wrong: the inscriptions are defective and partly retrograde, the depiction of the figures crude and clumsy, and there is no mint name on the reverses of 19a to 19d. Only on coin 19e can we read *manbij*. Most probably we are dealing with unofficial coins.

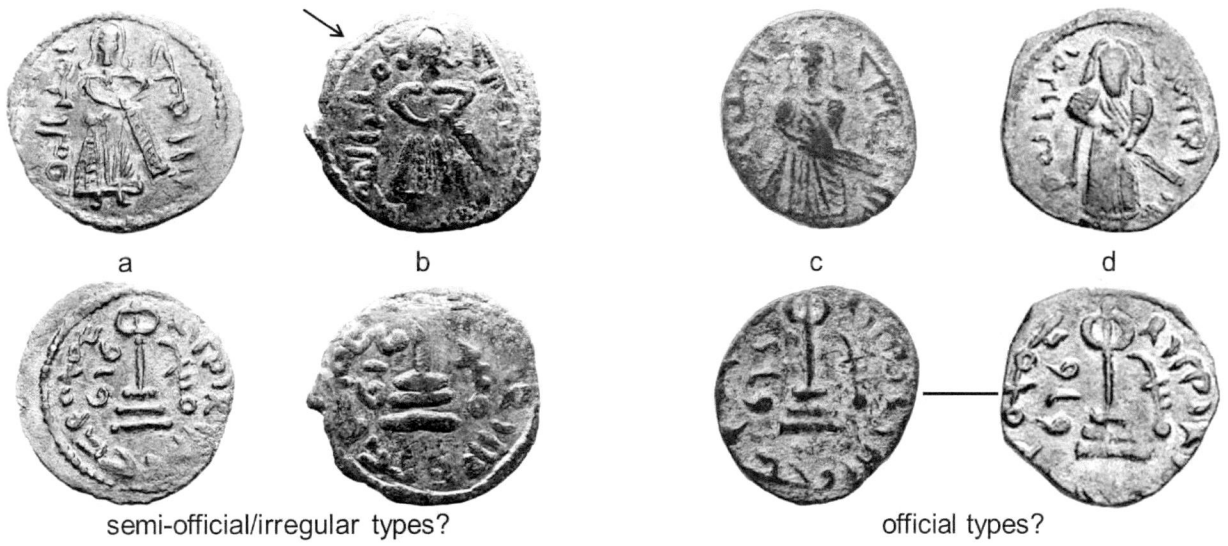

Figure 20

There is no doubt that the prototype of the extremely blundered series (figure 19) is a Manbij coin, for example the well-known Manbij obverse from the cover of the 2nd edition of Album's checklist (coin 20a). We know of only two obverse dies depicting the caliph in this very special and unusual way concerning the pattern of the robe and especially the position of the arms. In addition coin 20b shows the caliph with a curious hairstyle and a spelling mistake: the connection of the first two letters *alif* and *mim* (arrowed in figure 20). In the numismatic literature these coins 20a and 20b are unanimously described as official. However, considering their unusual appearance described above their official status must be called into question and I cautiously want to ask whether already these coins are products of either a semi-official mint or of an irregular mint. It might be that only coins 20c and 20d with a perfectly normal appearance of the caliph are the official ones. On the other hand the specimens presented in figures 19 and 20 are just some examples of a more complex problem than described so far. In private collections and FINT[34] there are a lot of more coins of the groups mentioned in figures 19 and 20. Among these there are even links between coin figure 20d and Ma'arrat Misrin coins.[35] An extensive die study is necessary to shed light on this problem.

Mintless – Amman

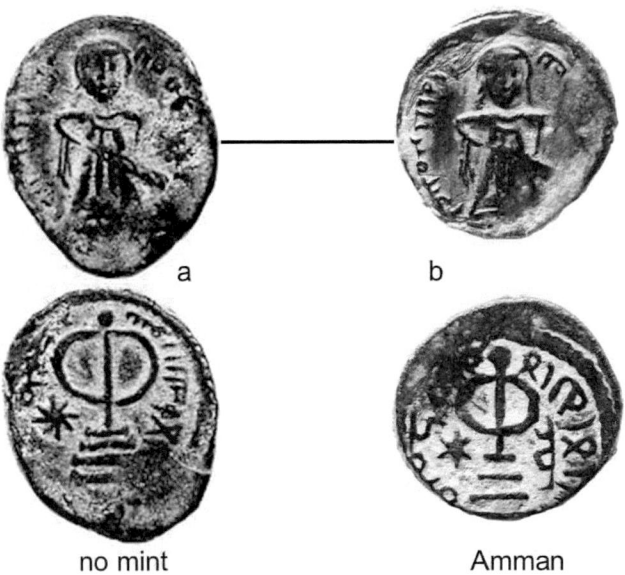

Figure 21

Moving South to Amman there are these two coins that have already been published by Tareq Ramadan.[36] Unfortunately he did not realize that both share the same obverse die. On the first coin, without mint name, the legend of the reverse starts at the unusual position of 4 o'clock, while the reverse of the second coin looks quite normal. The question of special interest should be, whether this reverse die is linked with other coins of Amman. The answer is given by the star: this one is only six-pointed, while on all coins of the official mint the star is eight-pointed. Thus, this pair seems not to be part of the official coinage of Amman.

Mintless – Damascus

Figure 22

---

[34] Forschungsstelle für islamische Numismatik, Tübingen.
[35] Thanks to Tony Goodwin for this hint and providing me with pictures.
[36] Ramadan (2011).

Here we have a similar link: the same obverse die, one reverse without mint name but a star instead and one reverse with *dimashq*. The legends are heavily blundered and the overall appearance unofficial.[37][38]

Damascus – Filastin

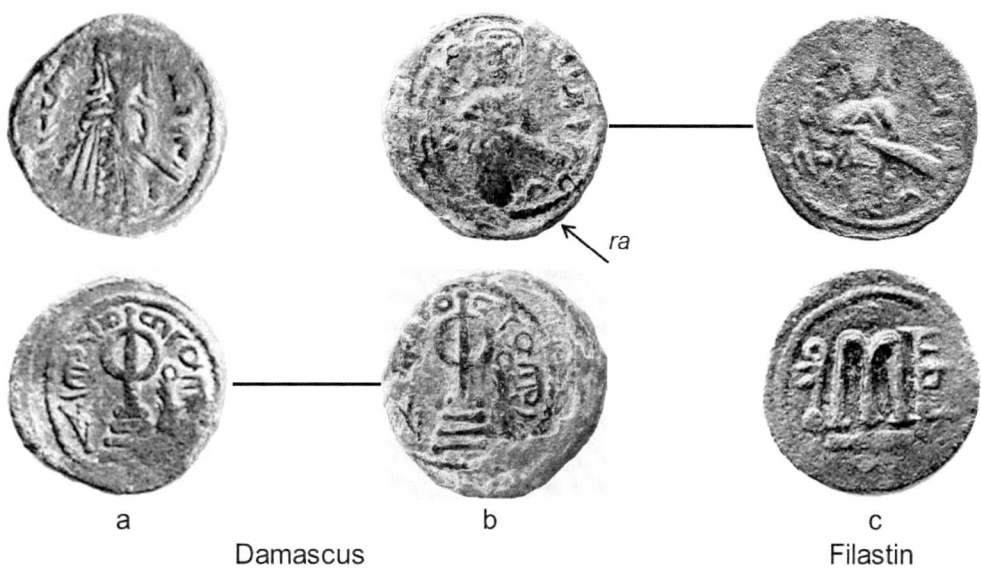

a
Damascus

b

c
Filastin

Figure 23

In this connection I have to come back to the die link that I have already published in the ONS Journal.[39] Nevertheless I would like to show it again in a compressed version, because it might have far-reaching consequences. In the literature the coin to the left (23a) with a completely blundered *shahāda* on the reverse is listed as a normal and regular coin of Damascus, connected by links or by style to the greatest part of the Standing Caliph coins of Damascus. The link shown here leads us to a Filastin looking obverse (23b) with the inscription *muḥammad rasūl allāh*, and finally this one is linked with a reverse in Filastin style with the cursive m, *filasṭīn* to the right and an undeciphered word to the left (23c). The most striking detail on the obverse is the position of the *ra*: on all other standing caliph coins from the jund Filastin the *ra* is on the left side. The last two coins must be attributed to an irregular mint, and consequently most of the coins of Damascus hitherto considered as regular become suspicious and may be products of this irregular mint. If we do not believe this – as Nikolaus Schindel does in a recent article[40] – we have to accept that in contrast to other small mints, the staff in the mint of the Umayyad capital was unable to write the *shahāda* without mistakes, at a time when the new coin type, the Standing caliph, was introduced by 'Abd al-Malik to demonstrate piety. It seems rather improbable that he would have accepted these coins. Or did he never see the products of his mint? I think the discussion of this topic will go on.

Īliyā – lillāh – Aylah/Allāh

Finally my last example of a curious die link:

On figure 24 we see six obverses of a standing caliph coin. Two small details prove that they all are struck from the same die: a faint line going diagonally upwards from the left eye and an unorthodox horizontal line beside the head (arrowed), which is possibly a die crack. Highly interesting are the

---

[37] Already published by Schulze I. (2010b) fig. 4 (obverses on p. 3, reverses on p. 4).
[38] Schindel (2013) and following him Goodwin (2013) speculate that the important mint name is missing because of lacking space and tend to attribute such coins as official.
[39] Schulze I. (2010b) fig. 10.
[40] Schindel (2013).

reverses (fig. 25). The first two pairs (25a and b, 25c and d) show the expected *īliyā filasṭīn* in different positions. The last two reverses to the right (25e and f) are enigmatic. They are from the same die and nevertheless different!

The upper coin (25e) appeared on the market in 2011 and shows to the left the word *lillāh*. On the coin below (25f) we see in the same position an additional stroke. This word is since 1985[41] interpreted as Aylah, the city on the Red Sea (now called Eilat).

Figure 24

Figure 25

Fortunately the *lillāh* coin was harshly cleaned and re-patinated. We are able to see the detailed work of an unskilled die-cutter; he was not able to cut a well-proportioned star, he was not able to

---

[41] Bank Leu, Zurich, auction 36, May 1985, lot 473.

cut a proper border, and he was not sure what to write on the left side; his first attempt was modified by an additional stroke. Thus the die above (25e) is the predecessor of the lower one (25f).

If the unorthodox line beside the head on the obverse is a die crack, we see no alteration to the obverse die. This means that all the reverse dies must have been in use at the same time in Jerusalem. Thus it is not surprising that the number of surviving specimens – apart from the *lillāh* coin – is similar for each reverse die (see the numbers in brackets in figure 25).

How can we interpret the *lillāh – aylah* phenomenon? We do not know what the unskilled die cutter had in mind. His first attempt *lillāh* was modified by an additional stroke, and the new word can be read as *aylah*, but just as well as *allāh*. This interpretation had already been suggested by Tony Goodwin[42] before the *lillāh* coin (25e) was known. In the light of the demonstrated change of the inscription on the same die, the interpretation of the word in question as *aylah* must be abandoned in favour of *allāh*, because the modification from *lillāh* to *allāh* seems to be the most probable.[43]

Conclusions

At the end of the discussion of enigmatic die links and puzzling coins I illustrate again the five Phase 2 reverses shown in figure 1, but now supplemented with the information indicating to which series they belong.

coin 8b   coin 12e   coin 9d   coin 2c   coin 9b

Figure 26

All these reverses are part of linked series, presumably struck in semi-official mints. A similar observation possibly goes for some of Phase 3 Standing Caliph coins (e.g. figures 18 and 20). Some of the specimens presented here might be irregular, but none of them were struck in the mint that is named on them.

As a consequence of this discussion we can tentatively say 'never believe at a first glance in the mint name which is written on an early Umayyad coin'.

It is a sort of modern reflex to believe in an efficient bureaucratic machinery. Not surprisingly, this was not the case in seventh century Syria. It is remarkable that the semi-official mint(s) link coins not only with different mint signatures but even from different *junds*, namely Dimashq, Hims and al-Urdunn, where curiously the most prolific mints of Phase 2 were located. Thus the suggestion of Lutz Ilisch to locate semi-official mints in *jund* Qinnasrin with no mints producing Phase 2 coins seems very attractive, although there is as yet no evidence from finds.[44] At least Ilisch's proposal is supported by the fact that by example none of the dies in figure 11 is represented in the Irbid hoard.[45]

---

[42] Goodwin (2005a) p. 94 fn. 17.
[43] In contrast to this: Ramadan (2010a). For the uncertainty in attribution see Album (2011) no. 3545A and p. 45 fn. 107.
[44] SICA p. 85 fn. 30.
[45] Thanks to Tony Goodwin for this tentative information.

Before speculating about number and location of semi-official mints we need a new basis for a differentiation within the Phase 2 coinage. Extensive die studies with attention to additional details and stylistic relationships need to be done. And we have to take another necessary step: we must stop applying double standards when judging a coin as official or unofficial. For example, if on a Hims coin we see a wrong letter, we are inclined to attribute it to an unofficial or irregular series. On the contrary we are used to describing *official* Damascus coins as 'blundered'. This double standard is dangerous and can lead us astray.

I propose to classify the Phase 2 and 3 copper coins of seventh century Syria into three groups:

1. Official coins looking correct – occasionally with minor faults in the die cutting – and not die linked to suspicious coins.

2. Semi-official coins, presumably struck by local authorities to avoid a lack of cash. These coins are produced to a high standard, but show by distinctive symbols clear differences from the official prototypes.[46] In other words, they indicate themselves as semi-official.

3. Unofficial/irregular/barbarous coins. These are those with senseless inscriptions or wrong depictions, presumably made by unskilled workers for private profit – probably contemporary forgeries.

The proposed subdivision is difficult. The prerequisite for a more detailed classification is to look at a lot of coins – not only from one mint – searching for die links, additional details and – what becomes more and more important – for stylistic relationships.

Bibliography

Proceedings 1	*Coinage and History in the Seventh Century Near East*. Papers from the Seventh Century Syrian Numismatic Round Table 2007 (held at the Barber Institute of Fine Arts, University of Birmingham on May 26th and 27th 2007), Supplement to JONS 193 (2007).
Proceedings 2	*Coinage and History in the Seventh Century Near East 2* (A. Oddy, ed.). Proceedings of the 12th Seventh Century Syrian Numismatic Round Table held at Gonville and Caius College, Cambridge on 4th and 5th April 2009 (London 2010).
Proceedings 3	*Arab-Byzantine Coins and History* (T. Goodwin ed.). Papers presented at the Seventh Century Syrian Numismatic Round Table held at Corpus Christi College, Oxford on 10th and 11th September 2011 (London 2012).
Album (2011)	S. Album, *Checklist of Islamic Coins*³ (Santa Rosa 2011).
Berman (1976)	A. Berman, *Islamic coins*, Exhibition Winter 1976 L. A. Mayer Memorial Institute for Islamic Art (Jerusalem 1976).
Bauden (2011)	F. Bauden, *Catalogo delle monete islamiche del Museo Bottacin*, Quaderni del Bolletino del Museo civico di Padova 9 (Padova 2011).
Foss (2008)	C. Foss, *Arab-Byzantine Coins, an introduction, with a catalogue of the Dumbarton Oaks Collection* (Washington D.C. 2008).
Goodwin (1995)	T. Goodwin, '7th Century Arab Imitations of Byzantine Folles', *NCirc* (1995) p. 336 f.

---

[46] The idea that small details like stars, dots, crescents and others might be helpful to form groups and find different mint places is not new: it was already suggested by Lutz Ilisch (2010) for post-reform fulus.

Goodwin (2005a)	T. Goodwin, ***Arab-Byzantine Coinage***, Studies in the Khalili Collection, vol. 4 (London 2005).
Goodwin (2005b)	T. Goodwin, 'Countermarks from after the Arab Conquest', in: W. Schulze and T. Goodwin, Countermarking in Seventh Century Syria, ***Supplement to ONS Newsletter 183 (2005)***, pp. 41-54.
Goodwin (2010)	T. Goodwin, 'Die Links between Standing Caliph Mints in Jund Qinnasrin', ***Proceedings 2***, pp. 35-40.
Goodwin (2013)	T. Goodwin, Two more Standing Caliph Fulus without Mint Name, ***JONS*** 217 (2013) p. 7.
Ilisch (2010)	L. Ilisch, Lutz, 'Abd al-Malik's Monetary Reform in Copper and the Failure of Centralization', ***Money, Power and Politics in Early Islamic Syria – A review of current debates***, J. Haldon ed. (Farnham 2010) pp. 125-146.
Meshorer (1966)	Y. Meshorer, 'An enigmatic Arab-Byzantine Coin', ***Israel Numismatic Journal***, vol. 3 (1965-66), pp. 32-36.
Oddy (2007)	A. Oddy, 'The "Standing Emperor" Coinage of Emesa/Hims', ***Proceedings 1***, pp. 8-11.
Oddy and Pavlou (1995)	A. Oddy and P. Pavlou, 'A Barbarous Bronze from seventh Century Syria', ***ONSN*** 145, (1995), p. 3.
Qedar (1991)	S. Qedar, 'Copper Coinage of Syria in the Seventh and Eighth Century A. D.', ***Israel Numismatic Journal***, vol. 10 (1988-89), (Jerusalem 1991), pp. 27-39.
Phillips (2010)	M. Phillips, 'The Single Standing Figure Type of Tiberias/Tabariya', ***Proceedings 2***, pp. 61-77.
Ramadan (2010a)	T. Ramadan, 'The Standing Caliph Coins of Aylah-Filastin', ***JONS*** 203 (2010), pp. 3-6.
Ramadan (2010b)	T. Ramadan, 'A rare Arab-Byzantine Hybrid Coin of Damascus: An intriguing "Mule" bearing a Standing Emperor Obverse and a sphere through Pole-on-steps Reverse', ***JONS*** 203 (2010), p. 43 f.
Ramadan (2011)	T. Ramadan, 'A brief note on a "skinny" Standing Caliph Arab-Byzantine coin presumably from Amman', ***JONS*** 209 (2011), p.13 f.
Schindel (2013)	N. Schindel, 'A "standing caliph" fals without mint name', ***JONS*** 216 (2013), p. 7 f.
Schulze and Oddy (2012)	W. Schulze and A. Oddy, 'Terminology for the Transitional Coinage struck in 7th Century Syria after the Arab Conquest', ***Proceedings 3***, pp. 187-200.
Schulze I. (2010a)	I. Schulze, 'The *al-wafā lillāh* Coinage: A study of style (work in Progress', ***Proceedings 2***, pp. 111-121.
Schulze I. (2010b)	I. Schulze, 'The Standing Caliph Coins of Damascus: New Die Links – New Questions', ***JONS*** 204 (2010), pp. 3-6.
Schulze W. (2012)	W. Schulze, ' The Syrian "orans figure" copper coins', ***Proceedings 3***, pp. 131-144.
Schulze W. (2013)	W. Schulze, 'The Byzantine-Arab Transitional Coinage of Ṭarṭūs', ***NC*** 173 (2013), pp. 245-259.
Schulze W. (forthcoming)	W. Schulze, 'The Standing Caliph coins with the mint name Qūrus' (forthcoming).
SICA	S. Album and T. Goodwin, ***Sylloge of Islamic coins in the Ashmolean, Vol. 1, The Pre-Reform Coinage of the early Islamic Period*** (Oxford 2002).
Walker (1956)	J. Walker, ***A Catalogue of the Arab-Byzantine and Post-Reform Umaiyad coins*** (London 1956).

Details of coins illustrated

Fig.	Weight	Source
Fig. 2a	4.09g	Priv. coll.
Fig. 2b	4.95g	Priv. coll.
Fig. 2c	4.06g	Priv. coll.
Fig. 2d	5.81g	Priv. coll.
Fig. 2e	5.57g	Baldwin's Islamic coin auction 9 (2004), lot 3046
Fig. 3a	5.16g	Priv. coll.
Fig. 3b	4.60g	Priv. coll.
Fig. 3c	–	Trade
Fig. 4a	4.25g	Priv. coll.
Fig. 4b	3.84g	Priv. coll.
Fig. 4c	3.18g	Priv. coll.
Fig. 4d	3.39g	Priv. coll.
Fig. 5a	4.05g	Priv. coll.
Fig. 5b	–	Trade
Fig. 6a	5.1g	Trade
Fig. 6b	3.55g	Priv. coll.
Fig. 7 → Fig. 11		
Fig. 8 → Fig. 11		
Fig. 9 → Fig. 11		
Fig. 10 → Fig. 11		
Fig. 11a	3.7g	Baldwin's Islamic coin auction 24 (2013), ex lot 4068
Fig. 11b	4.41g	Priv. coll.
Fig. 11c	3.43g	Priv. coll.
Fig. 11d	2.98g	Album auction 10 (2011), lot 207
Fig. 11e	3.54g	Priv. coll.
Fig. 11f	2.33g	Priv. coll.
Fig. 11g	3.06g	Foss (2008), no. 63
Fig. 11h	3.01g	Priv. coll.
Fig. 11i	2.78g	Priv. coll.
Fig. 11j	3.19g	Priv. coll.
Fig. 11k	2.78g	Priv. coll.
Fig. 11l	3.27g	Priv. coll.
Fig. 11m	3.00g	Priv. coll.
Fig. 11n	3.48g	Baldwin's Islamic coin auction 24 (2013), ex lot 4062
Fig. 11o	3.01g	Trade
Fig. 11p	3.35g	Künker, auction 137 (2008), lot 4066
Fig. 11q	3.06g	Priv. coll.
Fig. 11r	3.40g	Priv. coll.
Fig. 12a	5.22g	Priv. coll.
Fig. 12b	5.36g	Berman (1976), no.13 (ex Slocum collection)
Fig. 12c	6.91g	Goodwin and Gyselen, The Irbid Hoard (forthcoming), 498
Fig. 12d	–	Stack's New York auction 14 (1999), lot 452
Fig. 12e	–	Ex Slocum collection
Fig. 12f	4.26g	Priv. coll.
Fig. 13/14a	4.03g	Priv. coll.
Fig. 13/14b	3.29g	Priv. coll.
Fig. 13/14c	–	Trade
Fig. 13/14d	5.09g	Priv. coll.
Fig. 15a	3.80g	Trade 2005 = Album auction 19 (2014), lot 244
Fig. 15b	2.82g	Priv. coll.

Fig. 15c	3.48g	Priv. coll.
Fig. 15d	5.25g	Priv. coll.
Fig. 15e	4.61g	Bauden (2011), no.1
Fig. 16a	3.84g	Barber Institute of Fine Arts, Birmingham, AB 45
Fig. 16b	4.38g	Priv. coll.
Fig. 16c	2.47g	Priv. coll.
Fig. 16d	–	Trade
Fig. 17a/1	3.65g	Priv. coll.
Fig. 17a/2	4.56g	FINT, LI-185
Fig. 17b	–	Priv. coll.
Fig. 17c	–	Trade
Fig. 18a	1.93g	Priv. coll.
Fig. 18b	1.42g	Baldwin's Islamic coin auction 9 (2004), lot 3162
Fig. 18c	2.03g	Priv. coll.
Fig. 18d	3.97g	FINT, 2006-7-14
Fig. 19a	2.37g	Priv. coll.
Fig. 19b	2.25g	Priv. coll.
Fig. 19c	2.50g	Priv. coll.
Fig. 19d	3.47g	ANS, 1998.25.82
Fig. 19e	2.49g	ANS, 1998.25.54
Fig. 20a	3.40g	CNG auction 79 (2008), lot 1350
Fig. 20b	2.77g	Priv. coll.
Fig. 20c	3.11g	Priv. coll.
Fig. 20d	3.08g	Künker, auction 137 (2008), lot 4070
Fig. 21a	3.4g	Ramadan (2011), p.13
Fig. 21b	2.97g	Priv. coll.
Fig. 22a	2.91g	Priv. coll.
Fig. 22b	2.95g	Priv. coll.
Fig. 23a	3.55g	Priv. coll.
Fig. 23b	2.46g	Priv. coll.
Fig. 23c	2.61g	Priv. coll.
Fig. 24/25a	3.15g	Bank Leu, auction 56 (1992), lot 15
Fig. 24/25b	3.16g	Priv. coll.
Fig. 24/25c	3.31g	Sternberg, auction 8 (1978), lot 1014
Fig. 24/25d	3.01g	Priv. coll.
Fig. 24/25e	3.06g	Gemini auction VII (2011), lot 1069
Fig. 24/25f	–	Ramadan (2010a), p. 4

Notes on Two Imperial Image Obverse Types:
The Falconer and the Seated Couple

David Woods [1]

Introduction

The purpose of this paper is to re-examine the origin and significance of the main images on two well known obverse types from the so-called Imperial Image phase of Arab-Byzantine coinage: first, the so-called falconer on the obverse of a group of coins conventionally attributed to the pseudo-Damascus mint and, second, the seated couple on the obverse of coins from the mints of Scythopolis and Gerasa.[2] It is my argument that one cannot properly understand the image on either type without fuller attention to the rich artistic and cultural environment within which they were struck, and that those who sanctioned or engraved these coins did not work in cultural isolation or focus solely upon the current or recent coin types from the Byzantine empire, but were open to older classical influences from a variety of media. These influences may have significantly affected how they adapted current or recent coin types or, even when there was little or no adaptation, re-interpreted them nonetheless. Curiously, this principle has been well observed in recent efforts to explore the significance of the bar or globe on a pole on steps as normally depicted on the reverse of coins of the so-called Standing Caliph type, but the same broad-minded and flexible approach has been noticeably absent in considering the significance of these other types.[3]

The Falconer

There is a great deal of variety in the depiction of the alleged falconer from one die to the next within this group of coins, but they generally agree in depicting a single figure standing face forward with a long cross in his right hand and a bird perched near the end of his outstretched left arm.[4] On some dies, he is depicted with a chlamys and robes descending freely down his body (Fig. 1a). On other dies, he is depicted without a chlamys and belted tightly about his waist so that his lower tunic flares out like a skirt (Fig. 1b). It is clear, therefore, that this figure was re-interpreted at least once and adapted accordingly. I will refer to these figures as the cloaked and belted figures

---

[1] David Woods is Senior Lecturer and Head of the Department of Ancient Classics, University College Cork, Ireland: d.woods@ucc.ie

[2] S. Album and T. Goodwin, *Sylloge of Islamic Coins in the Ashmolean 1: The Pre-Reform Coinage of the Early Islamic Period* (Oxford, 2002) [*SICA 1* henceforth], pp. 82-84, identify ten different obverse types within the Imperial Image series. The obverse types under discussion here correspond to their types 'IX. 'Hunting Figure'' and 'I. Justin and Sophia' respectively. For the most detailed argument in support of the identification of this 'hunting figure' as a falconer, see A. Oddy, 'Arab Imagery on Early Umayyad Coins in Syria and Palestine: Evidence for Falconry', *Numismatic Chronicle* 151 (1991), pp. 59-66.

[3] For efforts to explain the bar or globe on a pole on steps in terms of the Arab understanding of the universe, or of traditional Semitic astral symbolism, or of the classical architectural heritage (Roman monumental columns), see N. Jamil, 'Caliph and *Quṭb*. Poetry as a Source for Interpreting the Transformation of the Byzantine Cross on Steps on Umayyad Coinage', in J. Johns (ed.), *Bayt al-Maqdis: Jerusalem and Early Islam*, Oxford Studies in Islamic Art IX (Oxford, 1999), pp. 11-57; W. Schulze, 'Symbolism on the Syrian Standing Caliph Copper Coins: A Contribution to the Discussion', in A. Oddy (ed.), *Coinage and History in the Seventh Century Near East 2* (London, 2010) [*CHSC 2* henceforth], pp. 11-21; S. Heidemann, 'The Standing Caliph Type – The Object on the Reverse', in *CHSC 2*, pp. 23-34.

[4] For a collection of obverse dies at x1.5 - 2 actual size, see A. Oddy, 'Symbolism and Design on the Early Umayyad Coinage', in T. Goodwin, *Arab-Byzantine Coins and History* (London, 2012), p. 109-23, at p. 111, Fig. 1.

Figure 1a: 'the cloaked figure'   *Figure 1b: 'the belted figure'*

respectively. Here one should note two important differences between the cloaked and belted figures.[5] First, the bird stands upon an orb when depicted in association with the cloaked figure, but directly upon the hand or wrist of the belted figure. Secondly, the left arm is not explicitly depicted in the case of the cloaked figure, so that the orb with bird seems to be hovering in mid-air. It is clear, from the context, however, that an arm has to be understood. In contrast, the left arm is always very clearly depicted in the case of the belted figure.

Since no Byzantine coin depicts an emperor standing with a long cross in one hand and a bird in the other, it is clear that the originator of this basic type did not base it directly on one Byzantine coin. Consequently, two explanations have been offered as to the origin of this type. First, Oddy explained it as a development of an Imperial Image type produced at Damascus (Fig. 2).[6]

Figure 2

This type depicts a single figure standing face forward with a long cross in his right hand and a *globus cruciger* in his left hand. However, it also depicts what seems to be a large bird perched on a T-shaped stand in the field immediately to the left of the figure. Oddy argues that the originator of the type at the pseudo-Damascus mint simply transferred the bird from the stand besides the figure in the original Damascus type to the figure's left hand in his new type. The assumption is that both types depict a falcon, but with the standing figure in a slightly different pose in each case. In contrast, Schindel and Hahn offer a more complex explanation.[7] They argue that the originator of the type at the pseudo-Damascus mint derived the main standing figure from the depiction of the senior emperor from among a pair of emperors depicted either on a type of follis (Class 5) issued under Heraclius during the period c.629-40 (Fig. 3) or on a type (Class 8) issued under Constans II

---

[5] I identify A. Oddy, 'Symbolism and Design on the Early Umayyad Coinage', in T. Goodwin, *Arab-Byzantine Coins and History* (London, 2012), Fig. 1, nos 5-6, as clear examples of what I am calling 'cloaked figures' and nos 1, 2, 7, 8, 13, 14 as clear examples of what I am calling 'belted figures'. Other dies seem to represent intermediate stages in the evolution from one type to the next. Hence Fig. 1, nos 3-4, seem to retain cloaks despite their belted appearance otherwise.

[6] Oddy, 'Arab Imagery on Early Umayyad Coins in Syria and Palestine: Evidence for Falconry', *Numismatic Chronicle* 151 (1991). He defends this interpretation in his 'Symbolism and Design on the Early Umayyad Coinage', in T. Goodwin, *Arab-Byzantine Coins and History* (London, 2012), pp. 109-110.

[7] N. Schindel and W. Hahn, 'Notes on Two Arab-Byzantine Coin Types from Seventh Century Syria', *Numismatic Chronicle* 170 (2010), pp. 321-30.

during the period c.655-58 (Fig. 4).[8] They then argue that he decided to add a bird to this figure's left hand on the basis of a misunderstanding of a Victoriola depicted in the left hand of Heraclius on types of silver miliaresia issued c.620-29 (Fig. 5).[9]

Figure 3

Figure 4   *Figure 5*

Neither explanation convinces in full, but that by Schindel and Hahn is by far the weaker. They effectively ignore the occurrence of the cloaked figure with orb with bird (Fig.1a), and focus solely on a small number of specimens within the belted figure type where some head, or head-like object, seems to occur beneath the figure's left arm (Fig 1b). This naturally leads them to seek the origin of this type in some Byzantine type depicting two heads, that is, two figures alongside each other, but this is not hard to find in a period of Byzantine history when joint-rule of some sort was the norm. Furthermore, there is little real similarity between even the belted figure (Fig 1b) and the figure of the senior emperor in military dress on the two types of follis of Heraclius and Constans (Figs. 3 and 4), since the belted figure stretches his left arm well out from his body as he supports the bird, but the senior emperor on these folles holds his left arm akimbo. Nevertheless, the key point here is that the alleged 'severed head' coins only form a small sub-type within the standing figure with bird type, and their origin cannot be properly investigated except in the context of the other sub-types within this larger group also. As Oddy highlights, other coins seem to depict a bag hanging beneath the left arm rather than any sort of head or bust, and there must be a strong suspicion that the heads or busts result from a misinterpretation of this bag.[10]

The strength of Oddy's argument lies in its relative simplicity and in the fact that the engravers in the so-called pseudo-Damascus mint did imitate the coinage of the Damascus mint, which is why their mint has been so named. Indeed, the cloaked figure with the strangely hovering orb (Fig. 1a) clearly derives directly from the emperor with orb as depicted on the Damascus type with the bird to the left (Fig. 2). This type depicts the emperor holding the orb so close to his chest that only the

---

[8] For these two types of follis, see P. Grierson, ***Catalogue of the Byzantine Coins in the Dumbarton Oaks Collection 2: Phocas to Theodosius III, 602-717*** (Washington, D.C., 1968) [***DOC 2*** henceforth], pp. 295-300 and 454-55 respectively.
[9] Grierson, ***DOC 2***, p. 269.
[10] Oddy, 'Arab Imagery on Early Umayyad Coins in Syria and Palestine: Evidence for Falconry', ***Numismatic Chronicle*** 151 (1991), p. 61; id., 'Symbolism and Design on the Early Umayyad Coinage', in T. Goodwin, ***Arab-Byzantine Coins and History*** (London, 2012), p. 110.

left shoulder is visible, as in the Byzantine original, but at the pseudo-Damascus mint the orb slowly drifts away from the emperor's body until the point where someone finally felt the need to add the depiction of a left arm also. However, Oddy's argument also suffers from some serious weaknesses. First, it is not clear that the bird depicted perched on the apparent T-shaped stand on the issues from Damascus is in fact a falcon. It may have been intended to represent any of a large variety of birds from a Roman imperial eagle, although this had normally been depicted with open wings, or a Christian dove, to some bird native to Damascus or its greater environs.[11] The key factor leading Oddy to identify it as a falcon is the fact that it appears to be perched on a stand such as was typically used in falconry, although a variety of other domesticated or pet birds could have been depicted with a similar stand. However, as he helpfully catalogues, the same T-shaped object also occurs in association with two other objects, or combination of objects, on obverses associated with reverses bearing the Damascus mint mark in Greek, and in association with six other objects, or groups of objects, on obverses associated with reverses bearing the mint mark in Arabic.[12] This proves that there is no intrinsic connection between the bird, whatever its identity, and the T-shaped object beneath it. Indeed, it is worth noting that the pseudo-Damascus mint also produced a close imitation of this type, but without the T-shaped object beneath the bird (Fig. 6).[13]

Figure 6: Pseudo-Damascus Fals (© CNG, Inc.)

More importantly, the fact that the bird seems to have been but one of a series of variable symbols – including palm-branch, star, and crescent – used in the field to the side of the main image suggests that its real purpose was to distinguish one batch of product from another batch of product in the manner of the issue marks on the Roman coinage of the late third and fourth centuries AD. Hence there is no intrinsic connection between the bird and the main image, the standing figure. It was an engraver in the pseudo-Damascus mint who first made this connection when he decided to place the bird on the left hand of the standing figure instead.

A second weakness in Oddy's argument is that he does not distinguish properly between the cloaked figure with bird (Fig. 1a) and the belted figure with bird (Fig. 1b). These seem to represent two different stages of development in the depiction of this figure, and need to be treated separately. In the case of the belted figure, Oddy is probably correct to argue that he represents a falconer. The change from the ceremonial to the more utilitarian clothing supports this interpretation. More importantly, the fact that some dies depict the belted figure with a staff or a spear in his right hand rather than a large cross seems to confirm that he had indeed come to be understood as a hunter by

---

[11] For an example of the continued use of the eagle as an imperial symbol into the mid-seventh century, see W. Schulze, 'The Byzantine 'Eagle' Countermark – Re-attributed from Egypt to Palestine', *Israel Numismatic Research* 4 (2009), pp. 113-20, attributing the use of the eagle counter-mark to the besieged Byzantine defenders of Caesarea in Palestine c.637-40. It may not be irrelevant that the insignia of the *dux Arabiae* in the *Notitia Dignitatum*, dated c.400, includes two large birds, probably identifiable as ibises. See O. Seeck, ***Notitia Dignitatum. Accedunt Notitia Urbis Constantinopolitanae et Latercula Provinciarum*** (Berlin, 1876), p. 80.

[12] See Oddy, 'Symbolism and Design on the Early Umayyad Coinage', in T. Goodwin, ***Arab-Byzantine Coins and History*** (London, 2012), pp. 118-19, Fig. 11 and Fig. 13 respectively.

[13] See Classical Numismatic Group, eAuction 306, Lot 473.

this point (Fig. 7).[14] However, it is by no means certain that this was how the originator of the cloaked figure with bird had initially intended him to be understood. Indeed, the very fact that subsequent engravers seem to have felt the need to transform the depiction of the cloaked figure until he better resembled a falconer proves he was not initially a very convincing depiction of such a figure. One does not doubt that the Imperial Image type from Damascus with the bird to the side of the standing figure did play an important part in inspiring the engraver in the pseudo-Damascus mint that it would be acceptable to depict a bird in association with the standing figure, the Byzantine emperor presumably, but the crucial question here is whether this was the only image to influence him in this direction. Did some other image influence him to set the bird on the figure's left hand in particular rather than elsewhere?[15]

Figure 7

No investigation of the origin and significance of the depiction of an apparent falconer on Arab-Byzantine coinage can afford to ignore the fact that moneyers in England began to depict a similar standing figure with bird on the reverse of several groups of silver pennies, or sceattas, struck c. 720-30 (Fig. 8a and b).[16]

　　　　　　　　a　　　　　　　　　　　　　　　　　　b

Figure 8
a: *Anglo-Saxon Sceatta Series K, type 20* (© T. Abramson)
b: *Anglo-Saxon Sceatta Series L, type16/18 variety* (© T. Abramson)

Such are the similarities between the Anglo-Saxon and Arab-Byzantine types, that it has even been suggested that the Anglo-Saxon moneyers may have imitated Arab-Byzantine coins reaching

---

[14] See Oddy, 'Symbolism and Design on the Early Umayyad Coinage', in T. Goodwin, *Arab-Byzantine Coins and History* (London, 2012), Fig. 1, no. 2 (staff); Schindel and Hahn, 'Notes on Two Arab-Byzantine Coin Types', Fig. 10 (spear); T. Goodwin, 'The Chronology of the Umayyad Imperial Image Coinage: Progress over the Last 10 Years', in Goodwin, *Arab-Byzantine Coins*, pp. 89-107, Fig. 4, d; W. Schulze and A. Oddy, 'The Spear on Coins of the Byzantine-Arab Transition Period', in this volume.
[15] There were other possibilities. One notes that a type of Anglo-Saxon sceatta depicts what appears to be a large bird of prey perched upon the shoulder of the bust on the obverse (Series K, Type 42). See T. Abramson, *Sceatta List* (2012), pp. 123-24, Group 41 according to his new arrangement of the coinage.
[16] The relevant types are mostly attributed to what are conventionally known as Series K and L within the Anglo-Saxon corpus. See Abramson, *Sceatta List*, pp. 112-15, Groups 33 and 35 according to his new arrangement of the coinage. See also his Groups 23 and 112.

England as a result of commerce or pilgrimage.[17] However, there are two important differences between the Anglo-Saxon and Arab-Byzantine types. First, the Anglo-Saxon coins depict the figure with bird standing in a crescent-shaped object generally identified as a boat. This has no obvious equivalent upon any Arab-Byzantine type. One could perhaps argue that it represents a misinterpretation of the curved line representing his cloak on the cloaked figure type, but against this one notes that the dress of the standing figure on the Anglo-Saxon coins bears a far closer similarity to that of the belted- rather than the cloaked figure on Arab-Byzantine types. Secondly, the Anglo-Saxon coins depict the standing figure with his face turned towards the bird rather than with face forward in the manner of the Arab-Byzantine coins. At this point, one needs to bear in mind that Anglo-Saxon moneyers often based their obverse and reverse types on those of late Roman coins issued during the first half of the fourth century AD.[18] It is important to note, therefore, that their depiction of the standing figure with bird bears a closer resemblance to a standing imperial figure on a base billon type issued c.348-50 (Fig. 9a) than it does to any depiction of the standing figure with bird on Arab-Byzantine coinage.

Figure 9
a: *Centenionalis of Constans I minted at Antioch* (© CNG, Inc.)
b: *Centenionalis of Constantius II minted at Antioch* (© Wildwinds.com)

This particular late Roman type was produced at most of the operative mints across the empire as part of a series of coins whose common reverse legend proclaimed that they were celebrating the **FEL TEMP REPARATIO** 'The Restoration of Happy Times'.[19] It depicts the emperor in military dress standing facing left in a galley, and with a phoenix on a globe in his right hand outstretched before him and the labarum in his left hand behind him.[20] In other words, this type explains the two chief characteristics that serve to distinguish the Anglo-Saxon from the Arab-Byzantine types as already explained. It is obvious, therefore, that the originators of the Anglo-Saxon type imitated this late Roman type rather than an Arab-Byzantine coin.[21] This is not to claim that these Anglo-Saxon

---

[17] See e.g. P.D. Whitting, 'The Byzantine Empire and the Coinage of the Anglo-Saxons', in R.H.M. Dolley (ed.), *Anglo-Saxon Coins* (London, 1961), pp. 23-38, at 31; A. Gannon, *The Iconography of Early Anglo-Saxon Coinage, Sixth to Eighth Centuries* (Oxford, 2003), p. 95.

[18] E.g. some sceattas imitate the **VRBS ROMA** follis, with reverse depicting the wolf and twins, issued c.330-40, while several of the most common series imitate the **VIRT EXERCIT** follis, with reverse depicting a single standard bearing the legend **VOT/ XX** within its flag, issued c.320-21. See Gannon, *The Iconography of Early Anglo-Saxon Coinage*, (Oxford, 2003) pp. 145-47, 171-76.

[19] See J.P.C. Kent, *The Roman Imperial Coinage VIII: The Family of Constantine I, AD337-364* (London, 1981), Trier nos 212-17, 239-40; Lyons nos 69-78, 95-99; Arles nos 99-101, 116-17; Rome nos 107-35, 148-52; Aquileia nos 97-99, 108-09; Siscia nos 197-209; Thessalonica nos 107-13, 119-21; Heraclea nos 62, 66, 68; Constantinople nos 80, 83; Nicomedia nos 61, 64; Cyzicus no. 66; Antioch nos 121, 124.

[20] On the significance of the various types within this series, see e.g. K. Kraft, 'Die Taten der Kaiser Constans und Constantius II', *Jahrbuch für Numismatik und Geldgeschichte* 9 (1958), pp. 140-86. Even though the type with the emperor standing in the galley was produced in the names of both emperors at the time, the brothers Constans I and Constantius II, it is generally assumed that it probably refers to Constans' expedition to Britain during the winter of 342/43.

[21] I refer to originators because it seems to me that the surviving specimens may point to several independent attempts at copying the same model, whether by the same or successive engravers in the same workshop. One variant (Series L, Type 13) is unusual in that it depicts the figure with the bird in its left hand, in closer imitation of the Roman model

engravers, or their imitators, necessarily understood what they were copying. Indeed, the fact that some die-engravers added a T-shaped stand beneath the figure's left arm on some variants suggests that they did not (Fig. 8b). They saw a real bird rather than statue on a globe, interpreted it as a falcon, and then provided it with a stand. Other engravers decided to drop the bird and replace it with a second cross instead, so that the figure in the boat was actually depicted holding two crosses. They clearly saw something else in this figure whether a missionary saint travelling to proclaim the gospel overseas, a pilgrim travelling to or from the Holy Land, or the church in England on its journey through life.[22]

The fact that the originator of the standard figure with bird type in Anglo-Saxon England created a type so similar to the standing figure with bird type on Arab-Byzantine coinage by using a late Roman reverse type naturally raises the question whether the same late Roman reverse type did not play some role in influencing the originator of the standing figure with bird type on Arab-Byzantine coinage to depict the standing figure in the way that he did also. However, the possibilities were probably a little more complicated in the Byzantine East than they were in Anglo-Saxon England. By the time that Anglo-Saxon moneyers began the re-introduction of a common coinage in England during the late seventh and early eighth centuries AD, most of their late Roman inheritance had probably already been lost, the towns and associated infrastructures having been destroyed either by the climate or by the three centuries of invasion and civil-war since the Romans had abandoned Britain during the early fifth century AD. However, the situation in the Byzantine, or former Byzantine, East was quite different. It still preserved much of its Roman inheritance by the late seventh century thanks both to long continuity of Byzantine, or east Roman rule, before the recent Arab conquests and a climate better suited to preserve ancient monuments. Hence the inhabitants of late seventh century AD Syria would have been surrounded by constant reminders of the Roman past in the form of statues, frescoes, and mosaics, whether in public buildings such as baths, churches, or local administrative complexes, or in private dwellings. Many such art-works would have included some depiction of the emperor responsible for the construction, or restoration, of the relevant building. Most of these works may be presumed to have continued relatively unharmed until the rise of iconoclasm within the Islamic state under 'Abd al-Malik and the subsequent rise of iconoclasm within Byzantine society under Leo III, except perhaps when they also included some depiction of the Christian cross.

The relevance of this is that Constantius II, one of the two emperors responsible for the production of the late Roman type discussed above, spent much of his reign based at Antioch in Syria and was also a prolific builder who sought to strengthen the eastern frontier against the Persian threat.[23] The region would have been rich with art-works in his honour and when during the period c.348-50 the phoenix played as important a part in imperial iconography as it did, sometimes even appearing alone as the main device on the coinage (Fig. 9b), many of these works would probably have included some depiction of this bird in association with the emperor. It is my argument, therefore, that the originator of the cloaked figure with bird type at the pseudo-Damascus mint was primarily influenced to depict this figure with a bird in his hand because he was familiar with some antique local art-work depicting an emperor – probably Constantius II – with a phoenix on globe in his left

---

than usual, and has made a rather clumsy attempt to convert the galley into a chair. See Gannon, ***The Iconography of Anglo-Saxon Coinage***, (Oxford, 2003) p. 98.

[22] See C.E. Karkov, 'The Boat and the Cross: Church and State in Early Anglo-Saxon Coinage', in T. Abramson (ed.), ***Studies in Early Medieval Coinage 2: New Perspectives*** (Woodbridge, 2011), pp. 61-69.

[23] Antioch was his principal winter residence, after a summer spent campaigning in Mesopotamia, for the period 337-50. See T.D. Barnes, ***Athanasius and Constantius: Theology and Politics in the Constantinian Empire*** (Cambridge, MA, 1993), pp. 219-24. On his building activities, see N. Henck, 'Constantius ὁ Φιλοκτίστης?', ***Dumbarton Oaks Papers*** 55 (2001), pp. 279-304.

hand, a variation of the late Roman coin type.[24] However, there remains a more intriguing possibility that deserves, at least, to be mentioned.

The late Roman coin discussed above bore the reverse legend **FEL TEMP REPARATIO** 'The Restoration of Happy Times', and the reason why the emperor was depicted with a phoenix rather than an eagle or a Victory upon the globe, and why the phoenix itself formed the main image on another type within the same series, was that the phoenix was the great symbol of renewal acceptable both to pagans and Christians alike.[25] The relevance of this here is that Constans II (641-68) chose imperial renewal as the theme for the first part of his reign also.[26] Hence his folles struck at Constantinople during the period 641-56 (Classes 1-5) proclaimed the legend **ANANЄO'**, an abbreviation of the Greek *ananeosis* 'renewal', alongside the denomination mark on the reverse.[27] Unfortunately, relatively little Byzantine art survives from the seventh century, and almost none at all from the reign of Constans II, so it is impossible to tell what new imagery, if any, he used in an effort to broadcast this theme across his empire. However, the phoenix was an ancient Christian symbol of renewal, and he may well have circulated images of himself holding a phoenix upon a globe in the same manner as the fourth century emperors.[28] It is not impossible, therefore, that the originator of the cloaked figure with bird type at the pseudo-Damascus mint may have been influenced by some recent depiction of Constans II with phoenix rather than some ancient depiction of Constantius II with phoenix. He would not necessarily have to have understood the true significance of the phoenix in either case. However, the possibility that he recognised the bird in his model as the phoenix, and understood the significance of the same, deserves serious consideration. This would transform his decision to depict this bird in the hand of the standing emperor on his coin into a political statement, a celebration of some apparent upturn in the military and political affairs of the Byzantine Empire as a sign of renewal. This seems unlikely, but is not impossible. It is more likely that he saw the emperor with a phoenix upon a globe in his hand as nothing more than an interesting variant in the imperial image, with no real thought as to the identity of the bird or what exactly it signified.

The Seated Couple

As has long been noted, each of the five main mints engaged in the production of Phase 2 Arab-Byzantine copper used a different main obverse type, so that Damascus preferred a single standing emperor based on the obverse of the folles (Class 1-4) struck under Constans II during the period 641-48, Heliopolis preferred two standing emperors based perhaps on the obverse of a follis (Class 2) struck under Heraclius during the period 613-16, Tiberias preferred three standing emperors based perhaps on the obverse of a solidus (Class 4) struck under Heraclius during the period 632-

---

[24] T. Goodwin, 'The Chronology of the Umayyad Imperial Image Coinage: Progress over the Last 10 Years', in Goodwin, *Arab-Byzantine Coins,* pp. 93-94, suggests that the Pseudo-Damascus coinage was not a city coinage, but was struck for 'a tribal leader on the desert fringe'. This does not affect the present argument in that such a figure would very likely have occupied an abandoned Roman fort, if available, a suitable environment in which to discover frescoes of long deceased emperors. One thinks of the early 4th-century frescoes from the legionary shrine in the Temple of Luxor, Egypt, depicting Diocletian and his court. See I. Kalavrezou-Maxeiner, 'The Imperial Chamber at Luxor', *Dumbarton Oaks Papers* 29 (1975), pp. 225-51.

[25] In general, see R. Van den Broek, *The Myth of the Phoenix according to Classical and Early Christian Traditions* (Leiden, 1972).

[26] On this theme in general, see J.F. Haldon, 'Constantine or Justinian? Crisis and Identity in Imperial Propaganda in the Seventh Century', P. Magdalino (ed.), *New Constantines: The Rhythm of Imperial Renewal in Byzantium, 4th-13th Centuries* (Aldershot, 1994), pp. 95-107.

[27] See Grierson, *DOC 2*, pp. 442-51.

[28] It would be interesting to know how contemporary Byzantine propaganda presented the result of the naval battle of Phoenix c. 655 since, while it is usually described as a Byzantine defeat, it clearly resulted in large losses for both sides. See C. Zuckerman, 'Learning from the Enemy and More: Studies in "Dark Centuries" Byzantium', *Millenium* 2 (2005), pp. 79-135, at 114-15. News of this event may have provided an opportunity for a brief re-introduction of the phoenix within imperial iconography in a visual pun upon the location of this battle.

41, Emesa preferred a single imperial bust based perhaps on the obverse of solidi (Class 1-2) struck under Constans II during the period 641-51, and Scythopolis preferred two seated figures based on the obverse of the follis struck under Justin and Sophia during the period 566-78 (Fig. 10a and b).[29] So why did the mint at Scythopolis resort to a model so much older than that used at the other mints?[30]

Figure 10
a: Follis of Justin II minted at Nikomedia in 571/2
b: Fals minted probably by Muʿawiya at Scythopolis/Baisan c.670

This choice could simply reflect the fact that a relatively large number of the folles of Justin and Sophia seem to have been in circulation in the region about Scythopolis.[31] However, one must be careful not to exaggerate this phenomenon, since neither of the figures quoted for two excavations at Scythopolis, where this type numbers 104 out of 1,590 coins (6.5%) and 310 out of 2,163 coins (14%) respectively, suggests that it dominated within the local currency. More importantly, these figures are of little real value in themselves, since they do not tell us about the proportions of different coin types in circulation at the crucial period, the actual start of minting at Scythopolis. Alternatively, this choice could reflect the greater respect felt for the larger weight and diameter of this coin compared with more recent Byzantine issues. However, Justin reduced the weight of the follis from 1/18 pound (18.1g) to 1/21 pound (15.5g) during the first year of his reign, and to 1/24 pound (13.6g) during the fifth year of his reign, a weight standard maintained until 616.[32] Hence the coins of his predecessor Justinian I were heavier than his, while most of his were no heavier or larger than those of his successors. In other words, there was nothing particularly attractive or distinctive about the module of his follis compared with that of Tiberius II (578-82), Maurice (582-602) or Phocas (602-10).

Finally, one needs to consider the possibility that it was the nature of the obverse design itself that encouraged the mint at Scythopolis to choose this particular type of follis for imitation. Here one should note that if it was simply a matter of choosing, or being assigned, an obverse design different from those already in use at, or assigned to, the other main mints, then there remained other possibilities. For example, a double bust was used on the obverse of solidi and folles of the Heraclii during their initial revolt 608-10,[33] on the solidi of Heraclius issued at Constantinople during the

---

[29] As T. Goodwin, 'The Chronology of the Umayyad Imperial Image Coinage: Progress over the Last 10 Years', in Goodwin, *Arab-Byzantine Coins*, pp. 89-90, notes, this apparent level of organization does not necessarily point to central control or co-ordination. On these apparent models, see Album and Goodwin, *SICA 1*, pp. 82-83.
[30] The mint at Damascus, followed by the Pseudo-Damascus mint, also used an obverse type with single seated emperor which, as Album and Goodwin, *SICA 1*, pp. 82, have suggested, may have been loosely based on the obverse of a follis produced at Antioch c.529-33, or on 'a seal or some other non-numismatic source'. I suggest that it probably represents a halving of the seated pair on the follis of Justin and Sophia.
[31] As suggested by N. Amitai-Preiss, A. Berman, and S. Qedar, 'The Coinage of Scythopolis-Baysān and Gerasa-Jerash', *Israel Numismatic Journal* 13 (1999), pp. 133-51, at 136.
[32] See W. Hahn and M. Metlich, *Money of the Incipient Byzantine Empire Continued (Justin II – Revolt of the Heraclii, 565-610)* (Vienna, 2009) [*MIBEC* henceforth], pp. 9-10. There were some minor regional variations also.
[33] Hahn and Metlich, *MIBEC*, pp. 203-06.

period 613-31,[34] and on the solidi and hexagrams of Constans II issued at Constantinople during the periods 654-63 and 654-68 respectively,[35] just to mention the more obvious examples. Again, a group of three busts was used on the obverse of folles of Heraclius issued at Ravenna during the period 616-26, and on reverse of the folles of Constans II issued at Constantinople during the period 666-68.[36] The fact that the authority at Scythopolis did not resort to these other potential obverse types, despite their continued availability, suggests that it may have chosen the twin seated type for some more positive reason, and not simply because of a lack of other choices.

Perhaps the most interesting feature of the coinage of Scythopolis is the inclusion of the name of the mint to the left and right of the seated couple on the obverse (Fig. 10b) rather than in the exergue on the reverse (Fig. 10a). Since the third century AD, it had been Roman practice to include some abbreviated form of the name of the mint on the reverse, normally in the exergue. For the most part, the other Arab-Byzantine mints continued to inscribe the name of the relevant city on the reverse, although over time, and with the need to find space for extra Arabic legends on the reverse, the mint mark was sometimes displaced to the obverse, whether in Greek or Arabic.[37] None of the other main mints tolerated a 'frozen' mint mark on the reverse in direct imitation of their immediate Byzantine model.[38] Instead, they changed the mint mark of their model to reflect their real location. In contrast, Scythopolis retained the mint mark of its immediate model 'frozen' in the exergue of its coinage, whether **NIKO** for Nicomedia, **CON** for Constantinople, **KYZ** for Cyzicus, or varied corrupt efforts at the same, but replaced the obverse legend of its model with the real mint name instead. Hence it replaced the Latin legend **DNIVSTI – NVSPPAVG** with the Greek legend **CKYΘO – ΠΟΛΗC**. Most importantly, there is no evidence of any phase or variant at Scythopolis where some form of the Greek name of the city did occur on the reverse.[39] The decision to place the mint name on the obverse rather than the reverse seems to have been deliberate, and to have occurred from the very start of production. The big question, therefore, is why the mint at Scythopolis decided to break with the long accepted Byzantine usage continued by its contemporary Arab-Byzantine mints, and whether this is also related to the associated decision to imitate an obverse type so much older than those imitated by these other mints.

An obvious interpretation of the decision to place the name of Scythopolis on the obverse to the left and right of the two seated figures is that it was intended to identify one of these figures as Scythopolis, that is, as the personification of the city. Here one needs to remember that it had long been customary by the early Byzantine period to symbolise cities by means of their guardian spirit or *Tyche* and that this *Tyche* was normally depicted with a mural crown and seated upright on a chair.[40] The *Tyche* of Scythopolis had featured prominently upon the Roman provincial coinage of that city until it ceased production in 240/1, but she had been depicted in a number of different ways

---

[34] Grierson, ***DOC 2***, pp. 247-57.
[35] Grierson, ***DOC 2***, pp. 427-33, 440-42.
[36] Grierson, ***DOC 2***, pp. 374-75, 459-60.
[37] Damascus struck a type with obverse depicting a single standing emperor with the legend **ΔAMACKOC** to his right and reverse with the mint mark in Arabic in the exergue. See Album and Goodwin, ***SICA 1***, nos 566-68. Emesa struck a type with obverse depicting an imperial bust with the mint mark in Arabic to its right and reverse with the mint mark in Greek on either side of the denomination **M** and the Arabic *tayyib* 'good' in the exeregue. See Album and Goodwin, ***SICA 1***, nos 538-58.
[38] Diospolis struck an Imperial Image type with an obverse depicting a single standing emperor surrounded by the legend **ΔΙΟC – ΠΟΛΗC**. However, the associated reverse seems to imitate the reverse of a coin from Scythopolis. The idea of putting the mint mark on the obverse was probably copied from the same coin also. See T. Goodwin, ***Arab-Byzantine Coinage***, Studies in the Khalili Collection IV (London, 2005), p. 154.
[39] There was a variant where the name of the city in Arabic was placed in the exergue and, bizarrely, the 'frozen' mint mark was shifted to the left side of the denomination **M** in replacement of the date. See A. Oddy, 'The Early Umayyad Coinage of Baisān and Jerash', *ARAM* 6 (1994), pp. 405-18, at p. 417, no. 10.
[40] In general, see S.B. Matheson, ***An Obsession with Fortune: Tyche in Greek and Roman Art*** (New Haven, 1994).

over time so that it becomes clear that she had no fixed definitive form (Fig. 11a and b).[41] The practice of symbolising cities in this way had continued into the Christian period, despite what one might have considered the problematic pagan associations of such imagery, and a mosaic roundel from early sixth-century Scythopolis seems to depict a bust of its *Tyche* in traditional pagan manner (Fig. 12).[42] However, *Tychai* could be Christianized to some extent, as when the artist responsible for the depiction of the *Tyche* of Madaba in a sixth-century mosaic from a private residence in that town added a cross to the top of her long sceptre (Fig. 13).[43]

Figure 11
a: *AE of Scythopolis in name of Lucilla Augusta dated CY 239 (AD 175/6): Tyche standing right, foot on river-god swimming right, holding scepter and cornucopia.* (© CNG, Inc.)
b: *AE of Scythopolis in name of Gordian III dated CY 304 (AD 240/1): Tyche seated right, cradling the infant Dionysos.* (© CNG, Inc.)

Figure 12: Tyche from Scythopolis (© T. M. Kristensen)

---

[41] See R. Barkay, ***The Coinage of Nysa-Scythopolis (Beth-Shean),*** Corpus Nummorum Palaestinensium V (Jerusalem, 2003), pp. 133-39.
[42] In general, see B. Poulsen, 'City Personifications in Late Antiquity', in S. Birk, T.M. Kristensen, and B. Poulsen (eds.), ***Using Images in Late Antiquity*** (Oxford, 2014), pp. 209-26.
[43] For detailed colour photographs, see M. Piccirillo, ***The Mosaics of Jordan*** (Amman, 1992), pp. 51-67. For discussion, see R. Avner-Livy, 'A Note on the Iconography of the Personifications in the "Hippolytos Mosaic" at Madaba, Jordan', ***Liber Annuus*** 46 (1996), pp. 363-74.

Figure 13: Mosaic from the so-called Hippolytus Hall, Madaba

The relevance of all this is that the original depiction of Justin and Sophia seated upright together looks very much like a depiction of two *Tychai* seated together. The main change which the originator of the Arab-Byzantine type has made to their depiction is that he has removed the orb from his left-hand figure, Justin originally, and replaced it with a cross-sceptre, so that the two seated figures are now identically equipped. The obvious explanation for this action is that he believed that, as a symbol of imperial power and world-domination, the orb was inappropriate to the figure whom he wished to represent, the *Tyche* of a provincial city presumably, which, as even its proudest citizens would admit, did not possess such power.

It is my argument, therefore, that the originator of the two seated figures type at Scythopolis has subtly recast the original depiction of Justin and Sophia to represent two urban *Tychai* instead. Since he only names Scythopolis, the expectation seems to be that those handling the coins would have no difficulty in identifying this other town. It was not unusual to depict two or more *Tychai* together; this could be done for a variety of reasons. For example, the personifications of Rome and Constantinople, the Old and New Romes, were often depicted together in the fourth century AD because of the similarly elevated status of both the two great imperial cities of the empire.[44] Alternatively, two *Tychai* might be depicted together in order to emphasize a real friendship or association between two cities, as when Julius Terentius, commander of the *Cohors XX Palmyrenorum*, commissioned a wall-painting in a temple at Dura Europus in 239, depicting, among other things, the *Tychai* of Dura Europus and Palmyra sitting alongside each other (Fig.14).[45] Finally, it is important to note that not everything that looks like a *Tyche* is necessarily

---

[44] See J.M.C. Toynbee, 'Roma and Constantinopolis in Late Antique Roman Art from 312 to 365', **Journal of Roman Studies** 37 (1947), pp. 135-44; also G.W. Bowersock, 'Old and New Rome in the Late Antique Near East', in P. Rousseau and M. Papoutsakis (eds.), **Transformations of Late Antiquity: Essays for Peter Brown** (Farnham, 2009), pp. 37-50.

[45] In general, see L. Dirven, 'The Julius Terentius Fresco and the Roman Imperial Cult', **Mediterraneo antico** 10 (2007), pp. 115-27.

identifiable as such, since it is arguable that the two apparent *Tychai* which the artist depicted alongside the *Tyche* of Madaba in the above-mentioned mosaic were intended to personify urban virtues allegedly possessed by Madaba rather than the *Tychai* of two associated cities.[46]

Figure 14: Wall-painting from the Temple of Bel at Dura Europus

In this particular case, the possibility that the authority responsible for minting at Scythopolis may have wanted to flatter the city by associating it with some powerful city or individual is lessened by the fact that the two seated figures are depicted in the exact same manner as if equals. Hence if the obverse was intended to depict two *Tychai*, then they probably represent two cities of approximately similar status, so the second Tyche is unlikely to represent either Damascus, the capital of the caliphate, or Tiberias, the capital of the jund. However, one notes that there was clearly some form of close association between Scythopolis and Gerasa during the late seventh century. Coins struck in the name of Gerasa were of the same basic type and module as those struck in the name of Scythopolis, and are often dealt with together for this reason.[47] The main difference as far as the obverse is concerned is the that coins of Gerasa restore the *globus cruciger* to the left-hand figure in closer imitation of the original obverse on the follis of Justin and Sophia (Fig. 15). Furthermore, they usually depict a star between the heads of the two figures rather than the cross as depicted on the obverse both of the Phase 2 coins struck at Scythopolis and of the original imperial coins struck for Justin and Sophia. The transformation of the cross into a star suggests that the engraver did not really understand, or care, what he was copying, and encourages the belief that his restoration of the *globus cruciger* to the left-hand figure was probably the result of a similar ignorance or carelessness. Such an interpretation is consistent with the generally cruder style of these coins also. The suspicion must be that the coins struck in the name of Gerasa were struck in imitation of those struck in the name of Scythopolis.[48] Whatever the case, the fact that both mints

---

[46] D. Woods, 'Rome, Gregoria, and Madaba: A Warning against Sexual Temptation', **Studia Patristica** 64 (2013), pp. 9-14.
[47] See A. Oddy, 'The Early Umayyad Coinage of Baisān and Jerash', **ARAM** 6 (1994); N. Amitai-Preiss, A. Berman, and S. Qedar, 'The Coinage of Scythopolis-Baysān and Gerasa-Jerash', **Israel Numismatic Journal** 13 (1999).
[48] A group of coins of similar type and module to those of Scythopolis and Gerasa have been attributed to Abila, but none actually preserve its name clearly and fully. See A. Oddy, 'The Coinage of Abila in the Early Umayyad Period', **ARAM** 23 (2011), pp. 337-46. Even if these were attributable to Abila, however, their crude style and corrupt Greek suggests that they are poor imitations of the coinage of Scythopolis once more.

struck the same basic type of coin on the same unusual module proves some form of close association. Hence if the originator of the two seated figure obverse at Scythopolis did intend to depict two urban *Tychai*, as I have argued, that of Scythopolis itself together with that of some other town of similar status, then that town is most likely identifiable as Gerasa.

Figure 15: Fals of Gerasa minted in the 670s

Conclusion

A common theme emerges from this discussion of the production of two very different obverse types at two different groups of mints, that is, the brief flickering of an iconographic independence drawing inspiration from the classical past. An engraver at the pseudo-Damascus mint was probably inspired to add a bird to the imperial orb by some fourth-century depiction of an emperor holding an orb surmounted by a phoenix, while an engraver at Scythopolis was probably inspired by some ancient depiction of the *Tyche* of Scythopolis to recast the seated figures of Justin and Sophia as the *Tychai* of Scythopolis and some associated city, very likely Gerasa. There were limits to what these engravers could achieve in that they seem to have been expected to produce obverse types that resembled those already in circulation and looked appropriately 'imperial'. Nevertheless, they drew upon their classical artistic inheritance to push against these limits. Unfortunately, none of those who imitated either of their obverse types subsequently seems to have understood what these engravers had been trying to depict, so the emperor with orb surmounted by a phoenix was rapidly transformed into a hunter with falcon, and the *globus cruciger* was mistakenly restored to one of the *Tychai*. This incomprehension of, or worse still a lack of concern for, classical iconographic traditions points either to the emergence of a new generation of engravers less schooled in the ways of the past or the increased Arabicisation of the mints. In either case, our two engravers arguably represented the last of their breed.

The Phase 2 Coinage of Scythopolis under Mu'awiya and his successors

Andrew Oddy [1]

Introduction

The study of Arab Byzantine coins in the past 30 years has revolutionised our knowledge of the coinage in Greater Syria between the Arab conquest – complete by 640 – and the second coinage reform of 'Abd al-Malik in 696/7. But this is more than half a century, so do we have any 'fixed points' in this period?

The Arab Byzantine copper coinage of this half century can be divided into three main phases:
- Phase 1 – the Pseudo-Byzantine issues that mainly copy the three figure coins of Heraclius or the standing emperor coins of Constans II, although there are less common coins with a bust on the obverse and with two standing figures
- Phase 2 – coins which usually have mint names in Greek and/or Arabic
- Phase 3 – the 'Standing Caliph' coins (the first coinage reform of 'Abd al-Malik)

The search for 'fixed points' must start with the work of Henri Pottier and Ingrid & Wolfgang Schulze who suggested a dating framework for the Phase 1 (Pseudo-Byzantine) coinage that is based on metrology. They concluded that the Phase 1 coinage spans the period 638-c.670AD.[2]

However, the Phase 1 coinage includes some quite rare imitations of the Sicilian coinage of Constantine IV (668-685) (fig. 1a). These, therefore, can only have been produced from about 670 and, as they are die-linked to imitations of Constans II (fig. 1b), the Pottier/Schulze dating framework must be extended beyond c.670 – perhaps to c.673. The 'Constantine IV' Phase 1 coinage has been described by Oddy where the die links to Constans II imitations are documented.[3]

Figure 1: (a) Phase 1 coin based on a follis of Constantine IV struck in Syria early in the 670s, ANS 1987.126.1, 3.59g; (b) Phase 1 coin derived from a follis of Constans II, Private collection, 2.48g (scale approx. x1.5)

---

[1] Andrew Oddy is an independent scholar   waoddy@googlemail.com
[2] H. Pottier, I. Schulze and W. Schulze, Pseudo-Byzantine Coinage in Syria under Arab Rule (638-c.670), Classification and Dating, ***Revue Belge de Numismatique, CLIV*** (2008) 87-155.
[3] A. Oddy, Constantine IV as a Prototype for Early Islamic Coins, in (A. Oddy, ed.) ***Coinage and History in the Seventh Century Near East 2*** (henceforth ***Proceedings 2***) London, 2010, 95-109.

Only one Phase 1 mint has been tentatively identified and that is Emesa/Ḥimṣ.[4] Here, for stylistic reasons, it is possible to suggest a connection between a large 'group' of Phase 1 coins and those inscribed with the mint name of Emesa in Phase 2. No other Phase 1 mints have been located, and there is no reason to think that those that did operate all closed at the same time. With this proviso, it is probable that Phase 1 ends in the early 670s, so when and where does Phase 2 start and was there an overlap?

This paper will examine Phase 2 at the mint of Scythopolis, subsequently known to the Arabs as Baisān, and is based on a study of 295 coins known from private and public collections, and from dealers' lists and sale catalogues. All these coins have either the name Scythopolis on the obverse or the name Baisān on the reverse.

It is generally agreed that a coinage reform took place under Mu'awiya (661-680) with the introduction of minting at towns that can be identified by mintmarks on the coins. There are five main mints: Damaskos/Dimashq, Heliopolis/Ba'albek, Emesa/Ḥimṣ, Tiberias/Ṭabariya and Scythopolis/Baisān[5] (see fig. 2 in the paper by Schulze & Oddy in this volume) and a number of subsidiary mints whose output was small. This coinage is now known as Phase 2,[6] but formerly had no agreed terminology and was called by a variety of names such as 'Umayyad Imperial Image', 'Proto Umayyad' and 'Bi-lingual'.

Within the period of the Phase 2 coinage there have been several suggestions for dating groups of coins; in particular the *al-wafā lillāh* coinage[7] and the Pseudo-Damascus coinage[8] have been attributed to Arab tribes involved in the Second Civil War of 682 – 692.

The trouble is that these and other suggestions do not really help to date the coins of the 'regular'[9] Phase 2 mints – the five main mints and a number of less important ones with only a small output. The new coinage issued from the five main mints seems to have been issued piecemeal and not all at the same time (see below). The fact that each mint chose a different obverse design seems to indicate a desire for its coinage to be distinctive.

- Scythopolis/Baisān   two seated figures
- Emesa/Ḥimṣ   facing standing figure or a facing bust. The relationship between these two types has not yet been worked out although they appear to be concurrent.
- Tiberias/Ṭabariya   three standing facing figures
- Heliopolis/Ba'albek   two standing facing figures
- Damaskos/Dimashq   standing facing figure or a seated figure. The sequence of the various Damaskos issues is still a subject of debate.

---

[4] A. Oddy, The Christin Coinage of Early Muslim Syria?, *ARAM* 15 (2003) 185-196.

[5] In this paper, the names for the mints are written as they appear on the coins, rather than as they are known to modern geography, with the exception of Pseudo-Damascus which is the name given to one particular coinage issue. Thus Damaskos rather than Damascus, Gerasa rather than Jerash, etc.

[6] For this terminology see W. Schulze and A. Oddy, Terminology for the Transitional Coinage Struck in 7th Century Syria after the Arab Conquest, in (T. Goodwin ed.) ***Arab-Byzantine Coins and History*** (henceforth ***Proceedings 3***) London, 2012, 187-200.

[7] I. Schulze, The *al-wafā lillāh* Coinage: A study of style (work in progress), ***Proceedings 2***, 111-121.

[8] T. Goodwin, The Chronology of the Umayyad Imperial Image Coinage: progress over the last 10 years, ***Proceedings 3***, 89-107.

[9] The regular coins are those that are believed to have been produced in official mints. Some mints have what appear to be 'irregular' imitations associated with them. Emesa is a case in point where the irregular 'bust type' coins are very common. The perceived status of the Pseudo-Damascus and *al-wafā lillāh* coins awaits the publication of T. Goodwin and R. Gyselen, ***The Irbid Hoard of Arab-Byzantine Coins***, Royal Numismatic Society Special Publication, forthcoming.

The coins at Scythopolis are much larger and heavier than those of the other mints. Is this an argument to say that they were the first to be struck? This appears to be the position taken by John Walker in the British Museum catalogue[10] where he suggested c.650[11] for the start of the Phase 2 coinage as a whole, but he put the Scythopolis coins first because they were inspired by the earliest prototype, these being the very common large *folles* of Justin II and Sophia struck 565-578 (see below).

The purpose of this paper is to examine the coinage attributed to Scythopolis/Baisān from the points of view of:
- Design and style
- Metrology
- Overstrikes

The design and style of the Phase 2 coinage of Scythopolis

A typical early coin of Scythopolis is illustrated in figure 2a. The obverse has the two seated figures (derived from the regular Byzantine folles of Justin II and his wife, Sophia struck at Nikomedia) with a cross between the heads and both holding sceptres and the legend **CKVΘO ПОЛНC** (Scythopolis) starting at 7.30 o'clock. The reverse follows closely the regular coinage of Justin II struck at Nicomedia with a large upper case **M** (denoting a follis) with a cross above the **M** and a letter ◊ (for officina **A**) below the **M**, **ANNO** vertically to the left, the date **ЧII** (year 7) vertically to the right, and the mint name **NIKO** (originally for Nicomedia) in the exergue.

Figure 2: (a) Fals (follis) of Scythopolis dated year 7 (276/11/11)[12], Private collection, 14.00g; (b) Follis of Justin II minted at Nicomedia in year 7, Private collection, 13.96g; (c) Follis of Justin II minted at Antioch in year 7, Private collection, 13.28g (scale approx. x1.5)

---

[10] J. Walker, *A Catalogue of the Arab-Byzantine and Post-Reform Umaiyad Coins*, British Museum, London, 1956.
[11] Walker suggests 650 in the catalogue section of the book, but suggests 635 in the introduction.
[12] The notation (276/11/11) is used throughout this paper for Phase 2 Scythopolis coins to give the number in the author's corpus followed by the obverse die number and then by the reverse die number.

Although the reverse is very similar to the regular Byzantine issue of about a century earlier, there is an innovation on the obverse where both seated figures hold sceptres (fig. 2a). On the regular Nicomedia coinage of Justin II (fig. 2b) Justin holds a globus cruciger while Sophia holds a sceptre. At the mint of Antioch, however, both Justin and Sophia hold sceptres (fig. 2c) but the style is very different from the Nicomedia coins (and from the Scythopolis coins).

What is most noticeable about the Scythopolis coins is the presence of the mint name in Greek on the obverse in place of the name and titles of the ruler. This is a major innovation which breaks completely with Byzantine practice and is only followed at three other Phase 2 mints, Damaskos, Diospolis and Tiberias.

It has previously been argued[13] that these variations from the design of the original Justin II coin can be taken as deliberate and that, therefore the date may be read as a real date, the 7th year of Mu'awiya (667-8), especially as the date 7 on the Scythopolis coin is written ЧII (fig. 2a), unlike on the Justin II coin of Nicomedia where year it is written ςI (fig. 2b).

Why did the Arabs strike large, heavy coins at Scythopolis that are derived from the coinage of Justin II struck at Nikomedia between 566 and 578, and specifically year 7 (571/2) rather than being derived from the smaller *folles* of Constans II or from their imitations which made up a very large proportion of the Phase 1 Pseudo-Byzantine coinage and are found abundantly in Greater Syria and were in production up until (and beyond in some cases) the opening of the Phase 2 mints? Two reasons spring to mind:
- Large Justin II *folles* were still in circulation, at least in the Scythopolis region, a century after they had been minted and so the minting initiated by Mu'awiya followed the most popular coins in circulation, or those that were, on account of their high weight, most treasured by hoarders.[14]
- It was a conscious attempt at producing two denominations because the mint at Scythopolis also struck half *fulūs* (fig. 3a) which are similar in size to, although generally greater in weight than, the Phase 1 (Pseudo-Byzantine) coins (fig. 3b and c) that were already in circulation.

The weight range of the Scythopolis half *fals* is 2.2g to 6.2g. The weight range of the Phase 1 coins is approx. 1.5g to approx. 5g.

If it seems strange that the first Arab minting at Scythopolis should apparently have been inspired by a coinage that had been struck a century earlier, it is pertinent to ask whether there are any other possible models, and there are.

There is a series of coins that 'copy' the official *folles* of Justin II but that, on stylistic grounds, were clearly not struck at the official mints in spite of bearing pseudo-mint marks for Constantinople, Nicomedia, Cyzicus, Thessalonica, and Rome.

---

[13] A. Oddy, Symbolism and Design on the Early Umayyad Coinage in **Proceedings 3**, 109-123, esp. 113-114.

[14] The evidence for the large number of Justin II folles in circulation in Greater Syria in the post conquest period has, hitherto, been largely anecdotal, being based upon the impressions of those working in Greater Syria today. For instance Amitai-Preiss *et al* [N. Amitai-Preiss, A. Berman and S. Qedar, The Coinage of Scythopolis-Baysān and Gerasa-Jerash, **Israel Numismatic Journal** 13 (1994-99) 133-151] wrote "It seems that the original type [i.e. the folles of Justin and Sophia], which has been found in unexpectedly high numbers at numerous sites, was very popular in Trans-Jordan and adjacent regions". This statement appears to be based on the coins excavated in the Roman Theatre at Jerash. Now, however, there is plenty of hard evidence from the coins in the Israel Antiquities Authority database. Gabriela Bijovsky [***Gold Coin and Small Change: Monetary Circulation in Fifth-Seventh Century Byzantine Palestine***, Trieste, 2012, 260-272] has shown that after the end of the reign of Justinian I, there is an influx of folles of Justin II that are abundant at sites all over Israel.

Figure 3: (a) half fals of Scythopolis minted under Arab authority (191/102/122), Spink Zurich 22 (17th March 1987) lot 150, 5.19g; (b) and (c) Phase 1 (Pseudo-Byzantine) folles struck in (probably the southern half of) Greater Syria, Private collection, 2.92g and 3.49g   (scale approx. 1:1)

These have been attributed by Hahn,[15] and subsequently by Hahn and Metlich,[16] to a mint associated with the army which may have been mobile. They are known to numismatists as *Moneta Militaris Imitativa*. The coinage is very distinctive in appearance and is generally of comparable weight to that of the regular coinage. The coins with the pseudo-Nicomedia mint mark are known for years 8 and 10 (fig. 4a and b).

Figure 4: (a) Follis of the so-called Moneta Militaris Imitativa type struck during the reign of Justin II and dated year 8. Mansfield collection, 12.97g; (b) Follis of the so-called Moneta Militaris Imitative type struck during the reign of Justin II and dated year 10. Mansfield collection, 10.54g; (c) Follis struck in Syria in c. 616 during the Persian occupation. Private collection, 9.63g; (d) Follis struck in Syria in c. 621 during the Persian occupation. Private collection, 9.28g   (scale 1:1)

If this coinage in the name of Justin II really is struck in some official capacity, such as for the army as has been postulated, it is presumably dated to the reign of Justin II. That this is almost certainly the case is confirmed by the existence of *Moneta Militaris Imitativa* coins struck under both Tiberius II and Maurice and with their portraits and titles.

---

[15] W. Hahn. ***Moneta Imperii Byzantini: Band 3: Von Heraclius' bis Leo III***, Vienna, 1981.
[16] W. Hahn and M. Metlich, ***Money of the Incipient Byzantine Empire Continued (Justin II – Revolt of the Heraclii, 565-610)*** Vienna, 2009, 33.

However, when the *Moneta Militaris Imitativa* coins in the name of Justin II are compared with the 'two seated figure' coins of Scythopolis it is obvious that the distinctive style makes it very unlikely that they were the model for the Scythopolis coinage.

But there is also another series of coins bearing the image of Justin II and Sophia that were in circulation in Greater Syria at the time of the Arab conquest.[17] These were struck during the Persian occupation of Syria after the capture of Antioch in 610 and before the final withdrawal of Persian forces in 629/630. This was a local coinage, struck perhaps at Emesa,[18] that copied coins of several previous Byzantine emperors, including Justin II, Maurice and Phocas, as well as Heraclius, the current emperor. The Justin II coins are dated between Year 4 and Year 14, approximately 614 to 628 if it can be assumed that year 1 equates to 610, the year of the invasion (fig. 4c and d).

But the style of these coins also precludes them being the model for the Scythopolis coinage. Hence, it can only be concluded that the Phase 2 coinage of Scythopolis was, indeed, derived directly from an example of the year 7 coinage of Justin II struck at Nicomedia.

Although the vast majority of the Scythopolis coins bear the pseudo mint mark **NIKO** on the reverse, a few are known with **CON** (fig. 5a) and there are three unique coins with **ƆON** (fig. 5b), **CION** (fig. 5c), and with **KYZ** respectively (fig. 5d).

*Figure 5: Scythopolis coins with mint marks **CON, ƆON, CION**, and **KYZ**. (a) (178/18/19) Private collection, 11.25g 6.30h; (b) (174/61/92) Private collection, 10.80g 7.00h; (c) (221/34/72) Location uncertain, 13.24g;[19] (d) (302/16/100) CNG Jan 2011, 6.75g 7.00h. Note the Arabic countermark **tayyib** on the obverses of 5b and 5c. (scale 1:1)*

The reverse of 5a is die linked to three other reverses with a **NIKO** mint mark, as is the reverse of 5c, but the dies of 5b are so far unique. The KYZ reverse, 5d, is die linked to no less than nine other

---

[17] They occasionally turn up in parcels of Byzantine coins, sometimes also containing Phase 1 and Phase 2 coins, originating in the Middle East.

[18] H. Pottier, *Le Monnayage de la Syrie sous l'Occupation Perse (610-630)*, Cahiers Ernest-Babelon, Paris, 2004; H. Pottier, Le monnayage de la Syrie sous l'occupation perse (610-630): Complément, *Revue Numismatique* (2010) 447-476.

[19] There is a cast of this coin, which was in a now-dispersed private collection, at the American Numismatic Society where the weight is recorded as 13.24g. However, the coin appears to be identical with N. Amitai-Preiss, A. Berman and S. Qedar, The Coinage of Scythopolis-Baysān and Gerasa-Jerash, *Israel Numismatic Journal* 13 (1994-99) 133-151 no. A16 which is said to be in the collection of the Pontifical Biblical Institute in Jerusalem.

reverses with **NIKO** mint marks (fig. 6). The obverse of 5d is very common, with 56 specimens having been recorded. With two exceptions, the weights of these 56 coins lie between 8.32g and 4.79g.

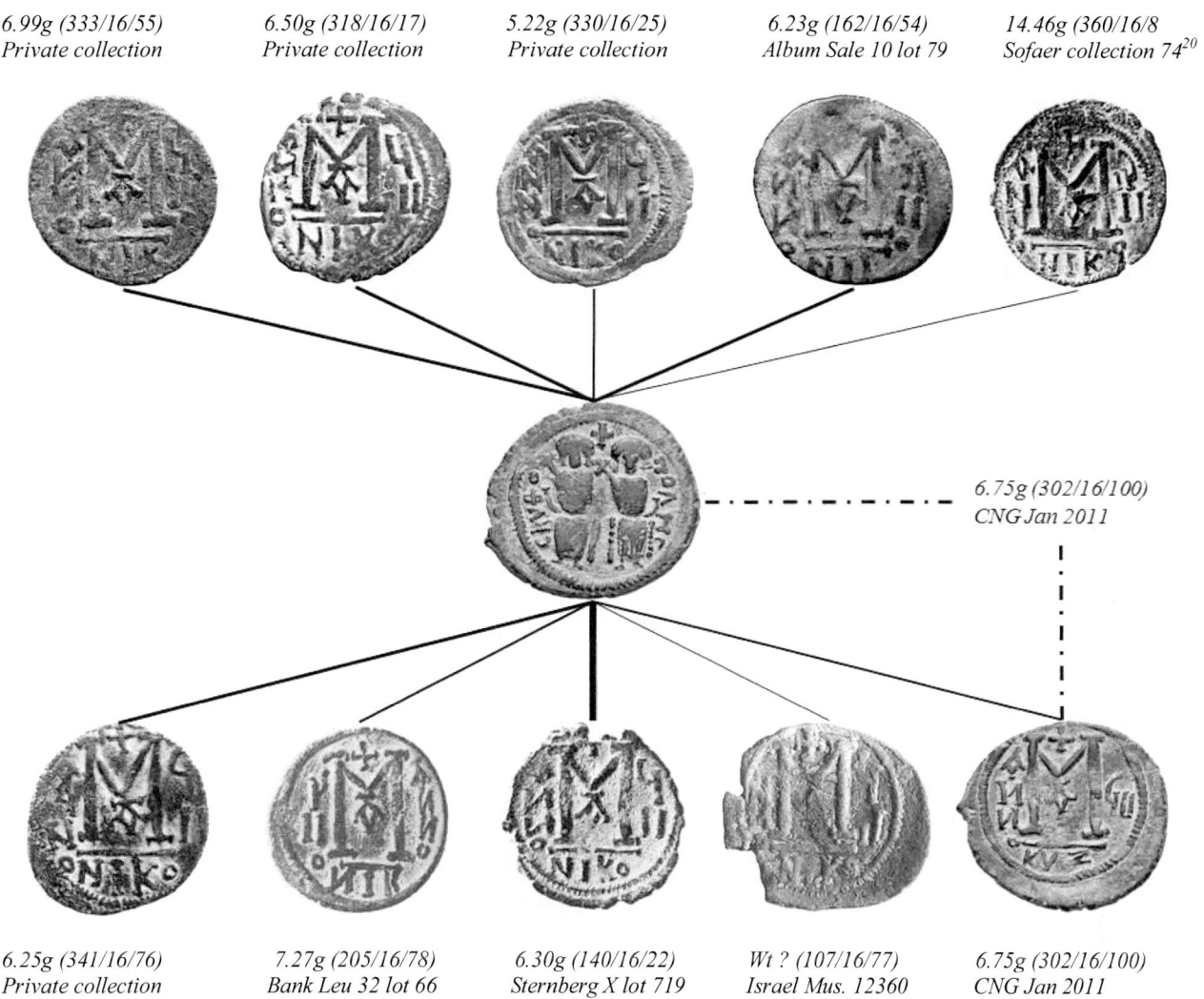

Figure 6: Die links for the KYZ reverse. The thickness of the connecting lines indicates the number of recorded die pairs. Note that the reverse dies almost all have retrograde letters or transposed legends (scale approx. 1:1)

Two things are noteworthy about the coins in figure 5. First they all have dates which are different from the **NIKO** reverse dies and, second, there are retrograde letters on the reverse of the **KYZ** coin indicating a degree of carelessness, incompetence, or illiteracy on the part of the die cutter. This type of mistake indicates that the coins are late in the sequence (see below). This is confirmed by the weight of the **KYZ** coin which is only 6.75g, about half that of the earliest of the Scythopolis coins (weights are discussed below).

It is however, important to ask if these dates (i.e. **XI** and **XII**) are significant in view of the opinion expressed above that the **ЧII** on the usual **NIKO** reverses may indicate the seventh year of Mu'awiya. The **CON** reverses are dated **XI** and **XII**, but are die linked via the obverse to **NIKO** reverses with the date **ЧII** and so if these dates (i.e. 11 and 12) are meaningful it is necessary to presume that the date **ЧII** became frozen for at least four years after its first introduction. However,

---
[20] Y. Meshorer, G. Bijovsky and W. Fischer-Bossert, *Coins of the Holy Land: The Abraham and Marian Sofaer Collection at the American Numismatic Society and the Isreal Museum*, New York, 2013, no. 74.

ЧII continues to be used with **NIKO** reverses as the weights of the coins decline with the passing of time (see below). Furthermore, it is noteworthy that the coinage of Gerasa,[21] as well as having meaningless dates such as **O/X/✱** and **X/O/U** written vertically, also appears to be dated year **XII** and **XIII**.[22]

In view of the low weight, the year ЧII on the **KYZ** reverse (fig. 5d) really cannot be meaningful.

So can anything be concluded from the various dates? It is a nice hypothesis that uses the Scythopolis coinage to date the inception of the Phase 2 coinage to the 7th year of Muʿawiya, but the hypothesis is put to the test by the coins of years 11 and 12 which are succeeded by many more light weight coins dated year 7 (see below). Until there is more evidence, Muʿawiya year 7 must remain only a hypothesis.

Neglecting the evidence of the hypothetical dates, what other factors can be used to indicate the start of minting Phase 2 coins at Scythopolis?

It must be remembered that Muʿawiya had been governor of Syria for twenty years before he became Caliph. During this time the only coinage struck in Syria was the Phase 1 issues at numerous towns that show no sign of central authority. In Iraq, however, the Arabs continued striking imitation Sasanian coins in the names of Yazdgard III and Chosroes II, some of which bore dates in the Yazdgard 'era'. The only concession to the change of regime was the addition of *bism allāh* (in the name of God) or *bism allāh rabbī* (in the name of God, my Lord) or *bism allāh al-malik* (in the name of God, the king) in the obverse margin. It is, therefore, strange that Muʿawiya did not attempt to Arabise the Phase 1 coinage struck in Syria during his governorship.

When Muʿawiya becomes Caliph, however, there is a change to the coinage in Iraq. Dates according to the Hegira, beginning in 42 H (662/3 AD), are introduced onto the silver dirhams which are also inscribed with the name of Muʿawiya or his local governor. This coinage reform, because that is essentially what it is, would be expected to be mirrored in Syria. This, however, does not seem to be the case. Even as the holder of supreme power, Muʿawiya does not grasp the coinage nettle in Syria.

One reason is that, unlike Iraq, there is no tradition of official coinage production on which to build a coinage reform. Another reason may be the fact that control of silver and gold coins had always been seen as far more important than the control of copper coinage. And a third reason seems to be that the unofficial Phase 1 production was working and seems to have been allowed to continue until c.670, or two or three years later. For whatever the reason, at about this time - the early 670s - Phase 2 coinage started, and it probably started at Scythopolis.

The dates and mint marks are one variable feature on the 'standard' design of the earliest coinage at Scythopolis (fig. 2a), but there are two other variants which although considered very rare a few years ago have become much more accessible in recent years as the Arab-Byzantine coinage becomes better-known in the antiquities trade in Greater Syria. These are known respectively as the '*mqsm*' type[23] and the 'udl' (undeciphered legend) type.[24]

---

[21] Gerasa, modern Jerash in Jordan, also issued large Phase 2 *fulūs* similar to, but stylistically different from, the coins of Scythopolis discussed here. The surviving coins of Gerasa are uncommon, but much less rare that was thought to be the case twenty years ago. 162 have been recorded as part of this project.
[22] N. Amitai-Preiss, A. Berman and S. Qedar, The Coinage of Scythopolis-Baysān and Gerasa-Jerash, *Israel Numismatic Journal* 13 (1994-99) 133-151 plate 21, C9 and plate 21, D4.
[23] 25 specimens are known.
[24] 21 specimens are known.

The '*mqsm*' type has the date on the reverse replaced by a legend in Arabic that has been read as *mqsm*,[25] meaning 'a part'. It is known with three obverse dies and two reverse dies (fig. 7)[26] and is die linked to the 'udl' type and to the **CON** and **CION** coins already described, as well as into the main Scythopolis series with date **ЧII** and mint mark **NIKO**.

Figure 7: '*mqsm*' type. *(a) (149/11/18) CNG 31.8.2011, 12.18g; (b) (236/11/62) Dumbarton Oaks 83, 12.36g; (c) (145/25/62) Münzzentrum Köln 30.11.1977 no.1818, 10.11g; (d) (041/18/62) ANS 2004.4.1, 11.77g (scale 1:1)*

The 'udl' type has the date replaced by an 'undeciphered legend' that has been the subject of several hypothetical readings. John Walker in the British Museum Catalogue wondered whether the 'udl' is "a cursive form of the date [in Arabic]",[27] a suggestion that has recently been revived in a Morton and Eden catalogue where the reading of Arabic *thalatha* (i.e. 3) is suggested.[28] Meanwhile Clive Foss read it as an illiterate attempt at writing *baisān*,[29] the name by which Scythopolis came to be known by the Arabs and which features in a literate form on the coinage a few years later,[30] presumably as a result of the deliberate 'Arabisation' of the legends (see below). The 'udl' legend was undeciphered by Amitai-Preiss *et al.*[31]

One other possibility is that 'udl' is a date in cursive Greek which was the language of the administration until the reforms of 'Abd al-Malik. Miles has briefly discussed the use of Greek/Coptic cursive letters to represent numerals on glass weights.[32]

In reply to an email asking whether the legend could be a number in cursive Greek, Frank Trombley sent a detailed opinion[33] in which he favours an Arabic interpretation of the legend and offers several tentative alternatives:

---

[25] N. Amitai-Preiss, A. Berman and S. Qedar, The Coinage of Scythopolis-Baysān and Gerasa-Jerash, **Israel Numismatic Journal 13** (1994-99) 133-151 esp. p.137.
[26] But see below for contemporary imitations of this type.
[27] J. Walker, ***A Catalogue of the Arab-Byzantine and Post-Reform Umaiyad Coins***, British Museum, London, 1956, p.2, Bel.1.
[28] Morton & Eden 66, 7th November 2013, lot 466.
[29] C. Foss in ***Arab-Byzantine Coins, an Introduction, with a Catalogue of the Dumbarton Oaks Collection***, Washington DC, 2008, p.52, although he does not repeat the suggestion with the catalogue entry on p.138.
[30] The date hypothesised below for the introduction of Baisān in Arabic onto the coinage is 75-6H, AD 693-6.
[31] N. Amitai-Preiss, A. Berman and S. Qedar, The Coinage of Scythopolis-Baysān and Gerasa-Jerash, **Israel Numismatic Journal 13** (1994-99) 133-151.
[32] G. C. Miles, ***Early Arabic Glass Weights and Stamps***, ANS Notes and Monographs 111, New York, 1948, 11.

'The range of possibilities is narrow. Speaking for myself, I do not think it represents a number, because even in the earliest Arabic papyri the numbers are spelt out in full. In bilingual papyri (Greek & Arabic) Greek letters are used for numbers, which are often then spelt out as well for the removal of doubt. There is an example of this in Document VIII of F R Trombley, Fiscal Documents from the Muslim Conquest of Egypt: Military Supplies and Administrative Dislocation, **Revue des Études Byzantines 71** *(2013) pp.5-38. (For examples of early Arabic writing and letter forms see A. Grohmann,* **Arabische Palaeographie II**. *Teil (Vienna, 1971), Schrifttafel II, between pp. 72-73.). I prefer to regard the mark in the reverse right field of the coin as an Arabic letter or letters. There are several considerations.*

1. Scythopolis was transliterated as B-Y-S-N in the earliest surviving Arabic sources. I have checked al-Tabari (ed. M. de Goeje, vol. 5, p. 2397, line 2). On the coin, the letter at the right is consistent with B-Y- (without points above and below the letters) and the first upward prong of an S or SH. It could thus be an abbreviation for the mint name.

2. It might simply be the Arabic 'sin' for S or 'shin' for SH (without the three points over the letter found in later classical Arabic texts – a common phenomenon in 7th c. epigraphy). If the mint name were intended, it could stand for S or SH of S-N or SH-N, the consonants of the second syllable of 'Baysan', 'Bayt Shan' or similar.

2. It could represent three letters, B-Y-T, written in defective script, i.e. without the points above and below the letters, giving the Arabic bayt or 'house'. If the 7th c. Arabs transliterated directly from the local Aramaic dialect, which is possible, they may originally have pronounced and written the place-name as 'Bayt Shan' (with a long 'a'), which is closer to the Aramaic and Hebrew, and not the 'Baysan' (with long 'a') that is recorded three centuries later in al-Tabari (ob. 923 AD).

3. As I now consider the problem, the bearer of the coin may have been expected to see the letter(s) as a doublet (two words superimposed, so to speak) represented in a single figure, first reading the B-Y-T, then reading S or SH, and making the connexion between 'Bayt' and 'S(h)an' (with a long 'a'). This would have involved mentally inserting the points above and below the letters to get B-Y-T, then mentally reading the letter a second time as S (or SH) as an abbreviation for S-N or SH-N.

The problem is, we know too little about how the 7th c. Arabs transliterated Hebrew and Aramaic place-names at the time of the Muslim conquest. The Hebrew is apparently 'Beth Shean' or 'Beth Shan' (with a long 'a'). Unfortunately the Arabic name of the town does not appear in any of the early 8th-9th c. inscriptions and grafitti found at Scythopolis, as edited by M. Sharon in the **Corpus Inscriptionum Arabicarum Palaestinae** *(CIAP) II (Brill, 1999), pp. 207-228.*

[I have also seen it] suggested that the letters represent B-B-Y (bi-Bay with vowels), 'in Baysan' with the place-name abbreviated.

[Sadly] there is too little evidence to construct decisive conclusions and there may be angles of argument of which I am unaware.'

Since no consensus has appeared, the abbreviation 'udl' will be retained in this discussion.

---

[33] E-mail Frank Trombley to Andrew Oddy 16th October 2014.

Two reverse dies are also known for the 'udl' coins, but these are paired with six obverse dies, which connect to the **CON**, **CION**, *mqsm*, and normal **NIKO** year Ч**II** reverses (fig. 8).

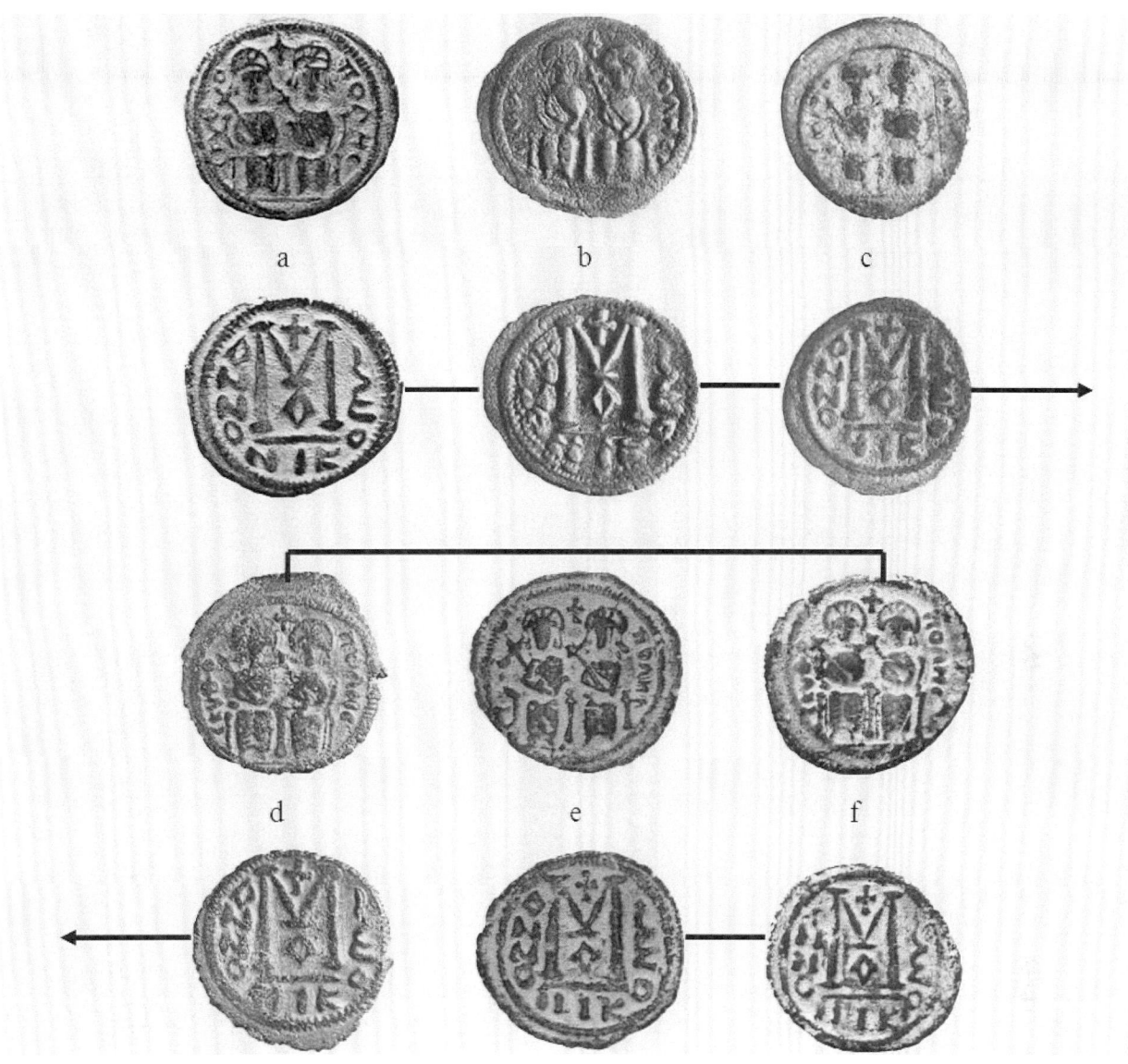

Figure 8: 'udl' type. (a) (142/14/28) ebay January 2013, 10.42g; (b) (113/52/28) Israel Museum 12366, weight unknown; (c) (062/48/28) Israel Museum 12332, weight unknown; (d) (235/11/28) Dumbarton Oaks catalogue 82, 10.11g; (e) (368/25/73) Morton & Eden Sale 66 (7 November 2013) lot 466, 11.10g; (f) (384/11/73) Private collection, 8.46g (scale 1:1)

So far this paper has considered the various varieties of the main obverse type described above and illustrated in figure 3a. Coins with the mint name Scythopolis on the obverse are relatively numerous and are known from at least 24 obverse dies and 43 reverse dies.[34] It is noteworthy that there is a small number of Scythopolis obverse dies known from only one specimen.[35]

---

[34] The uncertainties are due to the poor state of preservation of some coins, making the die identification difficult.
[35] A die study is in progress.

Scythopolis Coin Weights

Weights are recorded for 164 *fulūs* of Scythopolis. This number includes the *mqsm* and 'udl' varieties and those with **CON** (and variations) and **KYZ** on the reverse. Figure 9 is a histogram of the weights which range from 14.8g down to 3.69g. Looking carefully at this histogram it can be seen that the weights can be divided into four 'zones'. Zone 1 contains coins weighing more than about 12.5g. These suggest that the original weight standard was planned to be in the region of 14g, but that it quickly fell. Zone 2 contains coins weighing between 9.5g and 12.5g. Perhaps these represent an attempt to produce coins weighing about 11g. Zone 3 illustrates a rapid decline in weight until Zone 4 is reached. Zone 4 may represent a weight standard aiming at about 6g.

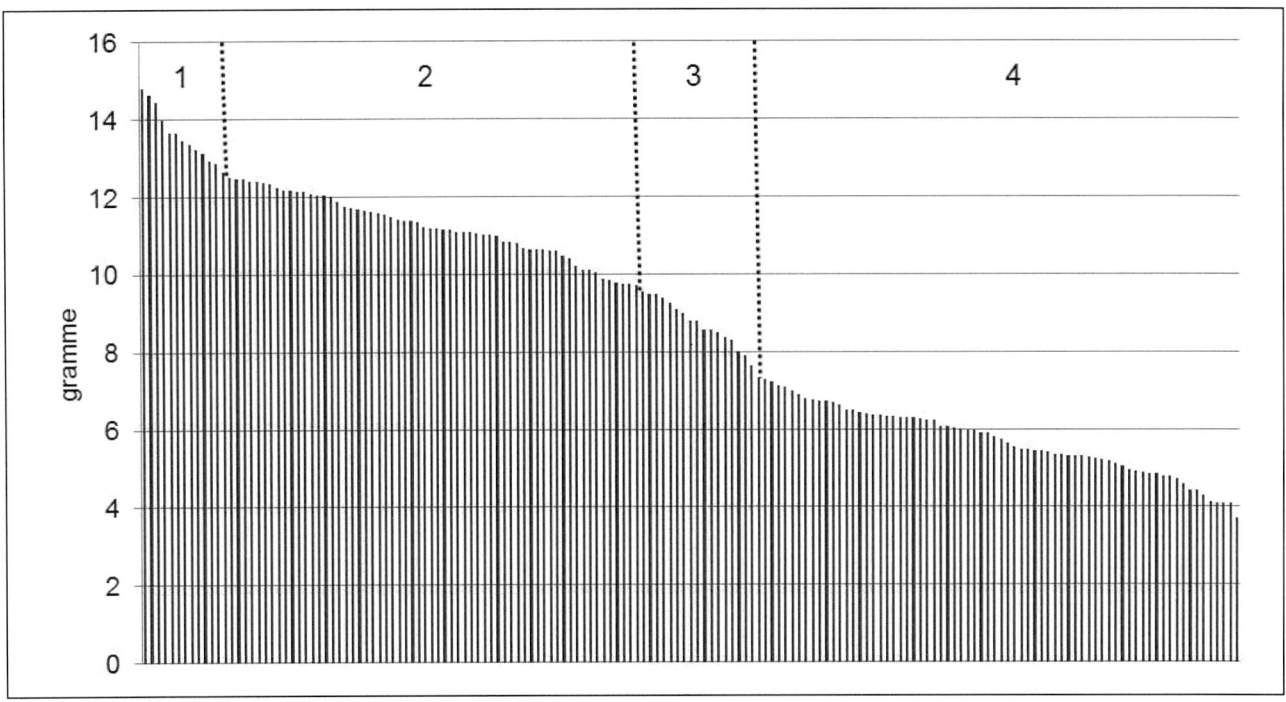

Figure 9: Histogram of the weights of 164 fulūs of Scythopolis ranging from 14.8g down to 3.69g

The first thing to note is that the *mqsm*, 'udl', and **CON** varieties are almost all at the heavy end of the histogram (zone 2), as can be seen from figure 10. This indicates that they are among the earliest issues at Scythopolis, but there is no indication that these varieties form a sequence with declining weight. For the moment, therefore, no rationale can be discerned to explain why four different reverses (i.e. **CON** year **XI** and **XII**, *mqsm*, 'udl' and **NIKO** year **ЧII**) were apparently used concurrently. Only four specimens of these four varieties lie outside zone 2. The two 'udl' coins weighing c. 8g are unremarkable, but the two light weight *mqsm* coins (weighing 4.86g and 6.35g) are probably contemporary imitations (see below).

When the actual Scythopolis coins are examined it is noteworthy that as the weight declines, so does the style and accuracy of the die cutting. In particular, legends on the reverse start to include retrograde letters and to have the left and right fields occasionally transposed. This can be illustrated by a selection of the coins (figs 11 and 12)

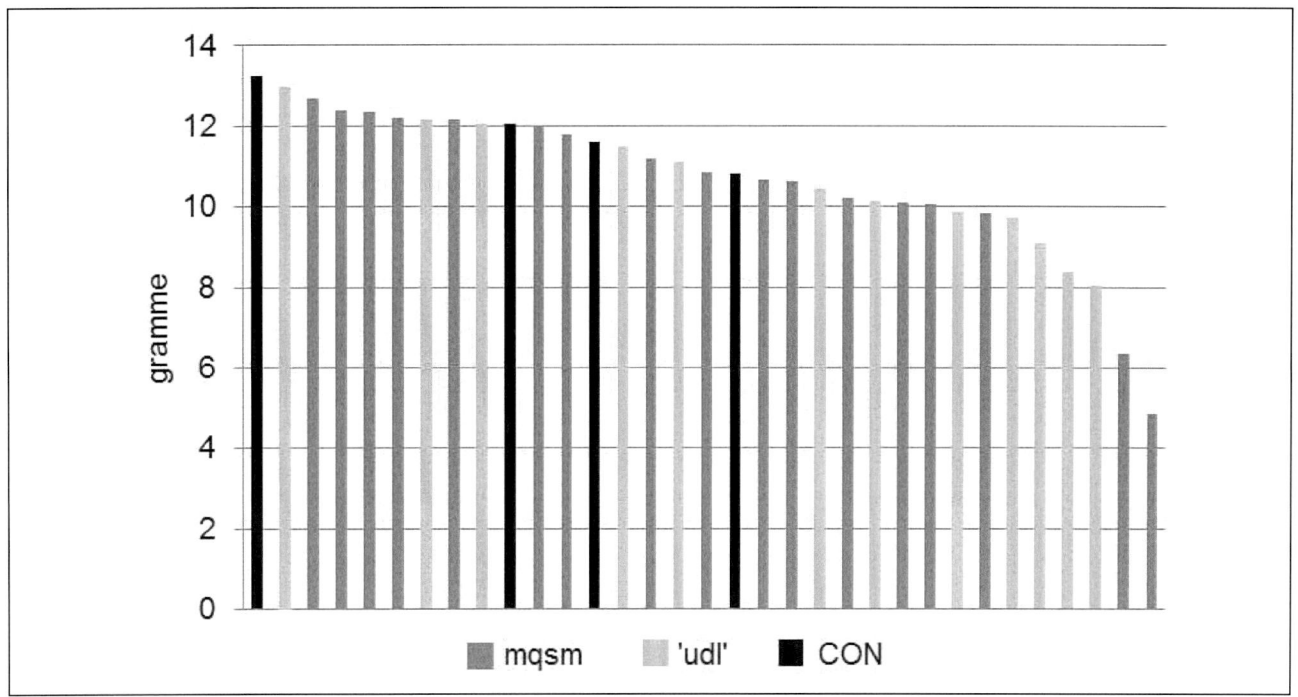

Figure 10: Histogram of the weights of fulūs of Scythopolis with reverse varieties mqsm, 'udl' and **CON**

What is difficult to suggest is the period of time over which this decline in weight took place and this must await a full die study.[36] A preliminary suggestion is to say that this must be a period of several years, and it is possible to identify different die cutters from a close observation of the coins.

The half *fals* of Scythopolis (fig. 3a) is much less common than the *fals*, being hitherto known from 23 specimens. Five obverse and five reverse dies have been identified (fig. 13). Weights and die identifications are available for 18 coins and they range from 6.2g down to 2.2g (fig. 14). When this histogram is examined there seems to be a gradual drop in weight and it is not possible to suggest any 'zones' except, perhaps, for the two lightest coins. However, when the dies are examined, the two lightest coins and the two heaviest are from the same obverse die (fig. 14). Furthermore, the only dies to show any evidence of incompetence or illiteracy, reverse 124 paired with obverse 104 (fig. 13d) and reverse 125 paired with obverse 105 (fig. 13e), are not the lightest in the group, although they are at the lighter end of the range (fig. 14).

What is noteworthy about the half *fulūs* is that the heaviest coins are about half the weight of the heaviest *fulūs* while the lightest half *fals* is about half the weight of the lightest *fulūs*. This suggests that as the weight of the *fals* declined, the weight of the half *fals* declined 'in step'. The fact that the same half *fals* obverse die was used for the lightest and heaviest coins can be explained if it is assumed that the production of the half *fulūs* was very much smaller than that of the *fulūs* (which is what the much smaller number of recorded specimens suggests) resulting in much less wear to the half *fulūs* dies.

---

[36] In preparation.

13.65g (132/11/26) Ponterio 136 (Nov 2005) lot 2101

12.42g (275/34/26) CNG (Sept 2012) lot 523

11.67g (279/18/45) Album 10 (April 2011) lot 73

11.20g (347/12/84) Private Collection

11.16g (177/12/13) Elsen 114 (Sept 2012) lot 1400

11.05g (256/48/11) Spink 31 (June 1989) lot 194

9.76g (137/66/26) Private Collection

9.75g (336/14/11) Private Collection

8.57g (170/34/38) CNG 285 (Aug 2012) lot 442

7.27g (205/16/78) Leu 32 (Oct 1982) lot 66

7.11g (086/13/16) Private Collection

6.88g (122/13/14) Private Collection

Figure 11   (scale 1:1)

6.70g (415/59/87) Gorny & Mosch 102 (2000) lot 664   6.57g (198/16/22) Baldwin 47 (2006) lot 249

6.50g (318/ 16/17) Private Collection   6.25g (277/58/91) Private Collection

6.08g (344/47/14) Private Collection   6.02g (354/44/44) Sofaer Collection 80

No wt. (474/16/54) Jordan Ahli Bank Mus.   No wt. (153/15/105) Jordan Ahli Bank Mus.

4.88g (320/59/57) Private Collection   4.85g (379/15/23) Album 19 (May 2014) lot 202

4.79g (385/16/55) Private Collection   4.71g (510/47/43) Kovacs 16 (Sept 2004) lot 393

Figure 12   (scale 1:1)

Figure 13: Half fulūs of Scythopolis illustrating the five known dies for each face of the coins. (a) (402/101/121) Bibliothèque Nationale, Paris, weight unknown; (b) (260/102/122) Spink 31 (20 June 1989) lot 195, 4.50g; (c) (237/103/123) Dumbarton Oaks 84, 5.82g; (d) (400/104/124) Private collection, 3.72g; (e) (047/105/125) Private collection, 3.51g (scale approx. ×1.5)

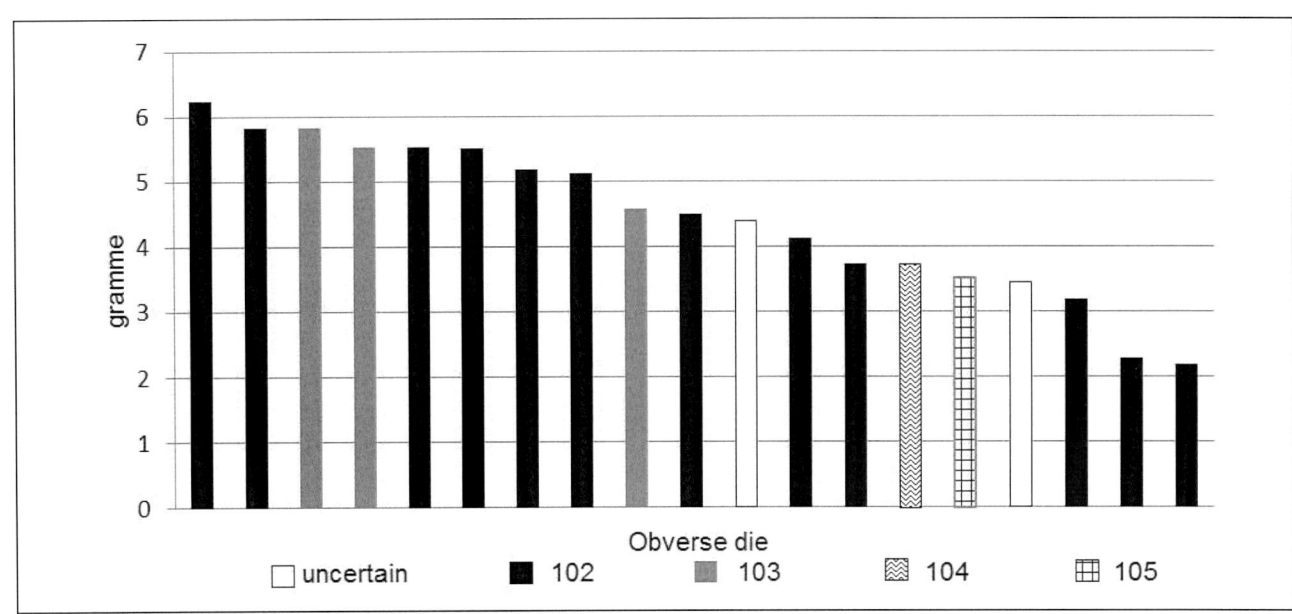

Figure 14: Histogram of the weights of 19 half fulūs of Scythopolis ranging from 6.2g down to 2.2g. The identification of the obverse dies can be seen from the shading of the individual weight columns. [One obverse die does not appear on this diagram as it is known from only one coin (fig. 13a) for which the weight is not available.]

The design and style of the Phase 2 coinage of Baisān

While the Scythopolis coinage was still in production, the name of the city reverted to Baisān, (which as Beth She'an had been the name of the place in pre-Hellenistic times) and this is reflected in the coinage on which the mint name Scythopolis remains on the obverse but the mint name Baisān (in Arabic) is introduced onto the reverse. Again, production consisted of *fulūs* and half *fulūs* but now it is the half *fals* which is the most abundant.

Eleven specimens of the *fals* with the mint name Baisān on the reverse are known being struck from two obverse dies and two reverse dies. These are all die linked together (fig. 15b, c, d and e). The obverse is unchanged from that of the coins of Scythopolis having two seated figures with the mint name **CKVΘO ΠOΛHC** reading clockwise from 7.30 o'clock. The Baisān obverses are not die linked to the Scythopolis coins but could be by the same hand as obverse die 15 (fig. 15a).

The reverse is where the change takes place with the **NIKO** legend being moved to the right field and Baisān in Arabic being introduced into the exergue. **ANNO** remains in the left field but without a date!

The weights of the Baisān *fulūs* range from 7.9g down to 5.1g (and are plotted as a histogram in figure 17), with an average of 6.4g. The weights of the Scythopolis coins with obverse die 15 range from 6.8g down to 4.1g, with an average of 5.2g. These similarities are highly suggestive of the two types being struck at more or less the same time.

The Baisān *fulūs* clearly belong in the equivalent of Zone 4 of figure 9, indicating that the Baisān coins were struck at the end, or towards the end, of the Scythopolis issues. However, the significant number of Scythopolis coins with weights below those of the Baisān coins rules out a definitive statement as to whether the Baisān coins were contemporary with the later Scythopolis coins or whether they followed the last of the Scythopolis issues, although the latter seems more likely. The forthcoming die study may shed light on this question.

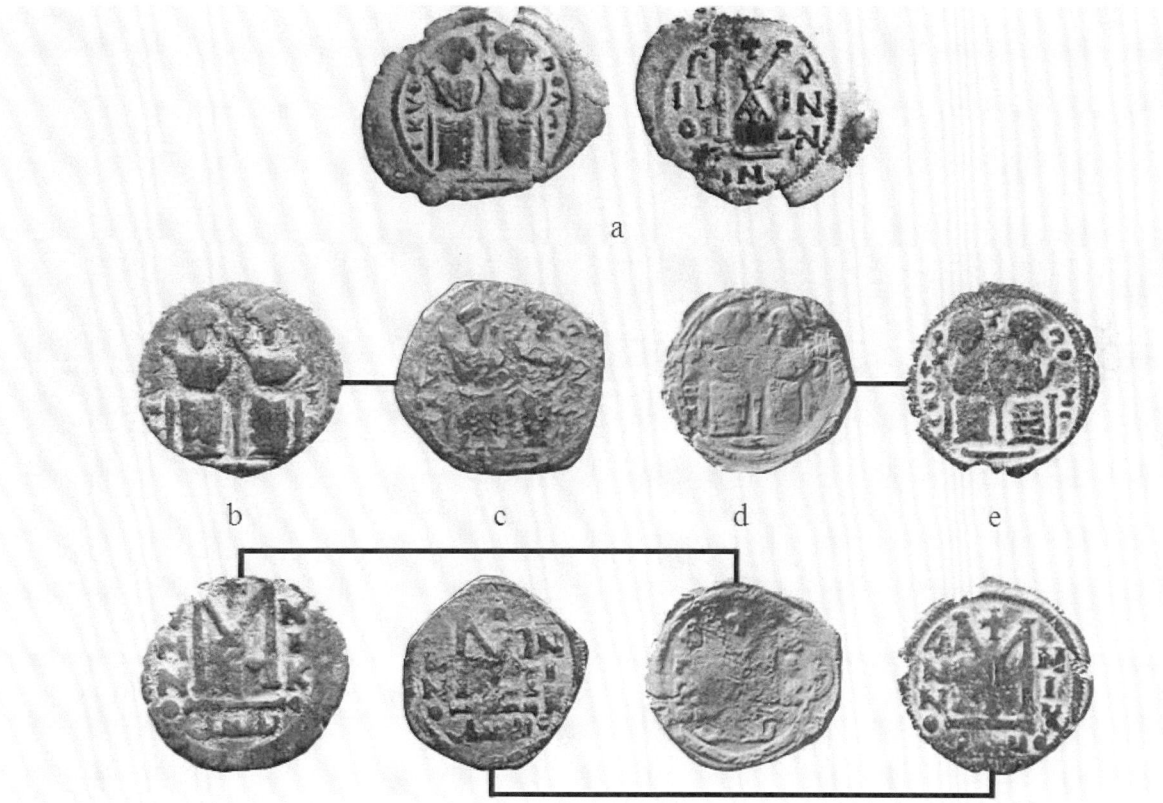

Figure 15: A fals of Scythopolis with obverse die 15 compared with four fulūs of Scythopolis/Baisān. (a) (461/15/23) Jordan Ahli Bank Museum, weight unknown; (b) (271/27/31) Private collection, 7.87g; (c) (268/27/93) Album 10 (April 2011) lot 72, 5.06g; (d) (034/62/31) Walker FN 5 no Bel.2, weight unknown; (e) (270/62/93) Private collection, 6.32g (scale1:1)

Figure 16: Half fulūs of Baisān. (a) Sofaer Collection 84, 3.78g; (b) Private collection, 4.11g; (c) Sternberg 7 (Nov 1977) lot 1306, 4.34g; (d) Khalili Collection 33, 4.92g   (scale approx. x1.5)

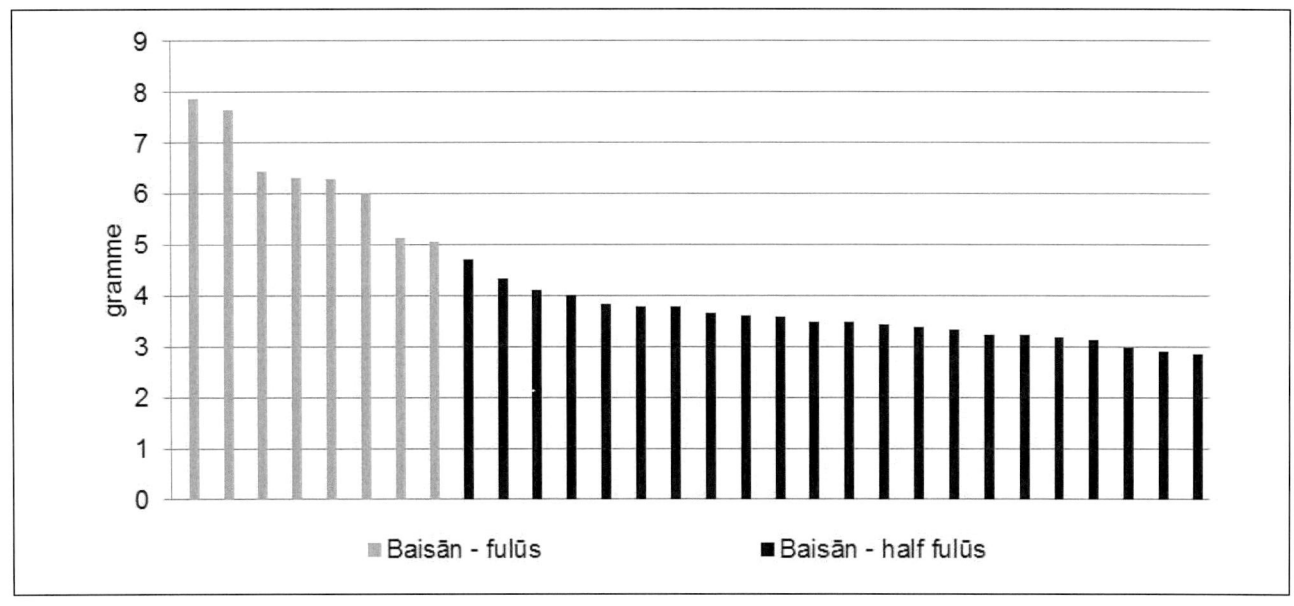

Figure 17: Histogram of the weights of fulūs and half fulūs with the mint name Baisān in Arabic on the reverse

The Baisān half *fulūs* are known from 43 examples, with two types of obverse die and three types of reverse. The first type of obverse die (fig. 16a and b), of which four specimens have been recorded (all from the same obverse die) has two seated figures holding sceptres with a rudimentary legend in the left field. This legend was read by Amitai-Preiss et al [37] as **CKYΘO**, but the lettering is too small for this to be certain, and there is no continuation of the name of Scythopolis in the right field. The second type of obverse dies (fig. 16c and d) is more stylistically similar to the Baisān *fulūs* (fig. 15b to e) but have no legend. Three reverse varieties have been recorded. All have a large letter **K** with *baisan* in Arabic to the left and a horizontal line to the right. One type has ᴗ above the **K** and **X** below (fig. 16a and c), another has **X** above and ⌒ below (fig. 16b) and the third has **+** above and ⌒ below (fig. 16d).

---

[37] N. Amitai-Preiss, A. Berman and S. Qedar, The Coinage of Scythopolis-Baysān and Gerasa-Jerash, ***Israel Numismatic Journal*** **13** (1994-99) 133-151 esp. 145 no. B2.

The weights of 22 half *fulūs* are recorded and their weight distribution is shown in figure 17, together with that of the *fulūs*. There *appears* to be a steady decline in weight of the Baisān half *fulūs* from 4.7g down to 2.9g. However, it is impossible to say with certainty whether this is a deliberate weight reduction with the passage of time or whether it is merely the result of poor quality control of the weight of the coins in the mint. In view of the fact that there is no clustering of weights (which would be indicated by level areas on the histogram), the latter is more likely. Hence it may be tentatively concluded that the theoretical weight of the Baisān half *fals* was approximately 3.6g. This is slightly more than half the average weight of the *fulūs* which is 6.4g.

The final Phase 2 coinage at Baisān – *the fals al-ḥaqq bi-baisān*

In 1984 an apparently unpublished coin was offered for sale by Hess.[38] This had a 'three figure' type of obverse, normally found only on the Phase 2 coinage of Tiberias, and weighed 3.02g. The reverse has an **M** with an **A** below and an 'anchor' symbol above. The Arabic legend reads *fals al-ḥaqq bi-baisān* which was translated as 'the legal *fals* in Baisān' in the Hess catalogue.

Figure 18: Three figure fulūs minted at Baisān. (a) Album 10 (April 2011) lot 149, 2.87g; (b) www in October 2013, 2.96g   (scale x2)

This issue was discussed by Amitai-Preiss *et al* [39] who prefer the translation 'the true *fals* [minted] in Baisān'. They illustrated a specimen excavated by the Hebrew University at Beth She'an (ancient Scythopolis/Baisān). Altogether 27 specimens have been recorded as part of this study with an average weight of 2.87g.

As Amitai-Preiss *et al* pointed out, the obverse copies the Phase 2 coinage of Tiberias, which was the capital of Jund al-Urdunn, the administrative district in which Scythopolis was situated. Because of its low weight, and because the design of the coins bear almost no relationship to the Scythopolis and the Baisān coinages already described, the issue of the *fals al-ḥaqq bi-baisān* coinage at Scythopolis must be the last Phase 2 coinage at that mint before it struck the epigraphic coinage of the second coinage reform of 'Abd al-Malik which took place in 77H (696/7).[40]

So why did the Scythopolis mint change its obverse design to follow that of the regional capital? It can only be seen as a move to standardise the weight and obverse design of the coinage within the jund. As Amitai-Preiss *et al* pointed out, the *fals al-ḥaqq bi-baisān* dies, and perhaps also the coins, may have been manufactured at the Tiberias mint.

When is this standardisation likely to have taken place?

---

[38] Adolph Hess 255 (September 1984) lot 4.
[39] N. Amitai-Preiss, A. Berman and S. Qedar, The Coinage of Scythopolis-Baysān and Gerasa-Jerash, *Israel Numismatic Journal* **13** (1994-99) 133-151 p.138.
[40] L. Ilisch, ***Sylloge Numorum Arabicorum Tübingen: Palästina: IV a Bilād aš-Šām I***, Tübingen, 1993, nos. 261ff.

In other junds to both the north and south of Jund al-Urdunn, the Phase 2 coinage comes to an end with the introduction of the 'Standing Caliph' coins (Phase 3) which are the result of the first coinage reform of 'Abd al-Malik. The date of this reform for the gold coinage is known because the coins are dated, the earliest one being 74H (693/4), although it is not known whether the copper coinage started at the same time – or later – or even earlier. As the mints of Scythopolis and Tiberias did not strike Standing Caliph coins, it is probable that the *fals al-ḥaqq bi-baisān* coins were struck in the years immediately before the second (epigraphic) coinage reform in 696/7. It may even be suggested that the type was struck 'in answer' to the manufacture of Standing Caliph coins in other junds, that is in or after 74H (693/4). Clive Foss, however, places these coins in the early years of the reign of 'Abd al-Malik, c.686-688,[41] but their low weight precludes this.

Overstrikes

Coins of Scythopolis are known overstruck on Phase 2 coins of Tiberias and Damaskos, and on a Phase 3 'Standing Caliph' coin from an unidentified mint.[42]

When the first of the overstrikes on a coin of Tiberias was identified in 1988 it was received at first with scepticism by some numismatists who found it difficult to believe that the Tiberias coins (fig. 19a) were not significantly later than the Scythopolis coins. This overstrike (fig. 19b), weighing 5.47g, was published as a 'Scythopolis on Tiberias' overstrike in 1994[43] and subsequently accepted as such by Amitai-Preiss *et al*[44] and Goodwin.[45] Amitai-Preiss *et al* also published a Scythopolis overstrike weighing 4.14g (fig. 19c) made from the same dies as figure 19b.[46] Althought they could not identify the undertype it seems very likely that it was also a three figure coin of Tiberias as others have since come to light weighing 5.28g (fig. 19d), 4.10g (fig. 19e)[47] and 5.36g.[48]

The weights (5.5g to 4g) show that the over-striking probably occurred towards the end of the two seated figures Scythopolis coinage (see fig. 9). Does this mean that the inception of the Tiberias coinage took place only when the weight of the Scythopolis coinage had declined from 12-14g down to 4-5g? This seems likely because if the Tiberias mint had been in production for some time at c.5g, the coins would have had a smaller intrinsic value than the heavier Scythopolis coinage struck contemporaneously in the same Jund. Of course, it is generally thought that the intrinsic value of copper coinage is not a factor of great importance in ancient mints,[49] but it is never a good idea for coins with the same face value, circulating in the same place, to have very different weights.

This raises the question of whether the Phase 2 Arab-Byzantine coinages *did* circulate outside the junds in which the mints was situated, or even outside the immediate hinterland of the mints themselves. Until recently the evidence for this was scattered, but Clive Foss made a start in

---

[41] C. Foss, *Arab-Byzantine Coins, an Introduction, with a Catalogue of the Dumbarton Oaks Collection*, Washington DC, 2008, 61-2.
[42] T. Goodwin, Arab-Byzantine Coins – the Significance of Overstrikes, *Numismatic Chronicle* **161** (2001) 91-109; T. Goodwin, The Chronology of the Umayyad Imperial Coinage: Progress over the last 10 years, *Proceedings 3*, 89-107, esp. 104-7.
[43] A. Oddy, The early Umayyad Coinage of Baisān and Jerash, *ARAM* **6** (1 & 2) 1994, no.18.
[44] N. Amitai-Preiss, A. Berman and S. Qedar, The Coinage of Scythopolis-Baysān and Gerasa-Jerash, *Israel Numismatic Journal* **13** (1994-99) 133-151, note to coin A8b.
[45] T. Goodwin, Arab-Byzantine Coins – the Significance of Overstrikes, *Numismatic Chronicle* **161** (2001) 91-109, no.47.
[46] N. Amitai-Preiss, A. Berman and S. Qedar, The Coinage of Scythopolis-Baysān and Gerasa-Jerash, *Israel Numismatic Journal* **13** (1994-99) 133-151, no.A8b.
[47] Album 7 (December 2009) lot 109.
[48] T. Goodwin, *Proceedings 3*, no.12.
[49] Although the availability of the raw metal was a factor in how many coins could be struck.

collecting it together in 1999.[50] His data was updated and made very accessible in the Dumbarton Oaks catalogue of 2008.[51] Now, however, the work of Bijovsky on the archives of the Israel Antiquities Authority has enabled her to publish distribution maps of the find-spots of Phase 2 coins in Israel.[52] Here it can be seen clearly that coins did travel away from the towns in which they were struck.

As the earliest Tiberias *fulūs* struck at c.5g are not common and appear to have rapidly declined in weight, it is unlikely that the larger coins would have persisted in the market place when the average size had been reduced. They would either have been hoarded or re-coined, hence their availability for over-striking would not have lasted for long.

Figure 19: Overstrikes of Scythopolis fulūs on fulūs of Tiberias/Ṭabariya.
(a) Ṭabariya, Private collection, 5.51g; (b) (326/22/24) Private collection, 5.47g;
(c) (208/22/24) Israel Museum 12339, 4.14g; (d) (331/15/23) Private collection, 5.28g;
(e) (311/63/95) Album 7 (December 2009) lot 109, 4.10g   (scale 1:1)

There is also an overstrike of a Scythopolis half *fals* on a small size Tiberias *fals* weighing 3.45g (fig. 20a).[53] This overstrike indicates that the weight of the *fals* at Tiberias did fall more quickly than at Scythopolis and soon reached the point where the Tiberias *fals* weighed only approximately half that of the Scythopolis *fals*. It is obvious that the minting authorities in Scythopolis could not allow these very light weight Tiberias *fulūs* to circulate at par with the heavier Scythopolis coins and so they were devalued by re-tariffing.

So few examples of overstrikes make the drawing of conclusions premature, but it certainly seems either that the monetary system at Scythopolis was more 'robust' than at Tiberias or that the monetary system at Scythopolis was out of step with that of the other main Arab-Byzantine mints. In fact both hypotheses may be true as the next overstrike illustrates a Scythopolis half *fals* on a 'Damaskos' (or Pseudo-Damascus) *fals* (fig. 20b). Thus it may be the case that the fairly rapid weight decline at Tiberias was not a local economic factor but part of a deliberate attempt to bring the coinages at Tiberias, Damascus, Emesa and Baalbek approximately into line as far as size and weight are concerned. Thus it would be the Scythopolis coinage which remained out of step but

---

[50] C. Foss, The Coinage of Syria in the Seventh Century: the evidence of excavations, **Israel Numismatic Journal** 13 (1999) 119-132.
[51] C. Foss, **Arab-Byzantine Coins, an Introduction, with a Catalogue of the Dumbarton Oaks Collection**, Washington DC, 2008, 61-2.
[52] G. Bijovsky, **Arab-Byzantine Coins from Excavations in Israel – an update**, this volume, figures 12-16.
[53] N. Amitai-Preiss, A. Berman and S. Qedar, The Coinage of Scythopolis-Baysān and Gerasa-Jerash, **Israel Numismatic Journal** 13 (1994-99) 133-151, coin B1a.

the minting authorities there were sufficiently independent to try and maintain their heavier denominations.

The overstrike on a 'Damaskos' coin (fig. 20b) is on the variety known as *jāza hadhā dimashq wāfiya*[54] which is the reading of part of the Arabic reverse legend and translates as 'current this (fals in) Damaskos, full weight'. Until recently, this variety was presumed to be a product of the regular Phase 2 Damaskos mint. Goodwin has now suggested, however, that the *jāza hadhā* variety was initially struck "by an unknown authority in Damascus" and that the reverse was then copied by the Pseudo-Damascus mint.[55] It is not possible to determine whether the under-type of figure 20b is a 'regular' coin or a Pseudo-Damascus coin.

Figure 20: Overstrikes of Scythopolis fals and half-fals on fulūs of Tiberias/Ṭabariya and of 'Damaskos' (or, perhaps, Pseudo-Damascus). (a) (225/dies uncertain) Israel Museum 12375, 3.45g; (b) (228/102/122) Private collection, 4.11g (scale approx. x2)

Finally, there is one more overstrike of great significance. This is a Scythopolis *fals* overstruck on a Standing Caliph (Phase 3) *fals* of an unidentified mint (fig. 21a).[56] The undertype is similar to the coin illustrated in figure 21c.

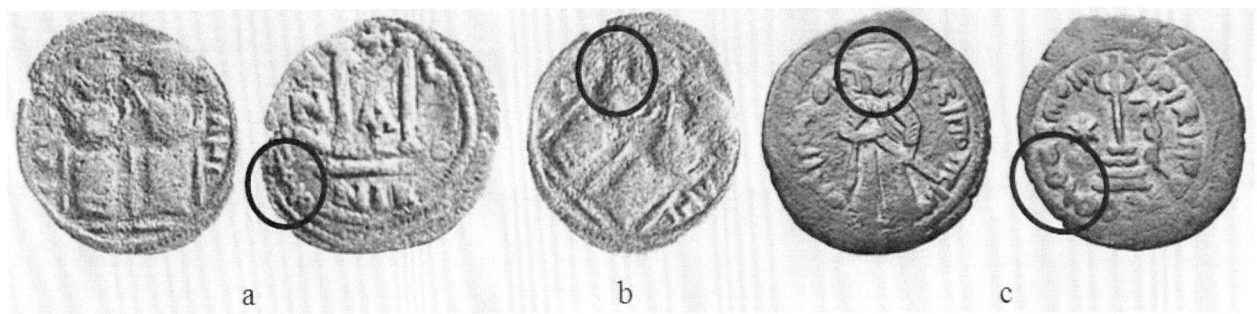

Figure 21: Overstrike of a Scythopolis fals on a 'Standing Caliph' (Phase 3) coin of an unknown mint. (a) (207/15/15) Franciscan Biblical School collection, Jerusalem, 4.08g; (b) Obverse of (a) rotated through 45°; (c) Standing Caliph (Phase 3) coin of Hims, CNG 282 (July 2012) lot 420, 4.45g (scale approx x1.5)

---

[54] S. Album and T. Goodwin, Sylloge of Islamic Coins in the Ashmolean: Volume 1: The pre-reform coinage of the early Islamic period, Oxford, 2002, nos. 564ff.
[55] T. Goodwin and R. Gyselen, **The Irbid Hoard of Arab-Byzantine Coins**, Royal Numismatic Society Special Publication, forthcoming.
[56] N. Amitai-Preiss, A. Berman and S. Qedar, The Coinage of Scythopolis-Baysān and Gerasa-Jerash, *Israel Numismatic Journal* **13** (1994-99) 133-151, coin B1a.

The Scythopolis obverse die (no.15) is known from 18 specimens combined with five different reverse dies all weighing between 6.8g and 4.1g. The same obverse die is also one of those used for the overstrikes on the Tiberias *fulūs*. Five specimens are known of this obverse die combined with the same reverse die (no.15 – see figure 21a). Again, the low weight range puts the use of obverse die 15 towards the end of the weight range of the Scythopolis coinage indicated by zone 4 on figure 9. Obverse die 15 is also the one that is most stylistically similar to the obverse dies of the Baisān coinage (fig. 15).

The evidence for the standing caliph undertype is indicated in the images in figure 21. On the reverse, part of the Arabic legend is clearly visible on the reverse of the Scythopolis coin, but on the obverse an 'eye of faith' is necessary. However, it is just possible to see the 'ghostly' head of the Caliph when the Scythopolis coin is rotated through 45° (fig. 21b).

That this overstrike uses a Standing Caliph coin as a 'blank' was first recognised by Amitai-Preiss *et al*[57] but they did not comment on the potential importance of this coin for dating the Scythopolis coinage. Goodwin, in his first publication on overstrikes,[58] did comment on the importance of this coin as a demonstration that the later coinage of Scythopolis was concurrent with the Phase 3 Standing Caliph coinage.

What this overstrike demonstrates is that the Scythopolis coinage was still being struck after the introduction of the Phase 3 Standing Caliph coinage at mints outside Jund al-Urdunn. From the fragment of the Arabic legend on the reverse the likelihood is that the Standing Caliph undertype was struck at Hims. Now it is known, because the coins are dated, that the gold Standing Caliph coins were first struck in 74H (693/4), but the copper coinage is undated. The conventional view has been that the copper Standing Caliph coins were also initiated in 74H, or soon after, although Goodwin has proposed that the Standing Caliph coinage at Īliyā probably preceded 74H. However, the Standing Caliph coins at Īliyā have a different reverse from the one over-struck at Scythopolis. The reverse of the latter is known as the 'symbol on steps' and Goodwin concluded that this type "possibly occurred just before the gold solidi were first issued [74H], but the two events were almost certainly very close to each other in time". This dating is supported by the recognition of the Scythopolis overstrike on a Standing Caliph coin, possibly minted originally at Hims. To fit the later coinages struck at Scythopolis into the available time period before the second coinage reform in 77 H (696/7), it is necessary for the Standing Caliph coins with the 'symbol on steps' reverse to have started at least by 74H, if not slightly earlier.[59]

A proposed time line for this period is outlined in figure 22. This is, however, only an outline in which the Hegira years are used as 'pegs' on which to hang the successive coinage issues without meaning to indicate that the author is committed to this dating in detail.

---

[57] N. Amitai-Preiss, A. Berman and S. Qedar, The Coinage of Scythopolis-Baysān and Gerasa-Jerash, *Israel Numismatic Journal* **13** (1994-99) 133-151, coin A8a.
[58] T. Goodwin, Arab-Byzantine Coins – the Significance of Overstrikes, ***Numismatic Chronicle* 161** (2001) 91-109, esp. 100.
[59] This discussion ignores the Standing Caliph coins struck in Jund Qinnasrīn and Jund al-Jazīra where the absence of mints for Phase 2 coins may indicate that the Standing Caliph type was used significantly before 74H. The differences between coin production and circulation in the two northern junds on one hand and the three southern junds on the other deserves an in depth study.

Coinage in Junds Ḥimṣ and Dimashq	Phase 2 Arab-Byzantine coins with mint names in Greek and/or Arabic	Standing Caliph *dinars* and *fulūs*	Standing Caliph *dinars* and *fulūs*	Standing Caliph *dinars* and *fulūs*	Standing Caliph *dinars* and *fulūs*	Epigraphic coinage of the 2ⁿᵈ reform of 'Abd al-Malik
	Pre 74H (693/4 AD)	74H (693/4 AD)	75H (694/5 AD)	76H (695/6 AD)	77H (696/7 AD)	77H (696/7 AD)
Coinage at Scythopolis/ Baisān	Over-striking by Scythopolis on three figure Ṭabariya copper	Over-striking by Scythopolis on Standing Caliph copper	*Fulūs* and half *fulūs* at Baisān	*Fulūs* and half *fulūs* at Baisān	*fals al-ḥaqq bi-baisān* copper at Baisān	Epigraphic copper at Baisān

Figure 22: Suggested approximate dating for the coinage of Scythopolis/Baisān in its final stages before the appearance of the epigraphic coinage of the second coinage reform of 'Abd al-Malik

Contemporary Imitations

Examination of figures 11 and 12 reveals that a significant number of Scythopolis reverse dies have retrograde letters or transposed legends. This raises the question as to whether these abnormal coins are regular issues of the Scythopolis mint or whether they should be classed as contemporary imitations/forgeries. Surprisingly, these errors in the reverse legends are usually combined with literate, or almost literate, obverse dies. Furthermore, a literate obverse die may be used with both literate and with illiterate reverse dies.

It is proposed, therefore, that most of these illiterate reverse dies should be considered as regular products of the Scythopolis mint in the latter years of its operation. Possible exceptions, however, are two obverse dies which have very large lunate headdresses and incomplete, or absent, obverse legends (figs 23 a-d and 23 e and f). One of these obverses has a reverse die of the *mqsm* type but with transposed reverse legends (fig. 23 a and b); there are two specimens known weighing only 6.35g and 4.86g. Because of the engraving errors and the very low weights compared with the *mqsm* coins of the early Scythopolis isssues (fig. 7) there is every reason to regard these coins as 'barbarous imitations' or 'contemporary forgeries'. However, their low weight makes it difficult to believe that they are contemporary with the regular *mqsm* issues which were probably struck in the early 670s. Yet, if they were struck some years later at a time when the weight of the Scythopolis fulūs had fallen to c.5.5g, why did the obverse imitate the original full weight *mqsm* obverse?

This question is complicated by the fact that the two 'barbarous' obverses are die linked together via a common reverse (fig. 23 d and e), but, and here is a problem, one of them is further die linked via two reverses (figure 23 e and f) to the 'twin Standing Caliph' coins (fig. 23 g-j), that have been attributed to the first year of 'Abd al-Malik (684/5) by Clive Foss.[60]

This whole group of coins (fig. 23) is enigmatic and no clear conclusions can be drawn about the time and place and authority of their issue. On the basis of two of the 'twin Standing Caliph' coins having been excavated at Gerasa, and the fact that the reverse of figure 23h has a decided 'flavour' of Gerasa in the style, Foss hesitatingly attributes the 'twin Standing Caliph' coins to Gerasa, an attribution following that of Goussous.[61] In 2004, Oddy first published the die link between the 'twin standing caliph' obverse and the 'Justin and Sophia' obverse (fig. 23 e and g). This seemed to

---
[60] C. Foss, The Two-Caliph Copper of Abd al-Malik, **Oriental Society Newsletter 177** (2003) 4-5.
[61] N. Goussous, **Umayyad Coinage of Bilad al-Sham**, Amman, 1996.

confirm Gerasa as the mint because the obverse of figure 23e has no legend and appears to be too barbarous to be a product of Scythopolis. Now however, a new die link to the other of the Justin and Sophia obverses featured in figure 23a-d raises a problem as the obverses of figure 23a–d have traces of what is obviously the Scythopolis legend ///**ΟΛΗC.**

Figure 23:
(a) (345/45/94) Private collection, 4.86g; (b) (436/45/94) Marot [62] plate XVI no.1447, 6.35g; (c) (469/45/30) Jordan Ahli Bank collection, weight unknown; (d) (319/45/30) www July 2013, 4.64g; (e) (316/26/30) Private collection, 3.81g; (f) (471/26/88) Jordan Ahli Bank Collection, weight unknown; (g) (233/56/30) Israel Museum 14610, 5.31g; (h) (387/56/88) Jordan Ahli Bank Collection, weight unknown; (i) (389/56/79) Hess (October 1983) lot 468, 5.85g; (j) (037/56/79) ANS 1998.25.13.9, 5.96g

If the 'twin Standing Caliph' coins are important official issue of 685, as Clive Foss postulates, then, presumably, none of the coins illustrated in figure 23 can be imitations/forgeries, unless the one and only known 'twin Standing Caliph' obverse die found its way out of the mint at the end of its life and was then used unofficially. An answer to this enigma awaits a die study of the Gerasa Justin and Sophia type *fulūs*.

---

[62] T. Marot, **Las Monedas Del Macellum De Gerasa**, Madrid 1998.

Summary

In order to aid the digestion of this paper, the main hypotheses, theories and conclusions are listed here:

- The Phase 1 (Pseudo-Byzantine) coinage of Bilad al-Sham was probably struck from very soon after the conquest until the early 670s. As it was being struck in a number of mints, they probably did not all shut down at the same time, but the use of a design based on the regular coinage of Constantine IV at only one mint suggests that Pseudo-Byzantine coins did not continue in production for long after his accession in 668. Perhaps of all the Phase 1 mints, the one that used the 'Constantine IV' obverse type was the last to close. This mint has not been identified

- The striking of Phase 2 coins in two denominations starts at the Scythopolis mint in the reign of Mu'awiya, perhaps in year 7 (667-80) but more likely in the early 670s.

- The early Scythopolis coinage had one obverse design but four reverse designs. Three of these reverses were only struck with one or two dies and were issued only for a brief period.

- The weights of the Scythopolis *fulūs* were reduced from an initial c.14g to a final c.4g. This weight reduction may have been gradual, but it is possible to suggest that there may have been an intention to strike initially at c.14g, but that this quickly fell to an intended c.11g and subsequently to an intended c.6g.

- The Scythopolis half *fals* has only one design with five known obverse dies and five reverse dies (two of which are retrograde). Although less common than the *fals*, the half *fals* was struck over the whole lifetime of the *fals*.

- Late examples of the Scythopolis *fulūs* were overstruck on early examples of the Phase 2 coinage of Tiberias. The most plausible explanation is that the Scythopolis coinage had been in production for some years before coining started at Tiberias. There is no independent date for the beginning of coinage at Tiberias, but because it is abundant a date before 690 seems likely.

- An example of a Scythopolis half *fals* overstruck on a Tiberias *fals* is known. This indicates that the weight of the *fals* at Tiberias fell more quickly than at Scythopolis making this devaluation necessary.

- A late Scythopolis *fals* is known overstruck on a Standing Caliph coin (of an uncertain mint, but possibly Ḥimṣ). The date of the introduction of the Phase 3 (Standing Caliph) copper coinage is unknown. In contrast, gold coins of the same design are dated and began to be issued in 696/7. It seems unlikely that the copper issues were initiated much before the gold, and so this overstrike must logically be dated to c.693/4.

- The Scythopolis coinage was probably followed by a *fals* and half *fals* with the mint name Baisān in Arabic on the reverse. The weights of the eleven known coins (from two obverse and two reverse dies) average 6.5g so it is not possible to be sure whether the Baisān coinage succeeded the Scythopolis coinage or was contemporary with its later stages. The half *fals* is more abundant and the average weight is about 3.5g. The suggested date for the Baisān coinage is c.694-696.

- The final Phase 2 coinage at Baisān was a small *fals* based on the design of coins being used at Tiberias. It has three standing figures on the obverse and *fals al-ḥaqq bi-baisān* in Arabic on the reverse and an average weight of 2.87g. This is not a common coin and its suggested date is c.696-697.

Acknowledgements

Collecting data on the coinage of Scythopolis and Baisān had been in progress for over 35 years and I am very grateful to the custodians and owners of all those public and private collections who have given me access to their coins and allowed me to take photographs or impressions for the subsequent manufacture of plaster casts. One of the largest collections, originally that of Dr Nayef Goussous in Amman, is now in the Jordan Ahli Bank Museum. It is a pleasure to record here the help given to me by Nayef Goussous on several visits to Amman over the years. His publications of part of the collection at the Ahli Bank are fundamental to the study of Byzantine-Arab coinage. The collection at the Israel Museum in Jerusalem is also very large and I am equally grateful to Dr Haim Gitler for supplying photographs of its Scythoplis coins many years ago.

In Europe and America I have benefited from my friendship with Charlie Karukstis, Mike Bates, who made the ANS collection available, Tony Goodwin, Susan Tyler-Smith, Marcus Phillips, Ingrid and Wolfgang Schulze, Gabriela Bijovski, Henri Pottier, Luke Treadwell, Steve Mansfield, and Frank Trombley who all furthered my research by supplying information and photographs and discussing unusual specimens. Among these names I owe an extra debt of gratitude to Ingrid and Wolfgang Schulze, Tony Goodwin and Steve Mansfield for reading and commentating on the penultimate draft of the manuscript. As a result some new ideas were generated, but I must say that I, and not them, am responsible for the wilder flights of fancy that may be detected by the long-suffering reader!

But most of all I dedicate this research to my wife, Pat, who has supported and indulged my obsession with coins for more than 50 years.

The Spear on Coins of the Byzantine-Arab Transition Period

Wolfgang Schulze and Andrew Oddy [1]

Introduction

Between the overthrow of the Byzantine provinces in the Near East in the late 630s and the introduction of an Islamic coinage by Mu'awiya (probably in the late 660s), several types of coins were struck in the geographical area that came to be known to the Arabs as Bilad al-Sham.[2] The iconography of these is mainly derived from the Byzantine coinage of Heraclius and Constans II, the most common obverse types being three standing figures (fig. 1a) and one standing figure (fig. 1b). Less common are two standing figures (fig. 1c) and a bust (fig. 1d). The reverses feature either an M or m. Standing figures usually hold a long cross in their right hand and to the left there is a *globus cruciger*, although these attributes are not universal. Bust type coins usually have a *globus cruciger* on the right of the figure (ie in the left field). These issues are known collectively as the *Phase 1 Coinage of the Byzantine-Arab Transition Period*.[3]

Figure 1

The importance of these coins is that they circulated alongside regular Byzantine coins and, although many of them are significantly barbarised in design, they are very conservative in their imagery.

However, with the coinage reform of Mu'awiya an abundant coinage began to be struck in five main cities that demonstrated innovation in design from the outset. The mints were Scythopolis (fig. 2a), Emesa (fig. 2b and c), Tiberias (fig. 2d), Heliopolis (fig. 2e) and Damascus (fig. 2f). Other,

---

[1] Wolfgang Schulze and Andrew Oddy are independent scholars: schulze@wg-s.de   waoddy@googlemail.com
[2] Sometimes known as 'Greater Syria' and consisting of the modern states of Jordan, Syria, Lebanon, Israel, the Palestinian Territories, and the south east part of Turkey
[3] For the terminology used in this paper see Schulze and Oddy (2012)

much less prolific, mints included Antaradus, Amman, Diospolis, Jerusalem, and Gerasa (but this list is not exhaustive).

Figure 2

In addition to these mints whose coins are readily identifiable because they have the name of the town or city of origin in either Greek or Arabic, there are two anonymous series known to numismatists as *al-wafā lillā* (fig. 3a and b)[4] and Pseudo-Damascus (fig. 3c and d)[5] respectively. Besides these two main anonymous series there are a number of smaller issues.[6]

---

[4] Schulze I. (2010)
[5] Goodwin (2007)
[6] Schulze W. (2012)

Figure 3

The Phase 2 coinage is full of innovative symbolism, and although the overall design – figure on the obverse, M/m on the reverse – is derived from Byzantine coins, the detail is often without any obvious parallels. It is with one aspect of this detail that this paper is principally concerned. Sometime and somewhere during the Phase 2 coinage of the Byzantine-Arab transition period in seventh century Syria, spears were introduced on the obverses of some coins at mints in Bilad al-Sham.

In fact, five, apparently separate, instances of the introduction of spears are known. In probable chronological order they are:
- The 'Twin Standing Caliph' issue of Gerasa
- The Pseudo-Damascus issues
- The 'orans' group
- The single standing figure follis of Tiberias
- The *miḥrāb* and *'anaza* drachm

In addition, there are two Arab-Sasanian coins with spears, minted outside Bilad al-Sham.

First, however, it is very important to ask what is meant by a spear in an Umayyad context. The coins in the five groups appear to show 'spears' with various shapes, but can they be better identified? In particular, do the coins illustrate spears or lances?

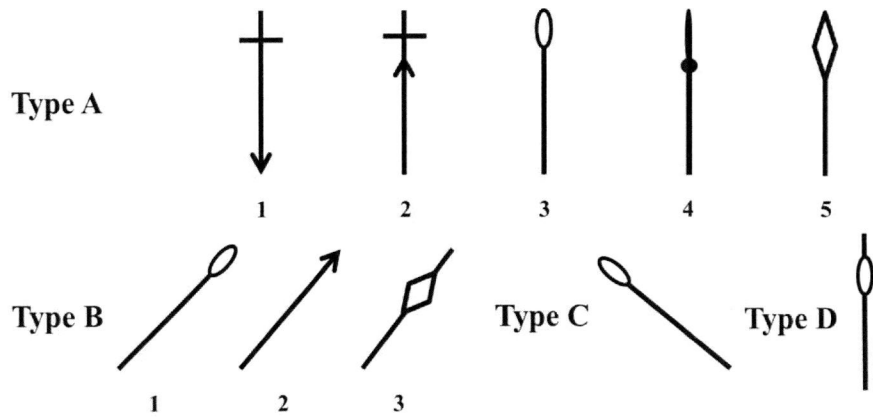

Figure 4

On Byzantine coins, the vertical form is sometimes described as a lance[7] but the definition of this in English[8] is "a weapon, consisting of a long wooden shaft and an iron or steel head, held by a horseman in charging at full speed".[9] Kennedy has found "no evidence of the use of heavy lances in mounted warfare" by the Arabs at the conquest period,[10] but they would have faced both Byzantine and Sasanian heavy cavalry who did carry long lances. That the Sasanian cavalry carried either spears (c.2metres) or lances (c.4metres), can be seen from illustrations on clay bullae[11] and rock reliefs. (figs 5 and 6).

Sasanain clay bulla of the spāhbed of the western part of the empire, late 6th century AD

Figure 5

Equestrian Combat of King Hormizd II in a rock relief at Taq e-Bustan. The king holds a lance in a 'couched' position for charging opposing cavalry.

Figure 6

---

[7] Morrisson (1970) p. 390, Pl. LX
[8] C T Onions (ed.), *The Shorter Oxford English Dictionary*, Oxford, 1973
[9] Although the Oxford Dictionary does not specify how the horseman held the lance, it was necessary that it was gripped very tightly and the best was to do this was to tuck it under the arm. In the later Middle Ages, armour was designed with projections on the breast plate to brace the lance and help to hold it firmly.
[10] Kennedy (2007) p. 59
[11] Gyselen (2007) p.268

Hence it remains to define what is meant by a spear in an Arab context and Kennedy describes the weapons of the early Muslim armies as follows:

> Along with the swords there were also spears. The long *rumh* was essentially an infantry weapon with a wooden shaft and a metal head, allowing it to be used as a slashing as well as a stabbing weapon. The shorter *ḥarba* appears in the early Islamic period and may have been used on horseback, ...

It therefore seems probable that the shorter *ḥarba* ('spear') is the weapon to be seen as the diagonal Types B and C (see fig. 4) that is carried over the shoulder and the long *rumh* ('spear') is the vertical weapon that has replaced the usual long cross in the right hand of standing figures (Type A) or is standing isolated (Type D). Thus the term 'spear' can be used for either type.

Apart from the coins, a number of contemporary illustrations of spears in Umayyad, Abbasid, Byzantine, Coptic and pre-Islamic contexts have been collected together by David Nicolle.[12] Some of these illustrate spears carried by horsemen or foot-soldiers which appear to be around 2metres in length. However, the only illustrations of direct relevance to Umayyad Syria are the fragmentary wall-paintings (dated to 725-744) at Quṣayr 'Amra in Jordan. Here foot-guards who stand to the left of the seated Amir (fig. 7a), carry spears with long blades, suitable for both stabbing and slashing, that are somewhat taller than a man, say c.2metres. In the same building is a hunting scene in which a huntsman carries a c.2metres spear with a short blade (fig. 7b). Both of these can be identified with the *rumh*.

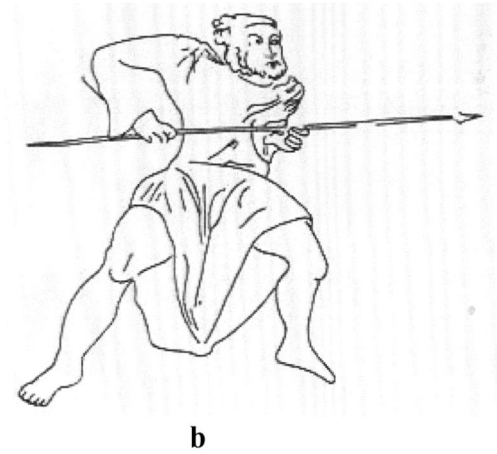

a   b

Figure 7

---

[12] Nicolle (1997)

The 'Twin Standing Caliph' issue of Gerasa

Figure 8

The Twin Standing Caliph coins are known from one obverse die and three reverse dies. They were first published by John Walker[13] after two examples (from the same dies, fig. 8b) and were discovered in the excavations at Jerash.[14] Walker translated the Arabic inscription on the reverses of Fig. 8b as 'In the name of Allah, [this coin is] of what the Servant of Allah, 'Abd al-Malik, Commander of the Faithful ordered'.[15] By 2004, ten examples of fig. 7b had been published and two other coins where the same obverse is combined with a similar reverse but with a garbled Greek legend instead of the Arabic.[16] The significance of the latter type was first realised by Nayef Goussous.[17] Andrew Oddy has published a die-link of one of the 'Greek' reverses with what is almost certainly a Gerasa obverse,[18] thus probably confirming the attribution of these Coins to Gerasa made by Nayef Goussous in 1996.[19]

From the Arabic reverse legend it is clear that the coins were struck in the reign of 'Abd al-Malik (AD 685-705; AH 65-86), but Clive Foss has argued that they were struck at his accession (685) and show 'Abd al-Malik himself, together with his brother, 'Abd al-'Aziz.[20] The brothers had been designated as heirs to reign in succession by their father, the Caliph Marwan ibn al-Hakam, during his brief reign of just under one year (684-685). Marwan called together all the Syrian leaders and made them swear an oath of allegiance to both his sons, thus hoping to establish a dynasty.

Of importance for this paper is the object between the two figures. Walker called it a "tall standard with globe", but also said that it resembles a spear.[21] Nitzan Amitai-Preiss et al described it as "a sharp, pointed, tall standard with a globe"[22] with which identification Clive Foss concurred,[23] although he changed his description to "a pointed staff with a globe" in 2008.[24]

Nadia Jamil, however, is unequivocal in calling the object between the two standing figures a "spear and globe" and backs this up with quotations about "the spear as a symbol of caliphal authority" in the poetry of the period.[25] The only reason *not* to identify this as a spear is the

---

[13] Walker (1935)
[14] Bellinger (1938) no.551 (two specimens)
[15] Walker (1956) p.ciii.
[16] One of these is Fig.4a taken from Goussous (1996) fig.70, and the second is illustrated in Amitai-Preiss, Berman and Qedar (1999) Plate 22 no D11
[17] Goussous (1993)
[18] Oddy (2004)
[19] Goussous (1996) p.81
[20] Foss (2003)
[21] Walker (1956) p.43, no.A5 and fn.2
[22] Amitai-Preiss, Berman and Qedar (1999) pp. 134-151, esp. p.148
[23] Foss (2003)
[24] Foss (2008) p.60
[25] Jamil (1999) pp.47 ff

presence of the circular object (globe) between the spearhead and the staff. It could be argued that this circular object, whatever it is, would interfere with the use of a spear in battle. However, this is a ceremonial coin and it is reasonable to interpret the circular object as a contribution to the spear as a symbol of authority in this case. Throughout history, spears have been used to display flags, pennants, and other military insignia on ceremonial occasions, and sometimes also in warfare.

If the dating proposed by Clive Foss is correct, this coin is the earliest example of the depiction of a spear on a coin struck in Umayyad Syria.

The Pseudo-Damascus issues

Figure 9

Apart from the twin standing caliph issue, there are two other types of copper coins on the obverse of which the figure carries a spear. On Type A the standing figure has a spear replacing the more usual long cross in his right hand (fig. 9a) and on Type B the standing figure holds a spear that rests on his right shoulder and passes diagonally behind his head with the spearhead above the left shoulder (fig. 9b).

Dies A1a and A1b

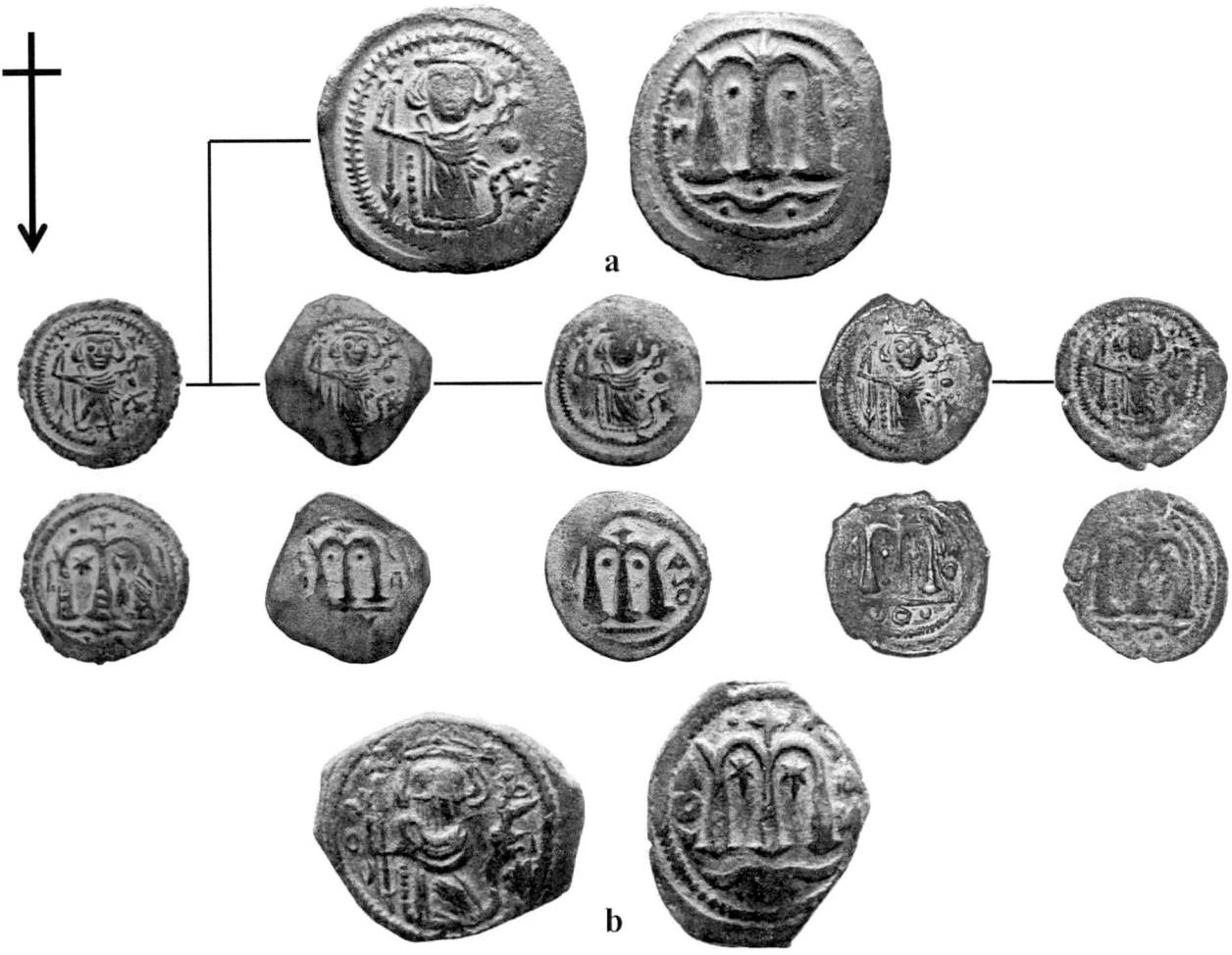

Figure 10

Obverse Die A1a: Facing standing figure wearing a long robe and a *chlamys* fastened at the right shoulder by a *fibula*. Three short 'tassels' hang from the waist on the left side of the figure. The face is beardless, but with long neatly dressed hair, the ends turning inwards. There appears to be a flat cap on the head. The right hand holds a long cross, with a spear head at its base. In the right field is a *globus* with a bird perched on it and a cross above. Below is a six-pointed star.

The presence of a bird in the right field (which usually perches on the outstretched left arm of the standing figure on other coins of the series) has led to the inclusion of this die in a series known as 'hunting' or 'falconry' coins.[26]

Die A1a is known with six different reverse dies all of which feature an m with either stars or dots within the arches of the m. Above is a cross or a trefoil and to the right and left and in the exergue are various dots, lines and letters.

Obverse Die A1b: Facing standing figure wearing a long robe and a *chlamys*. There are no tassels hanging from the waist. The face is bearded and moustachioed with long neatly dressed hair. He wears a flat crown surmounted by a cross. The right hand holds a long cross, with a spear head at its base. To the left are traces of a legend. In the right field is a bird on a globe, stars above and below.

---

[26] Oddy (1991) and Oddy (2012) pp. 109-111

Die A1b is only known with one reverse die having an ɱ with six-pointed stars in the arches. Above is a cross and to the right and left and in the exergue are various dots, lines and letters. This obverse die was unknown to Andrew Oddy[27] and brings the number of 'falconry' dies to 15.

Dies A2a and A2b

Figure 11

Obverse Die A2a: Facing standing figure wearing a long robe and a *chlamys*. There are three long tassels hanging from the waist of the left side of the figure. These are more prominent than on die A1a and end in small round objects – perhaps decorative pompoms. The face is bearded and moustachioed and has long flowing untidy hair with the ends turning outwards. In the right hand is a long cross with a spearhead placed just above the hand of the figure and pointing upwards. On the left of the figure is a *globus cruciger* with a letter O above.

Die A2a is known with three different reverse dies, two with a letter ɱ and one with M. All have a cross above the ɱ/M. There are various letters in the reverse fields and two of the dies have a rather badly written ΔAM, the mint mark for Damascus, in the exergue.

Obverse Die A2b: Facing standing figure wearing a long robe and a *chlamys*. There are three tassels ending in pompoms hanging from the waist of the left side of the figure. The face is bearded and moustachioed and has long flowing untidy hair. In the right hand is a long cross with a spearhead placed just above the hand of the figure and pointing upwards. On the left of the figure is a *globus cruciger* and to the right a six-pointed star.

Die A2b is known only with one reverse featuring an ɱ with dots and a cross above. Besides the ɱ are six-pointed stars and circles with dots. There are another four dots above the exergual line.

---

[27] Oddy (2012)

Die A3a

Figure 12

Obverse Die A3a: Facing standing figure wearing a long robe and a *chlamys*. There are no tassels hanging from the waist. The face is bearded and moustachioed and has long flowing untidy hair. He wears a dome-shaped cap (or ? crown). The right hand holds a long spear (*rumh*). In the right field the *globus cruciger* has been replaced by a cross on a base (or single step). Below the cross is a six-pointed star. In the left field are two 'Maltese' crosses arranged vertically with a letter O below with a pellet inside.

With this die the Christian symbol of a long cross has been discontinued, although crosses still remain on both obverse and reverse.

Die A3a is known with three reverse dies, all have dots in the arches of the m. To the right and left and in the exergue are various letters, lines and dots.

Die A3b

Figure 13

Obverse Die A3b: Facing standing figure wearing a long robe and a *chlamys*. There are no tassels hanging from the waist. The face is bearded and moustachioed and has long flowing untidy hair. He wears a dome-shaped cap (or ? crown). The right hand holds a spear (*rumh*). Adjacent to the left shoulder (in the right field) is a *globus cruciger*. The legend reads like a very blundered ENTOUTO NIKA.

Die A3b is known with three reverses each with a retrograde m with dots in the arches, a cross above, and various letters and symbols in the left and right fields and in the exergue.

Die A3c

Figure 14

Obverse Die A3c: Facing standing figure wearing a long robe and a *chlamys*. There are three long tassels ending in pompoms hanging from the waist of the left side of the figure (like those on die A2). The face is bearded and moustachioed and has long flowing untidy hair. He seems to wear a dome-shaped cap (or ? crown). The right hand holds a spear (*rumh*). Adjacent to the left shoulder (in the right field) is a *globus cruciger*. There are no other symbols in the obverse field.

Die A3c is known with 2 different reverses, both featuring an M, and with various letters and symbols in the field.

Die A4

Figure 15

Obverse Die A4: Facing standing figure wearing a knee-length tunic belted at the waist. The face is beardless, but with long neatly dressed hair. There appears to be a flat cap on the head. The right hand holds a vertical spear (*rumh*) and the outstretched left hand has a bird perched on the wrist. From the left arm hangs a severed head.[28] In the left field is a small circle with a cross on the top and above this is a palm branch.

The knee length belted tunic is typical of rural dress on depictions of Byzantine life in the seventh century[29] and this garb, together with the presence of a bird on the left arm, has led to the designation of this, and other related coins, as 'hunting' or 'falconry' coins. A palm branch in the field is common on the coinage of Damascus, where it appears to be just one symbol in a series.[30]

Die A4 is known with six different reverse dies, two of which have an M and four have m. The reverse fields and exergues have a range of different symbols which link to other obverses in the Pseudo-Damascus series.

---

[28] This device was first identified as a 'severed head' by Berman (1976), p.17, no.1, but interpreted as a bag for carrying game by Oddy (2012) p.110. Now, however, examination under a high magnification has revealed traces of eyes and of short spiky hair and a truncated neck. The identification as a severed head seems certain.
[29] For example the Byzantine mosaics at Argos illustrated in Åkerström-Hougen (1974)
[30] Oddy (2012) pp.118-119

Die A5

Figure 16

Obverse Die A5: Facing standing figure wearing a long robe belted at the waist and with tassels on the left side. The face has long flowing untidy hair. He wears a crown surmounted by a cross. The right hand holds a vertical spear (*rumh*) and the outstretched left hand has a bird perched on the wrist. Above the bird is a six-pointed star and below the left arm is a geometrical design whose meaning is unclear. In the left field is a cross.

It is unusual to see a full-length robe that is belted at the waist

Die A5 is unique but the reverse die links into the Pseudo-Damascus coinage.

Dies B1a and B1b

Figure 17

Obverse Die B1a: Facing standing figure wearing a long robe and a *chlamys*. There are no tassels hanging from the waist. The face is clean-shaven and has long flowing untidy hair. He wears a crown surmounted by a cross. The right hand holds a short spear *(ḥarba)* which rests on the right shoulder and passes behind the head with the spearhead visible above the left shoulder. Adjacent to the left shoulder (in the right field) is a small cross on a flat base (or single step) with a six-pointed star below. In the upper left field is a 'Maltese' cross.

Die B1a is known with two different reverses. The first has and ⅏ with a ✚ above, ΑO downwards in the left field and ՏN downwards in the right field. In both the arches of the ⅏ is • and Ϩ downwards and in the exergue is •••☉•••. The second reverse has a retrograde ⅏ with a ✚ above, with dots in the arches and with ϟN downwards in the left field and O in the right field. In the exergue is a row of dots.

Obverse Die B1b: Facing standing figure wearing a long robe and a *chlamys*. There are no tassels hanging from the waist. The face is clean-shaven and has long flowing untidy hair .There is a small cross on top of the head (but with no visible evidence for a 'cap' or 'crown'). The right hand holds a short spear *(ḥarba)* which rests on the right shoulder and passes behind the head with the spearhead visible above the left shoulder. Adjacent to the left shoulder (in the right field) is a small cross on a flat base (or single step) with a six-pointed star above and an O below. The left field is obscure on both specimens.

Die B1b is also known with two reverse dies. The first has an ɱ with a + above and with an eight-pointed star in the right arch. In the left field are the letters O N downwards. There is an unidentified countermark in the right field. The second reverse has a retrograde ɱ with a + above and a star in the left arch. The left field has ✶⊣ downwards and the right field has +ИХ downwards. In the exergue is a zig-zag line.

Die B2

A4

Figure 18

Obverse Die B2: Facing standing figure wearing a knee-length tunic belted at the waist. There are short tassels hanging from the waist. The face is beardless, but with long neatly dressed hair. There is a dome-shaped cap on the head. The right hand holds a short spear (*ḥarba*) that passes behind the chest so that the spearhead is visible over the left shoulder. The outstretched large left hand holds a *globus cruciger*, below which is an Є and a wavy line. In the left field is a long cross with a star at its centre (or a normal cross with a St. Andrew's cross superimposed), below which is a letter O. The same 'long cross with a star at its centre' appears on the reverse of one die associated with obverse die A4.

Die B2 is known with three different reverses, two of which have an ɱ and the third an M. There are various letters and symbols in the arches of the ɱ, in the field and in the exergue.

Die B3

Figure 19

Obverse Die B3: Facing standing figure wearing a long robe and a *chlamys*. There are short tassels ending in pompoms hanging from the waist. The face is bearded and has long neatly dressed hair. There is a small crown with a cross on top of the head. The right hand holds a short spear (*ḥarba*) which rests on the right shoulder and passes behind the head with the spearhead visible above the left shoulder. In the left field are the letters ATϹ arranged vertically, and in the right field there is a long cross with a star at its centre (or a normal cross with a St. Andrew's cross superimposed).

Die B3 is known with only one reverse featuring an M. The left and right fields are obscure, but above the M is a cross and the legend in the exergue appears to read *Dimasqh* (in Arabic). However, the reverse is very worn and all the details are not clear.

Die C – The 'orans' group

a   b   c

Figure 20

One obverse die with a standing figure holding a spear over his shoulder stands out from the others because the spear rests on the *left* shoulder and the style is very distinctive (fig. 20).

Obverse Die C: Facing standing figure wearing a long robe and a *chlamys*. The face is clean-shaven and has long fairly neatly dressed hair. There is a small crown with a cross on top of the head. A short spear (*ḥarba*) passes behind the head from the bottom right field with the spearhead visible in the top left field above the right shoulder. In both the left and right fields are hands holding a *globus cruciger*, but no arms are depicted.

The direction of the spear is sloping in the opposite direction from the spears on dies B1-3.

This obverse is known with two reverse dies, one with an **M** and the other with **m**. In the field are meaningless letters.

This coin is very significant because the reverse dies link to the Type I of the 'Orans' group that was published by Wolfgang Schulze in 2012.[31] The reverse with an **M** (figs 20a and 21a) is die linked to Type I reverse 3 of the 'Orans' group (fig. 21d) and the reverses with an **m** (figs 20b and c and 21b) to Type I reverse 1 of the 'Orans' group (fig. 21). Schulze originally thought that the Orans Group 'could be a product of the Pseudo-Damascus series, but it is more likely that it was produced by a small separate mint which borrowed stylistic elements of Pseudo-Damascus'. Now the discovery of the two coins illustrated in Figures 20b and c clearly show a spear over the shoulder (which was not certain from fig. 20a). As the Type I Orans Group is linked within itself and there are no links to other Pseudo Damascus coins, it is even more likely that this is a separate issue.

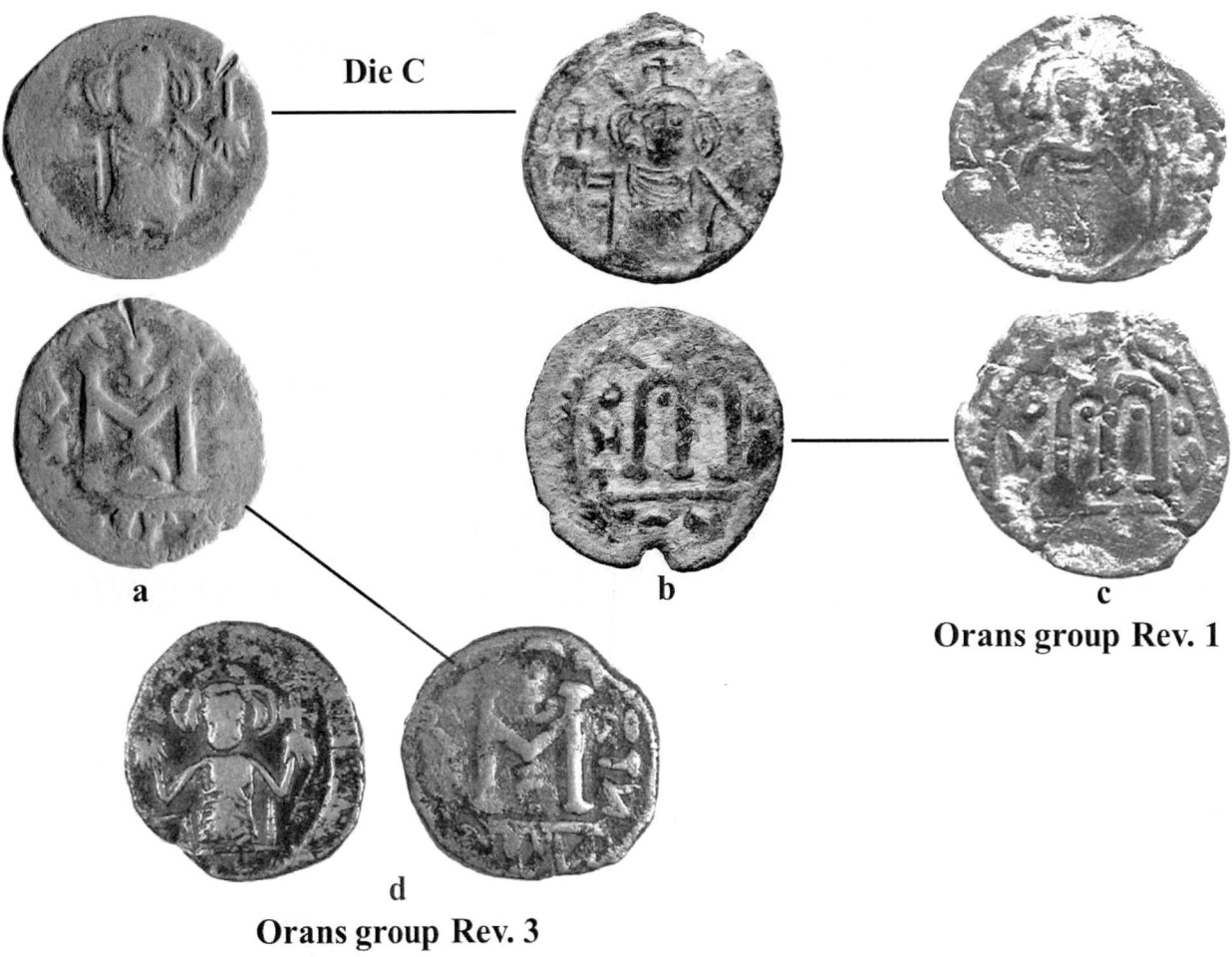

Figure 21

---

[31] Schulze W. (2012)

Die D – The single standing figure type of Tiberias

Figure 22

Obverse Die D: Facing standing figure wearing a long robe and with a cross on the top of the head. There are tassels hanging from the waist. Both hands hold a *globus cruciger*. In the left field there is a vertical spear (*rumh*). The legend beginning to right reads: TIBЄPIΔC/OƆ.
The reverse has a cursive m with a cross above. To the right: XΛNΛE, to the left AΛΛK(?), in the exergue: NOB (B retrograde).

This coin is from Meshorer's enigmatic series, discussed without definitive conclusion since 1839. Yaacov Meshorer was the first to attribute this coin type to Tiberias.[32] Marcus Phillips has cautiously dated this series 'late' in the seventh century.[33]

The coin illustrated here is from the collection of the Israel Museum and seems to be unpublished and unique. It is important for the spear series in so far as it is the only specimen with a spear not held by the standing figure. For the first time within the Phase 2 coinage we have a vertical spear standing alone and not replacing the usual long cross. Therefore it seems that the addition of the spear to the usual coin image is more than pure decoration, but the introduction of a new symbol with a clear message.

Prototypes for the Spear

The spear as a symbol of caliphal authority has already been mentioned, but it is difficult to associate the iconography of the coins of the Orans Group and of the Pseudo-Damascus issues with the person of the Caliph because of the presence of globus crucigers and crosses on the head and above the m on some of the dies. The origin of the design, however, is certain. It is quite clear that the die A and D coins with a vertical spear are not derived from the Constans II *folles* that are the 'inspiration' for so much of the Phase 1 and 2 Byzantine-Arab coinage. There are no Constans II coins with a spear, but there are coins among the *folles* of Constantine IV and of Justinian II (1st reign) of Syracuse (see fig. 23) where the standing figure holds a vertical spear.

For the Types B and C coins with a diagonal spear, the prototype must be a coin of Constantine IV struck in Constantinople, Carthage or Syracuse (see fig. 24) because neither under Constans II nor under Justinian II were coins struck with a diagonal spear. The Constantine IV coins with a diagonal spear, however, depict a bust and not the standing figure found on the coins catalogued above. Nevertheless they are the only possible contemporary prototypes and their use fits with the hypothesis that sees the Phase 2 coinage as being inspired by Byzantine originals rather than slavishly copying them.[34]

---

[32] Meshorer (1966). For further references cf. Karukstis (1999 and 2007).
[33] Phillips (2010)
[34] Oddy (2012)

Constantine IV 668 – 685
Follis of Syracuse

Justinian II first reign (685 – 695)
Follis of Syracuse

Figure 23

Constantine IV

Follis
of Syracuse

Hexagram
of Constantinople

Solidus
of Carthage

Figure 24

Dating the Orans Group, the Pseudo-Damascus coins, and the Tiberias coin with spears

The die cutters in Syria could have seen such Byzantine coins and used them for inspiration. This gives us a *terminus post quem* of AD 668 for the minting of the coins where the figure holds a spear. The *terminus ante quem* must be the inception of the Phase 3 Byzantine-Arab coinage usually known as the 'standing caliph' types. The rare gold coins of Phase 3 are dated, and start in AH74 (AD693/4),[35] but the bronze coinage is not dated and may have preceded the issue of the gold. Tony Goodwin has suggested that the standing caliph bronze coinage of Jerusalem probably started in the late 680s and spread to other mints in the early 690s.[36]

---

[35] Miles (1967)
[36] Album and Goodwin (2002) pp.106-7

However, 668 to c.690 is a long period and it is pertinent to ask whether there is any other evidence that contributes to suggesting a date for the coins with spears? As far as the Pseudo-Damascus coinage is concerned, on the basis of likely find spots in the northern part of modern Jordan and in adjacent parts of Israel, Tony Goodwin has postulated that the coins were struck by a leader of a Christian Arab tribe, the Kalb, who supported the Umayyads in the Second Civil War. This places the dating of the Pseudo-Damascus coinage in the period from about 685 to the early 690s.[37] For the Type I Orans Group, Wolfgang Schulze has proposed a date of around 690[38] as a reaction by 'Abd al-Malik to the religious slogan on the al-wafā lillāh coinage that is attributed by Ingrid Schulze to the pro-Zubayrid Ǧudam Tribe during the civil war leading up to the accession of 'Abd al-Malik in 684/5.[39] The single standing figure coin of Tiberias fits into the same period of time.

There is however, one feature of the design of the coins with spears that may be susceptible to a closer dating and that is the tassels that hang from the belt of the standing figure on seven (figs. 10a, 11a and b, 14, 16, 18, 19) of the 12 obverse dies of the Pseudo-Damascus coins illustrated here. The same symbol occurs on about 13 obverses of the 127 Pseudo-Damascus dies[40] and on 3 of the 93 obverse al-wafā lillāh dies.[41] The fact that tassels only occur on a small proportion of these two groups suggests the tassels are a late feature in both series.

a	b	c	d
Die A2	Die A3c	Tiberias	Justinian II semis

Figure 25

However, tassels with pompoms hanging from the waist also occur on the enigmatic series of standing figure coins of Tiberias (figs 22 and 25c). Marcus Phillips has dated these to post 693[42] because he thinks that the tassels have been derived from the end of the *loros* worn by Justinian II on his silver and gold coinage of Class III (fig. 25d) that Philip Grierson dates to 692-695.[43] If this is the origin of the tassels, it is not a question of copying something that is understood – ie a *loros* – but copying something that is *not* understood and has been interpreted as an ornament hanging from the waist. One thing about the *loros* that is noticeable is that it ends in two or three 'pompoms'[44] just like the tassels on the 'spear coins'.

---

[37] Goodwin (2012)
[38] Schulze W. (2012)
[39] Schulze I. (2010)
[40] We are grateful to Tony Goodwin for sharing with us the current number of Pseudo-Damascus obverse dies.
[41] We are grateful to Ingrid Schulze for sharing with us the current number of al-wafā lillāh obverse dies.
[42] Phillips (2010) fig. 7
[43] Grierson (1968) p.570
[44] Grierson (1968), Pl .XXXVII, nos. 7a.3-7h

Figure 26

It should also be pointed out that Ingrid and Wolfgang Schulze drew a stylistic connection between the *loros* on coins of Justinian II and the design of the scabbard on Standing Caliph coins of Ḥarrān.[45] The same pompoms are present at the end of the scabbard worn by the standing caliph on the rare silver dirhams probably minted in Damascus in AH 75[46] (fig. 26).

As far as the dating of the Justinian II Class III coinage is concerned, Philip Grierson suggests 692-695 in order to allow time for the first two classes of Justinian coinage to be struck after the start of the reign in 685. There is no documentary date,[47] but given that Class I is quite rare, there is no need to allow much time for this issue and so it follows that Class III may be earlier in its inception than suggested by Grierson, perhaps as early as 688.

To sum up the dating evidence for the coins with spears belonging to the Pseudo-Damascus coinage, it is certain that they post-date 668 and end – as do other Pseudo-Damascus coins die-linked with the spear coins – in the late 680s or around 690. Some of the coins with spears – especially those with tassels ending in pompoms could have ended slightly later.

The tassels with pompoms, whatever their origin, are another example of innovation in the design of the Phase 2 coinage. So, do they show a new trend of Umayyad clothing?

According to Yedida Kalfon Stillman:

> In the newly triumphant and wealthy *umma* … most Muslims abandoned earliest Islam's aversion to luxury garments. …The ruling Umayyad dynasty set the trend toward a more luxurious style.[48]

With this in mind it is possible that the die cutters simply reproduced a new trend of Umayyad dress on the coins and added tassels, sometimes with pompoms and sometimes without, to the clothing of the standing figure. If this is the case, it has to be admitted that the date of introduction of the coins of Justinian II on which he wears a *loros* is irrelevant for the dating of coins with spears.

---

[45] Schulze I. and W. (2010) p. 350
[46] Morton and Eden Sale No.54, 23 April 2012, lot 23
[47] But see the discussion on p.570 of Grierson (1968)
[48] Stillman (2003) p. 31 f

The same argument may be applied to the elaborated hairstyle, which is unusual for the illustration of a Byzantine ruler on coins. Another innovation is the depiction of the enigmatic St. Andrew's cross.

Are all these special features simply pure decoration? It is impossible to know for sure. If yes, it will not help for more detailed dating.

One thing that can be said for certain is that the inclusion of spears is a notable new phenomenon. So far there are 17 obverse dies with spears, and 39 associated reverse dies, making them a significant contribution to the coin production in Syria at the end of the seventh century.

Coins of Arab-Sasanian type with spears

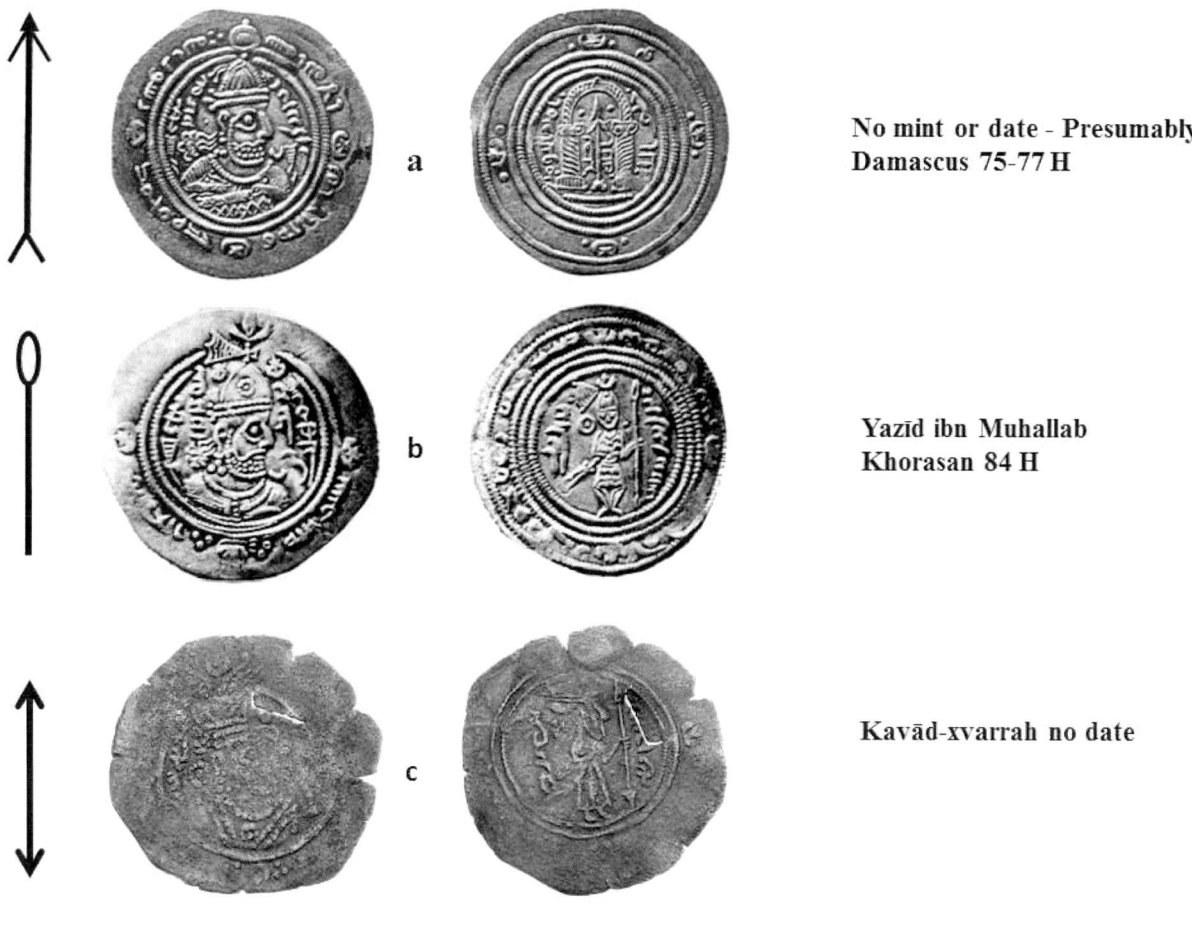

Figure 27

Finally, there are three coins with obverses based on Sasanian models that also depict a spear. But apart from the presence of a spear on the reverse, the coins are not related.

The first (fig. 27a) is the so called *miḥrāb* and *'anaza* drachm[49] showing a standing spear – a *ḥarba* or a *rumh* – within an arch representing the prayer niche or *miḥrāb* that indicates the direction of Mecca. The coin was first published by John Walker using the specimen acquired by the American Numismatic Society in 1944.[50] The coin has no mint or date but Luke Treadwell suggests that it

---
[49] Miles (1952)
[50] Walker (1941) p.24, ANS.5. The ANS inventory number is 1944.100.612.

was probably struck in Damascus around AH 75-77 (AD 694-697),[51] thus shortly after the proposed date of around 690 for the Pseudo-Damascus and orans types of copper coins discussed above.

Walker suggested that the arch was a *miḥrāb* containing a lance (sic) with two streamers, and in his full discussion of the coin, George Miles further identified the 'lance' as the *'anaza* of the Prophet which was used to indicate the direction of prayer.[52] There has been much subsequent discussion of Miles' interpretation of the reverse, which is summarised by Luke Treadwell in his recent full discussion of this coin type.[53] Suffice it to say that the representation of a spear cannot be contested, but some authors have reinterpreted the covering arch as the sacrum which was placed above the 'true cross' in Jerusalem and the spear as a generalised symbol of the triumph of the Muslim armies.[54]

Although not struck in Bilad al-Sham, there is another silver drachm that depicts a spear, but this one is held by an armoured warrior (fig. 27b). It was struck by Yazīd ibn Muhallab at Jūzjān in Khurāsān in AH 84 and so is several years later than the Syrian coins. It is, however, interesting, as it depicts a spear in the left hand of the standing figure, who wears 'scale' armour down to the knee, and the length of this spear is as tall as the top of the helmet crest – thus about 1.85metres. This is presumably a *rumḥ*, the longer of the two Arab shafted weapons. While depiction on a coin cannot necessarily be taken as an accurate representation because of the need to fit the warrior and his weapon into a circle, it does seem likely that this was the approximate length.

This coin was first published by John Walker[55] who merely described the figure on the reverse as 'a standing figure, facing, in armour, wearing helmet ... and holding in his left hand a spear, while grasping in his right hand a sword in its scabbard'. He discusses the Pehlevi, Arabic and Ephthalite legends in detail, but offers no identification for the bust on the obverse or the standing figure on the reverse. In 1952, the coin was in the collection of an Iranian collector, M Azizbeghlou, but now, according to Rika Gyselen, who has illustrated the coin without any discussion,[56] it is in Paris.[57] It is very surprising that the coin has apparently received no serious numismatic discussion in the past 60 years, especially as its armoured warrior (is it Yazid ibn Muhallab?) is one of the earliest depictions of an Arab warrior of the conquest period to survive.

Finally, there is a bronze coin with an unusual Sasanian bust to the right on the obverse. On the reverse is a figure in armour to the right holding a spear apparently with two spearheads,[58] one at each end of the pole (fig. 27c). In fact this must be a spear with an iron ferrule enabling it to be stuck upright into the ground. This could identify this spear with the *'anaza* of the Prophet used to indicate the direction of Mecca. The coin is anonymous and was minted in Kavād-xvarrah (kawad-khwarrah) in the Fars province of southern Iran.

Conclusion

In conclusion, it is certain that the introduction of spears onto coins during the reign of 'Abd al-Malik was no mere accident. Nadia Jamil has demonstrated that the spear was a symbol of caliphal power as well as a sign of power and religious legitimacy. It was also associated with the Prophet and the act of prayer.[59] These two interpretations satisfactorily explain the presence of spears if we

---

[51] Treadwell (2005), esp.p. 1
[52] Miles (1952)
[53] Treadwell (2005).
[54] For example Grabar (1957)
[55] Walker (1952) no. 3
[56] Gyselen (2009) Plate 15, no. XIII
[57] Bibliothèque Nationale de France, Cabinet des Médailles, inventory no. 1967.207
[58] Gyselen (2009) Type 109
[59] Jamil (1999) pp. 47 ff

assume that the spears on the 'Twin Standing Caliph' issue of Gerasa, the Pseudo-Damascus coins, the Orans coins, and the Tiberias standing figure coin are symbols of authority and power, while the spear in a niche alludes to the 'anaza of the Prophet. The two Arab-Sasanian coins with figures holding spears may well represent the conquering power of the Arab armies.

The period in which the spear coins were struck was after the second civil war. The introduction of spears can be compared with the introduction of the sword-bearing Standing Caliph, the symbol on steps,[60] and the orans coins,[61] all of which must be interpreted in the context of a numismatic experimental phase serving the development of the Arab government into a theocracy.

Acknowledgements

We are very grateful to Tony Goodwin for supporting us with important pictures, to John Haldon, Frank Trombley and Julie Hanson for information on late Roman and Byzantine armaments, and to Ingrid Schulze who invested a lot of time commenting and enriching early drafts of this article.

Bibliography

Åkerström-Hougen (1974)	G. Åkerström-Hougen: ***The Calendar and Hunting Mosaics of the Villa of the Falconer in Argos. A Study in Early Byzantine Iconography***. (Skrifter utgivna av Svenska Institutet I Athen 4, xxiii.) 2 vols, Stockholm: Svenska Institutet I Athens, 1974
Album and Goodwin (2002)	S. Album and T. Goodwin, ***Sylloge of Islamic Coins in the Ashmolean: Volume 1: The Pre-Reform Coinage of the early Islamic Period***, Oxford, 2002
Amitai-Preiss, Berman and Qedar (1999)	N. Amitai-Preiss, A. Berman and S. Qedar, 'The Coinage of Scythopolis-Baysan and Gerasa-Jerash', ***Israel Numismatic Journal*** 13 (1994-99), pp. 134-151
Bellinger (1938)	A. R. Bellinger, ***Coins from Jerash***, ANS Numismatic Notes and Monographs 81, New York, 1938
Berman (1976)	A. Berman, ***Islamic Coins***, Jerusalem, 1976
Foss (2003)	C. Foss, 'The Two-Caliph Bronze of 'Abd al-Malik', ***ONS Newsletter*** 177 (2003), pp. 4-5
Foss (2008)	C. Foss, ***Arab-Byzantine Coins***, Washington DC, 2008
Goodwin (2007)	T. Goodwin, 'The Pseudo-Damascus Mint – Progress Report on a Die Study', ***Coinage and History in the Seventh Century Near East***, Supplement to ONS Journal 193 (2007), pp.12-16
Goodwin (2012)	T. Goodwin, 'The Chronology of the Imperial Image Coinage: Progress over the last 10 years', ***Arab-Byzantine Coins and History***, T. Goodwin ed., London, 2012, pp. 89-107
Goussous (1993)	N. Goussous, 'A Unique Arab-Byzantine Coin', ***Yarmouk Numismatics*** 5 (1993) pp. 37-38
Goussous (1996)	N. Goussous, ***Umayyad Coins of Bilad al-Sham***, Amman, 1996
Grabar (1957)	A. Grabar, ***L'Iconoclasme byzantin: dossier archéologique***, Paris 1957
Grierson (1968)	P. Grierson, ***Catalogue of the Byzantine Coins in the Dumbarton Oaks Collection: Volume Two: Phocas to Theodosius III: Part 2***, Washington DC, 1968
Gyselen (2007)	R. Gyselen, ***Sasanian Seals and Sealings in the A Saeedi Collection***, Acta Iranica 44, Leuven, 2007

---

[60] Schulze W. (2010)
[61] Schulze W. (2012)

Gyselen (2009)	R. Gyselen, *Arab-Sasanian Copper Coinage*, 2nd edition, Vienna, 2009
Jamil (1999)	N. Jamil, 'Caliph and Qutb. Poetry as a source for interpreting the transformation of the Byzantine cross on steps on Umayyad coinage', ***Bayt al-Maqdis: Jerusalem and Early Islam***, J. Johns (ed.), Oxford, 1999, pp. 11-57
Karukstis (1999)	C. Karukstis, ***Meshorer's "Enigmatic Coin" Revisited***, ANS Arab-Byzantine Study Day 1999, unpublished article
Karukstis (2007)	C. Karukstis, 'Another Visit to Meshorer's Enigmatic Coin', ***Supplement to ONS Journal*** 193 (2007), pp. 40-42
Kennedy (2007)	H. Kennedy, *The Great Arab Conquests*, Da Capo Press 2007
Meshorer (1966)	Meshorer, Yaacov, 'An enigmatic Arab-Byzantine Coin', ***Israel Numismatic Journal***, Vol. 3 (1965-66), pp. 32-36
Miles (1952)	G. C. Miles, 'Miḥrāb and 'Anazah: a Study in Early Islamic Iconography', ***Archaeologia Orientalia in Memoriam Ernst Herzfeld***, New York, 1952, pp. 156-171
Miles (1967)	G. C. Miles, 'The earliest Arab Gold Coinage', ***ANS Museum Notes*** 13 (1967), pp. 205-229
Morrisson (1970)	C. Morrisson, ***Catalogue des Monnaies Byzantines***, Vol I, Paris 1970
Nicolle (1997)	D. Nicolle, 'Arms of the Umayyad Era: Military Technology in a Time of Change', ***War and Society in the Eastern Mediterranean, 7th-15th Centuries***, Y. Lev ed., Leiden, 1997, pp. 9-100
Oddy (1991)	A. Oddy, 'Arab Imagery on Early Umayyad Coins in Syria and Palestine: Evidence for Falconry', ***Numismatic Chronicle*** 1991, pp. 59-66
Oddy (2004)	A. Oddy, 'The Twin Standing Caliph Fals', ***Newsletter of the ONS*** 179 (2004), pp. 10-11
Oddy (2012)	A. Oddy, 'Symbolism and Design on the early Umayyad Coinage', ***Arab-Byzantine Coins and History***, T. Goodwin ed., London, 2012, pp. 109-123
Phillips (2010)	M. Phillips, 'Single Figure Coins of Tiberias/Tabariya with Bilingual Legends', ***Coinage and History in the Seventh century Near East 2***, A. Oddy ed., London, 2010, pp. 61-77
Schulze and Oddy (2012)	W. Schulze and A. Oddy, 'Terminology for the Transitional Coinage struck in 7th Century Syria after the Arab Conquest', ***Arab-Byzantine Coins and History***, T. Goodwin ed., London, 2012, pp. 187-200
Schulze I. (2010)	I. Schulze, 'The al-wafā lillā Coinage: A study of style', ***Coinage and History in the Seventh Century Near East 2***, A. Oddy ed., London, 2010, pp.111-121
Schulze I. and W. (2010)	I. and W. Schulze, 'The Standing Caliph Coins of al-Jazīra: some problems and suggestions', ***Numismatic Chronicle*** 2010, pp.331-353
Schulze W. (2010)	W. Schulze, 'Symbolism on the Syrian Standing Caliph Copper Coins: A contribution to the discussion', ***Coinage and History in the Seventh Century Near East 2,*** A. Oddy ed., London, 2010, pp.111-121
Schulze W. (2012)	W. Schulze, 'The Syrian 'orans figure' copper coins', ***Arab-Byzantine Coins and History***, T. Goodwin ed., London, 2012, pp.131-144
Stillman (2003)	Y. K. Stillman, ***Arab Dress. A short History: From the Dawn of Islam to Modern Times***, Leiden, 2003
Treadwell (2005)	L. Treadwell, 'Mirhab and 'Azana' or 'Sacrum and Spear'? A Reconsideration of an Early Marwanid Silver Drachm, ***Muqarnas*** 22 (2005) pp. 1-28

Walker (1935)		J. Walker, 'A New Byzantine Mint and some early Umaiyad Bronze Coins', ***Numismatic Chronicle*** 1935, pp. 120-126
Walker (1941)		J. Walker, *A Catalogue of the Arab-Sassanian Coins*, London, 1941
Walker (1952)		J. Walker, 'Some New Arab-Sassanian Coins', ***Numismatic Chronicle*** 1952, pp. 106-110
Walker (1956)		J. Walker, ***A Catalogue of the Arab-Byzantine and Post Reform Umaiyad Coins,*** London, 1956

Details of coins illustrated

Fig. 1a	7.77g	Priv. coll.
Fig. 1b	3.57g	Priv. coll.
Fig. 1c	5.69g	Priv. coll.
Fig. 1d	3.64g	Priv. coll.
Fig. 2a	7.11g	Priv. coll.
Fig. 2b	4.48g	Priv. coll.
Fig. 2c	4.05g	Priv. coll.
Fig. 2d	4.82g	Priv. coll.
Fig. 2e	4.48g	Priv. coll.
Fig. 2f	4.11g	Priv. coll.
Fig. 3a	4.36g	Priv. coll.
Fig. 3b	4.31g	Priv. coll.
Fig. 3c	4.49g	Priv. coll.
Fig. 3d	3.75g	Priv. coll.
Fig. 8a	5.8g	Goussous (1996)
Fig. 8b	6.10g	Israel Museum, Jerusalem, inv. no. 12374
Fig. 9a	3.95g	Priv. coll.
Fig. 9b	–	Ahli Bank Money Museum, Amman
Fig. 10a	3.53g	Priv. coll.
Fig. 10a (1)	4.31g	Priv. coll.
Fig. 10a (2)	4.06g	Priv. coll.
Fig. 10a (3)	5.76g	Priv. coll.
Fig. 10a (4)	2.9g	Goussous (2004) no. 139
Fig. 10a (5)	4.35g	Priv. coll.
Fig. 10b	3.43g	Priv. coll.
Fig. 11a	5.41g	Priv. coll.
Fig. 11a (1)	–	Spink Zurich 18/2/86, lot 84.3
Fig. 11a (2)	3.93g	Milstein INJ 1991, no. 75
Fig. 11b	2.60g	Priv. coll.
Fig. 12 (1)	3.20g	Priv. coll.
Fig. 12 (2)	3.44g	Priv. coll.
Fig. 12 (3)	2.78g	Trade
Fig. 13 (1)	3.29g	Priv. coll.
Fig. 13 (2)	4.06g	Milstein INJ 1991, no. 73
Fig. 13 (3)	4.23g	Priv. coll.
Fig. 14 (1)	3.95g	Priv. coll.
Fig. 14 (2)	3.18g	Priv. coll.
Fig. 15 (1)	–	Trade
Fig. 15 (2)	3.65g	Milstein INJ 1991, no. 132
Fig. 15 (3)	3.45g	Milstein INJ 1991, no. 133
Fig. 15 (4)	–	Trade

Fig. 15 (5)	4.46g	Oddy (1991) no. 21
Fig. 15 (6)	3.70g	Oddy (1991) no. 22
Fig. 16	3.83g	Priv. coll.
Fig. 17a (1)	–	Ahli Bank Money Museum, Amman
Fig. 17a (2)	–	Ahli Bank Money Museum, Amman
Fig. 17b (1)	2.69g	Priv. coll.
Fig. 17b (2)	2.96g	Priv. coll.
Fig. 18 (1)	4.32g	Image T. Goodwin
Fig. 18 (2)	4.17g	Image T. Goodwin
Fig. 18 (3)	3.3g	Goussous (2004) no. 132
Fig. 18 (A4)	3.45g	Milstein INJ 1991, no. 133
Fig. 19	6.79g	Priv. coll.
Fig. 20a	3.67g	Orientalisches Münzkabinett Jena inv. no. 303-C05
Fig. 20b	4.47g	Priv. coll.
Fig. 20c	4.30g	Priv. coll.
Fig. 21a	3.67g	Orientalisches Münzkabinett Jena inv. no. 303-C05
Fig. 21b	4.47g	Priv. coll.
Fig. 21c	–	Trade
Fig. 21d	3.91g	Priv. coll.
Fig. 22	5.22g	Israel Museum, Jerusalem, inv. no. 12530
Fig. 23 (1)	3.28g	CNG electronic auction 209, lot 444
Fig. 23 (2)	4.55g	CNG auction 73, lot 1053
Fig. 24 (1)	4.05g	CNG electronic auction 111, lot 232
Fig. 24 (2)	6.42g	Baldwin's Autumn Argentum Auction 2012, lot 43
Fig. 24 (3)	4.40g	CNG inv. no. 861022
Fig. 25a	5.41g	Priv. coll.
Fig. 25b	3.95g	Priv. coll.
Fig. 25c	4.51g	Israel Museum, Jerusalem, inv. no. 12534
Fig. 25d	1.96g	CNG electronic auction 208, lot 436
Fig. 26 (1)	4.33g	ArtCoins Roma, auction 4, lot 1148
Fig. 26 (2)	2.60g	Goussous (1996) no. 55
Fig. 26 (3)	3.47g	Morton and Eden, auction 54, lot 23
Fig. 27a	3.76g	Bibliothèque Nationale de France inv. no. 1967.209
Fig. 27b	–	Bibliothèque Nationale de France inv. no. 1967.75
Fig. 27c	0.61g	CNG electronic auction 155, lot 371

The Egyptian Arab-Byzantine Coinage

Tony Goodwin [1]

Background

Unlike its Syrian counterpart, an Egyptian Arab-Byzantine coinage was not properly recognised by 19thC numismatists, probably because none of the coins bear Arabic legends or symbols that are obviously Islamic. The first examples were published in 1862 by Sabatier, who provided reasonably accurate engravings of the **ABAZ** and **ΠAN** types, but interpreted them as Byzantine coins.

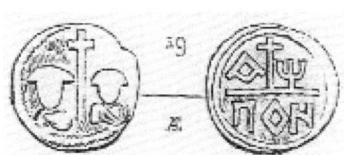 

Fig. 1: Illustrations from Sabatier 1862 of two Egyptian Arab-Byzantine coins, the first (Pl. XXX no. 19) identified as a coin of Heraclius from an uncertain mint and the second (Pl. XXXVI no. 22), misidentified as a Byzantine coin of Constantine IV.

Lavoix (1887) included two examples of facing bust coins in his catalogue of the Islamic coins in the Bibliothèque Nationale and followed Sabatier in identifying the bust as that of Constantine IV, although he included them under the early Islamic issues of Alexandria.[2] Wroth's British Museum Byzantine catalogue of 1908 illustrated several different types, but identified them as Byzantine coins of Heraclius, whilst mentioning the possibility that some of them may have been minted just after the Arab conquest.[3]

In 1956 Walker was surprisingly dismissive of the series. Despite the significant number of coins in the British Museum's collections he illustrated only one, commenting that "…there are certain barbarous imitations of Byzantine coins of Alexandria (Egypt), which quite conceivably were minted under the Arab usurpers".[4] This general lack of interest continued for over 40 years punctuated only by Henri Amin Awad's short, but important article of 1972. Awad had formed a collection of 180 irregular Byzantine-style coins, mostly found in Fustat (Old Cairo). He classified the coins into four main types and argued that they "are without doubt Arab imitations".[5]

In recent years the subject has received more attention and there are short overviews of the series in the both the Ashmolean (2002) and Dumbarton Oaks (2008) catalogues.[6] There have also been three significant publications, each of which has advanced the subject considerably. The first of

---

[1] Tony Goodwin is an independent scholar: a.goodwin2@btopenworld.com
[2] Lavoix 1887 Cats. 94 (Type II) and 95 (Type II or IV). Unfortunately neither is illustrated.
[3] Wroth describes and illustrates examples of Types II (Heraclius Cats. 304 and 305), III (Heraclius 285), IV (Heraclius 303) and V (315-322). My classification into five types is given in the next section of this paper.
[4] Walker 1956 p. 53.
[5] Awad's classification (Awad 1972) is somewhat confused. He illustrates 16 coins including examples of Types I (12, 16 and probably 13), II (3 and 4), III (10, 11 and 14) and V (1 and 2). Cat. 16 appears to be similar to a variant of Type I discussed later in this article and Cats. 5-9 are probably all regular coins of Heraclius.
[6] SICA pp. 107-108 and DOC pp. 99-105.

these, published in 2002, was the study of the American Numismatic Society collection by Lidia Domaszewicz and Michael Bates, which includes a large group of coins donated by Awad. In all 240 coins were identified as Byzantine and 382 as Arab-Byzantine, so the authors had a much larger group of coins to work with than any previous scholars. They concluded that all the 3-figure coins identified by Awad as Arab-Byzantine were in fact Byzantine issues of Heraclius and they identified three types of Arab-Byzantine coins (AI, AII and AIII – identical to Types I, II and III below). They accepted the suggestion, originally made by Awad and Bacharach,[7] that the **MACP** legend on Type III was a Greek transliteration of the Arabic *miṣr*, but concluded that the **ABAZ** legend on Type II was no more than a blundering of the Byzantine **ΑΛΕΞ**. Somewhat strangely they suggested that the coins with the legend **ΠΑΝ** (Type V below) were probably provincial Byzantine issues struck outside Egypt and copying the Heraclian coins of Rome, so that **ΠΑΝ** was merely a blundered rendering of the mint name **ROM**. In 2004 Michael Metlich and Nikolaus Schindel responded comprehensively to the Domaszewicz and Bates article, rightly dismissing the **ROM** suggestion,[8] whilst broadly supporting the classification of the Arab-Byzantine coins into three main types. They suggested that the **MACP** and **ABAZ** coins could be successive issues from the mint of Babylon/Fustat and they made the interesting suggestion that **ABAZ** might be a Greek transliteration of the Arabic *'Abd al-'Aziz*, 'Abd al-Malik's brother and governor of Egypt from 65 to 85AH.

The third significant publication was Daniele Castrizio's 2010 catalogue of the coins from Antinoöpolis in northern Upper Egypt, which included a high proportion of Byzantine and Arab-Byzantine coins, all properly catalogued and in most cases illustrated. This included 61 **ΠΑΝ** coins, an unprecedented number of what had previously been considered a rare type. Castrizio concluded that these coins must have been minted locally, almost certainly at Antinoöpolis itself, and at some time after the Arab conquest.

Thanks to this recent work we now have a much better basis for a proper classification of the Egyptian Arab-Byzantine coinage and this will be attempted in the next section.

However, before looking at the coins themselves it will be useful to briefly review the very meagre published excavation and hoard evidence from Egypt. Unfortunately Castrizio's publication is the only one to include Arab-Byzantine coins that approaches modern numismatic standards. In looking at older publications it is worth remembering that the 7thC Byzantine coinage was not properly classified until 1962 and that the Arab-Byzantine types not generally recognised before 1972,[9] so any earlier publications are likely to group all 7thC coins under Heraclius. The problem is exacerbated by inadequate descriptions and lack of illustrations. A little useful information can be gleaned from Milne's 1912 report on coins found during excavations of the monastery of Apa Jeremias at Saqqara, which lists 40 standing emperor coins, presumably of Constans II or Arab-Byzantine imitations, and 9 coins with a facing bust and palm branch which must be Type II (see below) Arab-Byzantine.[10] Rodiewicz's 1984 report on the coin finds from Kom el-Dikka (Alexandria) illustrates a number of Egyptian Byzantine coins, including several of the last issues of Heraclius, but includes no coins of Constans II and only one which may be Arab-Byzantine.[11] Lastly Noeske's monumental *Münzfunde aus Ägypten* of 2000 lists nearly 4000 coins from the pilgrimage site of Abu Mina situated in the desert to the west of Alexandria. The coins range from

---

[7] Bacharach and Awad 1981.
[8] See also my review of Domaszewicz and Bates' article (Goodwin 2003a).
[9] See Phillips 1962 and Awad 1972.
[10] J. G. Milne's classification of the coins seems to be competently done, given the state of knowledge at the time, but there are no illustrations. See Quibell 1912 pp. 37-42.
[11] Rodiewicz 1984, see particularly the illustrations on pp. 432-433. Cat. 340 is not very clear, but could possibly be a Type II Arab-Byzantine. At first sight Cat. 341 looks interesting and a drawing of the reverse shows a long cross with the letters **o-m** either side, but the coin in the corresponding photograph looks to be a worn post-reform fals.

Ptolemaic to Abbasid with a few later strays, and include two Type V **ΠAN** coins and 8 Arab-Byzantine coins which could be either Type I or III, but unfortunately none of the coins is illustrated.[12] Other sites, listed by Noeske appear to have produced no Arab-Byzantine coins at all, but clearly some examples may have gone unnoticed, given the poor understanding of the series until very recently.

The Main Types of Egyptian Arab-Byzantine Coin

The following classification is based on Domaszewicz and Bates' three types, but extended by three further types, one of which (Type V, their UII) they regarded as Byzantine. In order to minimise confusion I have kept their order of types and retained their use of Roman numerals for each type, so my Type I is the same as their Type A.I etc. It should be noted that this order of types does not imply any chronological order. All coins illustrated are from private collections unless otherwise stated.

Type I
(MIB Constans II X37 and X38, Domaszewicz and Bates AI)

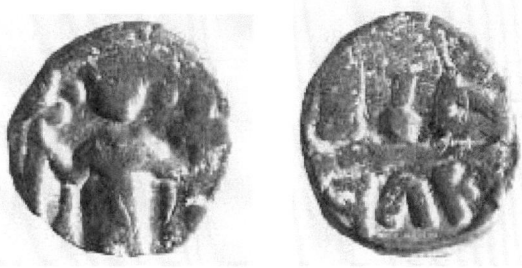

Fig. 2. Obv: Crude standing figure holding long cross and globus cruciger or cross.
Rev: **I-B** *with cross-on-globe between and blundered* **AΛЄΞ** *in exergue. 4.94g. 12h.*
(approx. 2x actual size)

This type imitates the last Alexandrian issue of Constans II which probably continued to be struck for a few years after the conquest.[13] However, the smaller, lighter Arab-Byzantine coins are quite distinct and appear to be the product of a separate mint. The style is always cruder, sometimes much cruder, and the exergual legend is almost always blundered. An interesting feature is the very wide range of weights from around 1g up to about 6g (see Fig. 3). Domaszewicz and Bates state that there are apparently two denominations,[14] but this needs to be checked by proper statistical analysis of a sufficiently large sample of weights.

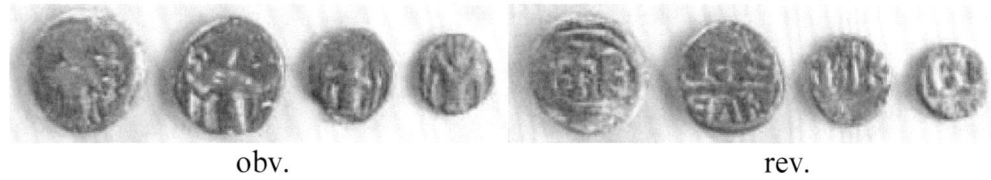

obv.   rev.

Fig. 3: Variation in size and weight of Type 1, l. to r. 5.19g., 4.94g., 2.05g. and 1.66g.
(actual size).

---

[12] Noeske's book is a work of considerable scholarship which also lists other coin hoards and excavation finds from the 4th to the 8th century. For most coin series, which are reasonably well understood and found in quite large numbers, illustrations are not essential to the main purpose of the book, but their absence is a serious flaw for the study of Arab-Byzantine coins, which occur in small numbers and may not have been recognised by excavators and cataloguers.
[13] See my article on Egyptian Byzantine coinage elsewhere in this volume.
[14] Domaszewicz and Bates p. 96.

Although the mint name is Alexandria, the mint may not actually have been located there as Rodziewicz does not record any examples from Kom el-Dikka. It appears to be the most common type in Awad's collection from Fustat and at Antinoöpolis it is the second most common type after the **ΠAN** coins, so perhaps the mint was located near Fustat or further south.[15]

Type II
(BMC Heraclius 304, MIB Constans II X35, Domaszewicz and Bates AII, DOC 140-141)

*Fig. 4. Obv: Facing bust with palm branch-on-globe to left, star to right and **A** to lower right.*
*Rev: **IMB** with **A** above, **ABAZ** in exergue. 7.39g. 6h.   (approx. 2x actual size)*

Type II is the most obviously Arab-Byzantine type with all crosses eliminated and the palm branch motif which is familiar from some Syrian Arab-Byzantine coins. The bust is distinctive with a flat crown and wide buns of hair on either side and is not a close copy of any Egyptian Byzantine coin. Examination of the reverse exergual legends on a number of specimens makes it clear that this is not just a blundered version of **AΛЄΞ** as the letter **B** is always clear. Unfortunately the last letter is almost always off the flan, but on the few specimens where it is readable it is clearly a **Z** rather than a **Ξ**. The example shown in Fig. 4 also seems to have a very small diagonal stroke after the **Z** which may be an abbreviation marker (as in the **ΔAM** mint name on many Damascus Arab-Byzantine coins). The **ABAZ** legend could possibly be a mint name, but Metlich and Schindel's suggestion of an abbreviated transliteration of 'Abd al-Aziz seems much more plausible. There are parallels on a few Syrian Arab-Byzantine coins which have governor's names in Arabic,[16] and Greek transliterations of 'Abd al-Aziz's name appear in Egyptian papyri, so there is nothing far-fetched in this interpretation. The actual mint was probably in the vicinity of Fustat as none are recorded from Antinoöpolis or Kom el-Dikka, whilst Awad lists 25 from Fustat and Milne records 9 examples from Saqqara, only a few kilometres from Fustat.[17]

---

[15] Unfortunately neither Awad nor Domaszewicz and Bates give the numbers of each type. Awad says that he has 100 examples of standing figure coins, but this includes the **MACP** type.
[16] For example *'Abd al-Rahman* at *Sarmīn*. An intriguing possible parallel to the Egyptian type is the Standing Caliph type of *Harrān* which has the name *Muhammad* on the obverse. This could perhaps be Muhammad b. Marwan, another brother of 'Abd al-Malik and governor of the Jazira province.
[17] Milne 1912.

Type III
(MIB Constans II X36, SICA 732 and 733, Domaszewicz and Bates AIII, DOC 131-139)

Fig. 5. Obv: Squat standing figure holding long cross and globus cruciger, star to lower right. Rev: **I-B** *with cross-on-globe between and* **MAC(P)** *or* **MAC(A)** *in exergue. 7.70g. 6h. (approx. 2x actual size)*

Although this type broadly follows the design of the last issue of Constans II the obverse standing figure is very wide in proportion to its height and often gives the impression of a three-quarter length figure due to the feet being off the flan. The mint name is usually read as **MACP**, but on specimens where the last letter is fully struck it usually looks more like **MACA** (see Fig. 6).[18] Occasionally a further letter is visible after the last **A** (Fig. 6d), but I have yet to find an example where this looks like a **P** and it is more likely to be an abbreviation marker. However, whatever the exact reading there is little doubt that this is a Greek transliteration of the Arabic *miṣr*, the name of the military town just outside Babylon which was the new administrative centre of Egypt.[19]

It is quite common to find examples of these coins with retrograde reverses and some of these may be contemporary imitations, but the few which I have examined are similar to the normal coins in style, fabric and weight, so the majority of these retrograde coins are probably products of the official mint.

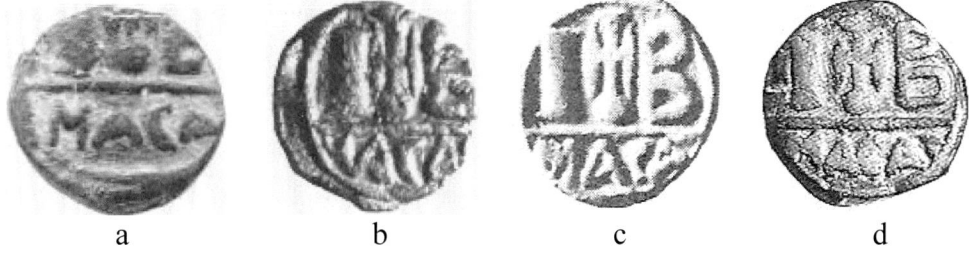

a   b   c   d

Fig. 6: **MACP**, **MACA** *or* **MACAP**? *Four coins with clear reverse exergual legends.*[20] *(all coins approx. 1.5x actual size)*

---

[18] See also Domaszewicz and Bates Cats. 32 and 33.

[19] "Babylon" was the name given to the Roman fortified town situated in Old Cairo. *Al-Fustāt*, the new Arab town, was probably founded in 642 and was generally known as *miṣr*, the name which persists today as the modern Arabic name for Egypt. It is usually pronounced "masr" in the Egyptian dialect. For details of the foundation and early history of al-Fustat see Kubiak 1987.

[20] Coin a. ANS collection, b. private collection, c. Ratto sale 9.12.1930 lot 1324, d. Spink Zurich sale 20.6.1989 lot 69.

Type IV
(BMC Heraclius 305, SICA 735)

Fig. 7. Obv: Crude facing bust with palm branch to left, uncertain object to right and Ԑ *to lower right. Rev:* IМB *with* **ABN** *in exergue. 7.06g. 6h.*
(approx. 2x actual size)

I know of only four examples of Type IV, struck from three different obverse and three reverse dies.[21] One obverse die (Fig. 8b) looks very much like the obverse of some Type II coins, but the other two dies are in a rather different style. The reverse is quite distinctive and all three dies bear the exergual legend **ABN**. The unusual rhomboid **A** on at least two of the reverse dies is found on contemporary Coptic papyri and also occurs on the Type V coins described below.[22] These are quite large heavy coins and the fabric is different from that of the **ABAZ** coins. The metal seems to be of better quality and the edges are smoothed on all the examples that I have seen. At first this smoothing made me rather suspicious that we might be dealing with modern forgeries, but the British Museum example has been in the collections since 1849 and was acquired by the British Vice Consul at Tunis in the 1830s or 1840s. At this time the Egyptian Arab-Byzantine coinage was completely unpublished, so it is highly unlikely that this is a forgery. **ABN** could be a mint name or another personal name, but at present I am unable to offer any suggestions and none of the known coins has a reliable provenance.

a　　　　　　　　　　b

Fig. 8a: The BM coin; as Fig. 7 but with the **N** *of* **ABИ** *retrograde (BMC Heraclius 303). 7.1g.*
Fig. 8b: The Ashmolean coin; as Fig. 7 (SICA 735). 9.25g. 6h.
(approx. actual size)

---

[21] Two are in a private collection, both struck from the same die pair. The British Museum and Ashmolean examples are illustrated in Fig. 8. There may also be a fifth example in the Bibliothèque Nationale - Lavoix Cat.95 is not illustrated and the exergual legend was apparently not readable, but the rest of the description fits Type IV. Unfortunately the coin is not at present accessible.

[22] When I catalogued the Ashmolean coin in SICA, I took this first letter for an **O**, but close examination shows that there is a circular punch on top of the **A**.

Type V
(MIB Heraclius X48, Domaszewicz and Bates UII, DOC 142-143)

a   b

Fig. 9a. Obv: Two crude facing busts with long cross between. Rev: A-Ⱳ with long cross between and ΠAN in exergue. 7.76g. 12h.
Fig. 9b. As above but cruder and all legends retrograde. 1.36g. 12h.
Both coins cast fabric (approx. 2x actual size)

These interesting coins have long been known and have usually been identified as irregular coins dating from the reign of Heraclius. The reverse exergual legend has sometimes been read as ΠON rather than ΠAN, but there is no doubt that the second letter is usually a rhomboidal A of the Coptic type, as is the A in A-Ⱳ. As early as 1897 Kubitschek suggested that the mint might be Panopolis in Upper Egypt, but this has not found general acceptance among numismatists, probably because Alexandria was the only known Byzantine mint and a mint located in Upper Egypt seemed highly improbable. Also the coins appeared to be rare and there was no published evidence of provenance. However, all this has changed with Castrizio's publication of the coins excavated at Antinoöpolis. Out of just under 300 Egyptian Byzantine and Arab-Byzantine coins no less than 61 were Type V, making it the most abundant of the various 7thC types and strongly suggesting that the coins were minted somewhere close to Antinoöpolis.[23] Castrizio concluded from excavation and hoard evidence that the coins were post-conquest and, although the arguments set out in his publication are not totally conclusive, I think that there is now little doubt about this dating. A slightly earlier date is not impossible, but it seems highly unlikely that such an irregular issue of coinage would have been tolerated under Byzantine rule. Castrizio also concluded that the mint was at Antinoöpolis itself and that ΠAN should be read as an abbreviation of ΠΟΛΙΣ ΑΝΤΙΝΕΩΝ. This is certainly possible as Antinoöpolis was the provincial capital, but the more obvious reading as an abbreviation for Panopolis, an important town just over 100km. to the south, seems at least equally likely. The answer will have to await the publication of coin finds from Panopolis itself, but for the present we can at least be sure that the mint was somewhere in northern Upper Egypt.[24]

The coins themselves are unusual in two respects. Firstly the absence of a denomination numeral on the reverse is unprecedented in 6th or 7thC Egyptian coinage and the novel A-Ⱳ design suggests a specifically Christian issuing authority such as a bishop or one of the major monasteries near Panopolis. Secondly almost all the coins appear to be cast. There are two varieties, the first (Fig. 9a) of reasonably good style and the second (Fig. 9b) of lighter weight, cruder style and with the legends almost always retrograde. The fact that this second variety has retrograde legends is slightly

---

[23] These figures exclude the coins from the San Colluto hoard which was deposited before the Arab conquest, and so contained no Arab-Byzantine coins.
[24] Noeske's 2009 publication of coin finds from the Monastery of Apa Shenute, just across the Nile from Panopolis, illustrates two Type V coins, but it is unclear whether these were actually found at the monastery. Noeske suggests that the coins could be an issue of the Patriarch Benjamin I (626-665), but argues that they can be dated no later than ca. 632 "because, as a rule, it was the most recent official issues that were imitated." This seems to me a very weak argument, as the "rule" is belied by the Type II coins considered above and also by the numerous Syrian and North African Arab-Byzantine coins which imitate Heraclius rather than Constans II, not to mention the earlier "Phocas" dodecanummia which imitate Justinian and Justin rather than Maurice (see my other article in this volume).

puzzling as the easiest way to create crude cast coins is to make clay moulds by simply impressing an existing coin into the clay. The resulting cast would of course have normal, not retrograde, legends. This was a common practice in late Roman Egypt and the pottery mould from Suhag recently published by Noeske shows that the practice was current at least as late as the end of the 6th C.[25] However, the mint at Panopolis appears to have adopted the more laborious method of actually engraving their crude clay moulds. The reasons for this are unclear, although conceivably they might have actually intended the legends to be retrograde in order to further differentiate the smaller half-unit(?) coins.

Type VI

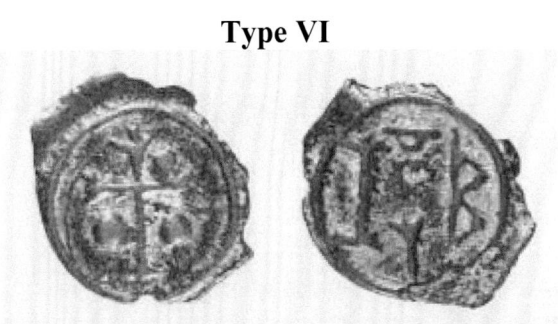

Fig. 10. Obv: Large cross on a horizontal base with trefoil terminations at the top and at each end of the cross bar, four globes (one very small) around. Rev: **I-B** *with uncertain design between, perhaps a heavily blundered cross-on-steps. 1.9g. 2h.*[26]
Cast fabric (approx. 2x actual size)

This rare type bears some resemblance to Type V, both in its cast fabric and in its obverse design which could possibly be a very debased copy of the Type V obverse. It was first published in 1950 by Miles who mistook the reverse design for an Arabic inscription,[27] but if his illustration is turned through 90°, it is clearly an **I-B** with a cross-on-steps between. I only know of three examples: the two recorded by Miles in the ANS collections and the one illustrated here from the Barber Institute. None of these has any details of provenance and the coin itself offers no clue as to the location of its mint.

Mints and Dates

Under Byzantine rule we only know of a single mint at Alexandria. In contrast by the end of the Umayyad period there were several mints located at Fustāt, Alexandria, Athrīb, Ahnas and one or perhaps two mints in the Fayyum.[28] It is not therefore surprising to find a number of different Arab-Byzantine mints in operation, although the existence of a mint in Upper Egypt is perhaps somewhat unexpected. At present only the attribution of the Type III **MACA** coins to Babylon/Fustāt is reasonably certain and the Type II **ABAZ** coins may well have been produced subsequently at the same mint. We can also be confident that there was a mint in northern Upper Egypt either at Panopolis or Antinoöpolis. The location of the other mints is very uncertain; it would be surprising if there was no mint at Alexandria, but at the moment we have no evidence that the Type I coins with the blundered **AΛEΞ** mint mark were actually struck there.

The dating is even more uncertain. The Arab conquest of Egypt was completed in 642 and I have suggested elsewhere in this volume that the new rulers continued to mint coins of Constans II at

---

[25] Noeske 2009 p. 211 fig. 45.
[26] The Coin Collection, Barber Institute of Fine Arts, Birmingham, Cat. No. AB 66, published in Goodwin 2003b Fig. 8.
[27] Miles 1950 Cats. 106 and 106a.
[28] I have recently seen, in a private collection, a post-reform fals similar to the Fustāt, Alexandria and Athrīb types, but with the mint name *Rashid* (Rosetta).

Alexandria for the next few years. Perhaps this stopped after the brief re-occupation of Alexandria by the Byzantines in 645/646, so the earliest date for an Arab-Byzantine coinage would be in the late 640s. The latest likely date is c.700 as the post-reform copper was probably introduced very shortly after the introduction of the new gold dinars in 77AH (696/697). Our only other real clue is the **ABAZ** type, which can be firmly dated to after 65ΛH (684/685) if we accept the association with 'Abd al-Aziz. This is also the only type which features the deliberate removal of crosses from the design and so it can perhaps be seen as a parallel to the Standing Caliph coinage in Syria. A tentative dating of c. 690-700 can therefore be assigned to Type II and, if Type III preceded it at Fustat, an even more tentative date of c. 670-690 can be assigned to Type III. The rare Type IV has a similar obverse design to Type II and was therefore probably a short-lived issue of the 690s. For the moment the date range for Types I, V and VI remains uncertain, although it seems reasonable to assume that they are all earlier than the "crossless" types. So the date range must remain as wide as c. 650-690, although it is highly unlikely that any of these types was struck for a period of more than 20 years.

Other possible Arab-Byzantine types

Could there possibly be other unrecognised Arab-Byzantine types? The answer must be "yes" and this section describes four other coins which could be additional types or varieties.

Fig. 11: A variant of Type I? Crude standing figure on the obverse and **I-B** *on the reverse but with an* **M** *replacing the usual cross-on-globe,* **AΛ**... *in exergue. 6.51g. 6h.*
(approx. 2x actual size)

The first very worn specimen (Fig. 11) appears to be closely related to Type I in both style and fabric, and so far as can be made out it has an identical standing figure on the obverse. However, the reverse is closer to Type II with a large **M** replacing the the normal cross-on-globe. It is also unusually heavy for a Type I coin. This coin should probably be classified as a second variety of Type 1, but a decision will need to await the discovery of better examples.[29]

The three coins shown in Fig. 12 all share the characteristic of an obverse copying Heraclius and a reverse which probably copies Constans II, or alternatively copies the reverse of the facing bust coins usually attributed to the period of Sasanian occupation. The first coin has an obverse of good style, although the cross between the heads is an unusual feature, but the blundered reverse exergual legend precludes the possibility that this is a hybrid variety made from two official dies. Its module is similar to that of the early issues of Heraclius and my feeling is that this is more likely to be an imitation from the Sasanian occupation period. The obverse of the second coin, which imitates the last issue of Heraclius, is of cruder style and the shape of the reverse cross-on-globe is closer to that on some of the Type I Arab-Byzantine coins rather than to the official coins of Constans II. It therefore seems probable that this is a post-conquest issue. The third coin has an obverse loosely

---

[29] Awad 16 is the closest that I have been able to find, but this has a small **M** below the cross. It was the only coin with this design of reverse that he recorded in his group of 180 coins and strangely it is not mentioned at all in Domaszewicz and Bates.

copying Heraclius, but it is also rather reminiscent of some of the best Type V Arab-Byzantine coins. It is an unusually thick coin, much thicker in relation to its diameter than any official coins of Heraclius or Constans II, so it seems unlikely that it was a contemporary forgery. It is much more likely to represent an attempt to produce a local "official" currency along the same lines as the Type V and VI coins. This last coin is therefore probably the best candidate for an additional Arab-Byzantine type, but at present I know of no other examples.

Fig. 12. 3 irregular "mules" with obverses copying Heraclius and reverses copying Constans II
12a. Obv: Busts of Heraclius and Heraclius Constantine with cross between heads.
Rev: **I-B** *with cross-on-globe between and blundered* **AΛЄΞ** *in exergue. 4.32g. 12h.*
12b. Obv: Three crude standing figures.
Rev: **I-B** *with cross-on-globe between and* **AΛЄΞ** *in exergue. 7.28g. 12h.*
12c. Obv: Crude busts of Heraclius and Heraclius Constantine with cross-on-steps between.
Rev: **I-B** *with cross-on-globe between and completely blundered legend in exergue. 9.93g. 12h.*
(all coins approx. 2x actual size)

Conclusions

The Arab-Byzantine coinage of Egypt can now be seen as considerably more diverse than was realised until recently. There are at least six different types, three of which probably have meaningful mint signatures or legends. The coins were issued at a number of different local mints and the emerging picture begins to look more like that in Syria than we might have imagined a few years ago. There are also a number of irregular coins which mix obverses and reverses of Heraclius and Constans II, a phenomenon also found in the Syrian Pseudo-Byzantine coinage.[30]

---

[30] I am very grateful to Eurydice Georganteli at the Barber Institute, Vesta Curtis at the British Museum, Michael Bates at the American Numismatic Society and Luke Treadwell at the Ashmolean Museum for allowing me to examine coins and make use of images. My thanks also to members of the Round Table who contributed to various discussions and particularly to Steve Mansfield who read a draft of this paper and made a number of helpful suggestions.

Bibliography

Album, A. and Goodwin, T., 2002, *Sylloge of Islamic Coins in the Ashmolean, Vol. 1, Arab-Sasanian and Arab-Byzantine coins*, Oxford, referred to as 'SICA'.

Awad, H., 1972, 'Seventh Century Arab Imitations of Alexandrian Dodecanummia', *ANS Museum Notes* **18** pp. 113-117.

Bacharach, J., and Awad, H., 1981, 'Rare Early Egyptian Islamic Coins and Coin Weights: The Awad Collection', *Journal of the American Research Centre in Egypt* **XVIII**, pp. 51-56.

Castrizio, D., 2010, *Le Monete della Necropoli Nord di Antinoupolis (1937-2007)*, Firenze.

Domaszewicz, L. and Bates, M., 2002, 'Copper Coinage of Egypt in the Seventh Century' in Bacharach, J. (ed.), *Fustat Finds*, pp. 88-111, Cairo.

Foss, C., 2008, *Arab-Byzantine Coins*, Washington, referred to as 'DOC'.

Goodwin, T., 2003a, Review of Domaszewicz, L. and Bates, M., 2002, *Numismatic Chronicle* pp. 417-420.

Goodwin, T., 2003b, 'Some Interesting Arab-Byzantine Coins from the Barber Institute Collection', *Numismatic Circular* **CXI** pp. 196-197.

Hahn, W., 1981, *Moneta Imperii Byzantini* **3**, Vienna, referred to as 'MIB'.

Kubiak, W., 1987, *Al-Fustat – Its Foundation and Early Urban Development*, Cairo.

Kubitschek, W., 1897, 'Beiträge zur frühbyzantinischen Numismatik 2: Verzeichniss der im Wiener Münzcabinet befindlichen byzantinischen Zwölfer aus der Münzstätte Alexandria' *Numismatische Zeitschrift* **XXIX** pp. 192-196.

Lavoix, H., 1887, *Catalogue des Monnaies Musulmanes de la Bibliothèque Nationale – Khalifes Orientaux*, Paris.

Metlich, M. and Schindel, N., 2004, 'Egyptian Copper Coinage in the 7th Century AD. Some Critical Remarks' in *ONS Newsletter* **179** pp. 11-15.

Miles, G., 1950, *Rare Islamic Coins (American Numismatic Society Numismatic Notes and Monographs* 118), New York.

Noeske, H-C., 2000, *Münzfunde aus Ägypten* I, Berlin.

Noeske, H-C., 2009, 'Finds of coins and Related Objects from the Monastery of Apa Shenute at Suhag', *Dumbarton Oaks Papers* **63**, pp. 210-219.

Phillips, J., 1962, 'The Byzantine Bronze Coins of Alexandria in the Seventh Century', *Numismatic Chronicle* pp. 225-241.

Quibell, J. E., 1912, *Excavations at Saqqara – the Monastery of Apa Jeremias*, Cairo.

Rodziewicz, M., 1984, *Les habitations romaines tardives d'Alexandrie: à la lumière des fouilles polonaises à Kôm el-Dikka (Alexandrie III)*, Warsaw.

Sabatier, J., 1862, *Description Générale des Monnaies Byzantines*, Paris.

Walker, J., 1956, *A Catalogue of the Arab-Byzantine and Post-Reform Umaiyad Coins*, London.

Wroth, W., 1908, *Catalogue of the Imperial Coins in the British Museum* **Vol. 1**, London, referred to as 'BMC'.

The Earliest Islamic Copper Coinage of North Africa

Trent Jonson [1]

Introduction

Given the scarcity of the earliest Islamic copper coinage (*fulūs*; sing. *fals*) of North Africa it is interesting that they appear in some of the late eighteenth and early nineteenth century catalogues, including Adler (1792),[2] and Marsden (1823).[3] These issues even captured the attention of the scholars and scientists who accompanied Napoleon's expedition to Egypt from 1798 to 1801, with several engravings of North African *fulūs* included in the multi-volume *Description de l'Égypte*, published in the years following the expedition (Figure 1).[4]

Figure 1: Two examples of engravings of North African copper coinage found in Description de l'Égypte. On the left, a Two Imperial Bust fals. On the right, an Imperial Bust fals. Description de l'Égypte ou Recueil des observations et des recherches qui ont été faites en Égypte pendant l'expédition de l'armée française. Tome II Etat Moderne. Plates i and h

The early catalogues describe some of the initial copper types of Muslim North Africa but do not provide any sort of detailed analysis of the coinage. This had to wait until Longpérier and Lavoix who, building on the groundbreaking scholarship of de Saulcy, took up the challenge presented by the North African *fulūs*. Of particular note are their studies of the bilingual (Latin/Arabic) *fulūs* of Ṭanja and the discussion of the coinage struck with the name Mūsā b. Nusayr.[5]

Despite the early identification of some of the copper types of North Africa, and the later efforts of Longpérier, and Lavoix, the earliest Islamic copper coinage of North Africa continues to be one of the least studied components of the Umayyad monetary system.[6] This lack of scholarship is not surprising, as the coins are quite rare and examples are housed in widely scattered locations in various collections, both public and private. They are also often poorly preserved and/or struck on flans that are slightly too small for the die, making their analysis difficult.

---

[1] DPhil Candidate, Khalili Research Centre, Oriental Institute, University of Oxford. tmaxvic@yahoo.com
[2] J. G. C. Adler, *Museum cuficum Borgianum Velitris, Pars II*; *Collection nova numerum Cuficorum seu Arabicorum veterum: CXVI continens numos plerosque ineditos e Museis Borgiano et Adleriano*, Hafniae, 1792.
[3] W. Marsden, *Numismatica Orientalia Illustrata*, London, 1823.
[4] E-D. Jomard et al., eds. *Description de l'Égypte ou Recueil des observations et des recherches qui ont été faites en Égypte pendant l'expédition de l'armée française*. Tome II Etat Moderne, Paris, Imprimerie royale, 1817.
[5] A. de Longpérier, "Monnaie bilingüe de Tanger", *Revue archéologique* 9, Paris, 1864, pp. 53-58; H. Lavoix, "Monnaie arabe au type Visigoth", *Revue numismatique Belge*, 1860, pp. 239-41.
[6] For the purposes of this paper the term 'North Africa' includes the territories of present-day Morocco, Algeria, Tunisia and Libya but excludes Egypt.

The only substantial investigation of the Islamic coins of North Africa is Walker's *A Catalogue of Muhammadan Coins in the British Museum (Vol. 2)*, published in 1956.[7] Walker's catalogue includes not only the early Islamic coins of North Africa housed in the British Museum, but also those found in other collections. It is therefore still immensely significant. Walker, however, did not have direct access to the majority of the coins he was describing, nor even, in approximately 30% of the cases, to illustrations, leading to errors in transcription and interpretation of the legends. Walker also classifies the coins first by language, type and metal, and only secondarily by mint and date. As Bates points out, although this arrangement has some advantages, "it obscures the evidence and hinders both numismatists and historians" as "superficially similar but historically unrelated issues are lumped together, while closely related coins are dispersed".[8]

This paper critiques the Byzantine (Latin) section of Walker's catalogue, which describes the earliest Islamic *fulūs* that can definitively be attributed to North Africa.[9] High-resolution digital imaging of the coins in Walker's catalogue, combined with a large number of new examples that either were unknown or inaccessible to Walker provide the opportunity to revise Walker's treatment of these coins. I will propose a new classification system for the early copper coinage based on mint location; revise the legends found on the examples in Walker's catalogue; provide, where necessary, new interpretations for the legends; offer the results of preliminary die studies for each of the coin series; advance the discussion of prototypes and chronology; and present the metrological data for each series.

An explanation of the abbreviations used in this paper can be found at the end.

Typology

The shortcomings of Walker's classification system are abundantly apparent in his treatment of the Byzantine (Latin) group. Walker divides the coins (both precious metal and copper) of this group into four classes according to their obverse imagery:

  I.   Two Imperial Busts (TIB)
 II.   Imperial Bust (IB)
III.   Imperial Head (IH)
 IV.   Portraitless

Walker allocates the early Islamic copper issues of North Africa to the first three of these categories. There are no copper coins of the Portraitless type, although Post-Reform copper coinage appears to have been struck in North Africa at the same time as the gold Portraitless coinage.[10]

Walker's TIB category lumps together both those copper issues struck in Tripoli and those struck at the main Muslim mint. The evidence, sparse as at is, also suggests that the Muslim administration struck the IB type in Tripoli, while they struck the IH *fulūs* at two further mints, Ṭanja (modern Tangier, Morocco) and Tilimsān (modern Tlemcen, Algeria). Walker's grouping of the copper issues in this manner therefore does not provide us with any historical or geographical information about the coinage. Instead, these subdivisions skip from place to place, and backward and forward in time.

---

[7] J. Walker, *A Catalogue of the Muhammadan Coins in the British Museum II, A Catalogue of Arab-Byzantine and Post-Reform Umaiyad Coins*, London, British Museum, printed by order of the Trustees, 1956, pp. xxxix-li, 58-64.
[8] M. L. Bates, "History, Geography and Numismatics in the First Century of Islamic Coinage", *Revue Suisse De Numismatique* 65, 1986, p. 235.
[9] The Post-Reform (Copper) section of Walker's catalogue contains several other types that may be contemporary with the coinage discussed in this paper. There attribution is still uncertain, however, and are therefore not considered here.
[10] See the examples in Walker, pp. 289-91.

A more useful classification takes the early *fulūs* of what would become the Umayyad province of *Ifrīqiya* and divides the coins by mint, and then by issuer and date if available. Following this system, the *fulūs* of North Africa can be divided into four groups:

I. North Africa – TIB
II. Tripoli – IB, TIB
III. Tilimsān – IH
IV. Ṭanja – IH

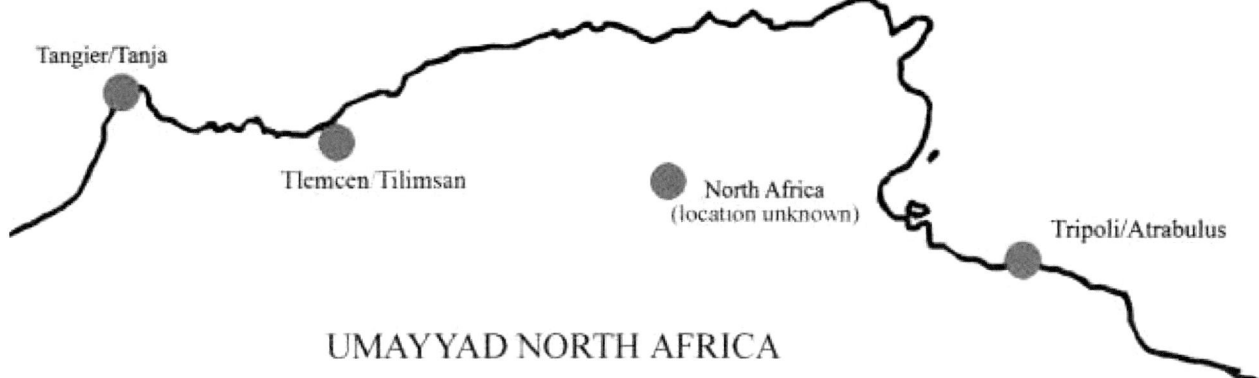

Figure 2: Locations of mints striking Copper Coinage in early Muslim North Africa

The location of the mint I have labelled 'North Africa' is unknown, but it struck the majority of both the precious metal and copper coinage issued by the Muslim conquerors after the conquest of the region. Walker suggests that this mint was located in Kairouan.[11] This is possible, although it may have been a mobile mint, travelling with the army,[12] and I have therefore adopted a generic label for this workshop.

Table 1: Comparison of the Number of Examples of the North African Fulūs in Walker's Catalogue and the Number of Examples Considered for this Paper

Walker	Mint	Walker	Known Corpus
TIB	North Africa	12	29
IB	Tripoli	6	22
TIB	Tripoli	6	9
IH	Tilimsān	1	6
IH	Ṭanja	3	9
	TOTAL	28	**75**

As can be seen in Table 1, in some cases a large number of new coins have come to light, in others only a few new examples are known.[13] Unfortunately, even with the additions to the known corpus it is still a relatively small sample size and many of the observations below must therefore be considered tentative.

---

[11] Walker, p. xlviii.
[12] Bates has persuasively argued that the North Africa mint accompanied Mūsā when he invaded the Iberian Peninsula in 93/712. See M. L. Bates, "The Coinage of Spain Under the Umayyads of the East, 711-750", *Actas III Jarique de Numismática Hispano-árabe*, Madrid, Museo Arqueológico Nacional, 1992, pp. 276-77.
[13] Walker knew of additional examples but did not describe them in his catalogue.

With the classification system set out, I will now discuss the copper coinage of each of the four mints, providing analysis of the imagery and legends found on each of the series. I will also discuss the results of preliminary die studies that have been carried out on the known examples.

North Africa

This mint must be considered the main, 'official' mint of the early Muslim conquerors of North Africa, striking both the earliest precious metal TIB coinage and the corresponding *fulūs* considered in this paper.

The dating and issuing authority of the earliest TIB *fulūs* (without a mint name, dates, or issuing authority in the legends) is uncertain. We do know that the Arab general and first North African Governor, Ḥassān ibn al-Nuʿmān al-Ghassānī, conquered Carthage for the second time in approximately 78-9/698. Walker suggests that Mūsā b. Nusayr replaced Ibn al-Nuʿmān as governor of North Africa in approximately 80/699-700 and, following Walker's chronology, Mūsā would have been in office when the Muslims struck the first TIB coinage.[14] This suggestion does not, however, explain the presence of the name 'al-Nuʿmān' and the date of 80 H on the IB *fulūs*. Walker sidesteps this problem by suggesting that 'al-Nuʿmān' did not refer to the North African Governor of that name, but instead his son, despite the lack of textual or numismatic evidence.[15] It seems much more likely that the governor Ibn al-Nuʿmān was the issuing authority for the IB coinage and, as I argue below, the iconography of the IB *fulūs* was modelled on that of the TIB coinage. This means that the TIB series preceded the IB coinage, and therefore Ibn al-Nuʿmān, and not Mūsā or Ibn al-Nuʿmān's son, must have been in office during the introduction of the TIB *fulūs*.

Significant questions remain regarding the exact dating of the TIB coinage, however. Although the *terminus post quem* for the TIB coinage struck under Ibn al-Nuʿmān is almost certainly between 76/695 and 79/698, prior to the striking of the IB series in 80/699-700, the *terminus ante quem* remains unknown. Did the production of this type end with the introduction of Latin-Epigraphic Portaitless precious metal coinage in North Africa in 84-5/703-4, or did it continue for an unknown period of time? Related to this is the question of attribution. We do not have any copper coinage that we can date to the same time as the earliest Latin-Epigraphic gold issues, and therefore the Arabs may have continued to strike the TIB *fulūs* after the introduction of the Latin-Epigraphic gold. This would then mean that at least some of the TIB *fulūs* without mint or governor name in the legend was struck under Mūsā b. Nusayr, the second governor of Islamic North Africa, who came to power at an unknown date but no later than the same year as the introduction of the Latin-Epigraphic coinage.

Two Imperial Bust (TIB) – Struck under Ibn al-Nuʿmān

The earliest TIB *fulūs* struck in the North Africa mint feature on the obverse busts of the Byzantine emperor Heraclius with his son and co-emperor Heraclius Constantine surrounded by a legend in Latin (Figure 3 below). The reverse shows a T-bar on steps surrounded by a second legend in Latin. Traces of a single beaded circle can be seen on the obverse and/or reverse of some of the coins.

---

[14] Walker, p. xlii.

[15] The exact date that Mūsā replaced Ibn al-Nuʿmān is unclear, with sources citing dates anywhere from 691 (Dabbāgh) to 85/704 (Maqqarī) (Ibn ʿAbd al-Ḥakam suggests 78/697-8). The coin evidence does not provide us with any definite answer to the question of the date of this transition, but both the Imperial Bust coinage and the fact that Portraitless, Latin-Epigraphic coinage was introduced in 84-5/703-4 suggest that the later date is more likely. See V. Christides, ***Byzantine Libya and the March of the Arabs towards the West of North Africa***, Oxford, British Archaeological Reports, 2000, pp. 49, 56, fn. 173; A-W. D. Ṭāhā, ***The Muslim Conquest and Settlement of North Africa and Spain***, London, Routledge, 1989, p. 72.

Figure 3: Islamic fals, struck at the main Islamic mint in North Africa, without date. Image courtesy of Classical Numismatic Group, Inc.[16] Mail Bid Sale 78, May 14th, 2008, Lot: 1916. (3.78 g)   (scale x3)

Figure 4: Islamic solidus, struck at the main Islamic mint in North Africa, without date. Image courtesy of A.H. Baldwin & Sons Ltd, London.[17] Baldwin's Islamic Coin Auction 24, May 9th, 2013, Lot: 4079. (4.23 g)   (scale x3)

The Byzantine mint in Carthage did not strike copper coins similar to Figure 3 and it is obvious from a comparison between Figures 3 and 4, that the copper *fals* was undoubtedly modelled on the earliest Muslim precious metal coinage of North Africa. This was a curious choice, as the creation of copper coinage almost exactly like the gold coinage must have been an invitation to forgers. Perhaps it was simply an expedient decision, as the Muslims struck the copper and precious metal coinage at the same mint. This is confirmed by the similar epigraphy on the two sets of coinage. As can be seen on the reverses in Figure 5 below, the shape of the O, A, S and E all suggest that the legends on the dies used to strike these two coins were engraved by the same engraver.

Figure 5: On left, reverse of Islamic fals, without date. Département des Monnaies et Médailles, Bibliothèque Nationale, Paris. L117. (4.63 g). On right, reverse of Islamic solidus, without date. Image on right courtesy of Classical Numismatic Group, Inc.[18] Triton VI Sale, January 13, 2003. (4.36 g)   (scale x3)

---

[16] Classical Numismatic Group, Inc. http://www.cngcoins.com/
[17] A.H. Baldwin & Sons Ltd, London. http://www.baldwin.co.uk/
[18] Classical Numismatic Group, Inc. http://www.cngcoins.com/

The most intriguing aspect of the TIB coinage of the North Africa mint, whether precious metal or copper, is their legends. These legends, not all of which have been satisfactorily interpreted, appear to be either various abbreviated representations of the *shahāda* in Latin or invocations to God. Unfortunately, the legends on these coins are in many instances difficult to read, and Walker must have had even more trouble before the advent of digital photography. As shown in Table 2, many of the new readings of the legends are substantially different from those recorded by Walker. Even with the aid of high-resolution photographs, questionable letters (enclosed by square brackets) remain for the examples described in Walker's catalogue.

Table 2: Comparison of the Legends in Walker's Catalogue and New Readings – TIB Type struck at the North Africa Mint under Ibn al-Nu'mān

OBVERSE		
Walker No.	Walker Reading	New Reading
W 156	......ANISES	[ƏƏP.CIN]........[M]ANI
W P.22=L115	....NMINE...	......[IASMAETONM]......
W P.23=L116	....SESOLCISN...	............[SESOLCISN]..
W C.5=Ø57	........OLCISETALIVS	........OLCISETAᴧIVS
W 157	6EVSNONESTAᴧIVS6S	GEVSNON.[ST]AᴧIVS6S
W 158	........TAᴧIVS6SNST	........[TA]ᴧIVS6S[NIT]
W G.3	........SVOᴧ⋅⋅⋅S6.	G..........[ETV]ONVS

REVERSE		
Walker No.	Walker Reading	New Reading
W 156	ESNCIPASMAETOMNI	.E[Ə]NCIPASMAETOMNI
W P.22=L115	ƏESNEIPASMAETOMNININM	[ƏE].N[CI]PIAS[MAE]TON[N]I[A]IN[M]
W P.23=L116	ƏENEIPASMAETOMNASNM	ƏENCIPI..M.ET[OMNAINN]
W C.5=Ø57	...CII·ASMAET	[ƏE]..[P]I[M]ASMAET[O]....
W 157	[IN]NOMINETVOV6S	G[EVSINNOM]INETV[O]V
W 158	..NOMINETV....	......NOMINETV...
W G.3	6EVSNONESTAᴧIVS6EV	GEVSNO[NES]T[Aᴧ]IVSGS[N]

Table 3: Obverse Dies used on the TIB Type struck at the North Africa Mint under Ibn al-Nu'mān, together with Weights

Ref. No.	Legend	Die	Wt. (g)
W 157	GEVSNON.[ST]AᴧIVS6S	1	1.763
ANS 1993.11.6	...[SN]..[ESTAᴧIVS6SN.]	2	2.051
PC	......ONE.TAᴧI.[S6S]..	2	2.21
W 158	........[TA]ᴧIVS6S[NIT]	3	2.487
PC	[6]EV.NONESTAᴧIVS[S]S	4	2.088
L119	[G]VSTV[E]............V.	5	1.80
SICA I 737	[6]VS[TV..............	5?	2.98
SICA I 736	...TVEC[G]VSETA[ᴧ]....	6	2.08
W P.22=L115	......[IASMAETONM]......	7	2.290
W 156	[ƏƏP.CIN]........[M]ANI	7?	2.443

L117	[NONES] .... [N .. ABE] .	8	4.634
CNG78, L:1916	.... PS[E]	8	3.78
L118	Unreadable	8?	2.470
PC	.... O[LCIS] ...	9	4.114
W P.23=L116	.... [SESOLCISN] ..	9	4.057
TOI 381	Unreadable	9?	2.86
PC	Unreadable	??	3.257
W C.5=Ø57	.... OLCISETAΛIVS	10	2.835
N78	[N]ONESTƆS[NIS] .. S[O]LCISE	11	2.329
BN, L:838	.... CTV[OVN]	12	2.18
icaL24, L:4064=Sp31, L:51	... SINNO .. E	13	2.83
PG 7003	G .... [ETV]ONVS	13	2.18
PC	Unreadable	??	1.81

Table 4: Reverse Dies of the TIB type struck at the North Africa Mint under Ibn al-Nuʿmān

Ref. No.	Reverse Legend	Field	Die
W 157	G[EVSINNOM]INETV[O]V	T/3	1
ANS 1993.11.6	[GE] .... ETVOVN	T/3	2
PC	.... [N]ETVOVNV[S]	T/3	3
W 158	...... NOMINETV ...	T/3	2
PC	GEVS .... E[T]VO .	T/3; p r	4
L119	I[NN]OMI[N]ETVG	T/3	5
SICA I 737	[E]VSTVE [CGVSET]AΛ[I]V	T/3; p r?	6
SICA I 736	INNOMI . NETVOƐS[PS]	T/3	7
W P.22=L115	[ə] . N[CI]PIAS[MAE]TON[N]I[A]IN[M]	T/4; p r	8
W 156	. E[ə]NCIPASMAETOMNI	T/3	9
L117	..... [I]ASOAET[O] ... [N] ...	T/3	10
CNG78, L:1916	[əE] ... P . MET[O]	T/3	11
L118	.... ETOMNN[IVIIV] ...	T/3	12
PC	[əEN]CIPI[AS] ... [T]OMNAINN	T/3	13
P.23=L116	əENCIPI .. M . ET[OMNAINN]	T/3	13
TOI 381	əE .... MAETOMN .	T/3	14
PC	.... ETOMN[A]	T/3	15
W C.5	[əE] .. [P]I[M]ASMAET[O]	T/3	16
N78	əəN .... [SM]	T/3	17
BN, L:838	GEVSINNO[M]IN[E]	T/3	18
icaL24, L:4064=Sp31, L:51	G[EVSNON]EST[AΛI]VSGSN	T/3	19
PG 7003	GEVSNO[NES]T[ΛΛ]IVSGS[N]	T/3	20
PC	EVSI[NNO] .... V . [B]	T/3	21

With the help of both new examples of the TIB *fulūs* (legends in Tables 3 and 4 above) and the related precious metal issues, however, the majority of the most common legends can now be unravelled. For the *fulūs* these legends are:

NONEST6SNISIPSESOLCSETNONABE[TV]
NON EST DeuS NISi IPSE SOLus soCioS ET NON hABETUr
There is no God but he alone, and he has no partner (legend usually truncated)

6VSTVS6VSETAΛIVSNONE
DeUs TuUS DeUS ET ALIUS NON Est
Thy God is God and there is no other

GEVSNONESTAΛIVS6SN
DEUS NON EST ALIUS DEUS Non est
There is no God except for God

DEVSINNOMINETVOVNVS
O God! In thy name alone

ƏEƏNCIPIASMAETOMNAINN
DEus Dominus NOster CIAS MAgnus ETernus OMNiA Noscens?
Tentative interpretation in Walker's catalogue (p. 54)

In most cases the above legends have been truncated due to a lack of space or have one or more errors within the legend, making both the transcription and interpretation of the legends difficult. These legends are also found on the corresponding precious metal coinage struck at this mint.

A die study of 23 examples of this type yields 13 obverse and 21 reverse dies. The large number of dies suggests that the TIB *fulūs* struck under Ibn al-Nu'mān at the North Africa mint was a substantial issue. Finally, it should be noted that every reverse field of this type has a T-bar on three steps, except for one example with a T-bar on four steps. Pellets to the right of the T-bar can be found on three of the reverse dies. The T-bar on steps is also found on all but one of the known TIB solidi (13 examples) and all of the known TIB tremisses (30 examples).

Two Imperial Bust (TIB) – Struck under Mūsā b. Nusayr

Figure 6: Islamic fals, likely struck at the North Africa mint. Walker 161. Image from Lane-Poole Add. IX, 23, 84. (2.44 g)   (scale x3)

Walker records five examples of the TIB *fulūs* struck without a mint name but bearing the name of Mūsā b. Nusayr, the governor of North Africa from c. 84/703 until 94/713. Like the previously described TIB type, this issue has on the obverse Heraclius and his son, while the reverse features a T-bar on steps. On this series the Byzantine Emperor and his co-Emperor are much more crudely rendered than on the earlier TIB coinage, and in many cases have become almost a caricature, as seen in Figure 6 above. In other cases, there is more similarity between the busts on this series and the earlier TIB coinage, although the senior Emperor has shifted from the left to the right of the field.

Table 5 below compares Walker's readings of the legends on this coinage with new readings. Unlike the legends of the earlier TIB coinage, differences between the two sets of readings are relatively minor.

Table 5: Comparison of the Legends in Walker's Catalogue and New Readings – TIB Type struck under Mūsā b. Nusayr[19]

	OBVERSE	
Walker No.	Walker Reading	New Reading
W 161	IN[......]VNVƧƏƧᵐV	..........NVƧƏƧᵐV
W 162	ƧƏƧ	ƧϿƧ..
W P.27=L120	INNƏMINIVNVƧƏƧᵐV	INNƏO . INIVNVƧƏƧᵐV
W 163	ƧƏƧ[.....]ƏNЄMᵒN . I	Ƨə[Ƨ].....]ƏNЄMON · I
W Cod.1	INNƏOMINIVNVƧƏƧᵐV	INNƏOMINIVNVƧƏƧᵐV

	REVERSE	
Walker No.	Walker Reading	New Reading
W 161	M[......]ƧIRAMIRA	.......[ƧIR]AMIRA
W 162	MVƧEFИVSIRAMIRA	M[V]Ƨ[EF]ИVS . RAMIRA
W P.27=L120	MVƧEFИVSIRAMIRA	ɱVƧEENVSIRA[ɱIRA]
W 163	[A]ɱIRARISVFƧSVɱ	[A]ɱIR[A]RISVFƧSVɱ
W Cod.1	ɱVƧEFNVƧIRAɱIRA	ɱVƧEFNVƧIRAɱIRA

As can be seen in the table, there is only one obverse and one reverse legend on this type, although in some cases errors occur with individual letters. Retrograde legends also occur on two of the examples. The obverse and reverse legends are:

Obv: **INNƏOMINIVNVƧƏƧᵐV**
　　　IN Nomine DOMINI UNUS DSEU (for DEUS?)
　　　In the name of the Lord, God Alone.

Rev: **ɱVƧEFNVƧIRAɱIRA**
　　　MUSE Filius NUSIaR AMIR Africae
　　　Mūsā b. Nuṣayr, Amir of Africa

The interpretation of the two abbreviated legends above is the same as those suggested by Walker.[20]

Like the previously discussed TIB type, the legend engravers continued to attempt to spell out in full as many of the words as possible, the only exceptions being *filius* and *Africae*. The obverse legend is similar to the legend *O Deus! In nomine tuo unus* found on the precious metal TIB coinage of this mint struck under Ibn al-Nu'mān. The use of the phrase *in nomine domini*, however, only appears with the advent of the Portraitless, Latin-Epigraphic precious metal coinage (most commonly as the legend *in nomine domini misericordis unus deus* (found on many of the gold fractionals), first struck at this mint in 84-5/703-4. The use of this phrase therefore suggests that this

---

[19] The 'F' on the reverse of W 163 is reversed.
[20] Walker gives full credit to De Saulcy (J. A. 1839, vii, p. 502) for providing the interpretation of the legend. De Saulcy deciphered the legend using coin W 163. Walker did note an alternative interpretation for the last four letters of the obverse legend – DSEU – DeuS EternUs. See Walker, p. 60, fn. 1.

copper type was contemporary with the Portraitless coinage. It may, in fact, be even later, as the appearance of the letterforms Ƨ and ə only occurs on the precious metal coinage beginning in 89-90/708-9. Could this coinage have been struck between 89/708 and 92/711, prior to the introduction of Arabic, post-reform *fulūs* in 91-92/710-11?[21] As with the majority of the coinage described in this paper, more precise dating will remain speculative until the appearance of hoard, excavation and/or overstrike evidence.

Table 6: Weights, Obverse and Reverse Dies of the TIB Coinage Struck under Mūsā b. Nusayr at the North Africa Mint[22]

Ref. No.	Obverse Legend	Die	Wt.
W Cod.1	INNƎOMINIVNVƧƏƧᵐV	1	N/A
W 161	.... NVƧƏƧᵐV	1	2.442
W P.27=L120	INNƎO . INIVNVƧƏƧᵐV	1	2.998
W 162	..... NIVNVƧƧƧ ..	2	2.115
N77	I .. [ƎO] ..... NVƧƧƧEV	2	1.850
W 163	ƧƎ[Ƨ] .....]ƏNEMON · I	3	2.429

Ref. No.	Reverse Legend	Field	Die
W Cod.1	MVƧEFNVƧIRAMIRA	T/3	1
W 161	.... [ƧIR]AMIRA	T/3	2
W P.27=L120	MVƧEFNVSIRA[MIRA]	T/3	1
W 162	M[V]Ƨ[EF]ИVS . RAMIRA	T/3	3
N77	MV]ƧEFИ[VSIRA]MIRA	T/3	3
W 163	[A]MIЯ[A]ЯISVFƎSVM	T/4	4

Walker describes five coins of this type in his catalogue, and I know of only one additional example. The six coins were struck from three obverse and four reverse dies. The small number of surviving examples, combined with the small number of dies, suggests that this type was never a large issue.

Walker argues that the Muslims struck this coinage at Tripoli, although it does not bear a mint name.[23] Although this series and the TIB coinage of Tripoli are superficially similar in their imagery, they differ in their legends and epigraphy (and it appears they also differ in their weights – see Metrology below). Due to these differences, I suggest that they were struck at different mints, although they may have been contemporary.

Tripoli

The *fulūs* of the Tripoli mint consist of two series, the IB type struck under Ibn al-Nuʿmān and a TIB type struck under Mūsā b. Nusayr.

---

[21] Although it is not certain as the dated post-reform fulūs do not have a mint name, current thinking suggests that this series was struck in North Africa. A-H. Fenina, ed., **Numismatique et Histoire de La Monnaie en Tunisie, Tome 2: Monnaies Islamiques**, Tunis, La Banque Centrale de Tunisie, 2007, p. 234.
[22] The 'F' on the reverse die of Walker 163 is reversed.
[23] Walker, p. xlviii.

Imperial Bust (IB) – Struck under Ibn al-Nu'mān

Figure 7: Islamic fals, likely struck at the Tripoli mint. Ashmolean Museum, Oxford. SICA I 738. Image by Jonson. (3.19 g) (scale x3)

The IB *fulūs* struck at the Tripoli mint features legends in Arabic on both the obverse and reverse surrounding imagery derived from Byzantine prototypes. The obverse legend is engraved vertically, beginning in the upper left hand corner downwards and then continuing in the upper right hand corner. This legend provides us with the only date on any of the earliest Islamic copper coinage of North Africa – *fī sanati / thamānīn* – in the year 80 (699-700). The legend frames a crudely drawn bearded and crowned figure. Despite the rough nature of the engraving, enough care has been taken in the preparation of the dies that the folds of the imperial *chlamys* (Roman/Byzantine cloak) and its *fibula* (fastener) can be clearly discerned on most of the known examples. The reverse of this series features a globe on pole on steps framed by a second legend – *bism Allāh hādhā amara bihi al-Nu'mān* – that translates as "in the name of God, al-Nu'mān ordered this". As discussed above, this undoubtedly refers to Ḥassān ibn al-Nu'mān al-Ghassānī. Traces of a plain outer circle on the obverse and reverse can be seen on some of the examples.

Although the legends on the coins of the IB type are in Arabic, Walker includes this type in the Byzantine (Latin) group, arguing that these issues "bear a distinct family resemblance" "not only in fabric and module, but also in style and portraiture" to other coinage in this group.[24] Walker is unclear on the Byzantine model for this coinage, but suggests that the prototype was probably a *semissis* of Constans II.[25]

Figure 8: Byzantine semissis of Constans II, struck at the Carthage mint. (2.20 g). Image from Wroth, Catalogue of the Imperial Byzantine Coins in the British Museum (scale x2)

---

[24] Walker, pp. xlii, (61-2).
[25] The example that Walker cites for his argument is in fact a solidus, not a semissis. See Walker, p.xlii (Wroth 288, no. 270, Pl. XXXII.19).

Walker's suggestion of a Byzantine *semissis* as the model for the IB coinage, tentative as it is, makes little sense for a number of reasons. The Byzantine mint of Carthage did not strike a *semissis* with a single outward facing Constans II bust, but instead struck *semisses* like the example in Figure 8 above. Nor does it appear that the Byzantine mint in Carthage struck gold fractionals in any great quantity. We only have a small number of surviving *semisses* from the reigns of Heraclius (610-41) and Constans II (641-68), with *tremisses* only from the latter.[26] A more likely Byzantine model, at least for the proportions of the figure on the obverse, is the Carthaginian *decanummia* (sing. *decanummium*) of Constans II.[27] As can be seen by a comparison of the *decanummium* bust in Figure 9 and the obverse of Figure 7 above, there is good congruency between the relative proportions of the figure. There even appears to be some similarity with the placement of the obverse legend on the two coins. This suggestion carries even more conviction when the similarities between the metrology of the Byzantine *decanummia* and early Muslim coinage are considered (see Metrology below).

Figure 9: Byzantine decanummium of Constans II, struck at the Carthage mint. Image courtesy of Classical Numismatic Group, Inc.,[28] Auction 61, September 25, 2002, lot 2251. (2.40 g)   (scale x3)

Figure 10: Islamic semissis, struck at the main Muslim mint. Walker C.1=Ø45. Image by Jonson. (2.03 g)   (scale x3)

The use of a single bust, and perhaps the general layout and proportions of the obverse of the Imperial Bust type has its origins in the Byzantine copper coinage circulating in North Africa at the time of the Muslim conquest, i.e. the Constans II *decanummium*. This attribution does not, however, explain some of the details of the obverse imagery on this coinage, nor the reverse imagery that is substantially different from that found on seventh century Byzantine copper coinage. Instead, the model for both the obverse and reverse imagery on this coinage appears to be Muslim, not Byzantine. The details of the imagery on the obverse of the IB type, in particular the vestigial beard and the trefoil design replacing the cross on the crown of a facing figure must have been derived

---

[26] P. Grierson, ***Catalogue of the Byzantine Coins in the Dumbarton Oaks Collection and in the Whittemore Collection***, Vol 2, Part 1., Washington, Dumbarton Oaks Center for Byzantine Studies, 1966, p. 43.
[27] For Stickel's selection of a Carthaginian follis of Constans II as the model for the prototype for the obverse see Walker, p. xlii. and fn. 2.
[28] Classical Numismatic Group, Inc. http://www.cngcoins.com/

from the busts on the TIB coinage.[29] Even more compelling evidence for this derivation is found on the reverse. The reverse of the Byzantine copper coinage invariably has a denominational symbol as the dominant imagery on the reverse, not a cross on steps (from which the globe on pole on steps must have been derived). The globe on pole on steps is, however, found on the reverse of the TIB type *semissis* (Figure 10 above). This suggests that the TIB coinage, at the very least the gold coinage, was already in circulation at the time of the striking of the coinage of the IB type.

Table 7: Weights, Obverse and Reverse Dies of the IB Coinage of Tripoli

Coll. No.	WT	OD	RD	Reverse Field
L92	4.518	1	1	G/3
SICA 1 739	2.54	1?	2	G/3
W 165	2.48	1?	2	G/3
W ANS.12=ANS 1917.215.3491	4.163	2	3	G/3
N64	3.699	2	3	G/3
L89	2.646	2	3	G/3
ANS 1959.152.1	3.872	3	1	G/3
W 166	3.575	3?	1	G/3
SICA 1 738	3.19	4	4	G/4
W 167	3.80	4	4	G/4?
L93	3.464	4	4	G/4
Tub 92-15-1	3.52	5	5	G/3
L90	3.107	6	6	G/3
W 164	3.256	6	3	G/3
N64	3.122	7	6	G/3
PC	3.26	7	6	G/3
Tub 271F6	3.03	8	3	G/3
L91	2.615	9	3	G/3
Nu63	2.33	9	6	G/3
Jena OMJ 305-A10= St36	3.06	9	3	G/3
W C.6=O58	2.146	10	7	G/3
Jena OMJ 305-B10=St37	2.21	11	2	G/3

The result of a preliminary die study on the IB coinage is set out in Table 7 above. The results suggest that this was not a large issue, with the 22 known examples having 11 obverse and seven reverse dies.[30] Eight of the 11 obverse dies appear to be closely linked, with only obverse dies 4, 5 and 10 not having reverse die links to the rest of the series. There is also little variation in the obverse figure, which you might expect if the Muslim's struck this coinage over a long period.

Further observations can be made from the results of the die study. Only one of the seven reverse dies (RD4) has a globe on pole on four steps, the rest having three steps.[31] The legends on all of the dies are clearly, albeit crudely, engraved with the legends on all but one (RD3) of the reverse dies rotating clockwise, a similar orientation to the legends in Latin found on the TIB coinage.

---

[29] The trefoil design does appear on Constans II copper coinage, but it is not a prominent feature. The type used by the Muslims could be Heraclius and Heraclius Constantine (MIB 90, illustrated in Figure 1), but the trefoil ornament adopted on Series 1 may have been borrowed from Constans II and Constantine IV solidi dated between 654/5 and 659/60 (MIB 67-69).

[30] Gaillard records an additional example. See GAILLARD 1854, p. 65, no. 1102..

[31] There is no evidence of a pellet in the right field on W ANS 12, although there is some discoloration that Walker could have misconstrued as a pellet. Walker, p. xliii, 62.

The use of Arabic and a single bust on the obverse, and a globe on pole as opposed to a T-bar on steps all serve to distinguish the IB type from the TIB type. In addition, the flans used to strike the IB type are different, usually more oval in shape and varying in diameter from 1.47 to 1.88 cm, with an average of 1.67 cm, larger than the TIB copper coinage.[32] The mean weight also differs, with the weights of the IB type higher than those of the TIB struck at the North Africa mint (see Metrology below).

Taking all of these features together, the evidence suggests that the IB type was struck at a separate mint from the TIB coinage of the North Africa mint. Walker suggested that the mint was located in Kairouan or at Carthage,[33] but I tentatively place the IB type in the Tripoli mint, for two reasons. First, the average weights (mean, median and mode) of the IB coinage is similar to that of the TIB coinage struck under Mūsā b. Nusayr in Tripoli. Secondly, the Archaeological Museum in Tripoli houses an example of the IB type, while none are found in the Bardo Museum in Tunis or in the Tunisian Mint Museum.[34] Perhaps this issue, struck immediately after the second conquest of Carthage by the Muslims, served to announce or commemorate the victory? Unfortunately, without hoard or excavation evidence the identification of the mint that struck the IB series must remain speculative.

Two Imperial Bust (TIB) – Struck under Mūsā b. Nusayr

Figure 11: Islamic fals, struck at the Tripoli mint. Département des Monnaies et Médailles, Bibliothèque Nationale, Paris. W P.24=L121. Image by Jonson. (4.48 g) (scale x3)

The early Muslims of North Africa also struck a TIB series in Tripoli. Like the TIB coinage struck in the North Africa mint, the TIB *fulūs* of Tripoli feature legends in Latin on the obverse and reverse margins with Heraclius and Heraclius Constantine in the obverse field and a T-bar on steps in the reverse field. The busts on the obverse are even more crudely rendered than those of the TIB type struck under Mūsā b. Nusayr at the North Africa mint and were undoubtedly modelled on the previous TIB coinage.

---

[32] The median is 1.66 cm, while the standard deviation is 0.1 cm.
[33] Walker, p. xlii.
[34] G. Cimino, "Storia e numismatica dell'Africa del Nord", **Rivista Coloniale** 20, Rome, 1925, p. 347-53.

Table 8: Comparison of Legends in Walker's Catalogue and New Readings – TIB type struck under Mūsā b. Nusayr at the Tripoli Mint

	OBVERSE	
Walker No.	Walker Reading	New Reading
W 159	…ΔMINVM[INT]RPLFAK[T]	. MINV[MINTRP]LFA[KT]..
W 160	….[T]RPLFAKT	……[TR]PL[ŁAK]T.
W P.24=L121	…ΔNINVMINTRIPFAK….VX	∇NINVMINTRIP.[F]A[K].[X]VX
W P.25=L122	….ΔMINVM..TRPLF..X	∇MIИ[VM]..[TRLF]….X
W P.26=L123	…MINTPLEAKT (sic)	…..MINT[R]ŁEAKT
W ANS.11	∇NI……..KT+VX	∇N[IN]……….KTXVX

	REVERSE	
Walker No.	Walker Reading	New Reading
W 159	[I]NNΔN[II]VƧIƍMVƧ…	[I]NNΔN..ƧIƍM[VƧ]….
W 160	…ΔNIIVƧIƍM	…ΔNIIVƧIƍ…..
W P.24=L121	INN∇NIIVƧIƍMVƧEAMIRA	AЯIMAƎƧVMƍIS[VI]IHΔNNNI
W P.25=L122	IHNΔN.MV..AMIRA	IHN[ΔN]……AMIR[A]
W P.26=L123	..NIIVƧIƍMVƧEA	IN.[Δ]….MVƧE[A]MI
W ANS.11	ЯIM..VMƍIS-VIINΔN..	…IM.[ƎS]VMƍISVIIN[ΔN]..

Walker's rendering of the legends on the Tripoli *fulūs* is largely accurate. His only significant error is his insistence that the obverse legend begins with *in nomine domini*, when in fact it appears to simply begin with *domini* (O Lord!). The most complete legends on the coinage of the Tripoli mint are:

    Obv: **∇NINVMINTRIPLFAKTXVX**
        DoMINi NUMus IN TRIPoLi FAKTus XVX
        O Lord! This numus made in Tripoli ???

    Rev: **INN∇NIIVSIƍMVSEAMIRA**
        IN Nomine DomiNI IUSsiT MUSE AMIR Africae
        In the name of the Lord, Mūsā Amir of Africa ordered (this)

Walker is unable to offer an interpretation of the final three letters/symbols on this issue – XVX, or perhaps +VX – and I am unable to suggest an interpretation. Some or all of these letters/symbols may actually be at the beginning of the legend, as in every other case with the TIB copper the legend begins at 12 o'clock.[35]

The full rendering of the legends on this type are found on the first obverse and reverse die shown in Table 9 below, although the legend on the reverse die is retrograde. The legends on the rest of the dies appear to be the same, but truncated due to the engraver's miscalculation of available space. Other engraver errors include missing or upside down letters.

---

[35] De Saulcy suggested (probably using W P.24=L121) that the obverse legend ended in a date: IN Nomine DoMINI IVSSIT MVSE AMIR Africæ NVMum IN TRIPOLi Anno VX DomiNI. Lavoix also suggested that this was part of a date. However, the letters XVX do not correspond to a date.

Table 9: Weights, Obverse and Reverse Dies of the TIB Coinage of the Tripoli Mint

Ref. No.	Obverse Legend	Die	Wt.
W P.24=L121	∇NINVMINTRIP . [F]A[K] . [X]VX	1	4.476
W ANS.11=ANS 1924.12.1	∇N[IN] . . . . KTXVX	1	2.90
W P.25=L122	∇MIИ[VM] .. [TRLF] X	2	3.341
W 159	. MINV[MINTRP]LFA[KT] ..	3	2.299
W 160	. . . . . . [TR]PL[ŁAK]T .	4	2.107
W P.26=L123	. . . . . MINT[R]LŁAKT	5	3.112
N79	. . . . . . [I]N . . . . [A]K[T]	5	1.933
Mun23	. . . . . . [TINTRLŁ]	5	2.96
L124	. . . . [P]LFAKT	6	3.238

Ref. No.	Reverse Legend	Field	Die
W P.24=L121	AЯIMAƎSVMƔIS[VI]IHΔNNNI	T/4	1
W ANS.11=ANS 1924.12.1	. . . IM . [ƎS]VMƔISVIIN[ΔN] ..	T/3	2
W P.25=L122	IHN[ΛN] . . . . . AMIR[A]	T/3	3
W 159	[I]NNΔN .. 2IƔM[VƐ]	T/3	4
W 160	. . . ΔNIIVƐIƔ	T/3	5
W P.26=L123	IN . [Δ] . . . . MVƐE[A]MI	T/3	6
N79	I .. [Δ]NI . . . . . E[A]MI	T/3	6
Mun23	. . . [Δ]NIIVƐIƔMVƐE . . .	T/3	6
L124	. . . NIIVƐIƔMVƐE[A] ..	T/3	6

There are two obvious differences between the *fulūs* of the Tripoli mint and that struck at the North Africa mint under Mūsā b. Nusayr. The first difference is found on the legends, which include on the obverse the mint name Tripoli, and on the reverse a shortening of the governor's name to Mūsā. The phrase *in nomine domini*, which is found on the North Africa TIB *fulūs*, is here reduced to *domini* on the obverse, perhaps to accommodate the mint name. On the reverse, *in nomine domini* has been inserted at the beginning of the legend, but with a different abbreviation method from that found on TIB coinage struck at the North Africa mint under Mūsā. The abbreviation method for this phrase on the Tripoli coinage is the same as that found on the Portraitless Latin-Epigraphic precious gold coinage first struck at the North Africa mint in 84-5/703-4.

The second obvious difference between the North Africa and Tripoli TIB coinage of Mūsā are the differences in the epigraphy. The coins of Tripoli use Δ for D, while those without mint names use both ∂ and ϭ. The E form is **E** in the coins with mint name, while it is both **E** and **Ɛ** in the second type. The **Ɛ** is also often reversed or turned horizontally so that the letter faces downwards. **S** is reversed in both types, but only some of them, and reversed and normal **S** may appear in the same inscription. In addition, the letterform **8**, that Walker read as **T** but is described by Grierson as a ligatured **OV**, appears in those coins with mint names.[36] These differences in letterforms all contribute to my suggestion above that the TIB coinage of Mūsā b. Nusayr without mint name was struck at a different mint from Tripoli.

---

[36] Grierson, p. 106

The nine known examples of the TIB coinage of Tripoli were struck from six obverse and six reverse dies, suggesting that this was never a big issue. Like the other TIB coinage struck at the NA mint, in most cases the reverse field shows a T-bar on three steps, except for RD1 that shows a T-bar on four steps.

Tilimsān

The exceedingly rare early Islamic IH *fulūs* of Tilimsān is quite simple in its design. A bearded face with hair parted in the middle and held back by a diadem faces outward on the obverse, while the reverse bears a simple legend in Arabic – *ḍuriba bi-Tilimsān*. Traces of a single beaded circle can be seen on the edge of both the obverse and reverse of some of the specimens.

Figure 12: Early Islamic copper coin of Tilimsān. Image courtesy of the Tonegawa Collection.[37] *(1.76 g)   (scale x3)*

The one example of the early Islamic coinage of the mint of Tilimsān that Walker includes in his catalogue was described in the Post-Reform (Copper) section (P.127, p. 240) and not with the Byzantine (Latin) coinage, but the author "closely linked" the coinage of this mint with the IH *fulūs* of Ṭanja discussed below, and I have therefore included it in this paper.[38] Although he describes only one specimen, Walker noted three other specimens – one at the American Numismatic Society in New York and two in Tunisia.[39] Two further examples are now known to exist, one in the Tonegawa Collection (Figure 12 above) and the other in the National Museum, Copenhagen (Ø748).

Walker's rationale for linking the Tilimsān *fulūs* to the IH coinage of Ṭanja is never explicitly stated, but it appears to be twofold. First, he notes the proximity between the two mints, even though they are over 400 km apart. Somewhat more convincingly, Walker argues that the obverse of the Tilimsān issue may have been modelled on the image on the reverse of the Imperial Roman coin whose obverse, in turn, may have been the model for the 'Imperial Head' found on the Ṭanja issue (Figure 13 below). The obverse of this coin is in Figure 15.

Walker's discussion of the obverse of this coinage is confusing. Initially, he identifies the figure as Hercules.[40] Later in the catalogue, however, he corrects this error, and correctly identifies the figure as that of Baal.[41] The confusion over the identity of this figure is compounded by the fact that the most recently published article on this coin type suggests that the face is a depiction of Alexander of

---

[37] The Tonegawa Collection. http://www.andalustonegawa.50g.com/
[38] Walker, p. xliv, xlix, 240.
[39] One of the Tunisian specimens is apparently in the Bardo Museum in Tunis. The other, at the time of Walker's catalogue, was owned by H. H. Abdul Wahab. It is this second Tunisian example that is illustrated in Walker's catalogue on p. xliv (fig. vii), and not the Parisian coin. I did not have access to either of the Tunisian coins for this study. Walker, p. lxix.
[40] Walker, p. xliv.
[41] Ibid., p. lxix.

Great. Unfortunately the authors of this article do not appear to have an understanding of either ancient or Islamic numismatics, particularly the common reuse of coin imagery used by previous societies. They use the image in Figure 12 above to suggest that the hair (which they describe as 'two helicoidal shapes') represents horns and this leads them to Dū'l-Qarnayn (Sura 18: 83-93), traditionally identified as Alexander and the association of Islamic authors centuries later of Alexander with the Straits of Gibraltar.[42] The common appearance of an outward facing Baal in the Punic, neo-Punic, and Imperial Roman coinage of this region, and the similarity between the face in Figure 12 above and the examples in Figure 13 below make it clear that the figure is a rendering of Baal found on the earlier coinage.

Figure 13: Left: Reverse of Imperial Roman copper coin of Tingi Mauretaniae featuring a facing head of Baal in the field. Image from Boyce, Coins of Tingi with Latin Legends, Pl. 2, No. 5. (18.21 g). Middle: Reverse of Imperial Roman copper coin of Tingi Mauretaniae, (ca. 27 BCE), featuring a facing head of Baal flanked by two branches. Numismatica Ars Classica NAC AG, Auction 72, lot 559 (11.85 g). Right: Obverse of neo-Punic copper coin of Lix, Mauretania, ca. 2nd-1st Century BCE, featuring head of Baal-Melkert. Image courtesy of Classical Numismatic Group, Inc.,[43] Triton V, January 15, 2002, lot 593 (4.15 g) [44]

In this coinage Baal is always heavily bearded and with his hair parted in the middle, similar to the Islamic coinage. Whether the model was Punic or Roman is unclear, but it does raise the question as to why the administrators of the Tilimsān (and also Ṭanja mint, see below) chose to revive such an ancient prototype. It is a difficult question to answer, but Walker notes that this was not a practice confined to North Africa.[45]

Table 10: Weights, Obverse and Reverse Dies of the Coinage of Tilimsān

Ref. No.	Wt (g)	OD	RD
TC Tilimsān	1.76	1	1
W P127=L77bis	3.179	1?	2?
Abdul-Wahab Collection	N/A	2	2?
ANS 1917.216.3537	2.115	2	2
Ø748	2.300	3	3

I was able to study images of five of the six examples of the Tilimsān *fulūs*, and tentatively suggest that they are from three obverse and three reverse dies (Table 10). The rarity of the surviving coinage, combined with the die links, again suggest that this was not a large issue.

---

[42] S. Peña and M. Vega, "Who is the "Warrior on Western Islamic Copper Coins? (A Quranic Key for an Unidentified Icon)," *Arabica* 55, 2008, p. 113-121.
[43] Classical Numismatic Group, Inc. http://www.cngcoins.com/
[44] The reverse of this coin features a six-pointed star in the field. Six, seven and eight pointed stars are found on the very common Umayyad copper coinage of al-Andalus.
[45] Walker points out a Roman coin of Maximianus Herculeus (286-305) of the mint of Antioch, which has been used as a flan for an early Post-Reform fals. See Walker, p. lxx.

Ṭanja

Like the copper coinage of Tilimsān, the IH *fulūs* of Ṭanja is extremely rare. Walker describes three examples of this type in his catalogue, two with the mint name Ṭanja, and one that he suggests does not have a mint name (this suggestion is discussed below), and notes three further examples.[46]

Figure 14: IH copper coinage of Ṭanja. Département des Monnaies et Médailles, Bibliothèque Nationale, Paris. L1678. Image by Jonson. (7.68g) (scale x2)

The obverse of this coinage features a barbarous copy of a head in profile, with a thin neck and a *chalmys* draping the shoulders. The bust is surrounded by a legend in Latin, while the reverse has an Arabic legend – *bism Allāh fals ḍuriba bi-Ṭanja* – translated as 'In the name of God, a fals struck in Ṭanja'. There is also a five-rayed star at the top of the reverse field and two rosettes, one to the left and the other at the bottom.

The extensive study of the Imperial Head coinage of Ṭanja began over 150 years ago, with both Lavoix and Longpérier writing papers on the subject, and it is the scholarship of Longpérier that Walker relies on for his own analysis of the coinage.[47] Longpérier studied W P.28=L125 and the coin now in the Fitzwilliam Museum in Cambridge (PG 13218-2006),[48] and it is this latter coin that in his view held the key to the legend, which he read as *domine deus quis tibi similis* (Lord God, after all like thee, (or who is like thee)). Longpérier was also the first to link this legend to similar wording found in the Vulgate, the late fourth century Latin translation of the Bible – in particular Psalms XXXIV, 10; LXX, 19; LXXXII, 2; and LXXXVIII, 9.

My study of the Ṭanja *fulūs*, however, reveals two obverse legends on this coinage. The Fitzwilliam coin (PG 13218-2006) does appear to have the legend suggested by Longpérier, but W P.29, when combined with other coins of the same dies and W P.30, reveals a different legend – DNEDSDVSTIV . SIMILIS. The translation of this legend is currently unclear.

---

[46] One of the additional examples is in the National Museum in Copenhagen (Ø56). Longpérier published the second example in 1864. If the reproduction of the obverse in this article is accurate, then this coin is the example now in the Fitzwilliam Museum in Cambridge (PG 13218-2006). The final example is overstruck, and is described in J. D. Brethes, ***Contribution à l'histoire du Maroc par les recherches numismatique, Casablanca***, Les Annales, Marocaines, 1939, p. 331.

[47] Longpérier, p. 53-58; Lavoix, p. 239-41.

[48] Longpérier, p. 53.

Table 11: Weights, Obverse and Reverse Dies of the Bilingual Copper Coinage of Ṭanja

Ref. No.	Wt.	Obverse Legend	OD	RD
SICAI 741	3.91	ᗡ[N]Eᗡ2[ᗡV2TI] . . . . . . LIS	1	1
W P.29=L1678	7.683	ᗡNEᗡ2[ᗡV2T] . . . . . IMILIS	1	1
Ø56	6.021	ᗡNE[ᗡ2ᗡV2]TIV . [2IM]ILIS	1	1
Tub 2010-10-1	6.91	Overstruck - Discussed below	1	?
W P.28=L125	5.50	ᗡHEᗡ2qVI[T] . . . 2IMILI2	2	2
W P.30=L126	2.410	. . [D . 2]PIVTIVI2	3	3
PG 13218-2006	6.87	. . . . 2qVITIBI2IMIL . .	4	4
Bre 331	5.75	Overstruck	N/A	

There are several other unusual features of this coinage in addition to the legends. The first is their bilingual nature, Arabic and Latin, which drove Lavoix to argue that the Muslims struck these coins at the same time as the bilingual precious metal coinage produced in North Africa and the Iberian Peninsula between 97/715 and 99/717. Walker reserved judgement on this argument, but I would suggest that these issues are the earliest coinage struck at the Ṭanja mint. Bilingual coinage was not new to the region, with the Romans striking bilingual Latin-Punic coinage sometime after 38 BCE.[49]

As Walker points out, it is this bilingual Latin-Punic coinage that was likely the model for the IH *fulūs*. Figure 15 reproduces the obverse of the coin cited by Walker, and I have included one other example. Both the coinage of Marcus Agrippa and that of Octavian as Augustus have spiky hair, one of the features that can be clearly seen on the Ṭanja coinage. What these examples do not show, however, is the thin neck and *chalmys* found on the Islamic examples. Perhaps the engravers did a profile bust from memory, or copied a bust from another type circulating in the region at this time.

Figure 15: Left: Obverse of Imperial Roman copper coin of Tingi Mauretaniae featuring Marcus Agrippa in profile. Image from Boyce, Coins of Tingi with Latin Legends, Pl. 2, No. 5. Right: Obverse of Imperial Roman copper coin of Tingi Mauretaniae, with Octavian as Augustus in profile. Numismatica Ars Classica NAC AG, Auction 72, lot 559. (11.85 g)

The final interesting feature of this coinage is the frequency with which these coins appear to have been reused, with eight of the nine examples clearly showing overstriking. Neither Walker nor the earlier scholars appear to have noticed this feature, but it is worth considering several of the overstruck examples.

---

[49] A. A. Boyce, "Coins of Tingi with Latin Legends", *Numismatic Notes and Monographs* 109, New York, American Numismatic Society, 1947, p. 6-7.

Figure 16: IH fals of Ṭanja. Walker P.30=L126. Département des Monnaies et Médailles, Bibliothèque Nationale, Paris. Image by Jonson. (2.41 g) (scale x3)

The first example is W P.30=L126, found in Figure 16. Although both Walker and Lavoix described this coin in their respective catalogues, neither of them picked up on the fact that both the obverse and reverse of this coin is overstruck. The middle of the obverse of this coin shows *lilāh* possibly followed by *lā*. The reverse consists of two legends. In the image above the original legend is upward at an angle, while the overstruck legend appears to be *bism Allāh, rasūl ??*, with *'abd* at the bottom of the field. The overstrike also shows a palm, characteristic of the earlier pre-Islamic coinage of the region.

Figure 17: Above: Drawing of obverse of IH fals of Ṭanja. Image from Longpérier 1864, p. 53. Below: IH fals of Ṭanja, PG 13218-2006, Fitzwilliam Museum, Cambridge. (6.87 g) (scale x2)

The second example is in the Fitzwilliam Museum in Cambridge (PG 13218-2006). This coin is the one originally describe by Longpérier.[50] Like Lavoix and Walker with the previous example, Longpérier missed the fact that both the obverse and reverse are overstruck. In the bottom left of the obverse field, just below the bust, the Arabic letters *mīm, ḥā', mīm* can be clearly seen. On the

---

[50] Longpérier, p. 53.

reverse, the overstruck legend is not discernable, but the beaded border from the overstrike is apparent at bottom right.

The last example, in the Tubingen collection, is clearly overstruck, but the top of the head of the figure can still be seen on the obverse, as well as part of the Latin legend. The overstruck legends on this coin are the same as the legends on W B.53, which makes this only the second example of these legends.[51] Walker reads these legends as *bism Allāh ālū fā' lilāh* (In the name of Allah; honesty is Allah's) (reverse) and *hadhā mā āmara bihi 'Umar bi-Ṭanja* (This is what 'Umar ordered in Ṭanja) (obverse). The obverse of this coin may be the same die as W B.53.

Figure 18: IH fals of Ṭanja, Tüb 2010-10-1, Forschungsstelle für Islamische Numismatik der Universität Tübingen (6.91 g) (scale x2).

Metrology

Several factors need to be kept in mind with any discussion of the metrology of copper coins. Copper issues tend to vary more in weight than precious-metal coinage, and this may be compounded by the fact that copper coins are often overstruck on earlier issues (as in our case with the Ṭanja *fulūs*). This makes drawing any conclusions regarding the weights of copper coins extremely difficult.[52]

Despite these problems, it is still interesting to compare the various average weights (mean, median and mode) of the early Islamic *fulūs*, found in Table 12 and in the histogram/frequency table in the appendix. Unfortunately, the use of the mode assumes a large number of examples, which we do not have available and, as can be seen by the 95% confidence intervals in the table, the information cannot be considered precise. Any discussion of the metrology of the early Islamic copper coinage of North Africa must therefore be considered a starting point for further research.

Table 12: Comparison of Weights of the Earliest Islamic Copper Coinage of North Africa

Mint	No.	Mean	Median	Min.	Max.	St. Dev.	CI (95%)	
NA Nu'mān	23	2.68	2.44	1.76	4.63	0.8	2.33	3.03
NA Mūsā	5	2.37	2.43	1.85	3.00	0.4	1.87	2.89
Tripoli (IH)	22	3.16	3.16	2.15	4.52	0.6	2.89	3.43
Tripoli (TIB)	9	2.93	2.96	1.93	4.48	0.8	2.31	3.56
Tilimsān	4	2.34	2.21	1.76	3.18	0.6	1.39	3.30
Ṭanja	8	5.63	5.89	2.41	7.68	1.73	N/A	

---

[51] Walker, p. 271.
[52] Grierson, p. 22.

Some initial observations can still be made. As can be seen in the table and in the appendix, the TIB coinage struck at the North Africa mint under the first two governors of the region shows similar metrological characteristics, with both the TIB coinage of Ibn al-Nu'mān and Mūsā b. Nusayr having the same mode (2.00-2.49 g) and medians. There is a difference of 3/10ths of gram between the two means, however, although this is not likely to be statistically significant. The weights of these two issues do appear to be similar to the weights of the *decanummia* circulating in the region at the time of the conquest, suggesting an attempt to produce coins of a roughly consistent weight/size as that circulating in the region.[53] As I have argued above, the IH and TIB coinage that I have attributed to the Tripoli mint also appear to have similar average weights, with little difference between the means and median and a similar mode. Finally, it is important to note the large variation in the weights of the six examples struck in Ṭanja. It is likely that the mint reused earlier copper coinage already circulating in the region.

Conclusion

The first Muslim mint in North Africa struck both precious metal and copper coinage. Copper coinage was also struck sporadically in Tripoli, and later mints were established in Tilimsān and Ṭanja. In all cases, the earliest *fulūs* were modelled on the coinage already circulating in the region, either Byzantine or, in the case of the Ṭanja issue, Imperial Roman coinage.

Although this paper advances the analysis of the earliest *fulūs* of North Africa, further work needs to be undertaken. Some of the legends still need to be interpreted and translated. I have also suggest Byzantine and earlier prototypes for the earliest Islamic coinage, but a more comprehensive study of the Byzantine and earlier coinage already circulating in the region is needed to confirm my suggestions. Dating of the issues also remains problematic, and a study of the linkages between this coinage and the post-reform coinage needs to be undertaken.

Abbreviations

Locations of Examples Found in this Paper

icaL24	Baldwin's Islamic Coin Auction 24 – The Horus Collection, May 9, 2013
PG	Fitzwilliam Museum, Cambridge, United Kingdom
BN	Emile and Sabine Bourgey Numismatique Collection N. K., October 27-29, 1992, Lot: 838
CNG	Classical Numismatic Group, MBS78, May 14, 2008 lot: 1916
ANS	American Numismatic Society, New York, United States of America
Jena	Orientalisches Münzkabinett der Universität Jena, Jena, Germany
L	H. Lavoix, *Catalogue des Monnaies Musulmanes* I, Paris, Bibliothèque Nationale, Paris (1887)
Mun	Staatliche Münzsammlung München, Munich, Germany
N	H. Nützel, *Königliche Museen zu Berlin. Katalog der Orientalischen Münzen*, edited by Staatliche Museen Berlin, Berlin (1902).
PC	Private Collection
SICA1	S. Album and T. Goodwin, *Sylloge of Islamic Coins in the Ashmolean. Volume 1: The Pre-Reform Coinage of the Early Islamic Period*, Ashmolean Museum, Oxford (2002)
TOI	T. Falk, *Treasures of Islam,* Sotheby's Publications, London (1985)
Tub	Forschungsstelle für Islamische Numismatik der Universität Tübingen, Tübingen, Germany
TC	Tonegawa Collection, Madrid, Spain
W	John Walker, *The Coinage of the Arab-Byzantine and Post Reform Umaiyad Coins*, British Museum, London (1956)

---

[53] Average weight of decanummia: Heraclius - 3.1 g (6 ex.); Constans II Class 2 - 2.9 g (3 ex.); Constans II Class 5 - 2.2 g (1 ex.). A large number of copper coins were struck in Carthage up until the end of the reign of Constans II, but are quite rare thereafter. The main issues under Phocas, Heraclius and Constans II are half folles and decanummia. Grierson, pp. 29-30, 43.

Ø	Østrup, J. *Catalogue de Monnaies Arabes et Turques du Cabinet Royal des médailles du Musée National De Copenhague*, Levin & Munksgaard, Copenhagen (1938)
St	Stickel, Johann Gustav, *Handbuch zur Morgenländischen Münzkunde,* Leipzig (1845)
Bre	J. D. Brethes, *Contribution à l'Histoire du Maroc par les Recherches Numismatique*, Casablanca, Les Annales, Marocaines (1939)

Other Abbreviations

OD	Obverse Die
RD	Reverse Die
RF	Reverse Field
T/3 (or 4)	T-bar on three (or four) steps
G/3 (or 4)	Globe on pole on three (or four) steps
NA	North Africa
IB	Imperial Bust
TIB	Two Imperial Bust
IH	Imperial Head
p r	pellet right
St Dev	Standard Deviation
CI	Confidence Intervals (95%)

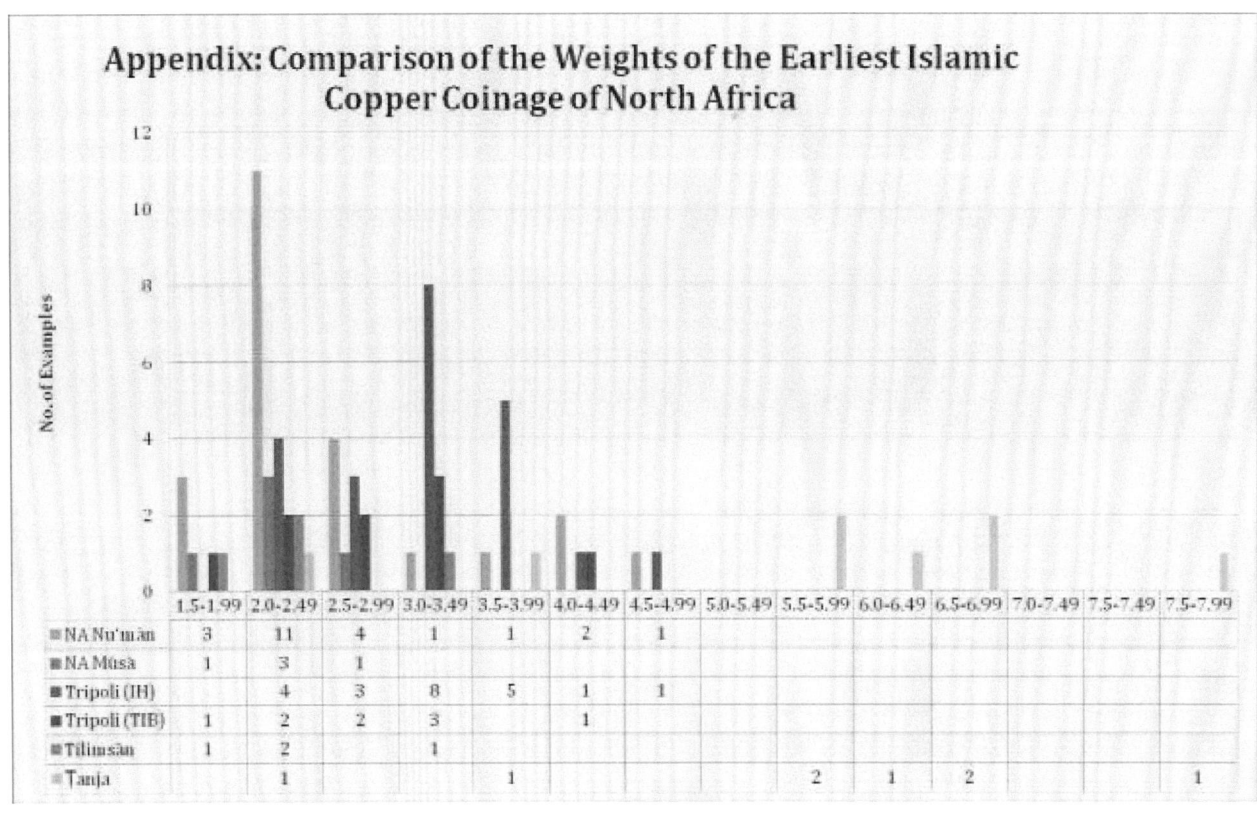

Appendix: Comparison of the Weights of the Earliest Islamic Copper Coinage of North Africa

	1.5-1.99	2.0-2.49	2.5-2.99	3.0-3.49	3.5-3.99	4.0-4.49	4.5-4.99	5.0-5.49	5.5-5.99	6.0-6.49	6.5-6.99	7.0-7.49	7.5-7.49	7.5-7.99
NA Nu'mān	3	11	4	1	1	2	1							
NA Mūsā	1	3	1											
Tripoli (IH)		4	3	8	5	1	1							
Tripoli (TIB)	1	2	2	3		1								
Tilimsān	1	2	1											
Tanja		1			1				2	1	2			1

Marks and isolated words on copper coins issued by the 'Treasury of Aleppo' in 146-148 H: a clue to the interpretation of marks on early Islamic coppers?

Lutz Ilisch [1]

By applying the relatively well documented emission system of 14th century Mamluk coppers [2] to the undocumented 8th century Umayyad coppers it becomes easier to understand the evidence of overstrikes and coin finds. Consequently it is possible to assume a very similar emission system with the high valuation of new copper coins within a limited area and period, followed by a possible reduction of value in course of circulation, and finally the declaration as 'old' fulūs, which may either demonetise them or allow the same coins to continue to circulate at their intrinsic value and which gives them the same status as foreign coppers. All this indicates an auxiliary status for copper coins outside the legal currency in Islamic law, which seems to originate with 7th century developments.

However, there is one feature which can be traced on 7th century and early post reform Umayyad, as well as on early Abbasid, copper coins, which is no longer found on Ayyubid or Mamluk coppers. That is the frequent occurrence of marks which differentiate an emission in a way which was not apparent to the contemporary average user of the coinage.[3] But the application of such marks did have a meaning to those who organised the emissions. The phenomenon is likely to reach back to Roman traditions as the same set of symbols which is predominantly found on early Islamic coins between North Africa and Syria, such as twigs, stars and crescents, occasionally accompanied the mint abbreviation in the exergue of Constantinian coins. And there is ample evidence of its use in the Byzantine copper coinage after the Anastasian reforms. Hahn advocated interpreting this as a dating system because these marks are placed to the sides of the valuation where later on the regnal year was to be found.[4]

Sasanian and post-Sasanian Iran used similar marking systems. With a relatively decentralized coinage, the silver mints generally did not need officina marks nor would dating marks be needed on coins inscribed with the actual year, except for the extremely productive Arab-Sasanian mint of Dārābgird and some other mints in Fārs, which needed subdivision. Here marks with dots and multiple dots in various positions of the reverse can be found on drachms from Fārs, al-Baṣra and Armenia[5] and later, after the reform, on early dirhams of the mint of Marw.[6]

---

[1] Director of Forschungsstelle für Islamische Numismatik University of Tübingen (FINT henceforth) lutz.ilisch@uni-tuebingen.de
[2] L. Ilisch, 'Abd al-Malik's Monetary Reform in Copper and the Failure of Centralization, *Money, Power and Politics in Early Islamic Syria*, ed. John Haldon, Farnham/Burlington 2010, pp. 125-127.
[3] A. Oddy, Symbolism and Design on the Early Umayyad Coinage, *Arab-Byzantine Coins and History*, Papers presented at the Seventh Century Syrian Numismatic Round Table held at Corpus Christi College, ed. Tony Goodwin, Oxford on 10th and 11th September 2011, London 2012, pp. 109-123 for an overview over such marks in the pre-reform copper coinage of Hims (pp. 115-116) and Damascus (pp. 118-119) still refraining from any interpretation.
[4] W. Hahn, *Moneta Imperii Byzantini* Vol. 1, Vienna 1973, p. 17 f.
[5] H. Gaube, *Arabosasanidische Numismatik*, Braunschweig 1973, pp. 55-57 for the use of marks in Fars.
[6] M. G. Klat, *Catalogue of the Post-Reform Dirhams, The Umayyad Dynasty*, London 2002, pp. 224-229, years 79-80 H.: no marks, 80 H.: three dots, 81 H.: one dot, 82 H.: two dots, 83 H.: three dots, four dots, annulet, 84 H.: three dots, annulet. Groups of dots and annulets reappear later on Samanid dirhams from Samarqand and ash-Shash around 302 H. and much later on Spanish Umayyad dirhams.

In Marw the use of marks placed behind or before the mint name in Pahlavi follows a clear sequence with irregular intervals which is best understood as referring to personnel, who either ran or controlled the mint and who were to be held responsible for its production.

It has to be borne in mind that the meaning of marks on coins is very varied. Regarding the large variety I refer to von Schrötter's Wörterbuch der Münzkunde[7] for the purposes of mint marks to which I have added a few from personal experience. No claim for completeness can be made.

mint administration:	mint, mint master / farmer, production personnel, controlling personnel, die engraver, die number, consignors of metal
fiscal administration:	tax collectors, money changers, chronological specification, value of coin/precious metal content

Apart from common mint marks referring to the place of minting, most of the other marks refer to personnel related to the production of the coins. Here those to be held responsible for the fineness and the exact weight of precious metal coins are particularly prominent, but as soon as it comes to copper coins that were unrelated to metal value, the reason for marking is different. However any attempt to identify the use of a single mark without documentary evidence or context is bound to fail.

After these general words about marks I would like to point to marks on late Umayyad and early Abbasid copper coins which can be found in Egypt and which have been listed carefully by George Miles in his article of early Arabic bronze coins from Egypt.[8]

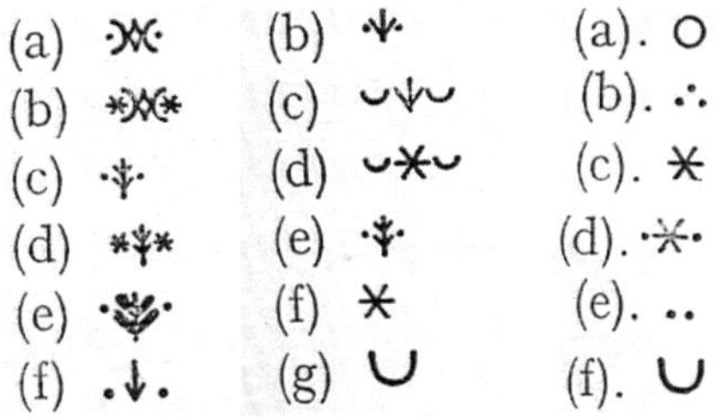

Figure 1: Marks on the Egyptian copper emissions of 116, 133 and 157 according to Miles

Following an interest in the wide variation of ornaments which he had listed previously for the Spanish Umayyad silver coinage of the 10th century,[9] Miles listed with a high degree of completeness what he called 'ornaments' on Umayyad/Abbasid coppers. For the fulūs emission of 116 H. in the name of the governor al-Qāsim ibn 'Ubayd-allāh he identified six different signs.[10]

---

[7] K. Regling and F. Frhr. von Schrötter, 'Münzbuchstaben', Friedrich Frhr. v. Schrötter (ed.), **Wörterbuch der Münzkunde**, Berlin² 1970, pp. 414 f., 426, 445.

[8] G. C. Miles, ***The Early Islamic Bronze Coinage of Egypt***, ANS Centennial Publication, New York 1958, p. 477

[9] G. C. Miles, The Coinage of the Umayyads of Spain, Part One, New York 1950, pp. 106-110 suggesting a relation between symbols and essayers.

[10] The date of the undated emission is established between the period of office and an overstrike of a dated fals from Ḥimṣ of 116 H., L. Ilisch, 'Die umayyadischen und 'abbāsidischen Kupfermünzen von Ḥimṣ', **Münstersche Numismatische Zeitung** X3, August 1980, p. 26 no. 4.

Figure 2: Egyptian fulūs of 116, 133 and 157 H with marks

For the first Abbasid issue from Egypt of 133 H., Miles again found six different 'ornaments' in addition to the rather common specimens without any such sign.[11] There is one type of copper coin emitted in the last year of Umayyad rule. These fulūs show no ornaments or marks but they bear the names of district capitals: Athrīb, al-Iskandarīya, Ahnās, Fusṭāṭ and Fayyūm.[12] Even if the number of ornaments (6) and the number of district names (5) are not exactly the same it would be tempting to assume a relation between the marks and the districts simply for the lack of marks in this emission. It should be noted however that in 133 H. only one of the ornaments is identical with those on the 116 H. emission. This could easily be explained by the assumption that Miles' 'ornaments' do not represent the actual districts, but that they refer to persons related to those districts. A change of most of the administrative personnel between 116 and 133, taking into account the change of regime from Umayyad to Abbasid, seems plausible. The fabric and style of the last Umayyad emission is rather uniform, with the exception of Alexandrian coins. It therefore seems possible that the district names do not refer to the actual mints but rather to areas where the coins were brought into circulation. Whatever may be the correct interpretation, a systematic use of such signs continued on Egyptian copper coinage for at least one more generation under the Abbasids.[13] The phenomenon needs further investigation on one hand with regard to the differences of marks, which in practice are not always as easily discerned as Miles' illustrations may suggest, and on the other hand with regard to distribution patterns among excavation coins from Egypt.

In Syria I am not aware of a similar use of signs in the same period, except for the isolated use of crescents, stars and twigs in the post-reform Umayyad copper coinage and early Abbasid continuation until aṣ-Ṣāliḥ ibn 'Alī, the brother of 'Abd-allāh ibn 'Alī, obtained the governorate of Aleppo. Both brothers had taken the lead in the Abbasid conquest of Bilād ash-Shām and Egypt. They had ended the Umayyad caliphate and while Ṣāliḥ led the goverment of Fusṭāṭ under the control of the Khurasanian general Abū 'Awn 'Abd al-Malik ibn Yazīd from Jurjān, who would also become his successor, 'Abd-allāh resided in Damascus, considering himself as heir apparent to the caliph aṣ-Ṣaffāḥ and as an independent ruler of the countries which he and his brother had conquered. Unlike in areas under the control of the caliph aṣ-Ṣaffāḥ and Abū Muslim, the power in Syria was still based on the Arabian aristocracy and not on Iranian and other *mawālī*.[14] It is therefore understandable that 'Abd-allāh ibn 'Alī had organized the massacre of the Umayyad family in order to win the allegiance of this Arabic aristocracy and place his own family in the footsteps of the Umayyads. However when aṣ-Ṣaffāḥ died and 'Abd-allāh made his claim for the caliphate, Ṣāliḥ was governor of Egypt and Palestine and hesitated to support his brother against the

---

[11] Miles op. cit. p. 481 no. 9.
[12] Miles op. cit. p. 477-480, J. Walker, ***A Catalogue of the Muḥammadan Coins in the British Museum***, 2, A Catalogue of the Arab-Byzantine and Post-Reform Umaiyad Coins, London 1956, p. 227 no. ANS. 37, p. 230 no. Kh. 9, p. 275 no. P. 140, p. 276 no. 910 and no. P. 141, both missing a reference to fulūs from Ahnās, first published by Henry Sauvaire in 1886 and republished and discussed by R. Curiel, 'Monnaie de bronze d'Ahnas-Miṣr', ***Revue Numismatique*** 1968, p. 131-137.
[13] Miles op. cit., p. 482 no. 11 appears with only one mark, p. 483 no. 12 and 13 were misattributed and date consirably later, p. 484 no. 14 is not Egyptian as shown below, p. 485 no. 15 has a wide variety of marks, while p. 486 no. 16, dated ca. 157-159 H., comes again with seven different marks.
[14] P. M. Cobb, ***White Banners, Contention in 'Abbasid Syria, 750-880***, Albany 2001, p. 22-26.

claims of as-Saffāh's son al-Manṣūr, who remained victorious in this struggle. This ensured the supreme position of the *mawālī* in the whole caliphate, but it left Ṣāliḥ ibn 'Alī in possession of Palestine and Egypt with rights of succession to his brother 'Abd-allāh in Damascus. By 141 H. Ṣāliḥ had lost all influence in Egypt[15] while he had won Syria, but was clearly at the mercy of the central government in 'Irāq. He became governor of Damascus in 136 to which he was able to add the jund Qinnasrīn in 137 H.[16]

The copper coins struck in his name began at the period when his brother 'Abd-allāh ibn 'Alī was murdered in prison by command of al-Manṣūr. It seems that no coinage ever named Ṣāliḥ before that. The mint mentions Ṣāliḥ's residence at that period, Aleppo, which was not simply named toponymically Ḥalab, but Khizānat Ḥalab, the treasury of Aleppo (with *khizāna* in *scriptio defectiva*). The emission continued from 146 to 148 H. and the basic type[17] can be described as follows:

obv.	لا اله الا الله وحده لا شريك له
marginal legend	بسم الله مما امر به الامير صلح بن علي اكرمه الله
rev.	محمد رسول الله
marginal legend	ضرب هذا الفلس بخزنة حلب سنة ست (سبع / ثمان) واربعين ومئة

By far the largest number of coins surviving from Khizānat Ḥalab are dated 146 H., mostly without marks or with a crescent above the reverse field. Thus out of six such coins in the Ashmolean Museum and Shamma collection, four, all of 146 H., have no marks at all, and one has a crescent mark, and one is a contemporary imitation (which I have excluded from the present research as it would disturb the recognition of structures of the marks).[18] However the coin type was continually struck with new dates from 146 to 148. This practice is in accordance with the earlier Abbasid copper coinage in Aleppo, where the first type of fulūs were struck in 133-135 H.[19] Then, in 135 H., a new type was introduced only to be replaced again after three years.[20] This next issue, however, was only struck in 138 H. or with the date 138 H. A break then follows until the issue of 146 H. started. What happened in between is not clear. Possibly Damascus coppers became acceptable for a while in Ḥimṣ and Ḥalab or perhaps privately manufactured cast imitations circulated for a while.

---

[15] See al-Kindī, ***Wulāt Miṣr***, Beirut n.d. (Dār Sādir), p. 127 on the gradual but systematic transfer of Ṣāliḥ northwards by the caliph al-Manṣūr. al-Kindī insists that even the third governorate of Abū-'Awn over Egypt was as deputy of Ṣāliḥ while in 141 H. Mūsā ibn Ka'b was directly nominated by al-Manṣūr.
[16] Cobb, op. cit. p. 27-33, 137 and 141.
[17] N. Lowick, ***Early 'Abbasid Coinage, A Type Corpus 132-218 H/AD 750-833***, edited by E. Savage, duplicated manuscript, London 1996, p. 318-321, nos. 186-206; older standard references: W. Tiesenhausen, ***Monety Vostochnogo khalifata***, St. Petersburg 1873, no. 758 (146 H.), 767 (147 H.); S. Lane-Poole, ***Catalogue of Oriental Coins in the British Museum***, vol. IX, Additions to the Oriental Collection 1876-1888, London 1889, p. 94, no. 90k (146 H.); H. Lavoix, ***Catalogue des monnaies Musulmanes de la Bibliothèque Nationale***, vol. I, Khalifes Orientaux, Paris 1887, p. 429 no. 1573-1578)146-147 H.); (H. Nützel) ***Königliche Museen zu Berlin, Katalog der orientalischen Münzen***, Berlin 1898, pp. 328-329 no. 2083-2087 (146-148 H.).
[18] N. D. Nicol, ***Sylloge of Islamic Coins in the Ashmolean*** Vol. 2, Early Post-Reform Coinage, Oxford 2009, nos. 1427-1432.
[19] Lowick/Savage op. cit. nos. 174-179.
[20] Lowick/Savage op. cit. nos. 180-183.

Figure 3: Fulūs of 146 and 148 H. with marks

The fulūs of Khizānat Ḥalab are worthy of special interest because after the first, and often unmarked, year the rest of the coins bear either marks on at least one side, either in the form of symbols or in the form of additional words. As there are no dies with both a symbol and a word we can assume that the words replace the marks and consequently we can expect to learn more about the character or intention of the marks by studying this group of coins. That this has not yet happened lies in the difficulty of reading those additional words with sufficient confidence, in spite of the fact that they are engraved on the coin dies at the same size as the rest of the inscriptions. Another reason may result from a relative rarity of such coins with additional words. Nicholas Lowick's record of Khizānat Ḥalab coppers, as edited by Elizabeth Savage was already a great step forward, although by listing some twenty varieties it was incomplete on one side, while it duplicated unnecessarily the descriptions of several varieties on the other side.[21] The material of this paper is essentially based on the FINT collection, which has an excellent representation of coins from Aleppo. There are about sixty fulūs from Khizānat Ḥalab in it and those are mainly selected with regard to variety, thus under-representing unmarked and over-representing marked coins. The collection does not claim any completeness. Varieties which are missing in the collection but are published have been included.

A list of words on fulūs 147-148 H.

The normal use of the extra words is to repeat the same word on both obverse and reverse. But it is quite common to find such a word combined with another one.

1. Ibrāhīm

One of the few securely readable words is the name Ibrāhīm. While it is tempting to think of Ṣāliḥ ibn 'Alī's son of this name, he is an unlikely candidate. The traceable *cursus honorum* begins only in 163 H., when he was dismissed as governor of Palestine to become governor of Egypt.[22] Therefore he was probably too young to figure on the coins of 147 H. and furthermore none of the other names on these coins can be related to the family of 'Alī ibn 'Abd-allāh. Consequently the Ibrāhīm of these coins remains unidentified.

---

[21] Lowick/Savage op. cit. nos. 186-206. It is unclear in which respect nos. 189-191 form varieties. Also nos. 192 and 199 are identical.
[22] Ṭabarī, ***Ta'rīkh ar-rusul wa l-mulūk***, ed. Muhammad Abū l-Fadl, Beirut n. d., vol. VIII, p. 148.

2. ASKLB

  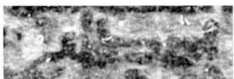

A rather mysterious word with a likelihood of non-Arabic origin (e.g. Asklepios) if the continued thick ground line is more than the die cutter's alignment for a straight line. While the first letter alif is clear the second may be a sīn or two rasm with a following yā or alif-maqsūra. In this latter case the three final letters could refer to the tribal group of the Kalb.

3. BRD 'Abbād

   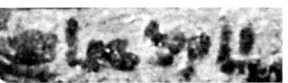

The words BRD and 'Abbād come in two varieties, one of which (no.3) renders the name in *scriptio defectiva*. A third variety (no. 4) adds at the beginning the preposition *ilā* (to/for), which may be related to the following *li* in *li-Dā'ūd*. The word BRD offers several readings like *burud* (plural of *barīd*, postal service) or *burk* (the fee in mills) or Turk. The identification of 'Abbād remains unknown.

4. li-Dā'ūd

 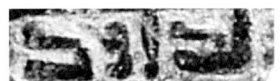

'for Dā'ūd' or 'by Dā'ūd' is one of the few absolutely clear words is this series. In Islamic coin inscriptions the use of the dative is extremely unusual. 'By Dā'ūd' is less plausible because 'authority' would be expressed on Abbasid coins of this period by *bi-'amr* and *'alā yaday*. Therefore I would prefer to interpret this, even without context, in the sense of 'for'.

5. Ibn Tamīm

  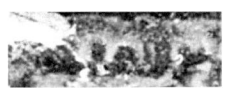

The reading 'Ibn Tamīm' could be rejected for the lack of the initial letter alif, which would be required when the nasab as a father's name or as a family name stands in isolation without preceding ism. It is however sufficiently common on early Abbasid dirhams,[23] so that this reading is unproblematic, while a preceding alif would have rendered the name nearly indistinguishable from the name Ibrāhīm. It is difficult to judge whether the Ibn Tamīm on the coin addresses an individual person or an administrative entity of the Banū Tamīm settling in the Jund Qinnasrīn, although the first seems more likely with regard to the individual *ibn* instead of *banū*.

---

[23] e.g. Lowick/Savage op. cit. nos. 684-684 for dirhams from Arminiya in 167 H.; nos 2367-2381 for dirhams of the same governor Ibn Hurraym from Sijistan; 2431, 2433, 2436 ff. for dirhams of the governor Ibn Tarka of the same province with the mint name Zaranj, 182-185 H.

6. ABRANY

This word is attested on two specimens from the same obverse die in the FINT collection, one linked to a reverse with li-Dā'ūd, the other with a crescent. Ibrānī (Hebrew speaking) may be one reading, which could correspond to the otherwise unknown Dā'ūd. There is however too much insecurity in this reading to regard it as a proof for any proximity of the Jewish community to the treasury of Aleppo.

7. Shams?

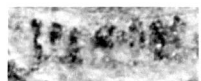

The word is rather indistinct, but Shams is a likely reading on the two known specimens which are both dated 148 H. and link this with a star and a crescent mark on the respective obverses. Shams (sun) could not be understood as a personal name at this period, being too closely linked to pre-Islamic paganism. Read in *scriptio defectiva* Shammās is attested as an Arabic name in the first generation of Islam but is unlikely later for the same reason as shams.

8. FRMA

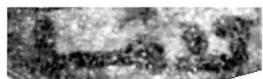  

A relatively common word on the coins of 147 H. has caused some misidentifications in the past. It was read as and attributed to Faramā, an Egyptian town in the Delta of the Nile.[24] A link between Faramā in Egypt and Ḥalab might be attributable to traders from Faramā maintaining a trading post in Ḥalab. But this is obviously very uncertain in the absence of other evidence. The ending of the word on alif (hamza) may give a hint to an Aramaic name, which would equally be possible for the enigmatic QLSA below.

9. Qusdār or Qasdīr?

The most commonly found word is among the most enigmatic. The reading benefits from the existence of several different dies rendering the same word with some variation. The first letter could be easily read as mīm on most coins, while at least two versions point rather to the letter qāf. The second letter is sīn or shīn beyond doubt, followed by a dāl or dhāl, as it is decidedly unconnected in some versions and therefore distinct from kāf. The following letter represents a

---

[24] Faramā is mentioned by Ibn Khurdādhbeh and Ibn al-Faqīh as an important hub of the Rādhānī-trade as it served as the link between the Mediterranean and the Red Sea, cf. M. Gil, 'The Rādhāite Merchants and the Land of Rādhān', ***Journal of the Economic and Social History of the Orient***, vol. XVII 3 (1974) pp. 304, 307. The potentially Jewish names of Dā'ūd and Ibrāhīm together with the lack of any safely Islamic names among these words may be worth consideration.

short stroke, unconnected to either side. The fact that this letter seems to be missing in one case confirms apparently the reading as alif with a *scriptio defectiva* version (last illustration), as has been observed for the name of 'Abbād before. The final letter reaches below the ground line and is likey to be a rā/zā or lām. If the first letter is a qāf then we have to read at least four radicals which point to a non-Arabic origin of the word. Lavoix[25] read the word as Qasṭar or qasṭar while Nützel[26] had opted for Miskīn. Regarding the initial letter as qāf as the more probable Lavoix may have been quite correct. Replacing the letter ṭā' by a dāl does not seem to present a major problem in a non-Arabic loanword.[27] The vocalisation of the word was unclear to the Arabic national dictionaries which render the word as *qasṭār, qisṭār* or *qusṭār* (plural *qasāṭīr*) as the term was no longer in use when they were written in the later Middle Ages but they describe it as a specialist for valuating coins, a *nummularius* as Freytag[28] renders it. The name of the office seems to be derived as a loan word from the Latin quaestor, designating during the early Roman Empire a financial advisor of a governor. The Persian derived term *jahbād* seems to have have taken lateron the place as the Eastern influence grew in the Abbasid administration.

Replacing the letter ṭā' by a dāl does not seem to present a major problem in a non-Arabic loanword.[29] *Qasāṭīr* are mentioned just at this time in 148 H. in al-Azdī's History of al-Mawṣil in a letter from the Abbasid central administration demanding that the tax administration in al-Mawṣil should register amongst others the activities of the *qasāṭīr* in tax collection for the treasurers (*khuzzān*) in registers (*daftar*).[30] This parallel relation of *qasṭār* and *Khizāna*, the office of the *khāzin*, evident both in the Mosul document and the contemporary copper coins from Aleppo supports the reading qasdār. Finally, the fact that this word is the most frequently observed individual word is in favour of the reading as qasdār = qasṭār, because these money changers clearly needed minor coins to balance payments with irregular precious metal coins.

10. Kūr?

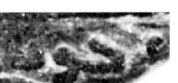 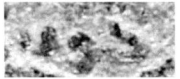

The word kūr is the plural of kūra, the district, which was an administrative unit of apparent importance in the emission system for copper coins at the period of the Umayyad caliph 'Abd al-Malik in the jund Qinnasrīn. The districts subsequently may have lost this earlier importance for the distribution system of copper coinage, which may explain why this word appears only on very few specimens of the 146-148 H. emission and why no names of jund capitals can be found any longer.

11. QLSA

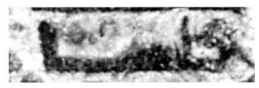

This word on the FINT coin was rendered as 'Kāsā?' by Nicholas Lowick[31]. While the graphic similarity with FRMA is puzzling, the differences in the second and third letters are clear.

---

[25] H. Lavoix op. cit. for the reading qastar cf. p. 431 no. 1578.
[26] H. Nützel op. cit. for the reading miskīn instead of qastar cf. p. 329 no. 2086.
[27] The exchangeability of dāl and tā in Ottoman toponyms is another example.
[28] G. W. Freytag, *Lexicon Arabico-Latinum praesertim ex Djeuharii Firuzabadiique et aliorum Arabum operibus*, 4 vols., Halle 1830-1837 (for the quotation of qastar cf. vol. 3, p. 443).
[29] The exchangeability of dāl and tā in Ottoman toponyms is another example.
[30] Abū Zakarya Yazīd ibn Muhammad al-Azdī, *Ta'rīkh al-Mawsil*, ed. 'Alī Hubayba, Cairo 1387/1967, p. 215; C. Robinson, *Empires and Elites After the Muslim Conquest: The Transformation of Northern Mesopotamia*, Cambridge 2000, p. 161.
[31] Lowick/Savage op. cit. p. 319 no. 199.

Table of marks (6=146 H., 7=147 H., 8 = 148 H.)

Finally the chronological sequence of the coins has to be discussed. At the beginning, in 146 H., coins without any marks were struck, but in this year coins with crescents on one or on both sides were produced. A total of 35 mark and date combinations have been found. Other simple symbols, like stars and dots on both sides, extend the series to 147 H. In this year words were introduced.[32] It seems that the names (Ibrāhīm, Dā'ūd, 'Abbād) are restricted to the year 147 H., while other words continue into the year 148 H. Identical names and words were primarily intended to appear on obverse and reverse, but in practice the obverse and reverse dies were very often mixed with, or shared between, different names/words. Thus the li-Dā'ūd reverse is not only to be found with a li-Dā'ūd obverse but also with four other names, while the li-Dā'ūd obverse is found only with the appropriate li-Dā'ūd reverse. In 148 H. the system was modified and only one side bore a word, while the other side bore a symbol.

Conclusions

Can those words in 147 and 148 H. be interpreted? As most of the words remain mysterious with only conjectural readings no simple interpretation can be offered. And as it seems that the system of marking underwent changes between the introduction of marks, the introduction of names and words, and the final conjunction of words and marks, it may be wrong to search for an easy

---

[32] The only coin with a name listed by Lowick/Savage (op. cit., no. 192) for the year 146 H has a reference to one specimen in the collection of the author, but this coin, now FINT collection 2002-20-1752, is clearly dated 147 H.

solution. At least twice we get Biblical names, which could theoretically belong to any of the religious groups present in Northern Syria, with a slight inclination towards a Jewish context, if the word Ibrānī is correctly interpreted. Two cases could be Islamic names, Ibn Tamīm and 'Abbād, but it is uncertain whether they refer to personal names or to tribal groups. The inclusion of a preposition 'li' or 'ilā' before names makes it almost certain that the persons or institutions represent recipients of the distribution process of the copper coins. Interpreted like this, then the other words which are better explained as administrative offices, like the qusdār, and the kūr/districts or villages may also be part of the process by which the coinage entered circulation.

The temporary inclusion of such recipients makes sense in the light of al-Manṣūr's demand to the judge of al-Mawṣil in 148 H. (see above word no. 10) when the quantities which were handed out or sold to these recipients to be registered and the coins themselves could be traced back to the recipients. Apparently it was hoped that the impact of money changers on the tax income could be controlled in this way by the central administration. Along these lines it may be tempting to link the caliphal decree of 148 H., to extend the book keeping in the tax registers, with the change in the marking system of the Aleppo coins in 147 H. But this change may equally be part of the older Egyptian system which also had copper coins without marks and copper coins with marks. Then both the marking of the copper coins in Aleppo and the demand of al-Manṣūr of 148 H. may be following a longstanding registration tradition of the Egyptian administration, which the central administration tried to introduce in the East. Within a short time it must have become clear that the administrative instruction did not bring the intended result. Thus the inclusion of offices and names that were recognizable to everyone remained an experiment that was never repeated in Islamic coinage. Marks, however, continued.

This is a superficial interpretation of the numismatic evidence which now has to await the discovery of improved and convincing readings of the largely mysterious words. It is hoped that through further contributions from linguists, papyrologists and specialists in Abbasid administration and taxation, the interpretations can be checked and the evidence can be securely interpreted.

The coinage of the Seleucia Isauriae and Isaura mints under Herakleios (ca. 615-619) and related issues

Frank R. Trombley [1]

The Seleucia and Isaura Mints

The mint of Seleucia (present-day Silifke on the south coast of Asia Minor), provincial capital of the province of Isauria, was first discussed by Philip Grierson.[2] He identified Seleucia and the associated mint of Isaura in the same province (present-day Zengibar Kalesi in the coastal mountains of southern Anatolia) as military mints founded to strike large numbers of *folles* to supplement the pay of the armed forces concentrated there during the Persian War of 603-629, observing:[3]

> Military requirements, however, might well provide such a special need [for a new mint], for the payment of troops always necessitated the provision of large supplies of coin, and particularly the provision of large quantities of small change. In a recent article I showed how during the revolt of Heraclius in 608-10 the rebels set up a temporary mint in Cyprus and perhaps another at Alexandretta… An emergency mint was again in operation in Cyprus in 626/7, 627/8, and 628/9, presumably in connexion with the final campaigns of the Persian War [of 603-629].

Grierson recapitulated his arguments in the Dumbarton Oaks catalogue of Byzantine coins.[4] His views have found universal acceptance as for example by Wolfgang Hahn in the *Moneta Imperii Byzantini* (*MIB*),[5] which refers to Seleucia and its associated mint at Isaura as *Militär-Subsidiärstätten* ('subsidiary military mint sites').[6] Apart from this, little systematic research has been done on the two mints, perhaps because of their short-term operation: the Seleucia mint operated in Herakleios' sixth to eighth regnal years (5 October 615 – 4 October 618) and that of Isaura in his eighth and possibly ninth regnal years (5 October 617 – 4 October 619).[7]

The 1981 edition of *MIB* 3 notes the existence of 57 coins from the Seleucia and Isaura mints in museums and private collections.[8] Grierson's pioneering study originally supposed that the operation of the two mints was confined only to the years 616/7 and 617/8 respectively, a consequence of a less than complete knowledge of this coinage, based on the relatively few known examples of these

---

[1] Frank Trombley is Professor of Byzantine and Near Eastern History in the School of History, Archaeology and Religion, at Cardiff University   trombley@cardiff.ac.uk
[2] Philip Grierson provides a detailed discussion of earlier theories about the 'Seleucia' coins and their false attribution to such diverse minting sites such as Antioch in Syria and even Ephesos: 'The Isaurian coins of Heraclius', *The Numismatic Chronicle*, Series 6, 11 (1953), 56-67. Idem, 'A new Isaurian coin of Heraclius', *ibid.* 13 (1953), 145-146.
[3] Grierson, 'Isaurian coins', 59-60 (as in note 2 supra).
[4] Philip Grierson, *Catalogue of the Byzantine Coins in the Dumbarton Oaks Collection and in the Whittemore Collection II. Phocas to Theodosius III, Part I. Phocas and Heraclius (602-641)* (Washington, D.C., 1968), 39, 329. Hereinafter abbreviated as *DOC* 2/1.
[5] Wolfgang Hahn, *Moneta Imperii Byzantini III. Von Heraclius bis Leo III. / Alleinregierung (610-720)* (Vienna, 1981), 107-108, 230, 290-291, nos. 192-197. Hereinafter abbreviated as *MIB* 3.
[6] *MIB* 3, 107.
[7] *MIB* 3, 230.
[8] The present article notes an additional 31 examples of these coins and two imitations.

coins at that time. Since then studies have been mostly conducted by numismatists and have as a rule concentrated on individual coins. In consequence, wider attempts at classification have not been attempted. Many more examples of these *folles* and half-*folles* have entered the public domain in recent years. It is the object of the present study to develop a fuller understanding of the characteristics of these coins and of their historical context by examining the contents of a private collection. For the background geography see Map 1.

Map 1: The Middle East in the Seventh Century after James Howard Johnston, Witnesses to a World Crisis (Oxford, 2010), Map. III

Historical and Numismatic Context: Second Phase of the Persian War c. 610-622

The First Phase of the phase of the Persian War of 603-629 ran from the accession of Phokas and rebellion of Narses at Edessa in Osrhoene until Herakleios' accession to the imperium on 4 October 610. The fighting during this period involved a generally successful defence of the frontier towns of northern Syria against Sasanid inroads.[9] The Second Phase of the war, the first decade of the reign of Herakleios, 610-622, was fraught with one military crisis after another and saw the loss of most of the eastern Byzantine provinces in Syria, Palestine and Egypt.[10] The Third Phase of the war involved Herakleios' military operations against Sasanid forces in Armenia and Upper Mesopotamia, culminating in the victorious battle of Niniveh on 12 December 627.[11] The mints of Seleucia and

---

[9] Persian military operations against the eastern frontier did not begin before March-April 603 (in the sixth indiction). Theophanes Confessor, **Chronographia**, AM 6095, trans. R. Scott and C. Mango (Oxford, 1997), 418-419, and note 3.

[10] Walter Kaegi rightly identifies the Second Phase, ca. 610-622, as a distinct period, giving it a separate chapter. Walter Kaegi, **Heraclius Emperor of Byzantium** (Cambridge, 2003), 58-99. The provinces in question included Cilicia I and II, Syria I and Syria II, Syria Euphratensis, Palaestina I, II and III, Arabia, Phoenice Maritima and Phoenice Libanensis, and all the provinces of the Diocese of Egypt. For easy reference, see F. van der Meer and C. Mohrmann, **Atlas of the Early Christian World**, trans. M. F. Hedlund and H. H. Rowley (London, 1958), Maps 15 a-b, 16 a-b, 17.

[11] Theophanes, **Chronographia** AM 6118 (Mango/Scott, 449-450 and note 4) (as in note 9 supra). Kaegi, **Heraclius**, 160-169. J. Howard Johnston, 'Heraclius' Persian campaigns and the revival of the East Roman Empire 622-630', **War in History** 6 (1999), 1-44. On the re-occupation of Roman territory in Oriens in the final years of the war, see O.

Isaura were in operation during the critical Second Phase of the war, when Sasanid armies were successfully besieging Byzantine cities (*inter alia* Antioch in 610, Damascus in 613 and Jerusalem in 614) and occupying provinces. The occupation of the Mediterranean littoral of Egypt in 619 cut off tax revenues and regular grain shipments to Constantinople, leading to a serious financial crisis *vis-à-vis* military pay and the welfare of the population of the capital.[12] In about 619-626 (but I accept Grierson's date of 615 as given in the Paschal Chronicle[13]) the church of Constantinople gave Herakleios permission melt down its gold and silver liturgical vessels and convert the bullion into coinage.[14] The superabundance of silver derived from this transaction undoubtedly dictated the minting of a new silver currency, the hexagram, and the adaptation of the fiscal system to it.[15] The Paschal Chronicle observes in this connection: 'In this year the silver coin of six grams (*nomisma hexagrammon argyroun*) was introduced by law; and during the same year official salaries (*basilikai rogai*) were paid in it at half the former rate'.[16] The reverse legend on the silver hexagram denotes the military crisis of the empire: 'God aid the Romans!' (*Deus adiuta Romanis*).[17] In a chronicle entry dealing with the departure of Herakleios' first expedition against the Persians in Armenia on 4 April 622 Theophanes Confessor observes:[18]

> Having taken the money of the holy churches in the form of a loan, pressed by difficulties, [Herakleios] seized the candelabra (*polykandēla*) and other service vessels of the Great Church and coined large numbers of *solidi* (*nomismata*) and *miliaresia*.

It must be borne in mind, however, that a great many liturgical vessels and other furnishings of this period were made of bronze alloys, as for example censers, candelabra and light-fittings.[19] It is possible that objects of these types were melted down and minted into *folles*, as shortages of copper and alloy metals arose at this time: during the earlier years of this currency reform (ca. 615-623) the flan size and weight of the bronze *follis* was reduced by ca. 20-25 percent.

The Nikomedeia mint continued to strike coins straight through until 618 (regnal year 8, ending 4 October 618), so the town seems not to have capitulated to the Sasanids.[20] The Sasanid army apparently by-passed Nikomedeia in Šāhīn's expedition of 615 and made directly for the Bosphoros, concentrating on raiding the coastlands of Bithynia opposite Constantinople.[21] The mint at Nikomedeia continued to issue coins. The five published examples of Herakleios' Class 3 *folles* (three standing figures) from regnal years 6 to 8 (5 October 615 – 4 October 618) in the Dumbarton Oaks Collection were struck on smaller flans of reduced weight, with an average diameter of 26.5mm and an average weight of 7.38g, well below the normative 30mm and 10g of regnal years

---

Schmitt, 'Untersuchungen zur Organisation und zur militärischen Stärke oströmischer Herrschaft im vorderen Orient zwischen 628 und 633', **Byzantinische Zeitschrift** 94 (2001), 197-230, with extensive bibliography.

[12] For estimates, see M. Hendy, **Studies in the Byzantine Money Economy c. 300-1450** (Cambridge, 1985), 620-621. On public bread for the population of Constantinople and the minting of ecclesiastical gold and silver vessels into coinage, see F. Dölger, **Regesten der Kaiserurkunden des oströmischen Reiches von 565-1453 I. Teil, 1. Halbband. Regesten 565-867**, ed. A. E. Müller *et alii* (Munich, 2009), nos. 173, 174. See also J. L. Teall, 'The grain supply of the Byzantine empire, 330-1025', **Dumbarton Oaks Papers** 13 (1959), 87-139., esp. 91-96.

[13] *DOC* 3/1, 17-18.

[14] Dölger, **Regesten**, no. 176.

[15] Hendy, **Byzantine Monetary Economy**, 494.

[16] **Chronicon Paschale**, 706; translation adapted from Hendy, *Byzantine Monetary Economy*, 494-495.

[17] ***DOC*** 2/1, 270-273 (nos. 61-67).

[18] Theophanes, **Chronographia** AM 6113 (Mango/Scott, 435). But see the Greek text, ed. C. de Boor (Leipzig, 1883), 302 line 34 – 303 line 3.

[19] See for example David Buckton (ed.), **Byzantium: Treasures of Byzantine Art and Culture** (London, 1994), 104-110 (nos. 113 a-b, 114, 116, 120).

[20] *MIB* 3, 106-107, 228 (nos. 174-176).

[21] Al-Tabarī, *Ta'rīkh, **The History of Tabari V. The Sāsānids, the Byzantines, the Lakhmids, and Yemen***, trans. C. E. Bosworth (Albany, 1999), 319.

1-5.²² The private collection, from which the coins for the present study were drawn, contains five examples from the mint of Nikomedeia dating from Herakleios' regnal years 6-8; they have an average flan size of 26mm and an average weight of 7.93g – comparable figures to the Dumbarton Oaks series. In contrast, the issues of *folles* from the Seleucia and Isaura mints for the same years 615-619 maintained a normal standard flan size and weight at ca. 30mm and 10g respectively. Philip Grierson offers no explanation for this phenomenon, nor does he explain why the normative flan size and weight at the Seleucia and Isaura mints was maintained between 615 and 619.

Although the principal Byzantine military commands – those led by the *magister militum per Orientem* and *magister militum per Armeniam* – remained in existence during the Persian war of 603-629, they are likely to have suffered manpower attrition in the great battle fought near Antioch in 613 so seriously that they could not undertake a frontal advance into northern Syria in the years between 614 and 622. The final solution to this problem was Herakleios' invasion of Armenia in 622: instead of attempting to win back the lost provinces by direct assault, Herakleios and his generals adopted the 'indirect approach' by redirecting the war into Armenia and Upper Mesopotamia, threatening the invasion of Persian soil from the north and acquiring many ethnic allies among the Armenian and Caucasian peoples. Seleucia and Isaura in the province of Isauria lay in the operational zone of the *magister militum per Orientem*. After the loss of northern Syria the army of Oriens, consisting of perhaps 10,000 to 15,000 men, established new billets in Asia Minor. One of these was Kaisareia in Kappadokia, which had an army factory (*fabrica*) and was a concentration point for Byzantine cavalry preparing to march across the Tauros mountains into Syria, at the eastern end of the Anatolia steppe whence the troops covered the strategic passes (*kleisourai*) coming down from the Tauros mountains.

Other formations appear to have taken up positions in Cilicia, ultimately retiring to the neighbourhood of Seleucia, which lies at the western end of the coastal plain where the Tauros mountains come down to the sea. The evidence for the presence of Byzantine troops at Seleucia consists solely of the coinage of the Seleucia and Isaura mints. Seleucia was the provincial capital of the province of Isauria. It was linked to Constantinople and Alexandreia by a continuous maritime traffic that ran along the south coast of Asia Minor until the Sasanids occupied Egypt in 619. It also enjoyed overland contact with the Anatolian steppe through a strategic defile or *kleisoura*, the Kalykandos river, which flows down from a source in the Tauros mountains in a south-easterly direction and pours into the Mediterranean on the east side of the *akropolis* of Seleucia.

Persian armies invaded Asia Minor a number of times during the Second Phase of the war. In 611 a Sasanid general led his force across the Tauros mountains and occupied Kaisareia in Kappadokia.²³ A large Byzantine force came up and blockaded the Persians in the town during the winter of 611-612. The following spring they broke out and headed back to Persian territory. Another Persian army, this one with Šāhīn, *pādhusbān* or civil governor of the West as its commander, entered the Anatolian steppe and made its way to the vicinity of Chalcedon on the Bosphoros opposite Constantinople, probably in the summer months of 615. They raided widely, and may have captured Kyzikos, whose mint stopped production of bronze coinage in the same year (Herakleios' regnal year 5, ending 4 October 615).²⁴

Only one other Persian incursion is known to have taken place in the Second Phase of the Persian War, sometime between 619 and 622. The Persians are said to have captured Ankyra on the central

---

²² **DOC** 3/1, 319-320 (nos. 162-164).
²³ Kaegi, **Heraclius**, 68-69 (as in note 10 supra). On Šāhīn's office, see al-Tabarī, *Ta'rīkh*, 146-147, note 375 with bibliography; 319, note 748.
²⁴ **MIB** 3, 106-107, 229 (nos. 183-185).

Anatolian plateau. Almost nothing is known about the circumstances of this event.[25] The only other known Persian penetration of Asia Minor was the Persian general Šahrbarāz's march to the Bosphoros in 626, but this falls in the Third Phase of the Persian war and is outside the chronological limits of the present discussion.

The character of these raids, and their possible impact on the coastal plain and mountains of Isauria, where Seleucia and Isaura lay, can be gauged only indirectly. The Arab historian al-Tabarī observes in very general terms that:[26]

> [Khusau II] ordered [his general Šahrbarāz] to devastate the land of the Byzantines, as an expression of his anger at the Byzantines' violence against [the emperor] Maurice and as an act of vengeance upon them for him.

As to the presence of Byzantine military formations in different parts of Asia Minor, there is a hagiographic text of some reliability about a Sasanid siege of Euchaïta in north-central Asia Minor in the anonymous *Vita, Educatio et Miracula S. Theodori*.[27] The key section, Miracle II, states:[28]

> The Persians who were still encamped in front the city being suddenly attacked by a Roman expeditionary force (*ekstrateuma*), blazing with rage, killed many of the captives in a death by the sword, and utterly burned the entire city including the church of the saint. But they could not escape at all, because the armour-clad saint fell upon them. Another Roman detachment of soldiers (*heteron rōmaïkon stiphos stratiōtōn*) attacking in the direction of the mountain called Ophalimos destroyed many [of them] and divine vengeance killed the rest when they reached the Lykos river as a multitude of hailstones was sent down from heaven, like lances, so that not one of those who did such things [as burning the shrine of the martyr] returned to his own land. In that place the Roman expeditionary force erected a new church in the name of the martyr as an act of gratitude because of the victory, as they had previously sworn, after finding him to be an advocate and helper, which [church] has stood there until the present day.

Whatever one makes of the miraculous details, the report contains a number of well-known geographical details (Mt. Ophalimos and the Lykos river) and indicates the presence of at least two Byzantine military formations that attacked the Sasanid besiegers of Euchaita. The soldiers were most likely subordinate to the *magister militum per Armeniam*, as Euchaita lay in the Helenopontos, a province in north-eastern Asia Minor. The text indicates that these formations were tactically active during one of the Sasanid incursions, although it is impossible to determine the most probable year, whether 615, 619-22 or 626.[29] There was of course no mint at Euchaita. In contrast, as here, there were surely substantial formations of troops at Seleucia and later Isaura for there to have been two mints operating between 615 and 619.

The Seleucia and Isaura Mints in their Historical Context

As far as the Seleucia and Isaura mints are concerned, substantial Byzantine forces appear to have been stationed in the province of Isauria to cover the *kleisourai* or strategic passes (particularly the Kalykandos river route) leading onto the central Anatolian steppe. There was in all probability a

---
[25] Theophanes, ***Chronographia*** AM 6111 (Mango/Scott, 434) (as in note 9 supra).
[26] Al-Tabarī, *Ta'rīkh*, 319 (as in note 21 supra).
[27] See the discussion in F. R. Trombley, 'The decline of the seventh-century town: the exception of Euchaita', ***Byzantina kai Metabyzantina*** 4 (1985), 65-90.
[28] Acta Sanctorum, Nov. IV, 53.
[29] The Sasanid force that reached Kaisareia in Kappadokia in 611-612 was too far to the east to have reached Euchaita.

Roman road running along the northern summit of the Kalykandos *kleisoura*, linking Seleucia to Klaudiopolis, Laranda, the Lykaonian plain and Ikonion beyond.[30] The military forces based round Seleucia would have been in a position to take the offensive against the conquered provinces of Cilicia and northern Syria further to the east. The coastal plain running eastward from Seleucia to Tarsos (which the Persians occupied soon after the battle of Antioch in 613) was agriculturally productive, and could have sustained a substantial number of troops.[31] The conventional cereal crops of wheat and barley are likely to have been extensively produced in this sector of the south coast of Asia Minor.[32] The Sasanid forces do not seem to have penetrated from Cilicia into Isauria in 613, to judge from a report of the Armenian history of pseudo-Sebeos:[33]

> A further battle occurred near the pass of the entrance to Cilicia. The Greeks smote the Persian force of 8,000 fully-armed men in the conflict, but then themselves turned in flight. The Persian army, strengthened, seized the city of Tarsus and all the inhabitants of the province of Cilicia.

In the 6th century there were thirty-three towns under the jurisdiction of the provincial governor of Isauria, of which Seleucia was the administrative capital.[34] It is doubtful that any of these towns were assaulted, particularly as they lay in upland districts covered by the great fortress of Seleucia at the mouth of the Kalykandos river. If pseudo-Sebeos is taken literally, only the two Cilicias (Tracheia and Pedias), and not Isauria, were occupied. Tarsos fell two to three years *before* the Seleucia mint began operating. Seleucia was itself an important hub of military activity, lying at the end of the Kalykandos *kleisoura*, being accessible by sea and having a *fabrica* or arms factory during the 7th century (*tēs phabrikos Seleukeias*).[35]

The Byzantine army defending the approaches to Isauria was certainly a detachment of the *magister militum per Orientem*, whose headquarters had been at Antioch until 610, when Persian forces seized that city. The Sasanid capture of the population of Tarsos does *not* mean that Byzantine military forces ceased to exist on the Isaurian plain east of Seleucia.[36] Pseudo-Sebeos' statement indicates the number of Persian troops operating on the Cilician-Syrian borderlands in 613 as about 8,000 men; a comparable force level of Byzantine troops would have been needed to garrison the wide Isaurian plain, which gradually narrows toward the west where the mountains come down to the sea just west of Seleucia and the Kalykandos river estuary.[37]

The sailing route of the Egyptian grain fleet passed along the south coast of Asia Minor, as early 7th century literary sources imply.[38] The Cilician plain could easily have been supplied by sea from Egypt

---

[30] F. Hild and H. Hellenkemper, **Kilikien und Isaurien**, Tabula Imperii Byzantini 5/1-2 (Vienna, 1990), 128, 131, 139-140 and Thematic Map.
[31] **Saint Anastase le Perse et l'histoire de la Palestine au début du VIIe siècle II. Commentaire**, ed. and trans. Bernard Flusin (Paris, 1992), 87.
[32] Naval Intelligence Division, *Turkey*, Volume II, March 1943, 134-139.
[33] **The Armenian History attributed to Sebeos**, trans. R. W. Thomson and J. Howard-Johnston I (Liverpool, 1999), 68. This is an important datum; unfortunately, pseudo-Sebeos' text next mentions Asia Minor only for Herakleios' decision to march against Persia in 622. The period of coin production at Seleucia and Isaura is thus not touched upon.
[34] Hild and Hellenkemper, **Kilikien und Isaurien** 5/1, 402-403 (as in note 30 supra).
[35] G. Zacos and A. Veglery, *Byzantine Lead Seals* I /2 (Basel, 1972), no. 1136.
[36] The commentators on pseudo-Sebeos do not expatiate on this key text. Pseudo-Sebeos, **Armenian History** II, 206-207 (as in note 33 supra).
[37] Pseudo-Sebeos does not mention Seleucia, hinting that Persian forces never penetrated that far to the east.
[38] On the normal sailing routes see Kaegi, **Heraclius**, 47-48. A great deal of circumstantial evidence can be found in M. McCormick, **Origins of the European Economy. Communications and Commerce AD 300-900** (Cambridge, 2001), 582-606 and Maps 20.2 and 20.3. The evidence for the sailing route along the coast of Cilicia and Isauria is also circumstantial, in the form of inscriptions mentioning traders in coastal towns such as Korykos and Korasion, but it is not possible to connect the persons named – mostly in funerary inscriptions – to the actual Alexandreia –

until Alexandreia fell in 619.[39] The seafaring capability of the Alexandrian grain fleet is likely to have remained intact until then, but even if not, the coastlands of Isauria and Cilicia produced an extensive range of natural and agricultural products: the vintage, olive culture, linen production, forestry, stock rearing and the maritime shipping trades were some of the industries needed to support an army detachment.[40]

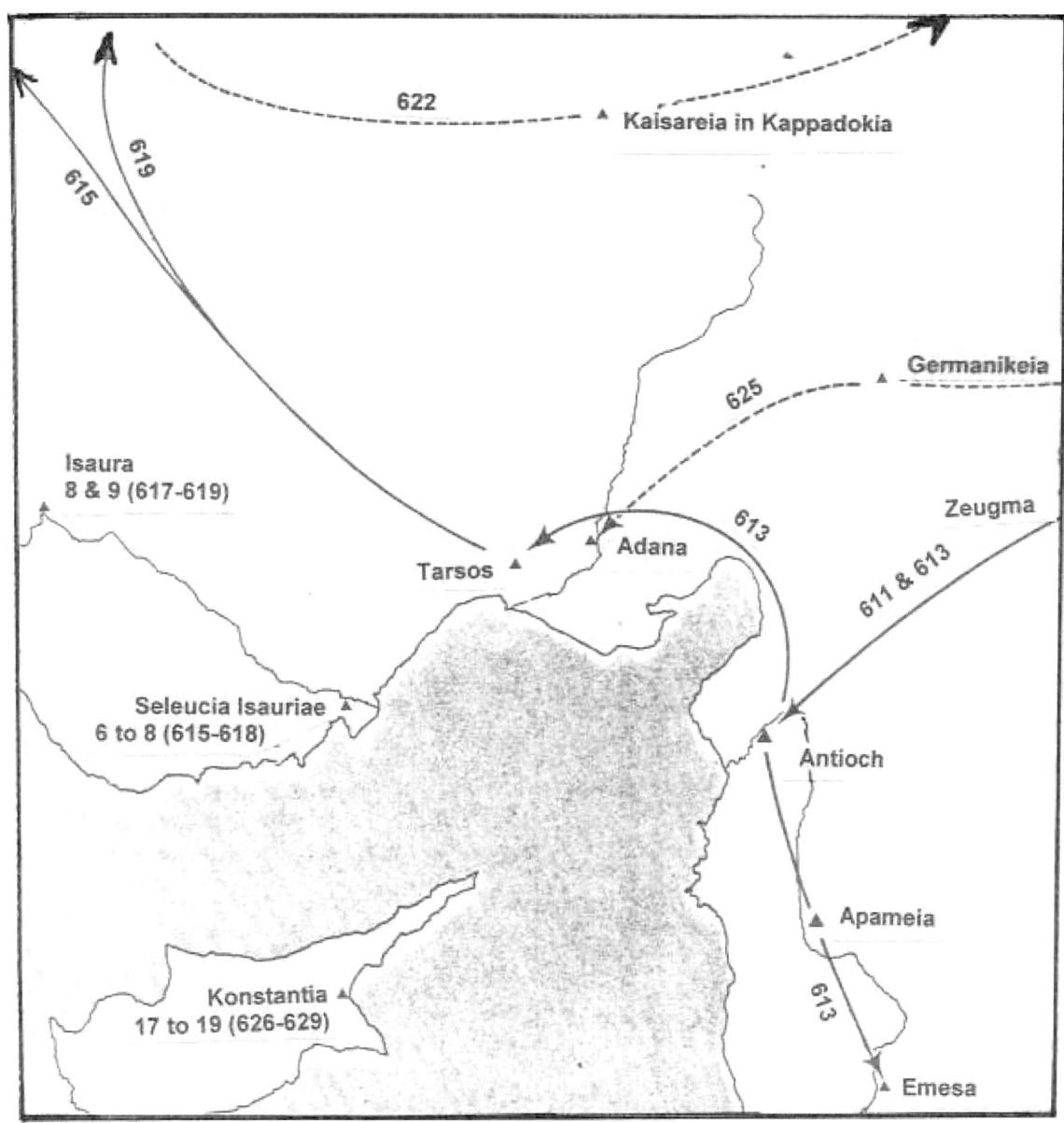

Map 2: The mint towns of Seleucia Isauriae and Isaura showing the Persian offensives into Syria and Anatolia, circa 615-620 after J C Balty "Un follis d'Antioche date de 623/624 et les campagnes Syriennes d'Heraclius", Schweizer Münzblätter (1970). Dotted lines are Byzantine troop movements, solid lines are Sasanain ones. Three towns are accompanied by the dates in which they issued coins of Heraclius. It must also be remembered that Emesa has been postulated as a mint issuing coins in the names of various recent Byzantine Emperors but under Persian rule.

Constantinople sailing route. Much of the data is contained in **Monumenta Asiae Minoris Antiqua III. Denkmäler aus dem Rauhen Kilikien**, ed. J. Keil and A. Wilhelm (Manchester, 1931). See inscription no. 340, which mentions a 'linen-' or 'sail-maker' from Egypt at Korykos. The inscriptions of Korykos and Korasion mention seven sail-makers (nos. 293, 303, 537, 582, 604, 633, 656), five customs-house officers (nos. 367a, 424, 433, 770, 750) and five ship-owners (nos. 179, 241b, 342, 663, 680).

[39] Kaegi, **Heraclius**, 91 (as in note 10 supra).
[40] Hild and Hellenkemper, **Kilikien und Isaurien** 5/1, 108-127.

It is of some interest that the latest coins in the Seleucia and Isaura series continue through Herakleios' 8th regnal year, which ended on 4 October 618.[41] No issues from the Isaura mint for Herakleios' 9th regnal year 618/9 are attested in *MIB* 3, *DOC* 2/1 or the British Museum Catalogue, but they might exist in private collections not noted in the published museum collections.[42] The synchronism between the fall of Alexandreia in 619 and the final issues of the Isaura mint in 618 or 619 suggests that the forces under the command of the *magister militum per Orientem* receiving military pay in the province of Isauria were logistically dependent on Egyptian grain and were forced to evacuate their positions after supplies of victuals from Egypt were cut off and local supplies proved to be insufficient. This is a *prima facie* argument for rather substantial army units having been based there. In 619 these forces could easily have retired up the road running along Kalykandos *kleisoura* to the Anatolian plateau. Philip Grierson and others have suggested that a Sasanid army may have besieged Seleucia in 616/7, in consequence of which the mint was transferred to Isaura, which lay in the more defensible mountainous interior in the province. It is certain that one of the Seleucia obverse dies became the principal (and probably only) obverse die used at the Isaura mint (see nos. 13, 14, 25-31 infra). The two mints were either in simultaneous operation in Herakleios' regnal years 7-8, or else the Seleucia mint retired to Isaura in the latter year. None of the other Seleucia obverse dies remained in use (Types 1-3, 5-6) after 617 at the new mint. This inclines to the inference that the Isaura mint started out as an auxiliary mint, then took over all minting operations once the Seleucia mint was closed. If Seleucia did in fact fall to the Sasanids in 617/8, all minting equipment and dies, including the crude Type 4, would have been destroyed. The Isaura mint must therefore have come into existence before any such event took place. One way or the other, this suggests significant military operations in the province of Isauria. The apparent closure of the Isaura mint not later than 4 October 618 (or 619 pace Sear) suggests the presence of substantial Byzantine forces in Isauria – few enough to be supplied from Egypt, but too many to be survive exclusively on grain and other supplies drawn from Cyprus and the coastal plain of Isauria.

There is another argument in favour of a large detachment of Byzantine soldiers being stationed in Isauria between ca. 615-619, and that is the very large number of obverse dies on the Class 2 coins (two standing figures) of Seleucia (Type 5 infra, nos. 15-22 and issued in Herakleios' 6th and 7th regnal years 5 October 615 – 4 October 617) by officinae A and B. This series has not been the object of die studies, but none of the Type 5 coins in the present collection can be convincingly shown to have come from the same dies. In other words, the mint output of Herakleios' 7th regnal year shows what appears to be very substantial number of obverse dies. D. M. Metcalf has suggested, in a study of *folles* from a later period, that a typical obverse die might produce as many as 10,000 coins.[43] Although his argument is admittedly speculative, the sample of eight Type 5 obverse dies in the present study might alone suggest something upwards of 80,000 *folles* being put into circulation, between October 615 and October 617, apart from the other types being issued. The figure is of course quite small compared to the number of *folles* likely to have been produced at the mint of Constantinople.

A very sizeable part of the output of the Seleucia and Isaura mints consisted of overstrikes of large *folles* from the reigns of Justin II, Tiberius Constantine, Maurice, Phokas and even Herakleios. This is suggestive of military pay, particularly as the module size of most coins from the other eastern mints at this time (Constantinople and Nikomedeia) began to be reduced radically from Herakleios'

---

[41] V. Grumel, *La Chronologie* (Paris, 1958), 356. *MIB* 3, 230.
[42] W. W. Wroth, *Catalogue of the Imperial Byzantine Coins in the British Museum* I (London, 1908), 221. This work hereinafter abbreviated as *BMC* I. But see D. R. Sear *et alii*, *Byzantine Coins and Their Values* (London, 1987), 182, where one or more issues by officina A are noted for regnal year 9. Its (or their) location is unknown.
[43] D. M. Metcalf, 'How extensive was the issue of *folles* during the years 775-820?', *Byzantion* 37 (1967), 270-310, esp. 278.

6th regnal year (5 October 615 – 4 October 616).[44] This numismatic fact coincides with the retreat of the Persian expeditionary force from Chalcedon on the Bosphoros in 615 and the closure of the Kyzikos mint.[45] From then onward the module size of most of the coins minted at Constantinople and Nikomedeia was reduced to a smaller flan size and lighter weight, as noted above. It seems probable that heavy *folles* with larger flans measuring ca. 28-33mm were being shipped to Seleucia and later Isaura for overstriking and issue to the army detachment there.

There are some exceptions to this rule but, apart from the mint of Thessalonikē, which consistently struck heavy *folles* on large flans from Herakleios' 3rd to 8th regnal years, the other mints seldom overstruck the large flans of the coins of previous emperors. Of the other mints, only those at Seleucia and Isaura were doing this between 615 and 619. The average flan size and weight of the Class 2 *folles* of Thessalonikē (two standing figures), as noted for years 3 to 8 in the Dumbarton Oaks Collection, are 29.0 and 10.71g respectively.[46] The private collection upon which the present study is based contains ten *folles* of the Thessalonikē mint from Herakleios' 3rd to 8th regnal years; their average flan size and weight are 31.0mm and 11.87g respectively, a reasonably close match to the Dumbarton Oaks figures. There is good reason to believe that the Thessalonikē mint was supporting military operations in Macedonia at this time. Paul Lemerle has put the Slavic occupation of northern Greece in Herakleios' fourth regnal year (5 October 613 – 4 October 614), which comes right in the middle of this series of large *folles*.[47] A Slavic naval attack on the coastlands of Greece and the nearer islands is likely to have taken place the following year, in 615.[48] In the Second Phase of Herakleios' Persian War, between 610 and 622, therefore, there appears to be a correlation between the overstriking of the large bronze *folles* of previous emperors and nearby military operations. The activity of the military mint of Cyprus in Herakleios' 17th-19th regnal years took place during Phase Three of the Persian War and is therefore of no direct concern to the present discussion, but it is worth noting that the flan size and weight of the coins minted there were much smaller than those of Phase Two at the Seleucia, Isaura and Thessalonikē mints.[49]

The 7th-9th century Byzantine sources make no mention of military forces operating out of Isauria between the years 615 and 618. Nevertheless, an army detachment under the command of the *magister militum per Orientem* consisting of perhaps some 5,000 men would have been in a position to make a direct advance against recently lost Tarsos in Cilicia and against Antioch in northern Syria. The positioning of an army in Isauria based on Seleucia may well be the explanation of why Sasanid generals made no advance against Constantinople or the central plateau of Anatolia after 615. It was not until 619, at earliest, the year of the fall of Alexandreia in Egypt and the last possible date for the closure of the Isaura mint, that they besieged and seized Ankyra. In the absence of documentation, it is nevertheless possible to infer that the province of Isauria had been under the control of surviving formations of the *magister militum per Orientem* until at least 619, drawing recruits overland from the Anatolian steppe via the Kalykandos *kleisoura* and from Constantinople by sea. This is a reasonable deduction from the ongoing activity of the Seleucia and Isaura mints, and it may explain the relative quiet in the years between Šāhīn's march on Chalcedon in 615 and the attack on Ankyra in 619; the Persian forces of the West stood on the defensive, guarding the north-western approaches to Syria because of the threat of the Byzantine army detachment in Isauria.

---

[44] See Grierson's analysis, ***DOC*** 2/1, 22-22 and Table 3.
[45] On the sources and chronology of these events, see Flusin, ***Anastase le Perse*** II, 83-93 (as in note 31 supra).
[46] ***DOC*** 2/1, 309-310 (nos. 134-138). ***MIB*** 3, 115-117, 231-232, (nos. 216-220).
[47] *Les plus anciens recueils des miracles de Saint Démétrius II. Commentaire*, ed. and trans. Paul Lemerle (Paris, 1981), 88-93, 99. Hereinafter cited as Lemerle, *Commentaire*.
[48] Lemerle, ***Commentaire***, 94, 99 (as in note 47 supra).
[49] ***MIB*** 3, 110-111, 230, (nos.198a-b).

The similarity between the busts of Herakleios and co-emperor Herakleios New Constantine[50] on the bronze coinage of Seleucia with that of the Alexandreia mint was possibly a consequence of Egyptian die-cutters being employed at the Seleucia mint.[51] There may be a somewhat different angle to this argument, however; it may be that the Alexandreian twelve-*nummi* bronzes with the bust of Herakleios and son circulated widely in Isauria because of the grain fleet supplying troops there, making a popular obverse iconography for the first coins of the mint at Seleucia starting in 615/16. The first issues of the new bronze coinage on large flans, even if overstruck on the issues of previous emperors, are likely to have been popular with the soldiery, particularly as the artistic quality of die Types 1-3 was high, providing large, handsome portraits of the emperors (nos. 1-11 infra). The heavy weight of these attractive *folles* will have guaranteed a high exchange rate in small transactions, in a manner similar to the large-module (38-40mm) bronze coinage of Justinian the Great from his 12th regnal year, 539/40, onward.[52]

The military crisis after the Persian advance on Chalcedon in 615 and the presence of large concentrations of troops in the environs of Seleucia was such that the local demand for bronze currency rapidly outstripped supply, so it became necessary to supplement the existing currency with an increased output of *folles*. The administrators of the Seleucia mint engaged a less skilled die cutter who produced the very crudely executed coins with two facing busts of the co-emperors, during Herakleios' 7th regnal year (5 October 616 – 4 October 617) (Type 4, nos. 12-14 infra). These crude types appear to have been minted exclusively in officina A. Other officinae – Γ, Δ and E – have been noted, and are represented by coin no. 23 infra from Herakleios' 7th regnal year. Fewer coins have survived from these latter officinae; their obverse iconography is quite crude and is restricted to obverses of the two imperial busts. *MIB* 3 and Sear note the activity of these officinae only in Herakeios' 6th and 7th regnal years, but none of them appear in the Dumbarton Oaks or British Museum collections.

The Sasanid threat to attack Seleucia was thus particularly serious in 615-618; alternatively Herakleios may have contemplated military operations against northern Syria to recover Tarsos and perhaps Antioch at that time. This refutes John Bagnall Bury's hypothesis that Herakleios languished in a state of military lassitude in the crucial decade between 613-622, before initiating offensive operations against Persian occupied Armenia and Upper Mesopotamia.[53] In 615-618 he was equipping an army in Isauria to confront Sasanid occupation forces in Cilicia and northern Syria. The termination of all minting operations in Isauria in 618 or 619 may indicate the failure of this enterprise or, as Philip Grierson originally suggested, the capitulation of Seleucia to the enemy in 618, followed by that of Isaura a year or two later.

In Herakleios' third regnal year (5 October 612 – 4 October 613) the Class 2 (two standing emperors) obverse was introduced at the eastern mints of Constantinople, Nikomedeia and Kyzikos.[54] This new obverse die was only introduced at the Seleucia mint in Herakeios' 6th or 7th regnal year (5 October 615 – 4 October 617) and thereafter became the most common obverse at Seleucia (Type 5, nos. 15-22 infra). The Type 2 and 3 obverse die (two facing busts) continued to be produced in Herakelios' 7th regnal year, as well as the very crude Type 4 (two facing busts) obverse die, which continued to be produced at Isaura during the two years of its operation, Herakleios' 8th, and possibly 9th, regnal year (5 October 617 – 4 October 619). The preponderance of the Class 2

---

[50] The correct form of the co-emperor's actual name was *Herakleios novus Constantinus* (III). Grumel, **Chronologie**, 356 (as in note 41 supra).
[51] Grierson, 'Isaurian coins', 61-62 (as in note 2 supra).
[52] E.g. **BMC** I, 55-58 (nos. 284-313).
[53] J. B. Bury, *A History of the Later Roman Empire from Arcadius to Irene (395 A.D. to 800 A.D.)* II (London, 1889), 208-209.
[54] **DOC** 2/1, 226-227, 278-286, 309-310, 317-319, 325.

coins of Seleucia noted in the present study belong to Herakelios' 7th regnal year (5 October 616 – 4 October 617). Some appear to belong to his 6th regnal year; it is not clear whether the latter was the actual date on the reverse die, or whether it was blundered because the under-type on the flan interfered with the overstrike (nos. 5, 20). Most of the coins of the Isaura mint have badly centred reverse strikes, so the date on the right side of the flan is frequently incomplete.

The fact that the Constantinople mint appears to have issued no coins in Herakleios' 8th regnal year (5 October 617 – 4 October 618) underscores the importance of the issues of the Isaura mint. The Nikomedeia mint issued its last bronze *follis* in that year – a reduced-module coin with the triad of Herakleios, Herakleios New Constantine and Martina on the obverse – and did not re-open until his 16th regnal year.[55] Except for Thessalonikē, which faced serious military threats, the Seleucia and Isaura mints were the sole Byzantine mints producing large-module bronze coinage in the years 617-619. The only other sources of large-module bronze coinage were the local mints operating at Sasanid-controlled Emesa and other sites in northern Syria, which produced imitations of Herakleios' coinage.[56] Coins no. 32 and 33 infra are likely to be Syrian imitations of the Seleucia coinage, but nothing is known of their provenance. This coinage is particularly important, because some issues have characteristics in common to the coinage of Seleucia such as pellet serifs. It is worth considering whether the same die-cutters – or men with the same training and skills – worked in the mints on both sides of the military frontier between ca. 615-619.

The survey which follows examines 23 *folles* and one half-*follis* from the Seleucia mint, 7 *folles* from Isaura and two imitations, 33 coins in all. The catalogue has been assembled from a private collection. It was not possible to consult all the coins available in the museums of the United Kingdom. An investigation of this type is envisioned in the near future. There is room for substantially more research in this area, in view of the continuing appearance of these types of coins in the commercial market. The conclusions drawn from the present survey must therefore be regarded as provisional.

CATALOGUE

I. COINS OF SELEUCIA ISAURIAE

TYPE 1
Obverse: large busts of Herakleios and co-emperor Herakleios Constantine with rectilinear thorax frame and long side-pieces on crown. The imperial images are designed for a large flan. Unlike later obverse dies, these have no *tavlion* at Herakleios' right shoulder, a stripe indicating high official status and rank. Reverse: Large **M** with Chi-Rho above and multiple **I** Roman numerals in date to right. Reference: *DOC* 179. *MIB* 192. Sear 844.

1.

---
[55] *DOC* 2/1, 320 (no. 165).
[56] Henri Pottier, *Le monnayage de la Syrie sous l'occupation perse (610-630)* (Paris, 2004).

Obverse: Legend corrupted in consequence of overstrike; image of co-emperor on margin of flan. Reverse: Chi-Rho above large **M** missing; officina **B**; visible date year **II II**. Exergue: Mint name **SELISU** is crudely incised. Overstrike: it is on a previous issue of the same mint, whose visible date to left of large **M** is year **II III**, giving date of 614/5). Flan size: 33mm. Weight: 13.97g. Patina is red-brown with black-green deposits in fields.

2.

Obverse: worn and pitted, but quite similar to no. 1, a possible die match; busts are well-centred; legend is illegible because of wear and proximity to flan edge. Reverse: poorly centred; large Chi-Rho above **M**; officina mark missing; **ANNO** and visible date at right only **II** (other numerals off flan). Exergue: **SE**[....]. Flan size: 32.5mm. Weight: 9.32g. Overstrike: *follis* of Phokas. Patina is natural copper alloy with black-green surface deposits.

TYPE 2
Obverse: large busts of Herakleios and co-emperor Herakleios Constantine are in draped garments with a trapezoidal shape below figures' right shoulders, a *tavlion* or stripe indicating high political and social rank. The face of Herakleios is youthful and un-bearded. They have medium length helmet straps. Crosses are atop their helmets and between figures. Reverse: large **M** with Chi-Rho above; **ANNO** with small **O** to left; regnal year to right using **G**; officina retrograde **B**; letters and numbers have pellet serifs. Exergue: **SELISU** elegantly cut. Reference: *DOC* 180. *MIB* 192. Sear 844.

3.

Obverse: legend missing; obverse die is similar or identical to nos. 4-6. Reverse: Large **M** with large Chi-Rho above; regnal year 7; regnal year **GI** is clear (616/7). Exergue: mint name obscured by head of imperial figure on obverse of under-type. Overstruck on *follis* of Maurice Tiberius **[MA]VRICI[VS]**, mint of Constantinople **CON**. Flan size: 32mm. Weight: 10.98g. Patina is dark-green with apparently sandy deposits in fields.

4.

Obverse: Herakleios Constantine off flan to right. Legend **DИИhEP**. Obverse die is similar or identical to nos. 3, 5 and 6. Reverse: officina retrograde **B**. Regnal year **ϚI** (616/7) is clear. Marks to right may be **O** from mint name of under-type split in half by latest strike - otherwise regnal year **ϚII** (617/8). Flan size: 32mm. Weight: 17.08g. Patina is dark-green with red-orange patina in fields.

5.

Obverse: legend: **DИИhP[--]NNCC**. Obverse die is similar or identical to nos. 3, 4 and 6. Reverse: regnal year **Ϛ** (615/6); nothing argues for **ϚI**. Exergue: **SELISU**. Overstrike: under-type unknown except for traces of beaded rim on reverse. Flan size: 33mm. Weight: 11.47g. Patina is black-green with smooth, dense dark orange deposits in fields.

6.

Obverse: legend: **DИИh[--]CSCE** (inverted **h**). Obverse die is similar or identical to nos. 3-5 supra. Reverse: regnal year **Ϛ**; material to right appears to be from under-type. Exergue: **SELIS[.]**. Overstrike: on observe, legend of under-type **MAUR** is mixed with most recent strike at upper left; on reverse, **[D]NMAUR** visible below exergue, and traces of consular robes, as in coins of Maurice Tiberius, mint of Antioch, at upper right (Sear 533). Flan size: 30mm. Weight: 9.74g. Patina is dark green throughout, with traces of copper and iron oxidation in surface pits and fields.

TYPE 3
Obverse: slightly reduced but well-executed busts of Herakleios and co-emperor Herakleios Constantine. Herakleios is clean-shaven and youthful-looking. Small, almost indistinguishable trapezoidal shape below emperors' right shoulders, a *tavlion* or stripe indicating high official and social rank. Medium-length crown helmet straps. Same crosses as Type 2. Reverse: large M with Chi-Rho above; officina **A**; **ANNO** with small **O** to left, regnal year **ϚI** to right; pellet serifs on letters and numbers. Exergue: **SELISU**. This series probably had the same die-cutter as Type 2, who produced the present type for official **A**. Reference: *DOC* 180a. *MIB* 192. *BMC* 274a. Sear 844.

7.

Obverse: legend **DDNN** is visible. Reverse: regnal year **ᐊI** (616/7). Exergue: **[.]ELISU.** Overstrike: struck on another coin of the same mint; the mint name of the under-type appears at top of reverse **[.]ELISU**. Possible trace of date **ᐊ** is at upper left of reverse. Chi-Rho of under-type may have obstructed impression of first letter of mint name in exergue of the over-strike. Flan size: 34mm. Weight: 11.29g. Patina is dark orange in fields.

8.

Obverse: legend obliterated on left, **ESC** on right. Smooth fields between figures. Reverse: year **ᐊI**. Exergue: **[.]ELIS[.]**. Overstrike: *follis* of Phokas **[D]NFO[C]A[S--]** (reverse lower right), year **II II** (obverse upper right), mint unknown. Flan size: 28mm. Weight: 8.15g. Patina is dark green with sandy or earthen detritus in crevices. An important feature of this particular coin is the nearly complete preservation of the facial features and garment outlines of both co-emperors.

9.

Obverse: similar or matching die with no. 7. Legend **UCESC** to right. Smooth fields between figures. Reverse: regnal year **ᐊI** or **ᐊII**. Under-type partially obstructs date. Exergue: **SELISU**. Overstrike: exergue of under-type has **SEL[...]** or **[T]HEU[P]** (obverse, left). This is possible evidence of the Seleucia mint overstriking its own coins. Flan size: 28mm. Weight: 10.19g. Patina is dark grey-green.

10.

Obverse: legend is faint, but letters **ESUCUCE** or similar appear at upper left; die is similar or identical to nos. 7-9. Reverse: officina **A**; regnal year **ᐊI** (616/7), with upper part of **I** perhaps visible to right of **ᐊ**. Exergue: degraded traces of **[S]ELI[SU]** visible; coin off centre at lower left. Overstrike: **[C]ON[--]** at upper left rim of reverse suggests under-type from reign of Tiberius Constantine. Flan size: 28.5mm. Weight: 10.35g. Patina is dark black-green, with an encrusted red-orange surface in fields.

11.

Obverse: badly worn and pitted with traces of under-type. Reverse: officina **A**; regnal year **ϚI**; strike is off centre at bottom. Exergue: traces of **SELISU**. Flan size: 28mm. Weight: 9.95g. Coin has been cleaned.

TYPE 4

Obverse: crude obverse busts of Herakleios and Herakleios Constantine. Co-emperors in garments drawn in long linear strokes and box-like helmet-crowns formed of pellets or thick lines. A large and distinct trapezoidal shape stands below Herakleios' right shoulder, a *tavlion* or stripe indicating high political and social rank. Herakleios has beard formed by crude vertical strokes. Reverse: officina **A**; **ANNO** with small **O**. Distinctly convex obverse and concave reverse. References: *DOC* 180a. *MIB* 192. Sear 844.

12.

Obverse: legend **DDNhERC**. Vivid eyes lie below line of brow and nose of senior emperor Herakleios. Reverse: officina **A**; regnal year **ϚI** (616/7). Pellet serifs on letters and numbers. Exergue: **SELISU**. Flan size: 30.2mm. Weight: 10.81g. Patina is red-orange in fields. Concretised black sediment lies over much of surface. The most important feature of this coin is the nearly complete preservation of the facial features and garment outlines of the co-emperors.[57] This obverse image appears to be unique in the numismatic literature.

13.

---

[57] Comment from Michael Braunlin (former Curator of Fleischer Coin Collection prior to its donation to Dumbarton Oaks): 'It looks to me as if the coin as found was uniformly covered by a heavy dark green-almost black concretion that has been for the most part removed, save for the inside of the M and above it, and on the obverse, at several points across the field. The bright copper color is I believe the original surface brightened by the cleaning. The very bright green spots to the left of the A/N/N/O are likely bronze disease, and may be possibly removed by picking at them with a wooden tooth pick. But the surfaces don't cause me to question its authenticity.' (Email of 17 December 2012).

Obverse: similar to no. 11, but with denser texture to the garments. Hollow crown-helmets formed by parallel lines. Reverse: Officina **A**; regnal year Ϛl (616/7). Exergue: **SELISU**. Flan is too small for obverse die. Overstrike: under-type unknown. Flan size: 30.5mm. Weight: 11.24g. This is the most common obverse design, appearing also in all known coins of the Isaura mint. Patina is alternately blackish and yellowish dark green.

14.

Obverse: same type as no. 13. Figure of Herakleios Constantine off flan. Reverse: officina **A**; regnal year Ϛ, but part of date may be missing. Exergue: mint name missing. Overstrike: *follis* of Maurice Tiberius or Phokas, year Ϛ, mint of Antioch **THEUP**. Flan size: 30.0mm. Weight: 9.30g. The coin has been cleaned.

TYPE 5

Standing figures of Herakleios and Herakleios Constantine; medium side-straps on helmet-crowns; elaborately furled garments with sometimes dangling feet. Reverse: large **M** with Chi-Rho above; **ANNO** to left, sometimes with small **O**; regnal date to right, invariably year Ϛl (616/7). Exergue: **SELISU**. Officinae **A** and **B**. References: *DOC* 181a-b. *MIB* 193. Sear 845.

15.

Obverse: Herakleios with crudely ruffled chlamys and arrow-shaped dangling feet. Co-emperor is partly off flan to right. Legend **DDИИhE** (**h** inverted, **E** without cross-bar). Reverse: officina **A**. Year Ϛl (616/7). Pellet serifs on some letters. Exergue: **SELISU**. Overstrike: perhaps Maurice Tiberius, clumsy large **M** and **A[NNO]**, unknown mint. Flan size: 32mm. Weight: 13.76g. Patina is black-brown and black-green, with sandy, bright tan-yellow deposits in fields.

16.

Obverse: ruffled chlamys. Feet of co-emperor are visible. Legend **DNИEЯACL[--]ACENII**. Reverse: officina **A**. Year Ϛl (616/7). Exergue: **S[--]**. Overstrike: *follis* of Phokas. Flan size: 32mm. Weight: 11.29g. Coin has been cleaned.

17.

Obverse: crude images of co-emperors. Legend **[--]IIhERAC** (cross) **VIΛΓEV**. Reverse: officina **A**. Year **ϚI**. Exergue: **S[.]LIS[.]**. Overstrike: large *follis* of Tiberius Constantine. Legend **[--]ONCTANT[--]**. Top of emperor's crown-helmet visible. Mint: **CON**. Flan size: 34mm. Weight: 13.93g. Patina is dark green with tan-yellow sandy incrustations. Provenance: Turkey.

18.

Obverse: legend badly worn and blundered. Chlamys of co-emperors crudely incised. Crown-helmets made up of pellets. Reverse: officina **A**. 'Year' is spelt **ANN**. Regnal year **ϚI** (616/7). Exergue: **[..]LISU**. Overstrike: no secure traces of under-type. Coin was hammered flat before re-striking, leaving splits in metal at rims. Flan size: 38.5 x 32.5mm. Weight: 11.25g. Dark green patina in fields; raised surfaces dark brown. Reference: Berk 575.

19.

Obverse: well-preserved figures of co-emperors. Legend **DNhERA** (**cross**) **INIVΛCEИI**. Reverse: officina **A**. Year **ϚI** (616/7). Exergue: **SELISU**. Overstrike: no direct traces of under-type. Flan size: 31mm. Weight: 10.70g. Red-brown patina with traces of dark green in fields.

20.

Obverse: Semi-bust of Herakleios in flowing *chlamys*; legend worn and pitted, with **ININΛhCEVS** or similar visible on right. Reverse: off centre; florid Chi-Rho; Officina **A**; regnal year **Ϛ**; pellet serifs.

Exergue: flattened with **[.]E[....]** possibly visible. Overstrike: traces of unknown under-type visible on obverse. Flan size: 30mm. Weight: 13.79g. Patina has red-brown earthen deposits in fields.

21.

Obverse: crude representation of co-emperors; legend is worn and pitted. Reverse: officina **B**; regnal year **GI** (616/7); pellet serifs on some letters. Exergue: **SELISU**. Overstrike: traces on obverse and reverse. Flan size: 32mm. Weight: 10.83g. Red-brown patina has oxidised green rims.

22.

Obverse: legend not visible. Obverse: Petals of crosses looped. Reverse: crude Chi-Rho; officina **B**; regnal year **GI** (616/7). Pellet serifs on letters. Exergue: **SELISU**. Overstrike: large **M**, year **II II** of previous emperor (Maurice Tiberius or Phokas). Flan size: 30.5mm. Weight: 12.22g. Dark green patina has red-orange deposits in fields.

TYPE 6
Obverse: well-executed but simplified busts of Herakleios and co-emperor Herakleios Constantine; Herakleios seems clean-shaven and youthful-looking; small, almost indistinguishable trapezoidal shape is below senior emperor's right shoulder, a *tavlion* or stripe indicating senatorial rank; medium-length crown-helmet straps; crudely shaped trefoil crosses, sometimes with split ends. Reverse: large M with Chi-Rho above; officina **A**; **ANNO** with small **O** to left, regnal year to right; pellet serifs on letters and numbers are lacking. Exergue: **SELISU**. This series probably had a unique die-cutter, who produced the present type for officina **E**. Officina **E** was active in Herakleios regnal years 6 and 7. Reference: *MIB* 192, 193. Sear 844.

23.

Obverse: legend too blundered to establish pattern; die too large for flan. Reverse: officina **E**; regnal year **GI** (616/7); Exergue: **SELISU**. Flan size: 31.5mm. Weight: 12.68g. Patina is dark green with sandy earthen deposits in fields. Provenance: Palestine.

TYPE 7

Obverse: simplified busts of Herakleios and co-emperor Herakleios Constantine, apparently modelled after Type 3 *folles* (nos. 7-11 supra), but with some characteristics in common with Type 6; Herakleios may be clean-shaven and youthful-looking; medium-length crown-helmet straps; crudely shaped trefoil crosses. Reverse: large **K** with trefoil cross above; **ANNO** with small **O** to left, regnal year **ϚI** to right; pellet serifs on some letters. Exergue: officina **A**; **SEL[ISU]**. This series may have had same die-cutter as Type 3. Reference: DOC *182a. *MIB* 195. Sear 846.

24.

Obverse: legend **ECCCE** or similar at upper right; strike is off centre to left. Reverse: regnal year **ϚI**. Exergue: officina **A**; **SEL**. Flan size: 25mm. Weight: 6.83g. Patina is dark red-brown, with light green, possibly corrosive deposits in fields. Provenance: Palestine.

II. COINS OF ISAURA

Bust of Herakleios and Herakleios Constantine, Herakleios with shaggy beard; image of co-emperor often on edge of flan; crown-helmet with outward-turned ribbons; vertical strokes between layers of crown-helmet; a *tablion* or trapezoidal, coloured cloth panel across the front of the chest, which displayed the political and social rank of the wearer through the colour or type of embroidery and precious stones on it. Reverse: large **M** with Greek cross above; officina **A**; **ANNO** to left with small **O**, regnal year to right. Exergue: **ISAVR**. References: *BMC* 267-268. *DOC* 183. *MIB* 196. Sear 848.

25.

Obverse: co-emperor on right edge of flan. Legend **DNhERΔCLER**. Similar to nos. 26-28. Reverse: Chi-Rho absent. Date missing. Exergue: **ISAS[.]**. Overstrike: coin of Maurice Tiberius. Legend **DNMAVRI[--]**. Year **Ϛ** visible. Flan size: 30.8mm. Weight: 12.17g. Red-brown patina. Image of Herakleios and legend are particularly distinct.

26.

Obverse: very similar to no. 25. Legend **DNh[--]**. Reverse: letters have pellet serifs. Date off flan. Exergue: letters at edge of flan consistent with **[..]AY[..]**. Overstrike: obverse legend **[--]AYDY[--]**. Flan size: 30mm. Weight: 10.88g. Patina is dark-grey with fine red-orange deposits in fields.

27.

Obverse: very similar to no. 25. Legend **DNhER[--]**. Reverse: Year **ϚII** (617/8). Some letters and numbers have pellet serifs. Overstrike: year **II**, Kyzikos mint **[KYZ]**. Line of bolts from *lorikos* (visible on obverse to right) suggests a previous emperor, probably Maurice, or Herakleios. Flan size: 31.82mm. Weight: 12.89g. Patina is red-brown with green corrosive areas in fields.

28.

Obverse: similar to no. 1. Legend **DNhER[--]**. Reverse: **ANNO** with filled **O**. Year **Ϛ** or **ϚI** (615/6 or 616/7). Exergue: mint name obscured by under-type of overstrike. Overstrike: *follis* of Justin II, Antioch mint **[THEUP]**. Flan size: 34mm. Weight: 15.12g. Patina is dark brown with medium brown deposits in fields. Coin was cleaned.

29.

Obverse: similar to no. 25, but with cruder figural elements and no vertical bars in Herakleios' helmet. Legend **DNhERΔ[..]hER** or similar. Reverse: year **Ϛ** visible. Exergue: mint name probably obliterated by overstriking. Overstrike: probably overstruck on an earlier *follis* of Herakleios,

Seleucia mint, whose obverse legend reads **[--]NCE[--]** or similar. Flan size: 33mm. Weight: 10.77g. Patina is grey with orange earthen deposits in fields. Provenance: Palestine.

30.

Obverse: similar to no. 29 with crude figural elements and co-emperor on right edge of flan; legend **DNhER[--]**. Reverse: **[.]N[..]** to left, year **Ϛ** visible to right; date is probably mostly off flan. Exergue: **[…]Y[.]**, with interference from under-type. Overstrike: under-type has large imperial bust of Justinian I or Tiberius Constantine (reverse at 270 degree angle); remnants of **ANNO** and **NIKO** of under-type are visible on obverse. Flan size: 31mm. Weight: 11.50g. Patina is brown with yellow-brown deposits in fields. Provenance: Palestine.

31.

Obverse: similar type to no. 25. Worn smooth. Reverse: date off edge of flan. Attribution certain because of Greek cross above large M. Exergue: mint name off flan. Flan size: 31.5mm. Weight: 10.19g. Dark- and light-brown patina. Coin was cleaned.

III. VARIANT TYPES

32.

Obverse: crude standing figures of Herakleios and Herakleios Constantine, Herakleios' chlamys consisting of vertical striations, co-emperor is taller here than on regular issues; helmet-crown is drawn with single line; legend **dNN[--]**. Reverse: large **M** with flaring legs with florid Chi-Rho above whose rho is either a pellet serif or retrograde; letters have pellet serifs; year **ϚII** (617/8). Exergue: off flan. Overstrike: faint traces of under-type. Flan size: 33mm. Weight: 11.60g. Patina is dark green with greenish-yellow earthen elements in fields. Coin appears to be imitation of the two-figure Type 5 of Seleucia Isauriae. Provenance: unknown.

33.

Obverse: crude standing figures of Herakleios and Herakleios Constantine; co-emperors' ankles and feet visible; cross of *globus cruciger* in Herakleios' right hand is exaggerated, having pellet serifs. The obverse is otherwise quite conventional. Reverse: large M with no discernible cross above or officina mark; **AИИ** to the left and possible year **V** to right. Exergue: no visible mint name. Overstrike: traces of unknown under-type or types. Flan size: 31mm. Weight: 12.33g. Patina is medium reddish-brown with grey particles in the fields. The coin may be a Syrian imitation of the standing figures Type 5 minted at Seleucia Isauriae.

Publications of the Seventh Century Syrian Numismatic Round Table

2007
Coinage and History in the seventh century Near East
Papers from the Seventh Century Syrian Numismatic Round Table held on 26th and 27th May 2007 at the Barber Institute of Fine Arts, University of Birmingham.
Supplement to ONS Journal 193 (2007)

- Numismatic Considerations of Byzantium's Maritime Border with the Caliphate
- (E. Georgeanteli and J. Shaw)
- Two Recent Heraclian Coin Hoards (M. Phillips)
- The 'Standing Emperor' Coinage of Emesa/Hims (A. Oddy)
- The Pseudo-Damascus Mint – Progress Report on a Die Study (T. Goodwin)
- The Muhammad-Drachms and their Relation to Umayyad Syria and Northern Mesopotamia (L. Ilisch)
- The Monetary History of the Bukharkuda Dirham ("Black Dirham") in Samanid Transoxania (204-395/819-1005) (L. Treadwell)
- Another Visit to Meshorer's Enigmatic Coin (C. Karukstis)
- An Overview of the Sources for the Coinage of Justin II and its Imitations (T. Vorderstrasse)
- Pseudo-Byzantine Coinage in Syria under Arab Rule (638-c.670): Classification and Dating. Preliminary report – summary (H. Pottier, I. Schulze and W. Schulze)
- Precious Metal Coinage of the Mint of Damascus AH 72-79 (L. Treadwell)
- Some New (?) Standing Caliph Coins (I. Schulze)

2010
Coinage and History in the Seventh Century Near East 2 (A. Oddy ed.)
Proceedings of the 12th Seventh Century Syrian Numismatic Round Table held at Gonville and Caius College, Cambridge on 4th and 5th April 2009
Archetype Publications (London, 2010)

- The Rise of Islam and Byzantium's Response (J. Howard-Johnston)
- Symbolism on the Syrian Standing Caliph Copper Coins – A contribution to the discussion (W. Schulze)
- The Standing Caliph-Type – The Object on the Reverse (S. Heidemann)
- Die Links between Standing Caliph Mints in Jund Qinnasrīn (T. Goodwin)
- A Standing Caliph Fals Issued by 'Abd al-Rahmān at Sārmīn (T. Goodwin)
- New Fakes of Standing Caliph Coins (I. Schulze)
- Heraclean Folles of Jerusalem (S. Mansfield)
- New Evidence for Coin Circulation in Byzantine and Early Islamic Egypt (T. Vorderstrasse)
- Single Figure Coins of Tiberias/Tabariya with Bilingual Legends (M. Phillips)
- More about the coinage in Syria under Persian rule (610-630): new specimens (H. Pottier)
- Numismatics and the History of early Islamic Syria (R. G. Hoyland)
- Constantine IV as a Prototype for Early Islamic Coins (A. Oddy)
- The al-wafā lillā Coinage – A study of style (work in progress) (I. Schulze)

2012
Arab-Byzantine Coins and History (T. Goodwin ed.)
Papers presented at the Seventh Century Syrian Numismatic Round Table held at Corpus Christi College, Oxford on 10th and 11th September 2011
Archetype Publications (London, 2012)

- The Crossless Folles of Heraclius (S. Mansfield)
- Travelling Across Borders: A Church Historian's Perspective on Contacts between Byzantium and Syria in the Second Half of the 7th Century (M. Jankowiak)
- The Mardaites (J. Howard-Johnston)
- The Import of Byzantine Coins to Syria Revisited (M. Phillips)
- A Preliminary Overview of Arab-Byzantine Coins from Excavations in Israel (G. Bijovsky)
- Ugly square flan coins – Another consistent group within the Byzantine-Arab Transition coinage (I. Schulze)
- The Chronology of the Umayyad Imperial Image Coinage – Progress over the last 10 years (T. Goodwin)
- Symbolism and Design on the Early Umayyad Coinage (A. Oddy)
- The Use of Pellets on Various Arab-Byzantine Issues (C. Karukstis)
- The Syrian 'orans figure' copper coins (W. Schulze)
- Byzantium and Islam in the late 7th century AD: a 'numismatic war of images'?
- (L. Treadwell)
- The Earliest Dated Islamic Solidi from North Africa (T. Jonson)
- Coinage and the Monetary Economy in 7th Century Nubia (T. Vorderstrasse)
- New fakes – an update (I. Schulze)
- The Standard Terminology in SICA 1 (T. Goodwin)
- Terminology for the Transitional Coinage struck in 7th Century Syria after the Arab Conquest (W. Schulze and A. Oddy)